MANA MĀORI AND CHRISTIANITY

MANA MĀORI AND CHRISTIANITY

EDITED BY
HUGH MORRISON
LACHY PATERSON
BRETT KNOWLES
MURRAY RAE

First published in 2012 by Huia Publishers
39 Pipitea Street, PO Box 17–335
Wellington, Aotearoa New Zealand
www.huia.co.nz

ISBN 978-1-77550-012-4

Copyright © the authors 2012
Cover image: CURAphotography/Shutterstock Images LLC

This book is copyright. Apart from fair dealing for the purpose of private study, research, criticism or review, as permitted under the Copyright Act, no part may be reproduced by any process without the prior permission of the publisher.

National Library of New Zealand Cataloguing-in-Publication Data
Mana Māori and Christianity / edited by Hugh Morrison ... [et al.].
Includes bibliographical references and index.
ISBN 978-1-77550-012-4
1. Maori (New Zealand people)—Religion—History. 2. Christianity—
New Zealand—History. 3. Christianity—Social aspects—New Zealand.
[1. Hāhi Karaitiana. reo 2. Hāhi Māori. reo 3. Whakapono. reo
4. Kōrero nehe. reo]
I. Morrison, Hugh Douglas. II. Title.
270.08999442—dc 23

Contents

Introduction   vii
Murray Rae

Part I

Chapter One: A Gifted People: Māori and Pākehā Covenants within the Presbyterian Church   3
Wayne Te Kaawa

Chapter Two: Te Ope Whakaora, the Army that Brings Life: The Salvation Army and Māori   23
Harold Hill

Chapter Three: Intercultural Exchange, Matakite Māori and the Mormon Church   43
Robert Joseph

Chapter Four: Māori and Pentecostal Christianity in Aotearoa New Zealand   73
Simon Moetara

Chapter Five: Māori Participation in the Assemblies of God   91
Philip Carew and Geoff Troughton

Chapter Six: The Rise and Significance of the Destiny Church   111
Peter Lineham

Part II

Chapter Seven: Kaikatikīhama: 'Our Most Precious Resource' 141
Nathan Matthews

Chapter Eight: Representations of Māori in Presbyterian
Children's Missionary Literature, 1909–1939 159
Hugh Morrison

Chapter Nine: The Rise and Fall of Women Field Workers
within the Presbyterian Māori Mission,
1907–1970 179
Lachy Paterson

Chapter Ten: Hihita me ngā Tamariki o te Kohu 205
Hone Te Rire

Chapter Eleven: The Subversive Theology of Rua Kēnana 223
Murray Rae

Chapter Twelve: Rātana, the Prophet: Mā te wā – the Sign
of the Broken Watch 243
Keith Newman

Chapter Thirteen: Translating the Gospel in the Māori Art
Tradition: The Works of Hapai Winiata 265
Bernard Kernot

Contributors 287

Glossary 291

Bibliography 297

Index 313

Introduction

Murray Rae

One of the persistent challenges for any nation as it develops and forges its identity is to acknowledge as truthfully as it can the reality of its past. This is no easy matter, for history is viewed differently according to the varied perspectives of those who conquered and those who were vanquished, of those who colonised and those who were colonised, of those who suffered injustice and those who were perpetrators of injustice, of those who were pioneers of a new social or political order and those who resisted such change. Even with the best of intentions, a single definitive story of the past is plainly impossible given the limitations of our varied perspectives. It is a sign of maturity in any generation, therefore, to acknowledge its need to attend to multiple voices: the voices of the poor as well as those of the wealthy, the voices of those who pioneered change and of those who suffered its adverse effects, and, in New Zealand, the voices of the tangata whenua (the people of the land) as well as those of tauiwi (the settler peoples). It is likely that more of the truth will emerge as the varied stories of history's cast are heard together and allowed to shape the present generation's collective sense of where it has come from and where it should now be heading.

It is in that spirit that the essays of this volume have been gathered together. They deal with a particular strand of our nation's history, namely the engagement of Māori with the religion of Christianity brought to our shores with the seal-hunters and whalers, the miners, the settlers and the missionaries. Some who have told the story of Christianity among the tangata whenua regard its impact as mostly destructive.[1] Others offer a more positive account of the influence of Christianity in upholding the rights of Māori to retain their land and to exercise tino rangatiratanga (self-determination).[2] Some speak of Christianity's corrosive effects upon traditional Māori culture and religion,[3] while others speak appreciatively of the missionaries' diligence in recording for posterity the stories of the 'old people' and thus preserving aspects of te ao Māori tūturu (the ancient Māori world).[4] A single definitive story is plainly impossible, and sweeping generalisations about either the benefits or the pernicious effects of Christianity among Māori are likely to obscure more than they reveal. The stories of Māori engagement with Christianity deserve a more careful and nuanced telling.[5]

In 2008 a group of academics at the University of Otago, independently working on a number of related projects, formed a research group called 'Te Whakapapa o Te Whakapono' (Lineages of Faith) to encourage and nurture the telling of those stories. Comprised initially of a theologian and three historians who were attached respectively to the university's departments of theology and religion, history, education and Māori studies (Te Tumu), the research group added to its membership others from around the country, including clergy, tertiary students and educators in law, education, Māori studies, history, religious studies and theology. One of the first fruits of the research group's work was a symposium held in Dunedin in 2009 at which participants presented a range of papers telling variously of missionary endeavours, of the work among Māori of particular churches, of particular individuals and of Māori reception and adaptation of Christian faith. Many of those presentations have subsequently been developed into the chapters of this volume, and some new papers have been added. The collection offered here is by no means comprehensive. Nor does it attempt any summary assessment. The editors have no pretensions to tell a single definitive story. We seek rather to bring to light just a few tiles in the mosaic of New Zealand history, intending thereby to contribute to a richer understanding of our past.

The contents of the book are presented in two parts. The first comprises a series of studies of the work among Māori of particular denominations or church traditions. There is a strong slant towards recent developments, and particularly toward independent churches whose work among and with Māori has been less well documented but, in the case of the Destiny Church, for example, has assumed a high public profile. Before coming to those more recent developments, however, the volume begins with an account, written by Wayne Te Kaawa, of the early days of Presbyterian mission among Māori. Presbyterianism was established in New Zealand, Te Kaawa argues, as the church of and for the Scottish diaspora. The first Presbyterian minister did not arrive in New Zealand until after the signing of the Treaty of Waitangi and his intent, unlike his Anglican, Methodist and Roman Catholic counterparts, was not to mount a mission to New Zealand's native inhabitants but to shepherd the flock of Scottish settlers. Te Kaawa explores the way in which a Presbyterian mission among Māori, focused especially in Te Urewera, developed from those beginnings.

In Chapter Two Harold Hill takes up the story of the Salvation Army and its work among Māori. That story is, Hill contends, a convoluted one that includes both 'noble endeavour and sad mistakes'. Hill explores, with respect to the Salvation Army in particular, a recurrent theme in the history of Christianity in New Zealand, namely, the extent to which the Christian gospel must be disentangled from its European cultural expressions in order to take root among Māori and so find an appropriate Māori expression. The Salvation Army, in common with other branches of the Christian Church in New Zealand, was conflicted over that issue. The annals of New Zealand church history reveal a wide range of views among Pākehā Christians about whether Christian conversion should entail the abandonment of tikanga Māori in favour of a new 'Christian culture', or whether the Christian faith among Māori could best flourish when adapted to and expressed within a Māori cultural framework.

That theme is apparent in the four following chapters. Robert Joseph confronts the question head on when he asks whether Mormons are Māori, and goes on to explore the doctrinal and historical parallels between Māoritanga and Mormonism. Simon Moetara in Chapter Four and Geoff Troughton and Philip Carew in Chapter Five chart the ways in which the Assemblies of God (Moetara) and the Pentecostal tradition more broadly (Troughton and Carew) have been inclined to the view, sometimes expressed quite uncompromisingly, that participation in the Pentecostal tradition requires that tikanga Māori be left behind. More recent developments, however, particularly the rapid expansion of Pentecostalism in Asia and in Africa, have encouraged much wider acceptance of and support for indigenous expressions of Christian faith within the Pentecostal tradition. Peter Lineham in Chapter Six explores the extent to which the Destiny Church should be regarded as a distinctively Māori religious movement, akin perhaps to Ringatū or Rātana. Lineham concludes that the Destiny Church draws upon a broad range of influences, political, cultural and religious, and holds together a number of contradictory elements. The Destiny Church provides a fascinating case study, therefore, of the complex multidirectional workings of cultural adaptation.

While consideration of the work of particular denominations or Christian traditions as a whole is not abandoned, the chapters of Part Two are distinguished by their focus upon the contributions of particular individuals or groups to the development of Christian faith among Māori. Nathan Matthews, in Chapter Seven, provides an account of the Kaikatikīhama, Māori catechists, working within the Marist mission in the latter half of the nineteenth century, who represented and preserved the Roman Catholic tradition of faith in outlying areas of the Wellington Diocese. Then, in Chapter Eight, Hugh Morrison offers a fascinating study of the engagement of children throughout the Presbyterian Church in New Zealand in supporting missionary work among Māori. Of particular interest are the ways in which Māori were portrayed in children's literature, specifically *The Break of Day* magazine, between 1909 and 1939. Morrison's study may be tightly focused, but it reveals a great deal about prevailing attitudes toward Māori among Pākehā New Zealanders, and about the convoluted story of race relations in this country.

Morrison's chapter is followed by a further account of Presbyterian Māori mission, this time focused on the women fieldworkers of the mission between 1907 and 1970. Lachy Paterson tells the story of the women who 'spearheaded the … expansion of the Presbyterian mission into the remote Māori communities of the central North Island'. Again, the narrow focus of Paterson's concern does not preclude the emergence of fascinating and more general insights about gender relations in New Zealand society at the time, the persistence of Victorian ideals through the early decades of the twentieth century, the slow emergence of Māori leadership and the processes of indigenisation of predominantly Pākehā institutions. Paterson observes also the gathering pace of Māori urban migration towards the end of this period that would have far-reaching effects, not just for the church, but for New Zealand society as a whole.

Paterson's chapter is followed by an account from Hone Te Rire, drawn largely from oral history, of one of the most widely respected and fondly remembered of the women workers in the Presbyterian mission, Sister Annie Henry. Te Rire gathers stories from those who knew 'Hihita', as she was usually called, and traces the enduring influence of this remarkable woman upon many who emerged as key leaders of the Tūhoe people in the mid- to late twentieth century.

Retaining the focus on Ngāi Tūhoe, Murray Rae in Chapter Eleven offers a study of 'the subversive theology of Rua Kēnana'. Rua was a controversial figure who came to prominence in the early decades of the twentieth century. Seeing himself as the rightful successor to Te Kooti Arikirangi Te Turuki, Rua proclaimed himself to be the Māori messiah appointed to deliver his people from Pākehā oppression. Rae explores the theological convictions motivating Rua's establishment of a 'New Jerusalem' at Maungapōhatu and argues that in spite of the unorthodoxy of some of Rua's theological claims, his denial of absolute sovereignty to the state had profound biblical roots.

Keith Newman, in Chapter Twelve, explores another Māori prophetic figure, Tahupotiki Wiremu Rātana, who likewise recognised the political ramifications of religious faith but chose quite different, less isolationist and adversarial, and arguably more successful strategies for pursuing the political aspirations of Māori. Rātana was also seen as a successor to Te Kooti, and took up the mantle of prophetic leader after a series of visions confirming his divine appointment. Rātana shared with Te Kooti and with Rua a strong reliance on the exodus motif of the Old Testament scriptures, and found in those scriptures a basis compatible with the Treaty of Waitangi from which to pursue the dream of liberation and equality for his people.

The book concludes with a study by Bernie Kernot of the work of Māori artist and Anglican priest Hapai Winiata. Kernot shows that whatever debates may have been going on in the missionary church about the degree to which kaupapa Māori should be abandoned or preserved following the conversion of Māori to Christian faith, Māori artists simply got on with the job of giving Māori artistic expression to their Christian faith. In Winiata's case, however, Māori culture and tradition were not seen as static, pristine entities to be preserved against all adaptation and change. They were fluid and evolving and able to be pressed into the service of new concerns. Neither was he averse to leaving behind aspects of his heritage that he found no use for. He saw a need for culture to adapt and be changed under the impact of the Christian gospel, and confessed his identity as Christian first and foremost. But precisely through his capacity and readiness to adapt the traditional art of Māori carving to the reality of Christian faith, Winiata has become an eloquent and powerful voice for a distinctively Māori art and a distinctively Māori expression of Christianity. His art is a compelling instance, therefore, of an encounter between Māori and Christian world views that leaves neither unchanged.

One of the consequences of our efforts as editors of this volume to encourage and nurture the telling of multiple stories is that we have not required the authors to conform to a single style of narrative. Some adopt the style of conventional academic discourse. Their writing is characterised by a degree of academic detachment and analytical intent. Some write as 'outsiders', curious about the lives and histories of groups to which they do not belong themselves. Others write from the inside. They are telling their own story, the story of their own people. Accordingly they are sometimes more bold in making judgements and show a more evident concern for where the story will turn next. Simon Moetara writing of the Pentecostal tradition and Harold Hill writing of the work of Salvation Army are cases in point. Some, like Hone Te Rire for instance, adopt the style of fond recollection. In Hone's case, as we have seen, the recollections gathered from among his own people refer to the much-loved Presbyterian deaconess, Sister Annie Henry, whose career in Te Urewera spanned more than half a century and who is recalled still with great affection. We have considered it appropriate as editors to preserve this diversity of style and tone. There is no single, correct mode of discourse for telling the stories of our past.

The stories told here are homogeneous in one respect, however, and that is that they are told in English. That is itself a limitation. There is no doubt that a richer appreciation of New Zealand history – and of our present reality – is available to those who are conversant in Māori as well as English, to say nothing of the many other languages that are now a part of New Zealand's cultural identity. Most of these chapters do use Māori vocabulary intermittently, however, in order to capture nuances not available in English. Translations are provided of Māori words at the point of their first occurrence in the text, but readers are referred also to the glossary at the conclusion of the volume.

The work of 'Te Whakapapa o Te Whakapono' has been greatly assisted by grants from the Centre for Research on National Identity at the University of Otago. We record our grateful thanks for this financial assistance and also for the wider interdisciplinary work of the Centre that has been a stimulus to our own work. We record too, our sincere thanks for the financial assistance for this publication provided by Te Tumu – the School of Māori, Pacific and Indigenous Studies at the University of Otago. Finally, we are grateful for the editorial assistance received from Dr Brett Knowles, and for the meticulous attention given to the text by Daisy Coles.

Endnotes

1 Keith Sinclair's oft-quoted assessment that the missionaries' 'ideas were as destructive as bullets' is a case in point. See the discussion in K Sinclair, *A History of New Zealand* (Harmondsworth, Middlesex: Penguin, 1959), 41–3.

2 See, for example, L Head, 'Wiremu Tamihana and the *Mana* of Christianity', in J Stenhouse and G A Wood (eds) *Christianity, Modernity and Culture* (Adelaide: ATF Press, 2005), 58–86 and K Newman, *Bible & Treaty: Missionaries among the Māori – A New Perspective* (Auckland: Penguin, 2010).

3 That attitude is evident in the work of Elsdon Best, for example. See the account of Best's work in J P Holman, *Best of Both Worlds: The Story of Elsdon Best and Tutakangahau* (Auckland: Penguin, 2010).

4 Michael Stevens, Ngāi Tahu historian at the University of Otago, has made this point in personal conversation. This phenomenon of missionary preservation of indigenous culture extends well beyond New Zealand's shores. According to Joseph Errington, Yale linguist and anthropologist, for example, 'missionaries count as the group which has produced the single largest body of knowledge about linguistic diversity around the world'. J Errington, *Linguistics in a Colonial World: A Story of Language, Meaning, and Power* (Oxford: Blackwell, 2008), 13. I am grateful to John Stenhouse for this reference.

5 A sensitive treatment of the multifaceted nature of the story can be found in T Ballantyne, 'Christianity, Colonialism and Cross-Cultural Communication', in Stenhouse and Wood, *Christianity, Modernity and Culture*, 23–57.

Part I

Chapter One

A Gifted People: Māori and Pākehā Covenants within the Presbyterian Church

Wayne Te Kaawa

The Presbyterian Church differs from earlier churches that arrived in a mission capacity to the indigenous inhabitants of Aotearoa New Zealand. In contrast, the Presbyterian Church bypassed the indigenous population and arrived as a predominantly settler church.[1] This assessment was offered by the then moderator of the Presbyterian Church of Aotearoa New Zealand, the Right Rev. Pamela Tankersley, during her Waitangi Day address at Waitangi in 2008. The Presbyterian Church dates its foundation in New Zealand to Rev. James Macfarlane's arrival at Pito-one (Petone) foreshore in 20 February 1840, a spot that is today marked with a Celtic cross.[2]

Since the signing of the Treaty of Waitangi the presbyteries have built up a 170-year history of mission and ministry to Māori. During that period of time Māori have evolved from being the subjects of mission to partners in mission. The constitution of the Presbyterian Māori Synod 115 years after the Presbyterians' arrival was a key landmark in this evolution. The transition has proven to be a difficult ongoing journey.

In this article, first presented to the 2009 Dunedin Symposium on 'Aspects of Māori Christianity and Mission' organised and hosted by the research group Te Whakapapa o te Whakapono, I will examine the history of interaction between Māori and the Presbyterian

Church from 1840 to 1899. This is an area that has fascinated me, particularly because there are very few surviving records from this period due to their destruction when the Whakatāne office of the Māori Synod was partially destroyed by fire in 1949. John Laughton, who was the superintendent of the Māori Mission at the time of the fire, comments that in spite of scant surviving records there is ample evidence of the Mission's success.[3] Due to the fire, however, he was unable to provide any documentary evidence to support his claim.

The intention of this article is to consider some of the few surviving records from this era as evidence of the work of the Presbyterian Māori missions, first in the North Island and then in the South. I will focus in particular upon some of the key people who were missionaries for the Presbyterian Māori missions during this period, notably the Rev. James Duncan, the Rev. Abraham Honoré, Mr George Milson and the young trainee missionary Mr Henry Fletcher, who between them undertook work in the Manawatū, Horowhenua and Whanganui areas. I will then consider the little-known and obscure South Island Māori missions that struggled to exist during the same period before quite literally disappearing altogether.

The North Island Presbyterian Māori Mission

The first Presbyterian minister to arrive in New Zealand was the Rev. James MacFarlane, who arrived in Aotearoa New Zealand fourteen days after the signing of the Treaty of Waitangi. Prior to his arrival the Anglican, Methodist and Roman Catholic churches had all sent ministers to these fair islands with the specific purpose of mission to the native inhabitants. MacFarlane was, according to George Budd, the first minister of any denomination sent to minister to the newly arrived settlers.[4]

Through his ministry to the settlers he also came into contact with local iwi, and developed an awareness and concern for their welfare. He noted the devastating impact of colonisation upon the local Māori population, and urged the establishment of a medical dispensary to treat those who were affected by the importation of new diseases. His social conscience led him to write to the *New Zealand Gazette* on the effects of British colonisation, and he became a critic of the New Zealand Company for their ignorance of Māori and their failure to set aside the promised tenth of land in Wellington to the local iwi.[5]

MacFarlane became embroiled in the Haerewaho controversy promoted by Edward Jerningham Wakefield. Haerewaho, a grand-nephew of Te Āti Awa leader Te Puni, had been arrested for stealing certain items of clothing. He had been committed to trial, the first Māori in the Wellington district to be tried under British law. Wakefield claimed publicly that Wi Tako and Moturoa had raised an army ready to strike settlers in Wellington should Haerewaho be found guilty and imprisoned. This proved to be incorrect, and Wi Tako enlisted the help of MacFarlane to refute publicly the allegations.[6]

Backed by his mission work and good relationships with Te Āti Awa and other local iwi, MacFarlane wrote to the Presbyterian Church in Scotland, appealing for them to send someone to establish a Presbyterian mission among Māori.[7] After two years of

Rev. James Duncan, Wellington, c. 1875. Photograph by J Kirkwood. Archives Research Centre, Presbyterian Church of Aotearoa New Zealand.

searching for an appropriate person, the Reformed Presbyterian Church of Scotland responded by sending the Rev. James Duncan to Aotearoa New Zealand with the specific purpose of mission to Māori. He arrived in Wellington on 18 April 1843 aboard the ship *Phoebe*. While en route to this country he began studying the Māori language. Duncan began his ministry in Wellington and, on occasions, at the invitation of MacFarlane, would assist him in his charge.

After more than a year of surveying possible opportunities, Duncan headed to the Manawatū area, where there was an estimated population of 2500 Māori. This was at a time when the Government were advising settlers to leave the Manawatū district, due to the Gilfillan murders.[8] Arriving at Te Marie in the Manawatū, Duncan's first contact was with the aging chief Taikapurua and his son-in-law Ihakara Tukumaru of the Ngāti Ngarongo and Takihiku subtribes of Ngāti Raukawa. The Anglican missionary Octavius Hadfield, who lived at Ōtaki, visited Te Awahou once every four months. Taikapurua and Tukumaru requested that Duncan stay with them and set up his mission among their people at Kapahaka, as they thought it more advantageous to have a resident missionary than an occasional missionary. He dedicated himself to learning the language and culture of those to whom he was ministering.

Before long the physical demands of missionary work took their toll upon his health. Added to the strains of his work, his house was burnt down, and then parts of his belongings, including his precious library, were lost during a shipwreck at the entrance to the Manawatū River. The population of the area began to decline as people moved to their other settlement of Matakarapa, across the river from Te Awahou (Foxton). Duncan returned to Wellington for medical treatment and there met John Inglis, who had also been sent by the Reformed Church as a missionary.

Duncan returned to the Manawatū, followed by Inglis, and they moved their mission station to Te Awahou. Together they established quite a following, between forty and eighty people attending classes for secular instructions once a week. This number increased to 120 during Sunday worship. Inglis taught some basic principles of trade and economics, including the use of weights, measures and prices, which aided the local hapū in trade and negotiations, a situation that was not appreciated by local Pākehā traders. Included in his teaching were agricultural skills. At one stage he prepared the soil and planted 60 acres of wheat: 40 acres for Māori and 20 acres for the settlers. In 1846, Inglis returned to Wellington, and then departed for Vanuatu.

Both missionaries had a background in the Reformed Presbyterian Church, and held similar theological and ethical views. These views led them into conflict with Octavius Hadfield, the Anglican missionary. Hadfield would visit the Manawatū area on a quarterly basis, baptising and delivering Holy Communion. This became a major point of difference between the two missionaries. Duncan believed that in order to receive the sacraments a complete transformation in both the personal and outward life of the person was required. After witnessing Hadfield and other missionaries he felt that people simply learnt the catechisms by repetition and did not understand the deeper meaning or significance of what a Christian life required. He refused to baptise or give communion to Māori on that basis, and is recorded as never having baptised or given communion to any Māori in his charge. Eventually Duncan and Hadfield fell out to the point of not acknowledging each other when in the same company.

Duncan maintained good relations with Māori, however. As evidence of this, Donald McLean reported that he had visited Duncan at home; he was invited in for dinner and was surprised to find a notable gathering of Māori chiefs already eating. Included as dinner guests were Te Rauparaha, Te Rangihaeata, Nepia Taratoa, Paoro Tukapurua (Taikapurua) and others.[9] This esteemed company demonstrates the status that Duncan was held in. Here was a person born in Scotland sitting down to dinner half a world away with some of the most influential people in the country at that time.

Sixteen years after his arrival in the Manawatū, Duncan withdrew as a missionary working for the Māori missions, due to a dispute with his rival Hadfield. Te Āti Awa had created a petition calling for the removal of Governor Gore Browne over the Waitara affair. Duncan accused Hadfield of conspiring with Te Āti Awa and of composing the petition himself. Hadfield responded by accusing Duncan of being a paid government informant receiving large grants of land for his services. Duncan successfully defended himself against these allegations but eventually withdrew from direct involvement in Māori work and confined himself to the care of the European congregation in Foxton.[10]

Although working now in a Pākehā church, Duncan continued his personal interest in Māori church affairs, and in 1862 he was appointed convener of the Foreign and Māori Missions. The Māori Missions Committee continued to develop and, ninety years later, it evolved into the Māori Synod, known today as Te Aka Puaho.

In 1864 Governor George Grey attacked Waikato, and soon the war spread to Taranaki. During these turbulent times Te Ua Haumene was promoting his own brand of Christianity called Pai Mārire, also known as Hauhau. This movement started to spread and to capture followers in the Taranaki and Manawatū regions. The Wanganui Presbytery memorial minute reported that James Duncan was credited single-handedly with stopping the spread of Pai Mārire to the Manawatū region.[11] Around the same time another missionary, Carl Völkner, was killed for opposing the spread of Pai Mārire in Ōpōtiki.

After withdrawing as a missionary to Māori, Duncan became moderator of the Northern Presbyterian Church, and served a further term as moderator in 1888 before retiring from ministry in 1897. Before he died he instructed his daughter to destroy all his journals and the early records of his time ministering to Māori.

Abraham Honoré

Abraham Honoré was part French and part Huguenot, and came from the Hamburg Mission House. The North German Missionary Society sent Honoré to support the Rev. Wohlers, who had established a mission for the society on Ruapuke Island. Arriving in 1847, Honoré remained with Wohlers until 1855 then moved to Stewart Island, where he worked until 1859 before finally moving to Aparima or Riverton in 1869. Völkner was a fellow mission worker of Honoré in the southern mission.

In 1871, Abraham Honoré transferred to the North Island, settling with his son, who was farming near Parewanui, close to the township of Bulls. Coming from the South Island Māori missions, Honoré had already built up a credible resumé of mission work among Māori. He began working between the Rangitikei and Whangaehu Rivers as an unattached missionary. Being in close proximity to Duncan, he joined him on a voluntary basis, and later Duncan handed over his Māori mission work to him permanently. The Foreign and Māori Missions Committee described Honoré as 'our friend', and he was accepted as their missionary in the Rangitikei, Turakina and Whangaehu districts.[12] This area was later extended to include the Manawatū and Horowhenua regions.

Honoré's acceptance into the North Island Presbyterian Māori Mission did not extend to financial support from the church, and he had to rely on the goodwill of his own friends and an annual grant from the Bremen Society, who were part of the North German Missionary Society. A number of congregations eventually held special collections to assist him. The Māori Missions Committee urged the church to assist Honoré financially, arguing that such support was due to him as an ordained minister of the Presbyterian Church. The appeal fell on deaf ears, and it was not until 1881, seven years after his acceptance by the Northern Presbyterian Synod, that financial support was finally granted to Honoré, at the princely sum of £10 per month.

Honoré had to confront two major challenges during his tenure. These were the spread of two very different forms of religion, Pai Mārire and Mormonism. Pai Mārire captured a wide following throughout the central North Island, and Honoré described its prophets as 'upstart false prophets'. He was dismayed at how easily anyone professing to be a prophet could obtain a hearing at various pā.

On his visits Honoré would spend much of his time countering the claims of those he considered false prophets, with some success. The 1890 report by the Māori Missions Committee to the General Assembly of the Presbyterian Church made particular reference to one incident in which a group from Parewanui was due to visit relations in Taupō: on finding that some of their relations had adopted 'Hauhauism' they promptly invited Honoré to accompany them and correct the ways of their relations.[13]

Some people also fell under the influence of visiting American Mormon missionaries, and had adopted their religion. Honoré readily dismissed Mormonism as a serious threat and placed the Mormons into the 'upstart false prophet' category. In 1890 he reported that the Mormons had a following of a grand total of four people.

Abraham Honoré is acknowledged for forging important links with the Rātana family, who were devout Anglicans and Methodists. Since 1830, Parewanui had become an important centre of Ngāti Apa tribal activities. The CMS missionaries Richard Taylor and John Mason frequently visited Parewanui, developing a preaching station and a small church. With the influx of settlers James Duncan also took an interest there, visiting settlers and taking services on alternative Sundays. Parewanui became a centre of indigenous religious activity that would be given its full expression under the leadership of Mere Rikiriki, a tohunga and leader of the Holy Ghost Mission. Rikiriki was an aunt to Tahupotiki Wiremu Rātana, and predicted the rise of her nephew as a noted religious leader.[14]

During his early years Tahupotiki Wiremu Rātana was fostered out to older relatives and raised as Presbyterian.[15] Ngahina, his grandfather, farmed land at Te Awahou, close to where James Duncan was settled. This brought Rātana into contact with his missionary neighbour, and when the Presbyterian Church's Turakina Maori Girls College was opened in 1905 he gave a substantial grant of £500 to the new school. His son Urukowhai married Ihipera, a convert to the Methodist Church. They lived at Parewanui, which was part of the district to which Honoré was assigned. In a newspaper interview in 1918, Rātana replied to a question as to his church affiliation that he was Presbyterian.[16]

Laurence Grace of the Māori Missions Committee requested Honoré to consider entering the Taupō district, and upon his agreement he was assigned with the young Henry Fletcher (discussed below) to conduct a survey of the area's population. Honoré was suffering from a medical condition, neuralgia, however, and in the event was unable to accompany Fletcher. In spite of this, he continued to conduct services until his death in 1894 from an attack of bronchitis. Despite the lack of initial support, Honoré had given twenty-five years of service in the North Island Māori missions and a further twenty-two years of service prior to that in the South Island Māori missions.

George Milson

George Milson of Dunedin, who had taken an interest in Māori missions, joined Duncan and Honoré in 1876. He was accepted on a voluntary basis and extended the work of the Presbyterian Māori missions as far as Hiruhārama or Jerusalem along the Whanganui River. Previously this settlement had been a Roman Catholic stronghold, but the wars had seen the mission station abandoned, like many others in the central North Island.

Milson's reputation as a teacher preceded him, and when he arrived in Hiruhārama in July of 1881 he was openly welcomed by Poutini, the leading chief of the village. Poutini was also the chairperson of the former school committee, and persuaded Milson to reopen the school. Major Kemp (Kepa Te Rangihiwinui), the leading authority along the Whanganui River, also supported Milson, supplying him with a free pass to travel unhindered along the Whanganui River. Milson saw this as an opportunity for the Presbyterian Māori mission to branch out from its traditional Manawatū base, making Hiruhārama the centre of mission activities. The Māori Missions Committee supported this idea, and convenor the Rev. Ralph Joshua Allsworth wrote to the minister for native affairs seeking permission to use the school buildings.[17]

The Hiruhārama School was reopened after a two-year recess. During the week Milson taught an average of forty pupils the standard subjects of reading in both Māori and English, writing and arithmetic. Added to this curriculum were religious instructions, which fitted in with Milson's weekend missionary work in surrounding pā. On other occasions he would visit the sick, treating them with homeopathic remedies, on which he soon became recognised as an authority. All was progressing well until the school was vandalised and literally destroyed. Before Milson could organise repairs to the buildings, people started moving away to other settlements along the Whanganui River, leaving Milson with only a handful of pupils. With a much reduced roll the Presbyterian Māori Missions Committee could not justify keeping Milson in Hiruhārama, and closed the school, re-appointing Milson to Koroniti, another Whanganui River settlement.[18]

Henry Fletcher

In April 1889, Henry Fletcher of Rangitikei took an interest in Māori, and towards the end of the nineteenth century he entered the Māori missions of the Presbyterian Church. Fletcher was born in 1868 at Denton, near Rochester, Kent in England. The family immigrated to New Zealand in 1874 and purchased a farm near Fielding from the New Zealand Company. On arrival they could not find the exact land so his father, William Fletcher, purchased a section in the town of Bulls.

Young Henry left school at thirteen years of age and joined a survey party. For seven years he travelled extensively throughout the Rangitikei region. On his travels he became acquainted with James Duncan. Fletcher felt quite drawn to Duncan, and experienced a vision in which he saw the beckoning hand of God calling him to go and minister to the Māori people.[19] At that time the General Assembly was looking for another worker for its North Island Māori Mission, and Fletcher was encouraged to apply for the position after relating his vision to Milson.

His application was approved in 1889, and he was posted to Te Reureu Pā near Turakina, specifically to start a school with a roll of between sixty and 100 pupils. During his time here he became a student of the Rev. John Ross, under whose tutelage he studied theology, Greek, Hebrew and Māori. He was also a keen student of astronomy, ethnology and hymnology. After his school closed due to lack of funds, in 1891 he was posted to a pā on the Rangitikei River. While he was still in training a decision was made that he would not be engaged to continue the Rangitikei mission and that a new field and a new beginning would be sought for him.[20]

Discussion centred on posting Fletcher to the Hawke's Bay to begin a new mission field there.

The New Zealand Wars had a marked effect upon missions throughout the North Island. Many Roman Catholic and Anglican churches had abandoned their stations with little or no intent of returning. In 1855, Thomas Samuel Grace established an Anglican mission in Taupō, but this suffered the same fate as other mission stations and was abandoned. Mr Laurence Grace, a descendent of Thomas, remained in Taupō and appealed to his church to reoccupy the station. After repeated requests were denied he turned to the Presbyterian Church, and sent a letter to the Rev. James Doull, convener of the Māori Missions Committee, appealing for a missionary to be sent to Taupō.[21]

In 1893, as noted above, Fletcher was appointed to conduct a survey of the Taupō area. He estimated the Māori population to be between 300 and 400; the Pākehā population he estimated to be around 300. In the entire Taupō region he found only one active minister, an elderly Māori Anglican curate. Once he had reported his survey findings, he was duly appointed to this new charge. Three days later he married Ada Morris at Hunterville, and the newly-weds set off for their new life in Taupō.

By canoe or on foot Fletcher visited most of the pā surrounding the great lake. Initially he faced much opposition due to the people's historic links to the Anglican and Roman Catholic churches. John Te H Grace, in his 1959 book *Tuwharetoa*, acknowledged that many of the older present generation of Ngāti Tūwharetoa knew Fletcher personally and had received much of their grounding in religious truth from Henare, as he was known.[22] Grace also acknowledged that Fletcher was a skilled craftsman in carpentry and engineering, and stated that many of the young tribesmen received training in those disciplines under tutelage in his workshop.

Te Waipounamu Presbyterian Māori Mission
The Presbyterian settlement of Otago began in 1848 as a cooperative venture between the Free Presbyterian Church of Scotland and the New Zealand Company headed by Edward

Gibbon Wakefield. Some of the well-known members of the Free Church who organised the exodus to the Edinburgh of the South included the Rev. Thomas Burns, who was appointed minister to the new settlement, John McGlashan as secretary of the Otago Association and Captain William Cargill, who was the agent for the New Zealand Company. The settlement was designed as a straight transplantation of the Scottish kirk system to the land of the long white cloud, a mode of Christian colonisation in which European civilisation was equated to the best of Christianity. According to Presbyterian historian Peter Matheson, within six years of their arrival in Dunedin they had established a presbytery, and within ten years had formed the Synod of Otago and Southland, complete with twenty-one churches with ministers, out-stations and schools.[23]

It is widely acknowledged that in the first year of arrival the settlers were at times dependent for their survival on Kāi Tahu living at the kāika at Otago Heads. At the time of colonial settlement the Māori population south of the Waitaki was estimated at 2000 people, but by 1868, on account of introduced diseases, it had declined to 500. Within a year after the arrival of the Presbyterian migrants in 1848, the Rev. Thomas Burns made contact with Kāi Tahu living on the Taieri plains. Te Raki, the leading chief of the Taieri, requested that Burns baptise his child. Two other children were also baptised at the same service.[24] These were the first recorded baptisms of Kāi Tahu people by the Presbyterian Church.

Mission work to Māori in the south was more the domain of another religious organisation, the North German Missionary Society. This missionary organisation was part of the Lutheran Church, which had taken an interest in Māori mission work after a German whaler returned to Bremen with a Māori crew member. The society posted the Rev. Wohlers to Aotearoa New Zealand as their missionary to Māori. However, they sent him without any financial support, as they believed that it was quite possible for him to make a living off the land. Arriving in 1844, Wohlers set up his mission on Ruapuke Island in the Foveaux Strait at the suggestion of Tuhawaiki, the chief of Ruapuke Island, whom he met in Port Cooper (now Lyttelton).[25] This was the beginning of a forty-one-year mission. In 1847, Wohlers appealed to his home church for help, and the Rev. Honoré was sent to assist him.

When the Dunedin Presbytery met in December 1854, concern was expressed at the state of Māori within the bounds of the presbytery. A committee was subsequently established, with William Will as convener, to enquire into the state of the natives within their bounds and to 'report any measures desirable for their "moral and social elevation"'.[26] The committee reported to the Presbytery expressing the wish that congregations take an active interest in the spiritual welfare of Māori living within their geographic areas. With the support of Presbytery they consulted the Otago Provincial Council, proposing, first, that stringent regulations be set up preventing Māori access to alcohol and, second, that an industrial school be established at the Otago Heads kāika.

The policy adopted by Will and his committee was one of pushing the government into action. There had been no positive response from the Provincial Council by 1859, so a society was established along the same lines as the committee. Captain William Cargill agreed reluctantly to be its president. Cargill denied that Māori had their lands unfairly taken and blamed their condition upon themselves, saying that they must become sober and industrious and lease lands not in productive use.[27]

Early in 1858 the committee sought the advice and support of the Wesleyan missionary stationed in Waikouaiti, the Rev. R G Stannard. They agreed to work together on common objectives, which included the establishment of an industrial school, obtaining a schoolteacher and pressuring the government for funds. They were successful in securing for three years the services of Mr and Mrs Baker, who began the industrial school at the kāika at the Otago Heads. They left in 1861 and died en route to Wellington when their ship ran into trouble and sank.

The controversial Johann Riemenschneider of the North German Missionary Society replaced the Bakers in 1862. In the same year the Synod gave a grant to support the teacher at the Otago Heads. Riemenschneider arrived after having served in Nelson and Taranaki. While in Taranaki, the Parihaka prophets Te Whiti and

Tohu Kākahi had attended his Bible studies, but Riemenschneider was compelled to leave when Pai Mārire developed, escaping a dangerous situation after having been rejected by his flock.[28] He stayed at the industrial school until his death in 1866 at the age of forty-nine. He is buried in Port Chalmers.

The untimely death of Riemenschneider left a gap in those working with Māori within the newly formed Synod of Otago and Southland. The Synod liaised with Wohlers for a replacement from the North German Missionary Society. The Society had other priorities, however, and recommended that the Synod should take over their mission and ordain Abraham Honoré, whose later work in the North Island has been surveyed above.[29] The Synod agreed to Honoré's ordination, and appointed him to work among Māori in Southland and the Otago Heads. Wohlers represented the Society at Honoré's ordination, and this initiated the folding of the work of the North German Missionary Society into the Synod of Otago and Southland. One year later the Society formally requested that the Synod take over its Māori mission work.

The Synod still wanted someone to operate the industrial school, so appealed to the church in Scotland for a replacement. The Rev. Alexander Blake MA, a missionary in Bangalore, India, was appointed, and arrived in 1869. As part of his mission he often visited Taranaki political prisoners in gaol in Dunedin. Among them were the prophets of Parihaka, Te Whiti and Tohu Kākahi. Throughout his term Blake also visited Kāi Tahu settlements in Waikouaiti, Moeraki and Taieri. People did not enjoy his laid-back and unstructured style of worship, as they had been conditioned by the Anglican and Methodist styles of worship and found it difficult to accept the change. In 1872, due to the ill health of his wife, Blake was released from Māori work and transferred to Kaikorai Valley.

Among the missionaries and teachers at the Otago Heads kāika, an unsung saint of this time was Patoromu (Bartholomew) Pu. He arrived at Ōtākou in 1854, and ministered for an unbroken period of fifteen years. The Synod assisted Patoromu with an annual grant of £10, providing the local Kai te Pahi hapū at the Otago Heads kāika could match that amount. To the Synod's embarrassment, the Kai te Pahi hapū not only matched the grant but bettered it by £1. Patoromu is described by T A Pybus as a person of considerable ability, a gifted preacher and good pastor.[30] In spite of his faithful service, he was only recognised as an assistant, and never a missionary in his own right. He assisted the Bakers, the Blakes, Riemenschneider and Honoré. In the transition period between missionary teachers he operated the mission on his own. Along with him at different times were other Māori catechists: Horomona Pohio, Rawiri Te Maire, Hoani Wetepi Koraki and Tare Weteri Te Kahu. They were the fruits of the Methodist policy of providing Māori catechists to carry the gospel message to their own people. The death of Patoromu Pu in 1877 signalled the beginning of the closure of thirty years of Presbyterian mission work among Māori in the lower South Island. The Anglican Church then moved into the Otago Heads and declared it their responsibility.

Mission work continued in localised areas, such as Stewart Island. In 1874, the Presbytery developed a concern for Māori of Stewart Island and approached Sir Donald McLean for financial support to appoint a teacher to the school. Mr Arthur Traill was appointed teacher; over the years he was supported by Rev. C Conner, Mr von Tunzleman and Mr Thomson (who would go on to become a minister).[31] Arthur Traill was to marry Gretchen, daughter of Rev. Wohlers, who spent his retirement with them, eventually dying on Stewart Island. In later years, the Synod gave a yearly grant of £25 to support Traill. Apart from this, after fifty years of missionary efforts to Māori in the South Island the nineteenth century was to end with neither a Presbyterian mission to South Island Māori nor any glimmer of hope on the horizon in the new century.

Conclusion

Today we have the benefit of hindsight in analysing both the North Island and South Island Māori missions of the nineteenth century of the Presbyterian Church. There are a number of similarities. In both cases there was a lack of finances, a lack of human resources, a lack of developed indigenous Māori agents and a lack of interest in Māori missions by the general populace of the Presbyterian

Church. In the South, there were a number of people and groups, including the North German Missionary Society, contributing to Māori mission. In the North Island, however, efforts were initially focused totally upon the efforts of one person, James Duncan. For a short while Duncan had help from Inglis, but when Inglis departed Duncan had to wait over twenty years for another helper. In the South, mission work was extended to the establishment of two schools at Otago Heads and Stewart Island, but they lacked a central figure, such as James Duncan, who could champion their mission.

In the southern mission it was difficult to find replacements when a missionary teacher moved on. Despite Otago's embarrassment of riches with respect to ministers, none were willing to extend their ministry to include Māori living in their bounds. The appeal by Will and his committee in 1856 for parishes to take an active interest in Māori mission raised little support. The only minister visiting Māori settlements in their bounds was the Rev. Thomas Burns, who criticised the southern church for its neglect of the Māori missions.[32] When a missionary was needed at the Otago Heads kāika, the replacements came either from Scotland or the North German Mission Society, regardless of the fact that there were ample Presbyterian ministers south of the Waitaki. The mission was to suffer greatly due to the constant turnover of its missionaries. The short-term nature of the service of the missionaries prevented them from getting into the fabric of Māori society.

One area that has not been highlighted is the lack of an indigenous missionary agency. George Budd notes that the Anglicans and Methodists sent mostly artisan missionaries to work with Māori.[33] The artisan missionaries all had a trade; they financially supported themselves, and thus could teach their converts a trade while developing an indigenous ministry. Wesleyans, Anglicans and Roman Catholics were quick to develop an indigenous lay ministry by ordaining Māori catechists who were charged with taking Christianity to their own people. This allowed them to get into the very fabric of the society to which they ministered.

By contrast, the Presbyterian Church sent ministers whose only trade was ministry. The idea was to rebuild the Scottish kirk among its immigrant population so that the church largely reflected the mother church in the Scottish homeland. The immigrants were determined to overcome the psalter's lament about not being able to sing the Lord's song in a strange land. Building an indigenous ministry to serve the indigenous population was beyond its theological capacity at the time. It was not until 1908 (sixty-eight years after the arrival of Presbyterianism) that Hakiaha and Manuaute of Taumarunui became the first Māori ordained as lay leaders in the Presbyterian Church, belatedly signalling the development of an indigenous agent; something that other churches had been much quicker to develop.

    Appeals for financial support went unanswered, and many times the Māori missions found themselves in financial debt, lacking any real financial benefactors to fund their mission. In the southern mission, there was little or no financial support for either the industrial school or the mission projects. When the Presbytery or the Synod did give grants, this amounted to a few pounds per annum and often, as with Patoromu Pu, conditions were applied to any funds that were granted. This lack of financial support for the southern mission was due, perhaps, to attitudes like that of Captain William Cargill, who contended, as we have seen, that problems of Māori were of their own making and that they had to help themselves first.[34]

    On a national scale, only twenty-five out of a total of eighty congregations contributed financially to the Māori Missions budget of £180 in 1889. James Doull, convener of the Māori Missions Committee, described this as pathetic, and publicly criticised his own church for its lack of support and encouragement, saying that other churches were doing more for Māori.[35] With such a small staff, he concluded that there was no reason for the Presbyterian Māori missions to be financially in debt. Towards the close of the century, the annual budget for the Māori missions decreased to £161, the majority of this amount going to support the sole remaining missionary. Church giving to Māori missions further decreased to £119, while contributions to foreign missions amounted to £602 annually. James Doull further stated publicly that charity begins at home before looking abroad.[36]

Credit has to be given to both the northern and southern missionaries for persevering with their mission with little support, either financial or in other resources. Only the Rev. Henry J Fletcher survived to see their sixty years of enterprise begin to show signs of blossoming at the beginning of the twentieth century, as the work was taken up by Edgerton Ward, the Rev. J G Laughton and an influx of deaconesses. Collectively, these missionaries would learn from the nineteenth century and build a healthy vibrant church, enabling Māori eventually to move into leadership and ownership of their part of the church.

Endnotes

1 Right Rev. P Tankersley (moderator, Presbyterian Church of Aotearoa New Zealand), Waitangi Day Address, Waitangi, 6 February 2008.
2 Archives Research Centre, Presbyterian Church of Aotearoa New Zealand, Register of New Zealand Presbyterian Ministers, Deaconesses & Missionaries 1840 to 2009, http://www.archives.presbyterian.org.nz/page143.htm, accessed 2 February, 2012.
3 J G Laughton, *From Forest Trail to City Street: The Story of the Presbyterian Church Among the Maori People* (Christchurch: Presbyterian Bookroom, 1961), 8.
4 G Budd, *The Story of Maori Missions: Being Five Studies* (Auckland: Presbyterian Women's Missionary Union, 1939), 9.
5 *New Zealand Gazette and Wellington Spectator*, II/68 (July 1841): 2.
6 Ibid, IV/318 (24 January 1844): 2.
7 Letter, J Macfarlane to Rev. Dr Welsh, 26 April 1841, in *The Home and Foreign Missionary Record*, November 1841, 405.
8 G S Parsonson, 'Duncan, James 1813–1907', in *Dictionary of New Zealand Biography, Volume One 1769–1869* (Wellington: Ministry of Culture and Heritage, 1990), 114–15. In 1847 a Whanganui chief was wounded by a junior officer in a shooting accident. As utu the Gilfillan farmstead was attacked. Mr. J.A.Gilfillan and his daughter were wounded, but his wife and three other children were murdered.
See James Cowan, *The New Zealand Wars: A History of the Maori Campaigns and the Pioneering Period: Vo1 (1845-64)*, (Wellington: R.E. Owen, 1955), 135.
9 W W Gibson, *The Rev. James Duncan: First Presbyterian Missionary to the Maori* (Auckland: Presbyterian Historical Society, 1975), 8.
10 Laughton, *From Forest Trail to City Street*, 8.
11 Gibson, *The Rev. James Duncan*, 19.
12 'Report of the Presbyterian Maori Missions Committee', in *Proceedings of the General Assembly of the Presbyterian Church of New Zealand* (PCNZ PGA), 1874.
13 PCNZ PGA, February 1890, 27.
14 J M Henderson, *Ratana: The Man, the Church, the Political Movement* (Wellington: Reed/Polynesian Society, 1963), 14.
15 K Newman, *Ratana Revisited: An Unfinished Legacy* (Auckland: Reed, 2006), 44.
16 Laughton, *From Forest Trail to City Street*, 9.

17 Letter, R J Allsworth to Hon. W Rollerston, Minister of Native Affairs, 26 August 1881, Archives, Home of Sisters of Compassion (AHSC), Wellington.
18 Letter, R J Allsworth to Ministry of Education, 11 January 1884, AHSC, Wellington.
19 J Irwin, 'The Rise and Fall of a Vision: Maori in the midst of Pakeha in the Presbyterian Church of New Zealand', PhD thesis, Victoria University of Wellington, 1994, 75.
20 Laughton, *From Forest Trail to City Street*, 11.
21 Budd, *Story of Maori Missions*, 14.
22 Te H Grace, *Tuwharetoa: The History of the Maori People of the Taupo District* (Wellington: Reed, 1959).
23 P Matheson, '1840–1870: The Settler Church', in D McEldowney (ed.), *Presbyterians in Aotearoa, 1840–1990* (Wellington: Presbyterian Church of New Zealand, 1990), 28.
24 Irwin, 'The Rise and Fall of a Vision', 55.
25 *Te Ao Hou* 57 (December 1966): 6.
26 Budd, *Story of Maori Missions*, 9.
27 Irwin, 'The Rise and Fall of a Vision', 60.
28 Peter Oettli, *God's Messenger: J.F. Riemenschneider and Racial Conflict in 19th Century New Zealand* (Wellington: Huia, 2008), 178-180.
29 Letter, F M Fahm (inspector of the North German Missionary Society) to Rev. T Alexander, 28 October 1867, Presbyterian Church of Aotearoa New Zealand Archives, Dunedin.
30 T A Pybus (ed. A W Reed), *Maori and Missionary: Early Christian Missions in the South Island of New Zealand* (Wellington: Reed, 1954), 142.
31 Budd, *Story of Maori Missions*, 12.
32 *Otago Witness*, 23 January 1869, 6.
33 Budd, *Story of Maori Missions*, 6.
34 T W H Brooking, *And Captain of Their Souls: Cargill & the Otago Colonists* (Dunedin: Otago Heritage Books, 1984), 123.
35 'Report of the Presbyterian Maori Missions Committee', in PCNZ PGA, 1889.
36 Ibid.

Chapter Two

Te Ope Whakaora, the Army that Brings Life: The Salvation Army and Māori

Harold Hill

On a number of occasions in recent years apologies have been offered to Māori because of past offences to their mana and invasions of their rights as tangata whenua. Ironically, the Salvation Army, a branch of the Christian church intentionally embodying the aggressive military metaphor, has recently apologised to Māori for its past retreat from involvement in their affairs. In the course of a hui held at Kaiwhaiki on the Whanganui River in October 2009, representatives of the organisation, including the territorial commander, Commissioner Donald Bell, and the rangatira of the Salvation Army Māori Fellowship, Captain Joe Patea, visited Hiruhārama to apologise for the Army's withdrawal of its officers from their mission on the river in 1899 and its failure to return. These expressions of regret were accepted by members of the whānau of Tamatea Aurunui, stalwart Salvationist of Hiruhārama in the late nineteenth century.

    A convoluted story lay behind this apology: one of noble endeavour and sad mistakes. The Army had, over the century, withdrawn not just from the Whanganui but from specifically Māori ministry in several other places in turn – from the Bay of Plenty, where it worked from 1896 to 1928, and from the East Coast, where it maintained a foothold from 1934 to 1992. This paper summarises the course of those efforts, as well as describing more recent activities on a national level. Finally, it attempts to draw some lessons.

The Salvation Army 'opened fire' in New Zealand in 1883, though it was not until five years later that an intentional mission to the tangata whenua was undertaken. The *War Cry* made few references to Māori in the intervening period. It is not clear why Salvationists lacked 'missionary' interest at this time, but it could be related to the fact that Māori were still overwhelmingly rural, while the Army began as an urban movement. Of the thirty-one centres of work established between 1883 and 1887, the majority were urban, and most rural corps opened were in the South Island – in places such as Waimate, Riverton, Leeston and Hokitika – which had a much sparser Māori population than in the north.[1] In a thesis on Baptist, Brethren and Salvation Army Māori missions, M K Smith points out that all three missions grew from a European demand for their presence in the new colony, and seem to have regarded the Pākehā population as their primary responsibility. The Army also had strong links with Britain, whereas the success of Māori missions seemed 'dependent on the extent to which the various groups and their members regarded themselves as indigenous'.[2] Certainly the appointment of a rapid succession of expatriate leaders was not calculated to indigenise the Salvation Army. Sheer lack of resources was doubtless another factor.

The key figure in the first phase of the Army's mission to Māori was Ernest Holdaway (Enata Horowe), 1863–1913. Jessie Munro in her life of Suzanne Aubert, the Catholic nun based for many years on the Whanganui River, notes that 'he was very tall, very handsome, very keen and put a lot of intelligent effort into learning Maori'.[3] The *War Cry* quoted him in 1889 as saying, 'I always think in Maori'.[4] His versatility as a musician also no doubt appealed to Māori – Suzanne Aubert established a Catholic brass band at Hiruhārama to counter the Salvationist influence.

Ernest Holdaway joined the Salvation Army in his home town of Nelson in 1884 and became an officer the following year. His first appointment saw him with a 'flying brigade' in North Canterbury, where he met the Māori Salvationist Hohepa Huria ('Māori Joe'

Solomon), followed by an interlude in Whanganui. Sent to pioneer the Army in Gisborne in 1886, he met Maraea Mohaki Morete (Morris), whose husband Pera Kararehe had been among those killed for utu by Te Kooti at Matawhero in 1868.[5] Escaping from the war party, Maraea testified in the 'treason trials' in 1869 and sought revenge for years before her conversion under Holdaway's ministry. She became the colour sergeant of the Gisborne Corps, and remained a Salvationist until her death in 1907.

Holdaway had a growing conviction of a calling to the Māori mission, and Colonel Josiah Taylor, colony commander, appointed him back to Whanganui in mid-1888, with his bride, Lizzie Edwards. They were accompanied by the part-Māori Lieutenant Henry de Blois and a Māori Salvationist, Wini Grey from Onehunga. They operated at first from a tent on the banks of the Whangaehu River, and held meetings with Māori camped for Land Court proceedings from January 1889. The *War Cry* claimed fifty conversions, and the Army gained such enthusiastic recruits as Piripi Pauro Tutawha and his wife Mere, and the heavily tattooed veteran Utiku Te Rangi Hikohia, known as 'Miro'.

Sadly, Lizzie Holdaway succumbed to typhoid fever in March, leaving her husband with a two-and-a-half-month-old baby girl, Eva Aroha. The child was cared for by friends for two years until Holdaway remarried and was joined on the river by his new wife, Agnes Alston.

In the meantime, Holdaway had met Tamatea Aurunui, a chief of the Te Āti Haunui-a-Paparangi, whose home was at Jerusalem (Hiruhārama). Formerly a Catholic catechist,[6] Tamatea threw his lot in with the Salvationists and invited Holdaway upriver, presenting him with a 24-foot canoe (which Holdaway named 'Rangimarie') for the purpose. The recently erected St Joseph's church at Hiruhārama had burned down before the Salvation Army arrived on the river, and Suzanne Aubert was away for a year collecting for its rebuilding so, as Jessie Munro observes, the Army 'by coincidence was almost occupying a vacuum'.[7] Relationships were not without friction: threats were made against the Salvationists, and Tamatea and Father Soulas later took each other to court with mutual accusations of sheep stealing (literal, not metaphorical, sheep were at stake).[8]

Tamatea had an iron-roofed house, still standing, with a full-length, dormer-windowed attic, which he made available for Salvation Army services. He accommodated the Salvationists and loaned them land for gardens. Holdaway was subsequently joined by a number of young men and women officers, whom he tutored in te reo and deployed further afield. Among these were John Nicholls, Walter Kemp, George Moore, Alexander Armstrong, Kate Bain, Margaret Wells, Agnes Scott and Hera Stirling. Recruits like Te Kare o Mahuru Te Tahua, a chief at Māwhitiwhiti, and Rikihana Te Taure at Ōtaki were influential supporters, and numbers of adherents grew.

At first Holdaway called his unit of the Army 'Te Taua Whakaora', but for some undocumented reason this 'war party that brings life' had by 1890 become 'Te Ope Whakaora'. Later, with the provision of a Māori song book and catechetical materials, a Māori division was formed on the basis of camps, such as Camp Jerusalem, Camp Manawatū, Camp Ngāti Awa and Camp Ngātiruanui in various places from the Taranaki down to Ōtaki. A 'division' is the Salvation Army equivalent of a diocese, and 'camp' was a Salvation Army term then current in the Australian outback, equivalent to a Methodist rural circuit.[9] At this time, therefore, the Army had, under the then colony commander Colonel Reuben Bailey, established parallel tikanga pākehā and tikanga Māori administrative structures at divisional level.

A 'Māori tribute' of one penny per soldier per month was levied on Pākehā corps for the support of the Māori work – though this was evidently not universally forthcoming. It is interesting to compare Holdaway's policy of cultural adaptation with that of Frederick Tucker in the initial phase of the Salvation Army's work in India in the 1880s, with his emphasis on learning the language, adopting of local names and dress, and 'living off the land' with the minimum of external financing.[10] Holdaway and his officers emulated early missionaries in traversing the back country on foot and on horseback, accepting hospitality where they found it.

Party attending the Salvation Army's sixth anniversary meetings in Christchurch, July 1889. Back: Mere Tutawha, Major Emmanuel Rolfe, Colonel Josiah Taylor, Captain John Nicholls. Front: Utiku Te Rangi Hikohia, Captain Ernest Holdaway, Maraea Te Kehu Te Waitaruna Tamatea, Piripe Pauro Tutawha. Seated, front: Tamatea Aurunui. *The War Cry*, 28 September 1889.

Lieutenant Robert Mackie was drowned when a canoe capsized in the Whakamataku Rapid; his body was never found.

The Salvationists also trekked out to celebrations such as the Army's sixth anniversary meetings held in Wellington in 1889, to which Holdaway took Miro, Piripi, Mere and the Tamateas; the same group undertook a fundraising tour in the South Island later that year.

In 1890, Holdaway took Miro, Maraea Tamatea and Maraea Morete to Melbourne to participate in meetings there. A group went to Wellington to greet General William Booth, the founder of the Salvation Army, on his first visit to New Zealand in 1891. In December 1891–January 1892 there was a hui at Parikino to discuss the extension of the railway line through the King Country. Te

Maraea Moana Mahaki Morete (Morris), Gisborne, 1887. Photograph by C P Browne, Salvation Army Archives.

Kooti attended, and the Salvationists were invited to hold a meeting outside his tent on Sunday 2 January. Holdaway and Maraea Morete had conversation with him – this was twenty-four years after Te Kooti had killed Maraea's husband.

In 1894, Colonel Bailey abolished the Māori Division on the grounds of expense and proposed that Pākehā corps would be responsible for evangelising Māori in their area – hardly practicable in that most Māori were rural. Holdaway was posted as divisional commander for the Auckland province and his specialist officers dispersed.

Later that year, however, Tamatea along with his daughter Maraea Te Kehu Te Waitaruna and Lieutenant Hori Aterea went with Holdaway to England, where an international congress was being held. Letters and the English *War Cry* reported that the Māori had been accorded a rapturous reception at the Crystal Palace. Among those present to greet them was Sir George Grey. In 1895–1896, Captain John Nicholls led a party consisting of Wini Grey, Hori Aterea, Maraea Tamatea and Hera Stirling on a seven-month evangelistic tour in Australia.

In 1896, a new commander, Brigadier W T Hoskin, reestablished the Māori Division, again with Holdaway as divisional commander. This time, however, Whanganui was inexplicably left out; the East Coast, Bay of Plenty and Ōtaki were included, and Holdaway's headquarters was to be in Gisborne. Nothing daunted, Holdaway pulled together some of his old team and reestablished a Māori officers' training programme there. Maraea Tamatea was one of his officers.

In 1899, yet another commander, Colonel W Estill, abolished the Māori Division once more. This time Holdaway was sent to Melbourne, and a Māori Regional Command, confined to the Bay of Plenty, was placed under an Irish officer, Adjutant Samuel Sadanand, who had served in India but did not speak Māori. Ivy Cresswell's *Canoe on the River*, an account of Holdaway's life, tells the anguished story:

> But what of the River Māori, whom Armstrong and Moore had come to love even as Horowe still loved them? Were they to be left without officers a second time, and perhaps for good? Armstrong pleaded the cause of the Māori, but to no avail. His D.O., who had been only a few years in New Zealand, did not seem to realise either the needs or the value of the Māori work; he evidently felt that pakeha work, which had problems enough of its own, should have the priority. Armstrong must proceed to Bulls. 'But what am I to do with the canoe?' asked Armstrong when he saw that further pleading was useless. 'Just tie it up at the bank', was the brief reply. With an aching heart Armstrong had to do as he was instructed.[11]

Discouraged, some of Holdaway's team resigned, including Captain John Nicholls (who became a Presbyterian) and Captain Arthur Seamer (who enjoyed a long career as a Methodist minister, superintendent of both Home and Māori Missions, president of the Methodist Conference and friend and advisor to both T W Rātana and Princess Te Puea). Ensign Hera Stirling became an Anglican lay worker, later marrying the Rev. Himepiri Munro, and was the first woman diocesan synodsperson in Waiapu (perhaps in the world) in 1922–1923. Envoy Emare Poraumati worked with both Presbyterians and Methodists before retiring to Rotorua, where she rejoined the Army.[12]

In 1902, Hera Stirling wrote of the Whanganui:

> I visited that district about two years ago. Maoris, who were formerly soldiers, still call themselves Salvationists. The Barracks at Jerusalem has never been opened for any purpose except Salvation Army meetings. The chief Tamatea will not open it for any other gathering, although his people often want him to do so. 'No', he says, 'I am waiting in faith for the Army to re-open at this place'. My eyes filled with tears when I stood and looked at the place that appeared to be forsaken. I am sure Tamatea's faith will not be in vain.[13]

By this time Maraea Tamatea had contracted tuberculosis and returned to Jerusalem to die. The *War Cry* reported her death in 1905. Thirty years later it was rumoured that 'there is a set of instruments at Jerusalem on the Wanganui River, in a hut near to the grave of the late Lieutenant Tamatea, which has been held by the Chief as "tapu" until such times as the Salvation Army returns to be their teachers'.[14] It did not happen.

Although Holdaway embraced ministry to Māori as his life's calling, he was able to spend just nine years directly responsible for the Salvation Army's Māori work in New Zealand: in 1888–1894 and 1896–1899. Having to watch the Māori Division dissolved not once but twice must have been deeply frustrating for Holdaway, but being a good soldier he saluted and got on with whatever other assignments he was given, both in New Zealand and in Australia. In such other appointments, however, he always managed to visit and support Māori and those still in that field when in New Zealand, or to introduce Māori cultural activities when in Australia. Five of his seven children were given Māori names – one of them 'Aurunui'. On his death at the age of forty-nine, he was provincial commander for Tasmania.

Not all Māori Salvationists were enlisted in the Māori Division, of course; people like Hohepa Huria and Maraea Morete were soldiers of predominantly Pākehā corps, at Kaiapoi and Gisborne respectively. There were urban Māori even at the turn of the century. At Petone, Hana Werohu Rangiwhaia Te Puni (1827–1913), widow of Henare Te Puni and daughter-in-law of Te Puni, who had welcomed Wakefield's settlers to Wellington, became a Salvationist in her sixties, attracted by the ministry of an outstanding woman officer, Captain Bessie Blincoe. The *War Cry* reported her as visiting Horowhenua, Whanganui and the Taranaki in support of Salvationist activities.

Some of Holdaway's protégés soldiered on. George and Catherine Moore in particular hung on in the Bay of Plenty, where in 1902 George was made regional officer for Māori work; he remained in this role until 1928. He shifted his base from Whakatāne to Tauranga in 1904 and began working with the Ngāi Tuwhiwhia, Ngāti Tauaiti and Te Whānau-a-Tauwhao hapū on Matakana and Rangiwaea Islands.

Concerned to provide impoverished local Māori with income from fishing, Moore established a Salvation Army fishing and fish-drying business on Rangiwaea, and then a freezing plant at Sulphur Point in 1907, marketing the fish in Auckland. This business, the Te Ope Fish Supply Company, was sold to Sanford in 1913. He had several assistants over the years, including Captain Robert Sampson (later a Presbyterian minister), his old Whanganui comrade Captain 'Kaha' Armstrong, his Māori convert Captain Joseph McCarthy (Motu Hinau), who died in 1906, and Captain Reg Watkins, who, as a volunteer stretcher-bearer, was killed on the Western Front in 1916. After the death of Envoy Kareti Karioi Taharangi[15] in 1917, Moore worked on alone.

Moore was more than an evangelist; in Cyril Bradwell's summary, 'he was doctor, chemist, veterinary surgeon, sanitary inspector and farming instructor, as well as spiritual advisor'.[16] He was a justice of the peace and held a first-grade interpreter's licence, often serving as court translator. He was seconded to the Health Department as a health inspector during smallpox epidemics in 1913 and 1923. He tried unsuccessfully to persuade banks to lend money to enable Māori communal farmers to enter the dairy industry and, while never getting involved politically, he regarded land confiscations as 'unfair'.[17]

In retrospect, Armstrong felt that Moore's varied activities left him insufficient time for evangelism.[18] Not surprisingly, the Army's leaders periodically expressed concern that their measures of success – statistics for converts enrolled as Salvationists and financial self-support – were not being achieved, however valuable Moore's services and however greatly they were appreciated by the Māori community.[19] Congregations declined. Moore resisted attempts to appoint him elsewhere, but the work was terminated by the territorial commander, Commissioner James Hay, in 1928. Moore took early retirement and went to work for Sanford, managing the Te Ope works, which he eventually bought back from them in instalments after they decided it was not viable in 1931. He continued with this as well as his welfare work in the district until his death at the age of seventy-six.

The Salvation Army's next foray into work among Māori was initiated in the early 1930s on the East Coast north of Gisborne. Basil and Mavyis Fairbrother, Salvationists teaching at the native school at Tokata-Te Araroa, began a Sunday school, and then another, and then a women's group, and then Sunday services. Finding they did not have time for these activities in addition to their teaching responsibilities, the Fairbrothers urged that officers be appointed to develop this work further.

When Lieut. Commissioner Frederick Adams arrived in New Zealand as territorial commander in 1934, he urged that some further effort be made to evangelise among the Māori. Lieut. Colonel Fred Burton was instructed to explore possibilities. This was a matter close to Burton's heart, as his wife Ruth, née Mogridge, had been one of Holdaway's officers. Burton interviewed Armstrong, Moore, Parker and Sansom, officers formerly engaged in Māori work, as well as the Rev. and Mrs Munro, and followed up officers who had earlier expressed an interest in working with Māori, such as Robert Prowse. He asked divisional commanders to report on which corps had substantial Māori populations in their areas, and what they were doing to contact those people. Burton's correspondence file for 1935–1936 includes over seventy letters and memos on Māori work prospects. Basil Fairbrother was gazetted an 'envoy' and made a marriage celebrant pending the appointment of officers.

Adjutant and Mrs Robert Prowse were appointed to Tokata-Te Araroa in 1936. They remained in the appointment until they retired in 1951, and lived in the community until they died; Bessie Prowse in 1962 and her husband in 1967. An ex-army hut was erected as a hall in 1946, and enlarged in 1948, in 1953 and again in 1964. Of the officers who followed the Prowses, Major and Mrs Harold Ingerson (1950–1958) and Major and Mrs Sam Medland (1958–1973) were the longest serving; Rex and Glenys Cross, Colin and Doreen Bell, James and Janet Cruden and Syd and Jean Rubie also worked there. Of local Salvationists, Henare and Nani (Ani Akuhata) Brown, early converts of Prowse, were best known.

Te Araroa was the focus of a very scattered community with a population of only a few hundred. It would appear that the Army's main emphasis in the area was on children's work – Major and Mrs Bell operated ten Sunday schools in outlying communities as well as Girl Guides groups in the late 1970s and early 1980s. However, Anglicanism remained the default religious profession of the community; the children may have gone to the Army Sunday school but went to church for confirmation and thereafter tended to drop out, and the Army never gathered a secure adult following. Young people had to move away for employment, and the population fell steadily. In 1987 the centre of East Coast work was shifted from Te Araroa to Tolaga Bay and renamed 'Te Ope Whakaora Regional Corps', but with depopulation the work became unsustainable. Although various options, such as relocating a Māori corps to Gisborne, were suggested, the work on the East Coast was closed in 1992 and officers withdrawn.

Subsequent Salvation Army attempts to relate to Māori have not been confined to specific localities. Since the 1980s endeavours have reflected a growing awareness of bicultural and multicultural issues in Aotearoa New Zealand, and a variety of attempts have been made to come to terms with these. In 1983, following Commissioner Dean Goffin's attendance at a confrontational Treaty workshop organised by the National Council of Churches Programme on Racism (and his own controversial public response in a sermon in St Paul's Cathedral, Wellington, at a service to mark the opening of a new session of Parliament), a Salvation Army Commission on Racism was set up.[20] Renamed the Council on Race Relations in 1986, it was replaced by a 'Cross-Cultural Ministries Council' in 1996.

Despite its focus on humanitarian, welfare and relief work, the Salvation Army had long shied away from involvement in 'political' questions – leading for example to strained relationships with the World Council of Churches in the early 1980s over that body's support for liberation movements in Africa. With the election of General Eva Burrows, an Australian who had worked many years in Rhodesia, to the international leadership of the Salvation Army in 1986, there was a renewed focus on principles of justice and equality. Burrows' 1987 'Agenda for the Future' urged Salvationists to champion the principles of justice and equality, and apply Christian solutions to all forms of racial and national prejudice. While Burrows was concerned particularly about apartheid, this statement encouraged liberal and activist attitudes elsewhere, including New Zealand.

In 1988 the Salvation Army became a founding member of the new ecumenical body the Conference of Churches of Aotearoa New Zealand, and assented to its 'bi-cultural partnership goal'. A 1989 statement on 'The Salvation Army and the Cultural Issue', prepared by the Army's Public Questions Board, incorporated the same principle. In 1990 church leaders, including the territorial commander of the Salvation Army, issued a statement about the Treaty, describing it as 'a key element in making us a unique nation and a living document affirming inalienable Māori rights and providing the basis for settlement, government and our life together as peoples of a Treaty'.[21]

The Council on Race Relations at Territorial Headquarters fostered training in Māori issues, held Treaty workshops, encouraged bilingual signage and promoted the development of Salvationist Māori fellowships, as well as keeping the issues before the Army's leadership.

Māori fellowships developed in Auckland and Wellington, and a working party in Auckland was formed to study and represent Māori issues in the Salvation Army. At the 1991 Congress Major Mavis Hirini was chosen as leader by the members of the Māori Fellowship meeting at the Victoria University marae, and in 1992 she was officially installed by Commissioner Earle Maxwell as the national convenor of the Army's Māori Fellowship. A bicultural advisory group set up in May 1996 became the Māori Strategy Council under her leadership. Some work was accomplished on Māori translations, for example of the 'Articles of War',[22] and a Māori supplement to the *Salvation Army Song Book*, during these years, as well as the building of community among Māori Salvationists.

In 1997 a policy statement was officially sanctioned by the Territorial Coordinating Council on 'The Salvation Army and the Treaty of Waitangi' that included mention of the Army's commitment to the goals of the Conference of Churches of Aotearoa New Zealand, and also contained this pledge:

> We will
> - affirm the importance of bicultural partnership,
> - provide a forum within the Salvation Army through which Māori voices and concern can be met,
> - include appropriately in worship, buildings and signage, the unique bicultural nature of our nation,
> - work towards ensuring Māori feel acceptance and safety within the Salvation Army.

In 1998 Captain Wayne Moses became the chairman of the Māori Strategy Council in succession to Major Hirini, who had retired. Moses felt that the bold statements and commitments made to Māori in recent years would lack credibility without the empowering of

Māori leadership. Over Labour Weekend 1999, a National Māori Hui was held at the Te Puea Memorial Marae at Māngere in Auckland, with Commissioner Ross Kendrew, the territorial commander, and Commissioner Fred Ruth from International Headquarters, London, in attendance. Commissioner Kendrew pledged dialogue and support for future 'partnership' in Salvation Army Māori work, and called for a twenty-five-year strategy.

One outcome was the appointment, in September 2000, of Captain Wayne Moses as leader responsible for Māori work in New Zealand, in addition to Wayne and Harriet Moses' existing appointment as corps officers at Mount Maunganui. Subsequently, the official Territorial Headquarters bulletin was for the first time printed in both English and Māori. In this 'transitional' role the Moseses promoted the development of Māori fellowships in such centres as Flaxmere, Mount Maunganui, Whanganui, Stratford, Foxton, Hamilton and Papakura. From June 2002 their base shifted to Whanganui, where they were additionally gazetted as assistant officers at Whanganui City Corps. The former Whanganui Corps Youth Hall was designated the national marae for Māori work, and was named 'Horoweiana' in honour of Ernest Holdaway.

A great deal was achieved during this period in encouraging Māori Salvationists and educating Pākehā Salvationists, as well as in representing the Salvation Army in the Māori world and in adding a Māori dimension to the Salvation Army's activities. Unfortunately the administrative arrangement whereby the national Māori leader was also responsible to divisional leadership and needed to carry the judgement of local leadership inevitably occasioned 'boundary disputes', so that, in Moses' words, 'The current strategy [whereby the rangatira was primarily responsible to a divisional commander because of his local corps responsibility] is a backward step and another gesture of disempowering Maori leadership … It sends messages of white Pakeha domination over Maori people'.[23] Moses was possibly hoping for a renewal of Holdaway's original 'tikanga Māori' mandate, but that did not eventuate; a period of transition without consensus on what it might lead to could not be sustained.

While in October 2003 Wayne and Harriett Moses were relieved of local corps responsibilities so that they could devote their time fully to work with the Māori Fellowship throughout the country, the underlying tensions were not completely resolved. The renewed association with Whanganui turned out to be a dead end. Unfortunately, because of a breakdown in health, Majors Wayne and Harriett Moses withdrew from Salvation Army officership in 2006. Since then the Māori Fellowship has functioned as a cultural association within the wider Salvation Army, with leadership provided by Joe and Nan Patea, at first on a part-time, voluntary basis and subsequently as full-time workers, based at Territorial Headquarters in Wellington. At a national hui in 2008, the Pateas were warranted as auxiliary captains. At that same event, Ernest Holdaway's piu piu and korowai, preserved by his Australian descendants, were received back as taonga of Te Ope Whakaora.

A number of themes are evident in the history of the Army's work among Māori. First, the frequent changes of policy and personnel in the early days allowed insufficient time for the work to take root and disillusioned those, both Māori and Pākehā, who had thrown their lot in with this mission. Decisions made on financial or administrative grounds by people who had no experience of or insight into Māori life adversely impacted on the work.

Second, it may be significant that the 1890s, as Andrew Mark Eason has shown, were also a period in which, in India and Southern Africa for example, the early Salvation Army missionary policy of cultural adaptation, exemplified also by Holdaway's mode of operation in New Zealand, was replaced by a greater emphasis on 'social salvation'. This assimilationist model saw indigenous culture as something to be left behind. Eason's argument is that the policy of adaptation to indigenous culture derived from the Booths' policy of adapting to working class culture in Britain, and that its attenuation was one of the consequences of the adoption of the 'Darkest England' social scheme in Britain.[24] The decision to disband the Māori Division for the first time in 1894 was taken at a conference in Christchurch, apparently for financial reasons, and while there is no evidence that the new policy was dictated from Melbourne or London, it is interesting that the same pattern of changes in both policy and personnel can be seen in other mission fields, in Southern Africa and in India, in this period.

Third, the Army was unable to capitalise on the opportunities presented by the post-Second World War urban drift and consequent weakening of the East Coast work. Discussions took place with Major (Rev.) K Harawira (vocational guidance officer) and Mr Athol Kirk (of the Department of Education) about the need for a hostel for Māori youth in Auckland after the Second World War, but a property could not be secured. Such a hostel was provided in Gisborne in the 1960s, but beyond this there appeared to be little vision or funds available for the possibilities opening up. A 'Maori Affairs Board' established by Commissioner Alfred Gilliard in 1961 was allowed to lapse by his successors. Pleas from successive Te Araroa officers for more pastoral care for young Māori relocating to cities did not always find an adequate response.

Fourth, leadership of Māori work long remained largely European, and the fostering of Māori leadership was not seen as a priority until recently. The small numbers of Māori associated with the Army over the years and the fact that very few became officers, and that most of those who did so tended to identify with Pākehā rather than Māori culture, meant that the available pool of indigenous leadership was limited.[25]

Fifth, despite the good intentions of leadership at various times, the Army in New Zealand remained monocultural and European in outlook. A rare reflection on this fact is found in Joan Hutson's history of the Gisborne Corps:

> A big question mark remains with regard to the Maori ministry in Gisborne. It began so well, only to fade into obscurity during those first decades. What happened? Were the cultures in the end too different? Were the Maori soldiery overwhelmed by the colonial mindset and then the Scottish flood of immigrants? Or did it come back to the vacillation of Army leadership with regard to Maori Mission policy?[26]

This Eurocentrism also meant that the expectations placed upon the Māori work, at least for much of the twentieth century, were for essentially Pākehā outcomes – uniformed soldiers, bands and songsters (choirs) as in Pākehā corps – though experienced workers like Moore and Prowse warned against such goals and urged greater understanding of Māori culture. Māori coming in from the country did not always find it easy to integrate into urban corps life. Eurocentrism also involved tokenism; expressions of Māori culture were an 'add-on' for special occasions without any connection with the actual life of the people, and no concessions were made to Māori ways of doing things when it came to decision-making.

Sixth, with the increased awareness of the significance of cultural issues over the past twenty-five years or so, and the increasing diversity of New Zealand society, there have been periodic attempts to promote multiculturalism as an alternative to biculturalism within the Salvation Army. This has happened partly because of a lack of insight into the significance of the tangata whenua as Treaty partners, arising both from the Army's internationalism and the fact that senior leadership was often from overseas and of relatively short tenure, as well as from a sincere recognition of the needs of other cultural groups in the New Zealand community. Māori have tended to feel that such moves undermine the prior commitment to the bicultural objective.

Seventh, the serious and well-intentioned efforts made in recent years to encourage Māori work have been undermined by residual tendencies to paternalism and the difficulty of reconciling the competing claims of local work and national aspirations. The administrative structure, requiring the Māori leadership to fulfil a dual mandate, to local corps and division as well as to national Māori responsibilities, was, unwittingly, set up to fail. The relationship between one divisional commander and Wayne Moses reprised the reluctance of two North Island Anglican dioceses to cooperate with Bishop Bennett in the 1930s and the refusal of the Bishop of Auckland to allow the Bishop of Aotearoa access to minister to Māori in the northern diocese from 1940 to 1960.[27]

This relates to an eighth general issue needing to be considered: the shape of a future Māori fellowship and its relation to the wider Salvation Army. Some churches – Anglican, Methodist, Presbyterian, Baptist – have developed parallel Māori and Pākehā administrative 'silos', while others, like the Roman Catholic Church, prefer to maintain some form of fellowship within the wider structure. In Holdaway's day, two brief attempts were made to establish a separate Māori division (and even separate Māori and Pākehā corps in Whanganui). The Army actually pioneered the former model, before returning to an assimilationist or integrationist policy. More recently it has attempted to find a middle way. Members of the fellowship have juggled loyalties and time commitment, to their local corps as well as to the wider Māori expression of the Salvation Army. Can the Army's ethos and structure accommodate the Māori way of doing things and aspirations to tino rangatiratanga? Can Māori influence the wider Salvation Army culture significantly?

The 1989 statement on 'The Salvation Army and the Cultural Issue', prepared by the Army's Public Questions Board, stated that 'there is no indication that today's Māori Salvationists desire any separate structure or function', and the Māori Fellowship Hui held during the 1991 Salvation Army Congress agreed. In that same year, however, the Army's Council on Race Relations recommended setting a goal to establish a Māori division and a Māori divisional commander by the year 2000.[28] Among both Māori and Pākehā Salvationists today there could be a range of opinion as to the most appropriate way to resolve this question, which has echoes of a wider, national political debate as well. About such matters there is a serious need for biblical and theological reflection, and not merely pragmatic accommodation to competing social and political ideologies.

In the more than 120 years since Ernest and Elizabeth Holdaway pioneered work among the Māori of the Whanganui district, some heroic and self-sacrificing work has been accomplished and some short-sighted decisions made. The views of Salvationists on bicultural relations are doubtless as various as those of any other citizens. There has been encouraging development in the Army's official attitudes to Māori, but a serious disconnection remains. Although Māori make up approximately 15 percent of New Zealand's population today, nationally 35 percent of people using Salvation Army social services are Māori; this figure is more like 50 percent in parts of the North Island. At the same time only a handful of Māori align themselves with the Salvation Army as a religious denomination or make it their community of faith.[29] With the revival of taha Māori and te reo Māori in recent years, the Salvation Army needs to continue to look for ways of relating more intentionally to Māori culture in order to secure a future with Māori.

As described in the introduction to this paper, in October 2009 a hīkoi of Salvationists was welcomed on to the lower marae at Hiruhārama, following which prayer was offered at the grave of Tamatea Aurunui and at his house above the marae. Responding to the Army spokesmen, Piripi Tamatea, great-great-grand-nephew of the old chief, said, 'That door is now closed; another door has now opened' (I te katinga o te tatau ka huaki te huarahi.)

Endnotes

1 A 'corps' is the basic Salvation Army unit, equivalent of a 'parish' or congregation.
2 M K Smith, 'Maori Missions – A New Wave: Baptist, Brethren, Salvation Army and the United Maori Mission 1880–1950', MA thesis, Auckland University, 1985, 1.
3 J Munro, *The Story of Suzanne Aubert* (Auckland: Auckland University Press/Bridget Williams Books, 1996), 195.
4 *War Cry*, 16 November 1889: 7.
5 This period of Maraea's life is described by Judith Binney in *Redemption Songs: A Life of the Nineteenth-century Maori Leader Te Kooti Arikirangi Te Turuki* (Auckland: Auckland University Press/ Bridget Williams Books, 1995).
6 *The Victory*, October 1898: 395–8.
7 Munro, *Suzanne Aubert*, 194.
8 Ibid, 289 and 432.
9 B Bolton, *Booth's Drum: The Salvation Army in Australia 1880–1980* (Sydney: Hodder & Stoughton, 1980), 82. Until 1913, the Salvation Army in New Zealand was part of an Australasian territory, with headquarters in Melbourne.
10 F B Tucker, *Muktifauj, or, Forty years with the Salvation Army in India and Ceylon* (London: Marshall Brothers, 1923). Māori costume was worn only for special occasions and concert performances in Holdaway's case, but that had long been true of Māori in general by that date.
11 I Cresswell, *Canoe on the River*, first published in *War Cry* in installments in 1971 and reprinted in H Hill (ed.), *Te Ope Whakaora, The Army that brings Life: A collection of documents on the Salvation Army and Maori 1884–2007* (Wellington: Flag Publications, 2007), 170. Cresswell probably heard this story from Armstrong. 'D.O.' signifies divisional officer or divisional commander.

12 Envoy is a non-commissioned rank in the Salvation Army; it was usually non-stipendiary at this time.
13 *All the World*, October 1903: 544.
14 Letter, Lieut. Colonel F Burton to Lieut. Commissioner F Adams, Territorial Commander, 7 May 1935, Salvation Army Archives, Wellington.
15 Son of Ngāi Te Rangi chief, Hone Taharangi, who had lost a leg in the battle of Gate Pā, and died in 1913.
16 C R Bradwell, 'Moore, George – Biography', from the *Dictionary of New Zealand Biography*, in *Te Ara – the Encyclopedia of New Zealand*: www.teara.govt.nz/en/biographies/3m58/1/1 (accessed 3 January 2012).
17 Correspondence and 'Notes of a Conference with Major Moore, 1923', Salvation Army Archives, Wellington.
18 Notes of interview with Lieut. Colonel F Burton, 22 February 1935, Salvation Army Archives, Wellington.
19 For example, correspondence and interview with the territorial commander, Commissioner Richards, July–August 1913, Salvation Army Archives, Wellington.
20 Goffin felt that the workshop required Pākehā and the church-leader participants in particular to accept responsibility for Treaty breaches; in his sermon he chose to criticise this approach and regretted the passing of an earlier time in which he felt race relations had been happier without such issues being raised.
21 Leaders' Statement, Conference of Churches in Aotearoa New Zealand (1990).
22 The 'Articles of War' or 'Soldier's Covenant' are signed by those becoming members of the Salvation Army. It is not known whether any copies of Holdaway's original translation survive.
23 Letter, Captain W Moses to Colonel R Redhead, 14 January 2002, Salvation Army Archives, Wellington.
24 A M Eason, 'Christianity in a Colonial Age: Salvation Army Foreign Missions from Britain to India and South Africa, 1882–1929', PhD thesis, University of Calgary, 2005. Stage Three of the 'Darkest England' scheme, never fully implemented, envisaged the relief of unemployment in Britain by large-scale emigration to occupy the 'empty lands' in the colonies. Booth did not take up the 10,000 acres offered in New Zealand (C R Bradwell, *Fight the Good Fight* (Wellington: Reed, 1982), 58). An interesting historical footnote is provided by a gift by Messrs Alexander and McGregor of land near Putaruru in the south Waikato, where a boys' home, named Hodderville, was built in 1920. Forty years later *Te Ao Hou* stated that 'One of the best training grounds for Maori farmers is the Salvation Army farm training school at Hodderville. The farm, covering 2060 acres, has 25 trainees who undergo a two-year course. Of 90 youths who have graduated so far, 28 have been Maoris.' *Te Ao Hou* 30 (March 1960): 14.
25 In the 1956 census only 136 people identified themselves as both Māori and Salvationist; in 1961, 153; in 1986, 492 and in 2001, 726.
26 J Hutson, *As For Me and My House: A Salute to Early Gisborne Salvation Army Families 1886–1952* (Wellington: Flag Publications, 2004), 227.
27 A Davidson, *Christianity in Aotearoa: A History of Church and Society in New Zealand* (Wellington: Education for Ministry Network, 1990), 132–3.
28 Report and minutes of these can be found in the Salvation Army Archives, Wellington.
29 In the 2006 Census, 0.063 percent of those who entered 'Salvation Army' as their religious denomination also described themselves as Māori.

Chapter Three

Intercultural Exchange, Matakite Māori and the Mormon Church

Robert Joseph

Kei muri i te awe kāpara, Behind the tattooed face,
he tangata kē. a stranger stands.
Nōna te ao – he mā. He will inherit the world – he is white.[1]

Introduction

According to Ngāti Whatua sources, the prophecy above was uttered by their tribal tohunga matakite (seer), Titahi, who foretold the bittersweet arrival of the Pākehā[2] and the subsequent impacts of European contact, which thrust the Māori world view into a state of perilous imbalance as had been prophesied. Land and natural resource loss through unjust wars, confiscations and other legal machinations wreaked havoc on the relationship between people and the natural environment. The forcible individualisation of land, property and world views in the Native Land Court disturbed the balance between members of kin groups. Introduced diseases and addictive substances – alcohol, tobacco, coffee, tea and sugar – decimated tribal populations and undermined Māori health and well-being. Christianity damaged in many ways the connection between the people and the gods, and the individualistic and economic assumptions of European capitalism and Western liberalism destroyed traditional tribal reciprocity economies, the equilibrium between kin, the physical and metaphysical world, the environment and the fundamental obligations to past, present and future generations.

In a Mormon historical view, a similar narrative is recorded by a rangatira who prophesied: 'When I depart from here to join my people who are waiting for me at home, weep not for me, but weep for yourselves; for the time is come and now is when alien white feet shall desecrate my grave.'[3] The first missionaries (often referred to as elders) of the Church of Jesus Christ of Latter-day Saints (LDS or the Mormon Church) arrived in New Zealand in the 1880s to live and proselytise among Māori over two centuries after Abel Tasman had first reached these shores. Notwithstanding the foretold calamities, Māori and the Mormon missionaries discovered that they had much in common, including a common heritage, spiritual beliefs, customary traditions and hope for the future. Many of the religious beliefs of these two peoples paralleled each other in surprising and initially inexplicable ways.

While this discovery was unanticipated by the LDS missionaries, Māori tohunga ironically predicted that a fullness of religious truth and salvation would also come to Māori from the Pākehā. It would be a combination of the natural similarities between these two groups, the dissatisfaction of Māori with other Christian churches in New Zealand, the respectful intercultural approach of the Mormon missionaries to Māori and the predictions of the tohunga matakite that would lead many Māori into the Mormon Church.

This chapter will analyse a subjective Māori Mormon view of the intercultural approach of the Mormon missionaries and the prophesied arrival of the Mormon message and messengers to a number of Māori tribes where it flourished. The author's narrative is subjective in that it represents the view of one who is Māori and has been brought up in the Mormon Church, with whakapapa going back to some of the original Mormon Māori converts in the 1880s. To balance this, however, the narrative will acknowledge other non-Mormon and, where appropriate, non-Māori alternative narratives. The use of primary sources allows the subjective views of those who were eye witnesses to events to further enlighten this analysis. I respectfully apologise in advance to those Māori Mormon whānau, hapū and iwi who are not discussed in this chapter. Time and space have precluded inclusion here, but it is hoped that these narratives will be analysed in subsequent works.

Why the Mormon Church?

Why did the Mormon Church appeal to some Māori tribes? Most Māori had been converted to the Protestant and Roman Catholic churches by the 1850s. However, when Māori were cheated in land deals by the laws and institutions of the state, they naturally responded by defending their lands, lives, liberties and tino rangatiratanga (self-determination rights). This tended to alienate them from other Christian sects, due to missionary involvement with the colonial Government during the New Zealand Wars period (1860s–1880s). Understandably, 'the only way it was possible for anyone to influence the Maoris at the time was to become as "Maorified" as possible'.[4] Mormon missionaries understood this injunction and the critical view recently expounded by Terry Warner, who opined that 'to influence, you must first be influenced'.[5] The Mormon missionary Oliver Cowdery Dunford recorded one of the reasons for his success among Māori in his journal in November 1889:

> As our Mission was to the Maori people, we soon became at home with the Maori. We spoke the Maori language, we ate the Maori food, we slept in the Maori huts, we slept in Maori beds, we studied Maori traditions, we studied Maori superstitions. In short as time passed, we began to think like Maori, to feel like Maori and no doubt look like Maori's.[6]

Commentary on the intercultural respect of the missionary John Ephraim Magleby[7] provides another insight into the successful efforts of the Mormon approach to Māori: 'Ephraim never refused any call for help from the Maori people. … He lived in their huts and ate their food, which pleased them to no end. … In essence, he followed the Maori way of life and in the meantime taught them the precious truths of the Gospel.'[8]

When William Bromley was called as New Zealand Mission president in 1881, his presiding leader in Utah, Joseph F Smith, directed him that the time was right to take the gospel to Māori.[9] The first successes among them came in 1883, but once the Māori and the Mormons got together, Māori converts flocked in large numbers into the Mormon Church from a number of tribes.[10]

After 1881, thousands were baptised into the Mormon Church. In August 1885, there were sixteen Māori and four Pākehā branches of the Mormon Church in New Zealand, and this number continued to grow steadily for the next fifteen years. At the close of 1887, there were 2573 Latter-day Saints. This means that in the year 1887 alone, 2055 Māori and 237 Europeans joined the Mormon Church.[11] At the turn of the century, there were nearly 4000 Māori in the Mormon Church, accounting for nearly a tenth of the total Māori population.[12] In 1901 there were seventy-nine Māori branches of the Mormon Church in New Zealand.[13]

This success has continued into recent times; there was a total of over 21,000 Māori members in New Zealand in 2001.[14] According to the 2006 Census, the main Christian denominations in New Zealand were Anglicans, Roman Catholics, Presbyterians and Methodists, with 'significant numbers' in the Mormon Church.[15] By 2010, the number of Mormons in New Zealand had increased to 103,802,[16] but it is difficult to track down the exact Māori population within that figure, given that ethnicity is no longer recorded in official church records. Still, from a cursory view, Māori numbers are still high in the Mormon Church in certain areas.

The Māori appear to have been prepared in special ways for the coming of the Mormon missionaries, at least in Mormon narratives.[17] To understand this preparation, one has to understand, respect and appreciate the traditional world view of Māori, te reo Māori (language), tikanga Māori (customs and traditions), mātauranga Māori (knowledge systems) and matakite Māori (seers). It was a combination of the effective intercultural approach of the Mormon Church towards Māori and the utterances of specific tohunga matakite Māori that was crucial in this preparation and in accurately explaining the success of the Mormon message to Māori.

Tohunga matakite Māori

Tohunga Māori or expert priests supervised worship and all else that was involved in the traditional Māori religious system that was based on tikanga Māori. Sometimes tohunga became mediums for the atua (gods) they served. In these roles, the tohunga would give oracles, cure diseases and admonish the people.[18] After the advent of Christianity, some tohunga continued to carry on the former practices, or blended the two. In some instances, kaumātua (family patriarchs and village elders) and rangatira (chiefs)[19] acted as tohunga matakite who were 'regarded with feelings of reverence, and were credited with possessing supernatural powers'.[20] Bronwyn Elsmore even asserts that prophecy was such a normal part of Māori tradition that nearly all rangatira could claim this designation.[21]

One must also remember the importance of direct revelation, which provided the foundation for the holy scriptures. In that same spirit, Joel 2:28–9 sheds light on this subject, in a way validating tohunga Māori prophesying future events. Referring to the last days, the scriptures state: 'And it shall come to pass afterward that I will pour out my spirit upon all flesh; and your sons and your daughters shall prophesy, your old men shall dream dreams, your young men shall see visions. And also upon my servants and upon the handmaids in those days will I pour out my spirit.' Numbers 12:6 further adds to this: 'If there be a prophet among you, I the Lord will make myself known unto him in a vision and will speak unto him in a dream'.

However, other Christian churches during the nineteenth century discounted the importance of revelation, dreams and visions, and Māori felt that Pākehā had lost the 'capacity for wonder or awe inspired by the unknown'.[22] Bronwyn Elsmore asserts that 'it seemed to the Māori that the Pākehā lacked contact with his God, for such agencies of communication as divination and dreams were condemned by them'.[23] Through the priesthood within the Mormon Church, direct revelation, visions and dreams could be legitimately acknowledged and restored to their fullness, and Māori appeared to recognise this.[24]

It is not surprising then that in 1880, the missionary George Batt wrote from New Zealand in a letter to the editor of the *Deseret*

News in Utah: 'I would like to call your attention to the Maories, the natives of this country. It strikes me very forcibly that they are about ready for the Gospel. They are firm believers in present revelation from God.'[25]

With this preface in mind, a number of tohunga matakite made significant prophecies concerning the coming to Aotearoa New Zealand of a true church. In the Mormon historic narrative, as a result of such prophetic utterances, a number of Māori in certain tribal areas ultimately joined the Mormon Church. Each instance of prophecy is therefore of great interest to Latter-day Saints. I will provide three detailed accounts in this chapter.

Arama Te Toiroa – Te Tai Rāwhiti tohunga matakite
In 1830, the year in which the Mormon Church was organised in Fayette, New York, by the young prophet Joseph Smith, an aged patriarch and tohunga matakite named Arama Te Toiroa gathered his whānau and hapū together in Te Māhia to advise them about a new church. Prior to 1830, Toiroa made a number of great prophecies. Three examples will illustrate the mana (respect) and veneration in which Toiroa was held by the people of Te Tai Rāwhiti (the East Coast of the North Island around Tūranga).

In the oral Tai Rāwhiti narratives, in approximately 1766, the spirit of prophecy entered into Toiroa, who foresaw the coming of strangers with red or white skin like the earthworm titipa. Toiroa named these people Pakerewha, possibly alluding to rewha (disease). Toiroa drew images of the Pakerewha in the sand with their ships, carts and horses, although he did not know names for these things at the time. He wove items of clothing out of harakeke (flax), including a little basket that, once finished, he placed on his head and called a taupopoki (hat). Toiroa then slit his cloak and turned it into pūkoro (trousers), which he wore.

Toiroa made a strange article from a kōkōmuka shrub and puffed smoke from the dried pōhata leaf; he named the article 'he ngongo' (a pipe). Toiroa also made a wooden sailing boat with a rudder, then took a small black mussel shell and set a fire burning within it (so that it looked like a funnel steamer), which he called ngātoroirangi (the fires of heaven). All of these tokens of a changing world Toiroa transported to the nearby pā (villages), including those in Tūranga (Poverty Bay), where the great British navigator James Cook would make his first landfall three years later.[26]

Toiroa made other prophecies, such as predicting who would survive and how opposition foe would die in tribal battles,[27] the birth of children[28] and counsel on religious matters. An example of the latter in the Ringatū Church narrative was given as follows: 'Te ingoa o tō rātou Atua, ko Tama-i-rorokutia, he Atua pai, otirā, ka ngaro anō te tangata. The name of their God will be Tama-i-rorokutia (Son-who-was-killed), a good God, however the people will still be oppressed.'[29]

To his people, Toiroa was considered a great tohunga matakite, so his whānau and hapū listened very carefully to what he had to say in Te Māhia in 1830. This was Toiroa's key prophecy in a Mormon context. It was recorded by one of his mokopuna (grandchildren), Hirini Te Rito Whaanga, who converted to the Mormon Church on 8 November 1884 in Nūhaka. Hirini actually recorded Toiroa's prophecy in 1902 while living in Salt Lake City, Utah, where he and his whānau had migrated:

> I desire to tell you of a prophecy of one of my forefathers, Arama Toiroa. Amongst our people this chief was regarded as a seer. … In the year 1830, this Arama Toiroa gathered his children, grandchildren and relatives together. At this time, most of his descendants had joined the Church of England, and the aged chief, addressing them, said: 'My dear friends, you must leave that church, for it is not the true church of the God of heaven. The church you have joined is from the earth and not from heaven.' Upon hearing this, his people asked, 'Where then can we find a church where we can worship the true God?'
>
> Arama Toiroa answered,
>
>> There will come to you a true form of worship; it will be brought from the east, even from beyond the heavens. It will be brought across the great ocean and you will hear

> of it coming to Poneke (Wellington) … and afterwards its representatives will come to Te Mahia. They will then go northward to Waiapu but will return to Te Mahia.
>
> When this 'Karakia', form of worship, is introduced amongst you, you will know it, for one shall stand and raise both hands to heaven.
>
> When you see this sign, enter into that church. Many of you will join the church and afterwards one will go from amongst you the same way that the ministers came even unto the land from afar off.[30]

Fifty-four years passed before Toiroa's utterances were fulfilled. In 1884, the Mormon elders Alma Greenwood and Ira Hinckley brought the Mormon message to the Pōneke area and then made their way to Hawke's Bay. There they were joined by President William Thomas Stewart, and together they all traversed the path Toiroa had predicted. It was at Korongata (now Bridge Pā,[31] Hastings), however, and not at Te Māhia, that Arama's descendants first accepted the Mormon message. Hirini Whaanga described the day when the gospel was first preached to some of Toiroa's people:

> In journeying northward they reached … Korongata, where many of us were assembled on the Sabbath day. Amongst the people who were there was a grandson of Arama Toiroa whose name was Te Teira Marutu.
>
> The meeting was conducted by Elder Stewart and his friends. The services were opened with singing and prayer, and a Gospel address was delivered, after which they sang again, and Brother Stewart arose to dismiss with prayer. In doing so he raised both hands and invoked God's blessing upon the people.[32]
>
> As soon as the grandson of Arama Toiroa saw this he arose and declared that this was the church of which his forefather prophesied which would surely be firmly established amongst the Māori people. He and his wife applied for baptism, and they and their children were thus initiated into the Church by Elder Stewart.[33]

Mel Tuati Whaanga recently augmented the narrative with these remarks:

> In 1884, Ihaka Whaanga [father of Hirini Whaanga] received word that a new religion had arrived at Korongata in Hastings. He sent his two eldest sons, Hirini and Ihaka (II) to investigate it. They arrived on the sabbath day. … At the end of the meeting Elder Stewart stood to offer the closing prayer and raised both hands above his head. This was the sign Toiroa had foretold. The two sons returned to Mahia and told their father what they had seen and heard. [Ihaka] Whaanga was pleased and gave permission for the new religion to come to Mahia, however he died before the missionaries arrived.[34]

On 11 April 1884, Elders Greenwood and Hinckley then visited Taonoke (near Omahu, Hastings) in response to a telegraphed invitation from Otene Meihana, which resulted in his baptism along with thirteen others on 27 April 1884. Mormon branches were subsequently established at Taonoke, Wairoa, Nūhaka, Te Māhia, Te Muriwai, Te Ārai, Gisborne and other areas of the East Coast.[35]

When the missionaries visited Te Māhia and held meetings with other descendants of Toiroa, after seeing the sign, these people said, 'This is indeed the church for us, for did not our revered forefather, Arama Toiroa, prophesy about it?'[36] Largely as a result of this prophecy, every person in Korongata and a large number of Māori in Nūhaka and Te Māhia were baptised into the Mormon Church. The final stanza of Toiroa's prophecy was the divine injunction Hirini Te Rito, his wife Mere Eia Mete and their whānau referred to, which mandated their migration to Utah in 1894.

One other incident worthy of discussion occurred when the Mormon elders visited Te Ārai (Manutuke) in 1886. When President Stewart and his missionaries arrived in Te Ārai, Te Hāhi Mihinare (the Church of England) was holding a diocesan conference with over 2000 Māori in attendance under the direction of Bishop William Williams. The arrival of the Mormon missionaries naturally created quite a disturbance. The Mormon historical narrative records that Bishop Williams welcomed the manuhiri (visitors) in his whaikōrero (welcome speech) as follows:

> Haere mai e te manuhiri tuarangi. I whea koe i te wa e hihi ana te kiko o te tangata i runga i nga kohatu o te umu? Whango rawa koe kai tau i a au to ai o ki runga i te mata o te whenua, ina rawa koe to haere nei, te takahi mai nei i taku patohe. Kati nei pea maku ko tenei.
>
> Welcome thou honoured guest. Where were you when the flesh of man singed on the stones of the oven? You have waited until I have made peace between man and man; then you have come trespassing on my preserves. As host I cannot but extend to you accommodation and food.

Bishop Williams had certainly issued a strong wero (challenge). President Stewart responded in his whaikōrero:

> I thank you most venerable Bishop for your welcome to me and my party. On all occasions when the Lord sent his servants with a message to the people of the world, he always sent some to prepare the way for them. In the meridian of time when he sent His only Begotten Son, he sent John and John came bounding from the wilderness, saying 'I am come to prepare the way for him whose shoes I am not worthy to unloose'. I am sent of the Lord with a message for these people, and you are my forerunner. You have prepared the way for me, and I congratulate you on your fine preparatory work. The flesh of man no longer singed on the stones of the oven. You have translated the Bible into Maori, and everything is in readiness for me. Again I thank you sir.[37]

Māori were very impressed with Stewart's response, and some asked to hear the message of these new ministers, to which Bishop Williams acquiesced. Some invited the elders to visit them in their homes after the hui. Subsequently, many of the Ngāti Konohi, Ngāti Oneone, Te Aitanga-a-Māhaki, Rongowhakaata and Te Muriwai people were converted to the Mormon Church.[38] Although unclear on the details, these people were familiar with Toiroa's prophecies, and rumours of new ministers with another message had spread into these areas.

Willard Amaru recorded that his tupuna (ancestor), Karaitiana Tuketenui Amaru, attended the Te Ārai hui, and he recorded that, following his response to Bishop Williams, President Stewart raised his hand to the square, greeted the people – 'tēnā koutou te Whare o Iharaira' (greetings to you the House of Israel) – then began to preach the restored gospel of Jesus Christ. The Amaru narrative added that when Karaitiana returned to Tolaga Bay (Uawa), he was aware of the prophecies (of Toiroa) about the true church for his people. He was baptised, and a large number of Te Aitanga-a-Hauiti entered into the Mormon waters of baptism.[39]

Before we leave Toiroa, two final points will be mentioned. All Māori (and non-Māori, for that matter) prophecies are capable of more than one interpretation, as alluded to above. The true tohunga matakite could not err. It was left to the interpreter to make mistakes.[40] Many of Toiroa's prophecies, including the narrative by Whaanga above, were interpreted by Te Kooti to establish his church Te Hāhi Ringatū – the Ringatū Church. Judith Binney in this respect recorded the following:

> Among the seminal narratives of Toiroa and Te Kooti, there is one concerning Te Kooti's visit to Nukutaurua when still a young man. … Toiroa then predicted to Te Kooti that he would see him coming from Turanga [Gisborne], weeping, and disappearing on a raupo raft beyond Papahuakina (Table Cape). But soon he would return, bearing the prayers of the faith with his hand upraised. Thus, in this narrative, Toiroa foresaw the coming of the new faith, the Ringatu or Upraised Hand.[41]

There are, therefore, contested narratives interpreting Toiroa's prophecies regarding the new church for Māori. Interestingly, Bishop Williams alleged that Te Kooti commanded his followers to 'avoid all intercourse with the Mormon teachers'.[42]

The last note I will make on Toiroa concerns Hamiora Mangakāhia, who, with Te Kooti, was another student of Toiroa. Mangakāhia considered that he too had been chosen to fulfil

Toiroa's quest for peace, which the prophet had articulated in 1858, following his death in 1867.⁴³ Mangakāhia quoted a prediction of Toiroa that it would be 'the distant descendant' (te Miha) – who would one day bring about this peace.⁴⁴ Mangakāhia later became the first premier of the Kotahitanga Māori Parliament, in 1892 at Papawai. In this manner, the lines of authority descending from Toiroa's mana were similarly alleged to have been woven into the Ringatū Church, the Mormon Church and the Kotahitanga Māori Parliament. Incidentally, Mangakāhia subsequently converted to the Mormon Church, as did many rangatira in the Wairarapa at Papawai, Te Ore Ore and Pirinoa, among other places. It is to the Wairarapa that we will now turn, to discuss another well-known prophecy, of the great tohunga matakite Paora Te Pōtangaroa.

Paora Te Potangaroa – *Wairarapa Moana tohunga matakite*

Paora Te Pōtangaroa was a tohunga matakite of the Wairarapa, and was recognised as such from the early 1860s. In the late

Paora Pōtangaroa. Reproduced with the permission of Rangi Parker of the Kia Ngawari Trust.

1870s, Pōtangaroa was preaching Christianity expressed in Māori concepts. When he appeared in public, people gathered around him for instruction, for which he spent much time in meditation. One such prophecy was recorded by Angela Ballara and Keith Cairns as follows:

> In 1881 Paora announced that he had experienced a prophetic dream; he called his people together to interpret his vision. His mana was so great that the crowd at Te Ore Ore in March 1881 was variously estimated at between 1,000 and 3,000. … On 16 March 1881 the gathering awaited Paora's prophetic utterance. About 1 p.m. he … presented his revelation in the form of a flag divided into sections, each bordered in black. Within each section were stars and other mystical symbols. It was raised to half-mast on the flagpole in front of the meeting house. … In spite of the scepticism and anger of those anxious for an immediate miracle, he refused to explain his meaning. The next day he appeared again and told the crowd: 'Look at the flag. Tell me what it means.' He made no further explanations. … Several weeks later Paora emerged from seclusion to make a declaration to his followers. [In the] future they should neither sell nor lease land, should incur no further debts and refuse to honour debts already incurred. … The black-bordered sections of the flag represented the huge blocks of land already alienated. The stars and other symbols represented the inadequate and scattered reserves, the sole remainder of a once great patrimony. Paora had been moved to prophecy by the failure of his people to understand the process by which they were dispossessing themselves.[45]

Pōtangaroa made a number of prophecies, it appears, at the same hui, which apparently lasted for three months. One key prophecy of relevance to the Mormon Church was also recorded by Ballara and Cairns: 'A new and great power was to come to the people from the direction of the rising sun. Various interpretations were made: it was believed to herald the arrival of the gospel of Jesus Christ, as interpreted by the Mormons; and it was believed that missionaries would come from the east and set in place a new church.'[46]

Bronwyn Elsmore recorded that Pōtangaroa prophesied that in two and a half years a prophet would appear after him and speak of matters concerning a new house, and would make them known to the people.[47] Elsmore added that while Māori found the churches at that time lacking, there was no rejection of the Christian message or hopes. Pōtangaroa's further instruction was that the different churches 'should be welcomed in the area because one would be influential in the future'.[48] Rimene recorded the following on this prophecy: 'There is a religious denomination coming for us; perhaps it will come from the sea, perhaps it will emerge from here. Secondly, let the churches into the house – there will be a time when a religion will emerge for you and I and the Māori people.'[49]

The Mormon narrative provides further context. Elder Matthew Cowley recorded that in March 1881, a large convention was held among Ngāti Kahungunu at Te Ore Ore. The hui had been called to discuss political, social and religious challenges facing Māori. The established churches were well represented, but the rangatira shared a feeling of discontent about the lack of unity among them. Why were there so many different churches within the bounds of Christianity? Which one should the Māori join so that unity could again be restored among them?[50] Pōtangaroa was asked the poignant questions, to which he responded: 'taihoa' (wait). He retired to his home and meditated, fasted and prayed about the problem for three days. When he returned to the convention, he addressed his people, stating in part:

> My friends, the church for the Māori people has not yet come among us. You will recognize it when it comes. Its missionaries will travel in pairs. They will come from the rising sun. They will visit with us in our homes. They will learn our language and teach us the gospel in our own tongue. When they pray they will raise their right hands.[51]

Pōtangaroa then referred to a number of key points in time: 'First, this day of fullness 1881, second, the year 1883 would be a year of the sealing; third, the year 1883 was a year of the honouring of great faith as it is written. Render therefore to all dues, tribute to whom tribute is due, custom to whom custom, fear to whom fear, honour to whom honour.'[52]

Apparently, Pōtangaroa then asked Ranginui Kingi to write down his words as he continued to answer the questions which had been put to him. He called the transcription of his words 'A covenant (kawenata) for remembering the hidden words which were revealed by the Spirit of Jehovah to Paora Potangaroa'. Cowley, who subsequently translated the document, opined:

> First, this is the day of the fullness (1881). Brother Cowley points out that later that year the fullness of the gospel was taken to the Māori. … Second, the year 1882 would be the year of the 'sealing' (or the year they would learn the sealing ordinances). Third, the year 1883 will be the year of 'the honoring' – of 'great faith' – as it is written: 'render therefore to all their dues: tribute to whom tribute is due; custom to whom custom; fear to whom fear; honor to whom honor'. (Romans 13:7). In that year, Māori began to honor the true God by rendering their dues to him and entering the Church of Jesus Christ of Latter-day Saints. Members of Ngati Kahungunu, especially, began to enter the Church in large numbers. The Te Ore Ore Branch was organized on December 16, 1883.[53]

Pōtangaroa's kawenata concludes with these words:

> This covenant is to be remembered by the generations which follow after us. And the fruits of that which is set forth above [in the covenants] are – we are the lost sheep of the House of Israel. [We will learn of] the scepter of Judah; of Shilo; of the king of peace; of the day of judgment; of the kingdom of heaven; of the sacred church with a large wall surrounding; of the increase of the race; of faith, love, peace, patience, judgment, unity. All this plan will be fulfilled by the people of the Ngati Kahungunu Tribe during the next forty years.
> March 16, 1881
> Ranginui Kingi[54]

Three months after the hui, in June, Pōtangaroa died.⁵⁵ The covenant, however, was sealed in a cement monument inside Nga Tau E Waru Marae (the meeting house) at Te Ore Ore that same year. A photographer from Masterton obtained permission beforehand to photograph the covenant, and the image subsequently made its way into Cowley's hands. A local Māori convert, Eriata Nopera, was present at the Te Ore Ore hui in 1881, and later identified the photograph in Cowley's possession as the covenant of Pōtangaroa.⁵⁶

Elder Cowley identified the 'sacred church with a large wall surrounding it' with the Salt Lake City Temple in Utah. He also pointed out that the only Māori to participate in all the ordinances of the Mormon gospel during the next forty years (until 1921), including the temple rites, were members of the Ngāti Kahungunu tribe. Later many members of other tribes participated in all blessings of the Mormon faith.⁵⁷

There is no question as to the authenticity of the prophecies of Pōtangaroa or of the document that Matthew Cowley used. Pōtangaroa was well known in his time. In fact, the Anglican hierarchy in New Zealand was aware of his activities, and concluded that he had not accomplished his ends.⁵⁸ Be that as it may, a prophecy is capable of more than one interpretation. Accordingly, Ballara and Cairns appear adamant that Pōtangaroa's prophecy was seen to herald not the Mormon Church but the Rātana Church: 'In 1928, when the religious leader T W Ratana visited Te Ore Ore at the request of the people, he removed the stone set up by Paora inside Nga Tau e Waru, repositioning it outside. The move silenced the medium. The coming of the Ratana faith is now widely believed to be the fulfilment of Paora's prophecy.'⁵⁹

Of course the Mormon historic narrative contests the above interpretation. At the close of 1883, for example, President William Thomas Stewart reported to his presiding leader, John Taylor, in Utah:

> Two or three years ago [the Maori] had a man here among them whom they regarded as a prophet, they say. He told them in 1883 that the true Gospel would be brought [to] them. …

Some of them firmly believe the Book of Mormon, being presented them in this year, to be the exact fulfilment of the predictions of their prophecy.[60]

In addition, Elder Alma Greenwood recorded in his journal on 6 April 1883 about a dream reported to him that John Rangitakaiwaho had had two days before. John said he saw in his dream a rope, one end of which was not finished. Elders Greenwood and Farr were standing by a group of natives and the native began trying to join the ends of the rope together. The elders said that the ends were not joined right but that they would show them how to fix it. They properly placed a piece that had been left out and then rolled the rope together, finding the piece to be a perfect fit. To him, and many others who heard this account, this was reason enough to join the Mormon Church.[61]

Greenwood added that while in the company of Brother and Sister Ihaia at Waihirere near Masterton, he met Samuel Pōtangaroa: 'This chief asked my opinion regarding the ancestors of the Maoris, their origin and where they came from etc. … Sometime ago a Maori prophet said that all the Sectarian Denominations were wrong and ere long another prayer would come which would be the truth. Many of the natives believe that Mormonism is the religion which was to come.'[62]

Furthermore, shortly after leaving New Zealand in 1884, Elder Greenwood wrote about Pōtangaroa's influence:

> Many of the natives were led to investigate the new and somewhat strange religion, which had come in their midst. This, too, was in accordance with some predictions previously made by a Māori prophet: that in 1883, a new religion would come. … The prophecy and its literal fulfillment gave the [Mormon Church] gospel prestige and influence [mana] among that people.[63]

Notwithstanding Pōtangaroa's prophetic influence on the local Māori to flock to the Mormon Church initially, what followed was also interesting:

The whole of Hamua Paora's own people joined the Church. But when the elders explained to them the Word of Wisdom – no tea, or coffee, no liquor, no smoking – they all went out again. 'Easy in, easy out' as the saying goes. However, the few who remained and complied with the tenets of the Church became the most faithful, the most understanding members of the Church.[64]

Consequently, on 26 August 1883, the first permanent branch of the Mormon Church was established at Papawai, Wairarapa, with Te Manihera Rangitakaiwaho as branch president.[65]

Another Māori Mormon stronghold was Tahoraiti, just south of Tamaki-nui-a-rua (Dannevirke); this was also influenced by Pōtangaroa's prophecy. Polly Kingi Marsh noted: 'In March 1881, a Maori chief, Paora Potangaroa, prophesied. ... Later in the year, the fullness of the gospel did come to our people, and everything that Paora Potangaroa prophesied did happen.'[66] Marsh underscored the influence of Pōtangaroa beyond the Wairarapa into southern Hawke's Bay, although the groups share common whakapapa links. To show that the Mormon message was similarly received among other tribes, we will now turn to the prophecies of the great Waikato matakite, King Tāwhiao.

Mormon elders and local Kahungunu and Rangitāne Māori at Aotea Marae, Tahoraiti (Dannevirke) 1914. Reproduced with the permission of Rangi Parker of the Kia Ngawari Trust.

King Tāwhiao – Waikato Taniwharau matakite

King Tāwhiao presided over the Kīngitanga movement during its most turbulent period, consisting of the Waikato Wars (1863–1864) and the subsequent land confiscations (raupatu) of 1.2 million acres of Waikato land – the Kīngitanga heartland. Consequently, Tāwhiao

Gottfried Lindauer, *King Tawhiao Potatau Te Wherowhero*, c. 1885. Christchurch Art Gallery Te Puna o Waiwhetu; gift of H G and A H Anthony, 1964. Reproduced with the permission of the Iwi and Cultural Office of Te Arikinui King Tūheitia.

and his followers isolated themselves from Pākehā, which provided ample time for meditation and speculation. It was during this period that Tāwhiao uttered numerous ohaoha or tongi (prophetic sayings). Michael King noted that Tāwhiao: 'absorbed and expressed an old testament view of himself as anointed leader of a chosen people wandering in the wilderness, but who one day would be delivered into their inheritance. His sayings most frequently repeated and remembered by his followers were of millennial character.'[67]

Tāwhiao proclaimed numerous prophetic utterances, one of which was as follows: 'He wa kei te haeremai ka puta he mihae no toku pito ake, he urukehu, kei a ia he whakaoranga. There will come a time when a messiah will emerge from amongst my own, fair skinned with a promise of salvation.'[68] Some interpreted the 1995 Waikato-Tainui settlement with the New Zealand Government of the raupatu land confiscations led by the late Te Arikinui Dame Te Atairangikaahu as the fulfilment of this prophecy.[69]

Another of Tāwhiao's famous tongi was as follows:

Maku ano e hanga i toku nei whare. Ko te tahuhu e hinau ko nga poupou he mahoe, patate. Me whakatupu ki te hua o te rengarenga, me whakapakari ki te hua o te kawariki.

I shall build my own house; the ridgepole will be built of hinau, and the supporting posts of mahoe and patate. Those who inhabit that house shall be raised on rengarenga and nurtured on kawariki.[70]

This vision, according to Elsmore, was that the house could be a symbolic reference to a royal 'house' built on the base of divine designation and mandate – an earthly manifestation of the heavenly kingdom.[71] Others held that the tongi was one of Māori unity: Māori as a people of one house, one nation, one dream and perhaps one faith.

The Mormon historical narrative claims that King Tāwhiao predicted the coming of the Mormon Church. In 1881, Elder John Ferris wrote that Māori had told him: 'more than a year ago the king [Tāwhiao] said a white man would come across the sea and preach to them the true gospel, and they affirm that they believe he [Ferris] is the man'.[72] Elder Ferris recorded in the *Deseret News* in Salt Lake City, Utah that three Māori chiefs considered him to be the man spoken of by King Tāwhiao two years before. He had come from 'a far country and would give them the good church'.[73] The text of King Tāwhiao's prophecy was later quoted in the *Improvement Era* in 1932:

> Our church is coming from the east – not a church paid with money. Its ministers go two by two; when they pray they raise their hands. They will not come to go among the Pakeha (Europeans) but will dine, live, talk, and sleep with you. The sign will be the writing of the names of males, females and children. … Those churches that have already come are nothing, but when these come that I speak about, do not disturb them – that will be your church![74]

The Mormon Church interpreted the 'sign of writing names' to be a reference to genealogical work and work for the dead, a unique Mormon doctrinal practice in temples.

Here, we digress to another relevant oral account provided by Roma Hoera Ruruku. Ruruku was Ngāti Koata from the Whāingaroa (Raglan)-Kāwhia areas in the Waikato. He travelled down to Rangitoto (D'Urville Island) with his tribe in the nineteenth century. It is believed in the Mormon historic narrative that Ruruku was present when King Tāwhiao in the 1860s (some say 1879) prophesied that the true ministers would come to New Zealand from over Te Moananui-a-Kiwa (the Pacific Ocean), travelling in pairs and teaching the people in their own tongue. Mitchell notes that the prophesy held that the true church would come in the future, and that the ministers of the church would travel two by two. King Tāwhiao added that 'they will not come to you and return to European accommodation, but they will stay with you, talk with you, eat with you, and abide with you'.[75]

For this Ngāti Koata branch of Waikato at Rangitoto, the first real contact with the Mormon Church came in the early 1890s; they heard the Mormon message at the funeral of John Hippolite in Porirua in about 1893. Ruruku saw the Mormon elders and

Roma Hoera Ruruku. Reproduced with the permission of Rangi Parker of the Kia Ngawari Trust.

their mode of teaching in the Māori language, and was baptised in 1893.[76] Ruruku then contacted Elder Joseph Groesbeck, who travelled to Rangitoto and baptised between twelve and fifteen men, women and children.

Another interesting experience was that of Ruruku's daughter, Wetekia Ruruku Elkington, who was also a matakite. It is recorded in the Elkington whānau whakapapa (genealogy) that Wetekia:

> … had a dream where she was lying on her back looking up and she saw a bird flying across the sky. The wings of the bird turned into a book and she heard a voice saying in Māori:

> O House of Israel, how oft have I gathered you in as a hen gathereth her chickens under her wings and ye would not. … I will gather you as a hen gathereth her chickens under her wings, if ye will repent and return unto me.

Not long after her vision, a tangi was held at Ohanga and a family from the North Island brought a book with them, the Book of Mormon. When Wetekia saw the book, she told her father Roma that it was the book she saw in her dream. After the tangi, Roma Ruruku travelled to Wellington and brought back the Mormon missionaries to Ohanga who taught the people, then baptised the whole pa into the Mormon Church.[77]

Wetekia learned to read from the Book of Mormon, and was married to John Elkington by President William Thomas Stewart.

Returning to King Tāwhiao, another Mormon missionary, Elder Charles Anderson, visited Waotu (around Putaruru in the Waikato) on 3 December 1884, and there gained an audience with King Tāwhiao:

> I have had the pleasure of presenting the Gospel message to King Tawhiao, the king of the Maoris in New Zealand and obtained his permission to go into his country and preach to his people. He also invited me to come to his headquarters … a favour which has never been granted to missionaries of any denomination heretofore, as there is a feeling of hostility between the Maori King and the English government. The King's people have not as yet been initiated into any of the sects, for the simple reason that no ministers have been allowed to enter in among them.[78]

A year earlier, a Wairarapa newspaper had provided an interesting report regarding King Tāwhiao's visit in 1883. The account appears to be exaggerated somewhat, because it is recorded that Tāwhiao opined: 'I was some time ago converted to a belief in the Mormon faith, and I now altogether hold to it. My people in the North are believers also in Mormonism, and it is my wish that all the Maori should be of that faith.'[79]

Whether that is true or not, what followed were significant conversions to the Mormon Church in the Waikato. On 18 February 1883, Thomas Cox presided over a special meeting of twelve Waikato Māori converts to the Mormon Church in Waotu to ordain the rangatira to the Aaronic priesthood.[80] The rangatira decided that Hare Te Katera should be ordained to the priesthood, because the others felt they were not yet worthy and Te Katera was the eldest among them. Consequently, Te Katera was also set apart as the president of the Waotu branch, the first (albeit temporary) Māori branch of the Mormon Church in New Zealand. During the years 1885–1886, seven Mormon branches comprising 537 souls were established in the Waikato.

Furthermore, the Kīngitanga historically respected the Mormon Church by allowing the missionaries to preach to the people, and convene hui ā-tau (annual meetings) at Kīngitanga marae (meeting houses) including Tūrangawaewae and Waahi.[81] Princess Te Puea (King Tāwhiao's granddaughter) even offered the Mormon Church Waikato land to build the Mormon high school, the Church College of New Zealand, in the 1950s.

Notwithstanding the different narratives, it was alleged by John Gorst that King Tāwhiao once remarked when asked about the Catholic Church, 'I approve of all religions in the world'.[82] It is appropriate then to mention another of King Tāwhiao's tongi:

> Ahakoa ngā mano huri atu ki te hāmaritanga, mahue mai ki a au kotahi mano, e rima rau, rima tekau, tekau mārua. Ko ahau kei roto ko te Atua tōku piringa ka puta ka ora.
>
> Regardless of the multitudes who seek salvation elsewhere, even if I am left with a thousand, five hundred, fifty or twelve, I am secure for God is my refuge and we shall overcome.[83]

Appropriately then, one Haimona Patete emerged as a religious and political leader in the 1890s in Rangitoto about the same time Ruruku was baptised into the Mormon Church. Following a vision he had during an illness, he established Te Hāhi o te Ruri Tuawhitu o Ihowa (the Church of the Seven Rules of Jehovah), which incorporated the teachings of the prophet Paora Te Pōtangaroa. Interestingly, this church also had followers in Rangitoto, among Ngāti Koata, Wairarapa and Ngāti Kahungunu, it appears, for a short time.[84] However, notwithstanding the differences in interpretation of the various matakite prophecies, the contested histories and the differences in religious tenets and personal opinion, the Pirinoa rangatira Piripi Te Maari left a poignant narrative on the Mormon influence in the Wairarapa in the 1880s that in a way succinctly summarises why the Mormon message appealed to many Māori:

> Two strange men came to our home. They were unheralded by any pomp or display. … There was something very different about them from our ministers. … They said: 'we are your fellow servants, we are here to do you service, your equals not your superiors. Let us eat with you and of what you eat.'
>
> They had with them a new book, which they explained was the history of my people before they came to this land.
>
> These men were very humble and would not accept any of our lands as pay; nor did they meddle with our women, but spent day and night in preaching and teaching us. We soon accepted the Gospel, and cannot tell you half our joy and how the Holy Spirit was poured out upon us. … We received that long-looked-for something that we had before lacked.[85]

Some formative conclusions

The Mormon message and the messengers appealed to Māori for a number of reasons. There was a general absence in their actions of implied (and overt) racial and cultural arrogance towards Māori. Māori were also impressed by the aroha (compassion, love) the Mormon missionaries showed to them. The intercultural exchange of the Mormon missionaries and leaders was significant where they were prepared to assimilate into the Māori world by eating Māori food, living like Māori, speaking Māori, thinking Māori, abiding with Māori and becoming Māori to influence Māori. This intercultural exchange enabled the Mormon Church to become incredibly successful historically in its proselyting work in Aotearoa New Zealand among Māori. The Mormons understood, appreciated and respected Māori for where and who they were.

The Mormons taught that Māori were chosen people of God through the house of Israel, so they expected Māori to accept their message and to assume their rightful place as leaders in the Mormon Church. Many were subsequently baptised, were ordained to the priesthood and became local and now international church leaders. In this way, the Mormon Church became Māori's own church, where Māori led, taught, blessed and guided their own whānau, hapū and iwi and others through personal revelation.[86]

Things did not always go the Mormon way, however. The Mormon Church did not have a monopoly on revelation, truth, goodness and Māori. They did not gain converts in all tribes; not all who joined remained faithful; matakite prophecies were reinterpreted to fit other churches; and some missionaries were persecuted for their message. But the Mormon Church did and still does appeal in significant ways to certain Māori groups.

The effective Mormon-Māori intercultural approach was accompanied by significant prophesied karakia signs: particularly the raising of either both hands or the right hand to the square in certain religious rituals. Moreover, the key prophetic utterances of at least three tohunga matakite – Arama Te Toiroa, Paora Te Pōtangaroa and King Tāwhiao – appeared to make a significant difference in establishing the lines of authority descending from the mana of these matakite into the Mormon Church. It is acknowledged that prophetic utterances are capable of more than one interpretation, and they were. But if tikanga embodied core spiritual values and principles that reflected doing what was and is right, correct or appropriate, then at least for some Māori tribes, it was and still is tika to embrace the Mormon message, apply the Mormon gospel and live the Mormon life in harmony with tikanga Māori.

It is also tika, and in this respect there may be lessons for current and future Mormon Church leaders and missionaries, to reflect on this history and today apply a similar intercultural approach of the former Mormon missionaries to Māori – to influence, you must be influenced, and you must understand, appreciate, respect and even celebrate the world view of others to influence them effectively. The Mormon missionaries and leaders were prepared to be influenced by Māori to influence Māori, and both were transformed in the process.

'Mehemea karekau ana he whakakitenga, kia mate te iwi. Where there is no vision, the people perish' (Proverbs 29:18).

Endnotes

1 R Mahuta, 'Tawhiao's Visions', presentation, Centre for Māori Studies and Research, University of Waikato, 20 June 1990, 3 and P Buck, *The Coming of the Maori* (Wellington: Whitcombe & Tombs/Maori Purposes Fund Board, 1962), 537.
2 The term 'Pākehā' (non-Māori) is used respectfully throughout this chapter.
3 R Davis, 'The Maori Temple or Whare Wananga', in *Te Karere* (August 1953): 275–7.
4 H M Wright, *New Zealand, 1769–1840: Early Years of Western Contact* (Cambridge, Massachusetts: Harvard University Press, 1967), 134.
5 T Warner, *Bonds That Make Us Free: Healing Our Relationships, Coming to Ourselves* (Salt Lake City, Utah: Shadow Mountain Press, 2001), 67.
6 A R Dunford (ed.), 'Missionary Journals of Oliver Cowdery Dunford & Ida Ann Osmond Dunford, 1889–1892' (Hamilton: New Zealand Mormon Church History Centre).
7 Magleby served among Māori in 1885–1889, 1900–1903 and 1928–1932. A wharenui (meeting house) was even named after him in Kaikou near Whāngārei, and still bears his name – Eparaima Makapi. See 'A Journal Record of John Ephraim Magleby' (typescript of three journals, 25 September 1898) and J E Magleby: 'Eparaima Makapi' (third mission journal collection, 1928–1932), New Zealand Mormon Church History Centre, Temple View, Hamilton.
8 'Ephraim Magleby: He Came to Serve', in G Rudd (ed.), *New Zealand: A Short Collection of Items of History to add to our Memories and Appreciation* (Salt Lake City, Utah: privately published, 1993 with additions in 2007), 3–4.
9 R L Britsch, *Unto the Islands of the Sea: A History of the Latter-day Saints in the Pacific* (Salt Lake City, Utah: Deseret Books, 1986), 263.
10 R L Britsch, 'Māori Traditions and the Mormon Church', in *New Era*, June 1981: 38.
11 'The Book is Translated', in S W Kimball (ed.), *New Zealand Church History* (Hamilton: New Zealand Division Seminary & Institute Department, 1974) and Britsch, 'Māori Traditions and the Mormon Church', 38.
12 G Underwood, 'Mormonism and the Shaping of Maori Religious Identity', in G Underwood (ed.), *Explorations in Mormon Pacific History* (Provo, Utah: Brigham Young University Press, 2000).
13 Britsch, 'Māori Traditions and the Mormon Church', 38.
14 Department of Statistics, New Zealand, *2001 Census of Population and Dwellings*, Māori Tables. Available online at www.stats.govt.nz (accessed June 2010).
15 Statistics New Zealand, Tables 28 ('Religious Affiliation') and 19 ('Languages Spoken by Ethnic Group'), in '2006 Census Data – QuickStats About Culture and Identity – Tables (XLS)', in *2006 Census of Population and Dwellings*: http://www.stats.govt.nz/ Census/2006CensusHomePage/QuickStats/quickstats-about-a-subject/culture-and-identity.aspx (accessed 2 February 2012).

16 Church of Jesus Christ of Latter-day Saints New Zealand Service Centre, Hamilton, December 2010.
17 Britsch, 'Māori Traditions and the Mormon Church', 38.
18 E G Schwimmer, *The World of the Maori* (Wellington: Reed, 1966), 61.
19 In many, if not all, Māori tribes, women were also rangatira.
20 H Whaanga, 'A Maori Prophet', in *Juvenile Instructor* 37 (1902): 152–3.
21 B Elsmore, *Mana from Heaven: A Century of Maori Prophets in New Zealand* (Tauranga: Moana Press, 1989), 86.
22 S P Smith, *The Lore of the Whare Wananga* (New Plymouth: Avery, 1913), 894.
23 Elsmore, *Mana from Heaven*, 86.
24 I Barker, 'The Connexion: The Mormon Church and the Maori People', MA thesis, Victoria University of Wellington, 1967, 35. The founding Mormon prophet, Joseph Smith, dictated in 1842 the Mormon creed in Article of Faith 9: 'We believe all that God has revealed, all that He does now reveal, and we believe that He will yet reveal, many great and important things pertaining to the Kingdom of God.' Thus the Mormon and Māori world views firmly believed in continuing revelation and prophecy from God.
25 Rudd, *New Zealand: A Short Collection of Items of History*, 13.
26 J Binney, *Redemption Songs: A Life of the Nineteenth-century Maori Leader Te Kooti Arikirangi Te Turuki* (Auckland: Auckland University Press/Bridget Williams Books, 1997), 11–12. There are several versions of this story in Paora Delamere's manuscripts, especially on pages 11–12 and 45–6. Delamere was poutikanga (leader) of the Ringatū Church from 1938 until his death in 1981.
27 See P Te H Jones and A Ngata, *Nga Moteatea*, Part One (Wellington: Polynesian Society, 1945–1957), 138; J Wilson, *The History of Hawke's Bay* (Wellington: Reed, 1939), 100; and A Ballara, 'Te Hapuku', in Department of Internal Affairs, *The People of Many Peaks; The Māori Biographies from the Dictionary of New Zealand Biography, Volume 1, 1769–1869* (Wellington: Bridget Williams Books, 1991), 159.
28 Binney, *Redemption Songs*, 12.
29 Delamere, cited in ibid, 45.
30 Whaanga, 'A Maori Prophet'.
31 Korongata or Bridge Pā was settled by Māori from Nūhaka who migrated there in the nineteenth century. Hence the people of Nūhaka and Te Māhia are Toiroa's people, as are many from Korongata.
32 Early in the Mormon Church, both hands were often raised when a prayer was given. The practice was later to change to only the right arm being uplifted when blessing the sacrament or dedicating a grave. Both practices were later discontinued.
33 Whaanga, 'A Maori Prophet'.
34 M T Whaanga, 'On the Rock Our Fathers Planted', unpublished manuscript, 8 September 2010, 1.
35 S Meha, 'A Condensed History of the Church of Jesus Christ of Latter-day Saints in New Zealand', unpublished manuscript,New Zealand Mormon Church History Centre, Temple View, Hamilton, n.d.
36 Ibid.
37 See S Meha, 'A Challenge Met', in Rudd, *New Zealand: A Short Collection of Items of History*.
38 Meha, 'A Condensed History'.
39 W Amaru, 'Karaitaina Tuteketenui Amaru', unpublished manuscript, n.d., 1–2.
40 Buck, *The Coming of the Maori*, 537.

41 Binney, *Redemption Songs*, 24–5. The Ringatū Church dates its origin from the revelations given to Te Kooti while he was imprisoned in the Chatham Islands in 1867. During acute bouts of fever, Te Kooti had strange visions in which the 'spirit of God' (some say the angel Gabriel) raised him up. On 4 July 1867, Te Kooti escaped and told the people that they would no longer kneel at prayer. Their homage to God would be the raising of the right hand at the end of prayers, from which the Ringatū derive their name. See also J Binney, 'Te Kooti Arikirangi Te Turuki', in *People of Many Peaks*, 194–201.
42 W Williams, *East Coast (N.Z.) Historical Records* (Anglican Church, 1895), 79 and 84. See also W Greenwood, 'The Upraised Hand, or the Spiritual Significance of the Rise of the Ringatu Faith', in *Journal of the Polynesian Society* 51 (1942) 1–80, 34–5.
43 A Ballara, 'Hamiora Mangakahia', in Department of Internal Affairs, *The Turbulent Years 1870–1900: The Māori Biographies from the Dictionary of New Zealand Biography, Volume 2* (Wellington: Bridget Williams Books, 1994), 53.
44 A Ballara, 'Hamiora Mangakahia', in *Te Puke ki Hikurangi*, 7 June 1898. At this time, Mangakāhia stated that he was the person to whom Toiroa had told his predictions for peace. Binney, *Redemption Songs*, 13.
45 A Ballara and K Cairns, 'Paora Potangaroa', in *People of Many Peaks*, 226–8.
46 Ibid.
47 Elsmore, *Mana from Heaven*, 248–9.
48 P Potangaroa (trans. J Rimene), 'The Prophecies of Paora Potangaroa, 4 April 1881', unpublished manuscript, 3, New Zealand Mormon Church History Centre, Temple View, Hamilton, n.d.
49 Ibid, 4.
50 M Cowley, 'Maori Chief Predicts Coming of L.D.S. Missionaries', in *Improvement Era* 53 (September 1950): 697.
51 Ibid. See also A Bennion, *Matthew Cowley Speaks* (Salt Lake City, Utah: Deseret Book Company, 1954), 755–6, 200–5.
52 As cited in Elsmore, *Mana from Heaven*, 251–3.
53 Cowley, 'Maori Chief Predicts Coming of L.D.S. Missionaries'.
54 Ibid.
55 Ballara and Cairns, 'Paora Potangaroa', in *People of Many Peaks*, 226–8.
56 Te W Naera, 'Tape about Maori Prophecies, in possession of Lewis Mousely', as cited in B Hunt, *Zion in New Zealand: A History of the Church of Jesus Christ of Latter-day Saints in New Zealand 1854–1977*, 2nd edition (Temple View: Church College of New Zealand, 1977), 22.
57 Cowley, 'Maori Chief Predicts Coming of L.D.S. Missionaries'.
58 *Proceedings of the Diocesan Synod of the District of Wellington*, First Session of the Ninth Synod, October 1881, 16. See also Barker, 'The Connexion: The Mormon Church and the Maori People', 40.
59 Ballara and Cairns, 'Paora Potangaroa', in *People of Many Peaks*, 226–8.
60 Letter, W T Stewart to J Taylor, 31 January 1884, as reproduced in M S Lee and M S Peterson (eds), *History of William Thomas Stewart* (Provo, Utah: Grant Stevenson, 1972), 25.
61 A Greenwood, 'Mission Journal for 1883', unpublished manuscript, 1883. Original holograph in Brigham Young University Archives, Provo, Utah.
62 Ibid.
63 A Greenwood, 'My New Zealand Mission', in *Juvenile Instructor* 20 (1885): 222.
64 Cited in Hunt, *Zion in New Zealand*, 35. See also R MacFarlane, 'The History of Henare Haeata Ngakuku' (unpublished manuscript privately held by the Haeata whānau,

Masterton), 1–2; and E S Maunsell's Report to the Native Department, 25 April 1886, in *Appendices to the Journal of the House of Representatives*, 1886, G-1, 18.
65 A Jensen (ed.), *Church Chronology* (Salt Lake City, Utah: Deseret News, 1914), 113.
66 P K Marsh, 'Church History in the Tamaki Branch', unpublished manuscript, Church College of New Zealand Manuscript Archives, Hamilton, n.d., 1.
67 M King, *Te Puea: A Biography* (Auckland: Hodder & Stoughton, 1977), 27. Refer also to P Te H Jones, *King Pōtatau: An Account of the Life of Pōtatau Te Wherowhero: The First Māori King* (Auckland: Polynesian Society, 1959).
68 See also Mahuta, 'Tawhiao's Visions', 11.
69 C Kirkwood, *Te Arikinui and the Millennium of Waikato* (Hamilton: Turongo House, 2001), preface.
70 Letter, Tāwhiao to A Matete, 15 April 1866, New Zealand Mormon Church History Centre, Temple View, Hamilton.
71 Elsmore, *Mana from Heaven*, 238.
72 W Bromley, 'Journal', June 16, 1881, Archives, Historical Department of the Church of Jesus Christ of Latter-day Saints, Salt Lake City, Utah. See also F Hodgson, *None Shall Excel Thee: The Life and Journals of William Michael Bromley* (Yorba Linda, California: Shumway Family History Services, 1990).
73 *Deseret News*, 23 November 1881: 683.
74 N P Olsen, 'New Zealand: Our Māori Home', in *Improvement Era* 35 (May 1932): 446.
75 H Mitchell and J Mitchell, *Te Tau Ihu o Te Waka: A History of Maori of Nelson and Marlborough: Volume II: Te Ara Hou – The New Society* (Wellington: Huia, 2007), 110–11. See Hunt, *Zion in New Zealand*, 4.
76 Recounted in Church of Jesus Christ of Latter-day Saints, *The Mormon Temple* (Hamilton: Church of Jesus Christ of Latter-day Saints, 1958), 7.
77 J Hippolite, 'Wetekia Ruruku Elkington 1879–1957', in C MacDonald, M Penfold and B Williams, *The Book of New Zealand Women: Ko Kui ma te Kaupapa* (Wellington: Bridget Williams Books, 1991), 205–7.
78 C Anderson, 'Labors among the Maoris', in *The New Zealand Mission*, 18 February 1885.
79 *Wairarapa Standard*, 7 March 1883.
80 Church of Jesus Christ of Latter-day Saints, *Manuscript History of the New Zealand Mission, Volume 1* (Salt Lake City, Utah: Church of Jesus Christ of Latter-day Saints, 1883).
81 David O McKay was the first Mormon apostle to visit New Zealand in 1921 at Waahi, in Huntly. In 1938, George Albert Smith, the second apostle, attended hui ā-tau at Tūrangawaewae and was received by Te Puea.
82 Cited in J Gorst, *The Maori King; or, the Story of our Quarrel with the Natives of New Zealand* (London/Cambridge: Macmillan, 1864), 199.
83 Mahuta, 'Tawhiao's Visions', 16.
84 A Patete, 'Patete, Haimona – Biography', from the *Dictionary of New Zealand Biography* in *Te Ara – the Encyclopedia of New Zealand*: www.teara.govt.nz/en/biographies/3p14/1 (accessed 4 January 2012) and also A Ballara and P Sciascia, 'Te Atua, Henare – Biography', from the *Dictionary of New Zealand Biography* in *Te Ara – the Encyclopedia of New Zealand*: www.teara. govt.nz/en/biographies/3t12/1 (accessed 4 January 2012). See also A E Duffy, 'Te Haahi o te Ruuri Tuawhitu o Ihowa', BA research essay, Victoria University of Wellington, 1973.
85 G Lambert (ed.), *Gems of Reminiscence*, 17th Faith Promoting Series (Salt Lake City, Utah: George C Lambert, 1915), 186–9.
86 L Gunderson, 'That long looked for something that we before lacked', unpublished manuscript, Kia Ngawari Trust, Hamilton, , n.d., 21.

Chapter Four
Māori and Pentecostal Christianity in Aotearoa New Zealand

Simon Moetara

There has been a perceptible shift in Christianity's geographical and cultural centre of gravity, from the northern to southern regions of the world. As Kenyan theologian John Mbiti puts it, 'the centres of the Church's universality [are] no longer in Geneva, Rome, Athens, Paris, London, New York, but Kinshasa, Buenos Aires, Addis Ababa and Manila'.[1] According to Barrett and Johnson, in 2004 there were 1227 million Christians in Asia, Africa, Latin America and Oceania, comprising 62 percent of the world's Christians, while those of the two northern continents represented only 38 percent, illustrating the radical shift of Christianity from north to south. Anderson notes that if present trends continue, by 2025, 69 percent of the world's Christians will live in the south, with only 31 percent in the North.[2]

This southward swing is more evident in Pentecostalism than in other forms of Christianity. Pentecostals represent perhaps a quarter of the world's Christians, with conceivably three-quarters of those residing in the majority world.[3] The greatest growth in Pentecostalism has taken place in sub-Saharan Africa, South East Asia, South Korea and Latin America.[4] The phenomenal growth of Pentecostalism in Latin America has led to scholars arguing that the continent is well on the way to becoming a Pentecostal, rather than a Catholic, one.[5] In Asia, large growing congregations in cities such as Seoul, Manila and Singapore, and the 'wild-fire growth' of the house churches in China, have Asian theologian Hwa Yung declaring that some two-thirds of Asian Christians are caught up in the renewal, and that 'one cannot understand the church in Asia today without coming to terms with the Pentecostal-Charismatic movement'.[6] In Africa, Johnstone and Mandryk estimate that 16 percent of the continent's Christian population was Charismatic or Pentecostal in 2000, and state that even if this is a rough estimation, these movements 'undoubtedly are fast becoming dominant forms of Christianity on the continent'.[7]

It has been customary to understand Pentecostalism as a Western phenomenon originating in Topeka, Kansas in 1901, or at the Azusa Street revival in Los Angeles in 1906. However, many scholars now argue for a 'multiplicity of fountainheads' in which Pentecostal revivals actually occurred before, or transpired independent of, events in the United States.[8] Examples of pre-Azusa Street Pentecostal-type movements include the revival in Tamilnadu, India, in 1860–1861, led in part by the Tamil Church Mission Society evangelist John Christian Aroolappen, and the healing/deliverance ministry of Hsi Shengmo (1835–1896) in China.[9] Examples of Pentecostal revival independent of Azusa Street took place in Pyongyang, Korea in 1907; in Valparaiso, Chile in 1909; and in Lagos, Nigeria, described as 'arguably the most Pentecostal city in the world', in which healing movements date back to the influenza epidemic of 1918.[10] This brief description reveals a worldwide charismatic move of God, dating from the mid-nineteenth century through into the first decades of the twentieth century, which occurred prior to or independent of the United States experience, and led to explosive growth among indigenous peoples.

Similar phenomena were evident in Aotearoa New Zealand. The origin of the Pentecostal movement in New Zealand is generally traced to the evangelistic campaigns of Smith Wigglesworth between 1922 and 1924. However, prior to Wigglesworth's arrival there is evidence of a 'fountainhead' of God's global work on these shores, as supernatural, Pentecostal-type signs clustered around a local figure – Tahupotiki Wiremu Rātana, founder of the Rātana Church. On 8 November 1918, Rātana received a divine call from the holy spirit to be the mouthpiece of God, and to 'unite the Māori people, turning them to Jehovah, of the thousands, for this is his compassion to all of you'.[11] His ministry exhibited healing,[12] prophecy,[13] confrontation of dark forces[14] and even glossolalia.[15] This is not to argue for Rātana as Pentecostal; rather, it is fascinating to ponder his ministry in light of global indigenous Christian experience in the early decades of the twentieth century.

A number of reasons have been put forward for the astonishing growth of Pentecostalism among indigenous peoples in the majority world (that is, the less-developed world within which most of the world's population lives, in contrast to the wealthy (and less populated) developed world) – and these factors suggest that Pentecostal Christianity would have been an attractive faith expression for Māori.

First, Pentecostalism in the majority world has been accepting and supportive of indigenous culture expression and practice. Anderson points out that Pentecostals in this part of the world have been affected by several factors, including the desire for a more contextual and culturally relevant form of Christianity, the rise of nationalism and a reaction to what are perceived as 'colonial' forms of Christianity.[16] Cox claims that the great strength of Pentecostalism lies in 'its power to combine, its aptitude for the language, the music, the cultural artefacts, [and] the religious tropes … of the setting in which it lives'.[17] Venn's[18] 'three-self' formula for indigenisation – self-governing, self-supporting and self-propagating – was easily and naturally realised by Pentecostal mission movements long before it was by older western mission churches.[19] Anderson believes that 'a sympathetic approach to local life and culture and the retention of certain indigenous religious practices' are undeniably key reasons for the appeal, 'especially for those overwhelmed by urbanization with its transition from a personal rural society to an impersonal urban one'.[20]

Pentecostal churches have established order, security and hope for those dislocated through rural-urban migration. According to David Martin, most analysts ascribe the explosive growth of Pentecostalism in Latin America to 'the desperate immiseration and social chaos' resulting from extensive migration from rural areas into megacities.[21] Pentecostal churches supply places of spiritual refuge and caring communities for those affected by mobility and change, often functioning as 'extended surrogate families'.[22] Wonsuk Ma also observes that in many non-Western continents Pentecostal believers have achieved social upward mobility, and this has been viewed as God's special blessing.[23]

Additionally, Pentecostal belief in a spiritual world resonates with indigenous beliefs. In the Pentecostal world view there 'is no sharp dividing line between the natural and supernatural world … the two interpenetrate and are inseparable'.[24] Jaichandran and Madhav believe the major Pentecostal distinction to be the belief that 'God continues to work in the church through supernatural means'.[25] Prophecy is part of religious experience, healing is accessible by faith and evil spiritual forces are exorcised and not merely demythologised. McGee states that Pentecostal perspectives on the spiritual realm 'have proved unusually compatible with non-western worldviews', and have 'contributed to the gradual Pentecostalization of Third World Christianity in life and worship'.[26] Pentecostals have responded to the void left by rationalistic Western forms of Christianity that had 'unwittingly initiated what was tantamount to the destruction of indigenous spiritual values'.[27]

These three traits suggest that Pentecostal expressions of worship should have been an appealing proposition for Māori. The Māori population also underwent rapid urbanisation after World War Two. Prior to the War, almost 90 percent of Māori lived in rural areas. In 1945, 25.7 percent of all Māori lived in the cities, and this figure had jumped to 83 percent by 1996. Belich notes that population explosion and urbanisation were traumatic for many Māori, devastating many traditional Māori communities and causing massive dislocation.[28] In little more than a generation, Māori had become a significantly urban people. This process led to greater education and employment opportunities for some, and cultural and emotional dislocation for others.[29] On the other hand, urbanisation also led to the rise of mana Māori, allowing Māori culture and values to impact upon the entire nation. The Māori renaissance of the 1970s led to a cultural resurgence, including renewed interest in te reo Māori and the establishment of a Māori language education system, the broaching of historical grievances via the Waitangi Tribunal, and the management of Māori-owned or iwi-based commercial assets.

Furthermore, Māori spirituality traditionally acknowledges that the natural world and the spirit world interact with and influence each other. Kernot comments on how the natural environment acts as a medium of communication between the human and the divine, where 'Natural events are interpreted as signs from the other world'.[30] Maori Marsden describes the Māori world view as 'at least a two-world system in which the material proceeds from the spiritual, and the spiritual (which is the higher order) interpenetrates the material physical world'.[31] Māori generally consider the natural and spiritual realms to be integrated and supernatural forces to both direct and affect the affairs of people. Faith healing was a prominent part of pre-European Māori religion[32] and of the numerous Māori reactions to Christianity.[33] Haami maintains that deliverance from the effects of transgressions of tapu was a major driving force behind the move of Māori ancestors and Māori themselves to follow Christianity.[34] The origins of the work among Māori by the older Pentecostal churches were associated with signs and wonders. There was growth in the influence of the Apostolic Church among Māori in the 1930s when, according to Pastor John Maxwell, Kui Rora Te Amo was raised from the dead at Waitangi Marae in Te Puke, leading to the salvation of many of her whanau.[35] In the Assemblies of God, British evangelist Stephen Jeffreys prayed in 1928–1929 for a Māori chief dying of cancer who was subsequently healed, and those present 'simply fell on their faces and cried to God to be saved'.[36] In what would become the New Life Movement, a Māori woman was sovereignly healed of blindness at a meeting led by Rob Wheeler in the isolated Hicks Bay-Rangitukia area in 1958, which led to the establishment of four new Māori 'Full Gospel' churches there in 1959.[37]

In light of such findings, one would expect that the Pentecostal/Charismatic approach might have held tremendous appeal for Māori, as it has for indigenous peoples in the majority world. However, the impact seems to have been less than one might have hoped for.

According to Manu Pohio, the hindrance for the Pentecostal churches has been Māori culture.[38] Kim Workman of the Elim Church tells of one prominent evangelist who would 'pray the Māori spirit out of people'. Workman also shared an incident from the mid-1990s in which the findings of a spiritual mapping exercise were presented in the church he attended. Areas identified as satanic that needed to be 'prayed against' included urupā, marae and Māori carvings.[39] Another former Elim Church leader shared his story: 'At times I wished I was Pakeha to fit in, to be part of it, to feel at home … I feel that the Church is trying to save us from being Māori. It's as if being Māori's the problem; we need to change that, then we're really saved …'[40] Lloyd Martin, author of *One Faith, Two Peoples*, identifies a similar attitude, but sees it also as an issue for the wider evangelical church:

> In some churches, Maori spirituality has been seen as demonic … but Pentecostal churches haven't been alone in that … I've heard it expressed one way – 'Come out from your culture because Christianity is the culture, the church is the culture', but sometimes the people saying that they have wanted Maori to come out of their culture […] haven't examined their own culture.[41]

One Māori minister interviewed said there is now a move away from 'pushing culture' to an emphasis on establishing a biblical foundation for church governance and practice in his movement. He was positive about this move, believing that culture needs to be expressed from a biblical foundation, rather than being the basis from which Christian faith is articulated: 'The Bible is what we believe in, and we can express [culture] from that foundation.'[42] He believed there would then be room for biblically appropriate cultural expression.

According to a number of leaders, there appeared to be an unwillingness to release Māori leaders with an independence that allowed them to lead in their own way. Workman states that many Māori leaders in the past struggled to exercise a leadership role within Pentecostal and evangelical churches. Due to the conflict between being true to their cultural values and being faithful to responsibilities to the church, many became itinerant evangelists because it took them out of the formal church structure and away from politics, allowing them to function 'in a much more free and honest way in terms of who they were and what they believed in'.[43] One experienced leader says, 'That's been an issue, Māori leadership that's relevant to Māori. Pākehā have been so used to being the bosses around the place, anything like that comes up, you become a threat.'[44]

Glen Tupuhi, a member of the ACTS Churches for more than twenty-five years and an elder at Graceway Church (ACTS), Hamilton, raises another issue, maintaining that Pentecostal churches have had great success among those Māori who can be described as having notional or compromised identities.[45] However, Tupuhi observes that often those Māori who enter their Pentecostal salvation journey from a notional or compromised identity often reach a plateau in their Pentecostal experience, tend to 'embark on an identity-affirming journey' outside of the church, and end up 'a compromised or notional church attendee'. Tupuhi notes that there are now avenues outside the church that will provide these Māori with the ability to become upwardly mobile. Treaty settlements, employment prospects in Australia or education opportunities, while not replacing the ultimate 'redemptive lift' of salvation in Christ, do provide opportunity for Māori to advance their economic and social prospects apart from the church.[46]

As the comments above indicate, there is much that has been challenging within the Māori Pentecostal experience. In New Zealand, older mainline churches have sought to address issues of biculturalism in their own policies as a means of addressing historical grievances and injustices. However, among the Pentecostal and Charismatic churches, Māori leadership structures are not as clearly discernible.

Three prominent Pentecostal movements will now be briefly considered.

The Assemblies of God
The New Zealand Assemblies of God never had any significant impact upon Māori from its inception in 1927.[47] A notable exception was the ministry of Ray Bloomfield and Frank Houston

among rural Māori in Waiomio in Northland about 1955–1956. Although this revival was highly successful and continued until 1959, it remained only an isolated episode, and had little effect outside one or two local areas.[48] A national Māori conference was held at Raglan in 1988 to consider how to better reach Māori for Christ. It was noted that in the past Pentecostal churches had shown 'an unhealthy rejection of Māoritanga' and now needed to 'adopt a more sensitive attitude'.[49] In 1993, only 7 percent of Assemblies of God adherents were Māori, compared with 24.5 percent of Apostolic Church attendees.[50] Executive member Peter Hira led seminars on ways to evangelise Māori at the Assemblies of God annual conferences in 1996 and 2000. However, these seem to have made little impact. In 2006, there were 1301 Māori adherents out of a total of 15,300 Assemblies of God members.[51]

In 2007 the Assemblies of God Annual Conference in Lower Hutt made note of the lack of Māori attendance within the denomination, and Peter Hira was commissioned to investigate reasons for the limited presence of Māori and ways to address it. Hira says that the process is still ongoing, but he has identified as key areas of concern the lack of freedom for cultural expression at movement and local church levels. He also sees a need for the leaders to acknowledge their actions in marginalising Māori and to 'front up' to what has occurred, and is concerned about a lack of development of Māori leadership.[52] Ian Clark, former overseas missions' director of the Assemblies of God, likewise attributes the lack of significant impact upon Māori by the Assemblies of God to the lack of Māori pastors and leaders over the years.[53]

According to Carew, biculturalism and its notions of partnership and special treatment are perceived within the Assemblies of God movement with suspicion, and regarded as a potentially divisive ideology. On the other hand, there is a preference for multiculturalism, which is considered congenial and consistent with Christianity unity.[54] Ian Clark says 'It's not that the Assemblies of God is anti-Māori. I believe they are just blind to them. They don't see Māori as a mission field; they never have. They have never embraced it. We have a tokenism towards Māori … that's what it is.'[55]

The ACTS

The ACTS Churches (formerly the Apostolic Church Movement) had their origins in the Welsh Revival of 1904–1905. The Apostolic Church in Wales was founded in 1916, the church arriving on New Zealand's shores in the early 1930s. Alfred Greenway was the first in the Apostolic Church to minister to Māori, at Waitangi Pā, Te Puke in 1934.[56] The first Apostolic Māori Mission church was opened at Waitangi Pā on Labour Weekend in October 1937, and became the centre of the church's Māori Mission work.[57] A policy for training workers was soon set out, stating that Pākehā ministers 'must seek to make themselves competent in the Māori language'.[58] A Māori Mission Advisory Panel was formed, which in 1965 became the Māori Advisory Committee, a new body with a nationwide focus that answered to the Executive.[59] The late 1990s were a time of expansion. In 1990, the sesquicentennial year of the Treaty signing, Superintendent Ron Goulton wrote:

> It is important for us as a church to realise that whether we like it or not – and let's face it, we have no option not to like it – the Maori were here before the European arrived and we all have to work in partnership doing all we can to see that the righteousness of God is revealed in our communities and in various difficult decisions that have to be made to correct injustice.[60]

After discussions regarding potential structural change, the Māori-Pacific Island Council (MPIC) was established in 1997.[61] The MPIC's mission was 'to empower and facilitate local churches in the evangelisation and Christian development of Māori and Pacific Island people in the community'. According to one former Council member, the original intention (in terms of Māori) was to increase the influence of Māori leadership in decision-making in order to impact Māori for Christ in a greater way. 'Te Akoranga', a training program to develop 'practitioners', was also initiated in 1997, and by 1999 between 50 and 60 people were in ministry training around the country. The MPIC recommendation for a national marae at Rotorua was endorsed by the executive in 1998. In order to explore the relationship between the MPIC and the national leadership team and general council further, a 'Commission of Release' was established in 2000 to discuss the biblical mandate for partnership between Māori and Pākehā, and how that might find expression within the movement. However, heightening tensions and differences in understanding eventually led to the dissolution of the MPIC in October 2002.

Lloyd Martin notes findings from an informal survey of New Zealand biblical and theological colleges in 1990 that the Apostolic denomination at that time was training more Māori leaders than any other institution.[62] Clark speaks highly of the number of Māori in the Apostolic Movement who had been outstanding leaders and held positions of importance at both local and national levels.[63] Sadly, statistics show that the percentage of Māori adherents for the New Zealand Apostolic/ACTS Movement decreased from 25.1 percent in 2001 to 13.3 percent by 2009.[64]

Destiny Church

Destiny Church is a movement with eleven churches and an estimated 9000 adherents.[65] Brian Tamaki left the Apostolic Movement in 1994 and moved from Lake City Church in Rotorua to launch Destiny Church in 1998 (the church was then known as City Church Auckland). Tamaki became aware of 'a very strong anointing' to reach Māori in 1990, and now approximately 75 percent of Destiny Church's adherents are Māori. Tupuhi maintains that the classical Pentecostal denominations abrogated their responsibility to Māori, which has in turn contributed to the success of Destiny.[66] Religious historian Peter Lineham says the movement 'is Māori at heart, although not tribal Māori ... perhaps appealing particularly to detribalised Māori'.[67] Lineham elsewhere speaks of the potent combination of 'pentecostalism, fundamentalist values and "black power"'.[68] Tamaki is heavily influenced by the African-American Pentecostal/Charismatic experience and the style of his 'spiritual father', Charismatic mainline minister Bishop Eddie Long. Like Tamaki, Long is noted for his theological stance on the importance of the role of the father and male authority in the home, outreach programs for the poor and at risk in the community, and his bold and overt modelling of 'a personal aesthetic of economic empowerment'.[69]

Tamaki has a high view of the Treaty of Waitangi – a unique position among Aotearoa New Zealand Pentecostal denominations – seeing it as a covenant between Māori and the Crown, with God as the third party. He believes that the Treaty cannot fulfil its purpose unless all parties are faithful to God: 'Until we as a nation humble ourselves before the One True Living God, the true spirit of Te Tiriti o Waitangi will not be restored. This process must start with the church and the Crown.'[70] Tamaki also has a high view of Māori as the first people of this country, and believes they must feature in any move that God has planned for this nation:

> Māori have a huge place to play in the role of the kingdom of God in New Zealand because they are the first people of the nation and if God is going to do something it is my express belief that he can't really bypass the first people. And so the indigenous people of New Zealand, the Māori must figure in any great moves of God that'll be in this country.[71]

Lineham suggests that Destiny Church's strong moral stance has an appeal to those who have been stung by modern society, saying that those drawn to churches like Destiny tend to be people 'who have been broken by the circumstances of life', and 'the levels of violence, broken homes and drug and alcohol abuse add relevance to the message'.[72] Lineham also sees Tamaki as the latest in a tradition of charismatic Māori leaders who 'offers hope and love to the disaffected and the poor ... the followers believe in him', and likens him to T W Ratana, who said he would 'attract the Morehu, the nobodies', and 'give them a sense of purpose and a voice and a meaning'.[73]

Despite Destiny Church's extensive community work and the transformed lives of its members, critics often voice disapproval of the bishop's 'lavish lifestyle' and the perceived 'cult of personality' inherent in the stress on submission to the bishop as God's chosen man.[74] Regardless, it is clear that Destiny Church has had a major impact on a number of Māori believers in the last decade.

Some concluding thoughts

The Pentecostal approach in Aotearoa New Zealand in general seems to be to reject attempts at bicultural expression. Other than Destiny Church, the current Pentecostal/Charismatic churches appear to show little acknowledgement of prior and preeminent bicultural commitments to Māori as tangata whenua. While mainline churches have endeavoured to redress historical injustices perpetrated by both state and church, Pentecostals have not taken this approach. The importance of the Treaty within the Destiny movement has not resulted in any formal change in structure, but its large proportion of Māori may mean such change is not necessary. A multicultural approach seems to be the preferred option of many Pentecostal churches. One can understand the appeal of this approach, in light of this nation's increasingly diverse ethnic make-up and the church's desire not to alienate other ethnic groupings. The debate is not a simple one. Advocacy of multiculturalism can also be problematic, potentially relegating Māori to the position of a single group among many. May acknowledges a scepticism among Māori about multiculturalism, and states that support for a multicultural approach can arise less out of a valuing of diversity or a concern for the interests of minority groups, and more 'from a fear of possible fulfilment of Māori bicultural aspirations'.[75] The document *Puao-te-Ata-Tu (Daybreak)* states that policies rooted in the concept of multiculturalism 'are commonly used as a means of avoiding the historical and social imperatives of the Māori situation'.[76] O'Sullivan states that multiculturalism 'became a popular tool for discrediting the respect for Māori that biculturalism offered', and that it 'masks prejudice'.[77] Carew points out that unless supported by the proactive encouragement of constituent cultures, multiculturalism 'effectively becomes a vote for the mono-cultural status quo'.[78] While acknowledgment of diversity of cultures within the New Zealand context is imperative, this commitment to multiculturalism rather than biculturalism has proven to be a barrier in developing a robust ministry with and for Māori.

The organisational structures of Pentecostal/Charismatic churches tend not to reflect a bicultural approach, but there is hope for connection and growth along more relational-organic lines. Within the ACTS/Apostolic Church the emphasis on 'apostolic streams' – networks of churches in relationship with a senior leader – offers the chance for Māori leadership and congregants to flourish in a number of possible settings without resorting to institutional structures. Likewise, Carew finds no opposition to a 'Māori stream' within the Assemblies of God movement, but observes that, as with other ethnic streams, the impetus must come from Māori, of whom there are few in the movement.[79]

The desire to establish a biblical foundation to church governance and practice is of supreme importance. Pentecostals affirm the inspiration and authority of scripture, upholding the Bible as the infallible, authoritative rule of faith and conduct, and believe that it is imperative that our world views are transformed in light of scripture. However, one must be cautious of equating biblical models and modes with the forms of one's own culture. As Lloyd Martin states, 'There is no such thing as a "Christian culture" that we can all join. When someone talks about Christian culture, he or she usually turns out to be talking about a version of his or her culture.'[80] Having learned the gospel within the mores of our own culture, it is easy to assume that our culture is the biblical culture. One must seek to avoid the ever-present danger of constructing a 'supra-cultural' church that simply exalts the dominant culture, inadvertently enforcing a monocultural agenda. In such a case, as Anderson notes, 'the "gospel" … is confused with "culture", it has been "colonialized" and a spurious "Christian culture" is offered in place of a genuine Christian message'.[81] As one leader shared, 'As long as Christian means Pākehā, we will not be accepted. To be Christian in our church means you're a Pākehā. It's like they've been a Pākehā all their lives, then they attach the name of Jesus to it, and now they're a Christian. Nothing else has to change. Māori, we can't do the same.'[82]

Newbigin believes that the growth of the church has often been hindered by the failure to recognise and honour differences of culture, where conversion 'separates the converts from their own culture, robs them of a great part of their human inheritance, and makes them second-class adherents of an alien culture'.[83] Steps must be made to ensure that the gospel is separated from cultural trappings, so as to ensure that a choice to follow Christ does not simply mean relinquishing one's culture for another.

Lineham believes that ethnicity will be the dominant mode of social organisation in Aotearoa New Zealand churches in the future, having seen it already manifest in present-day movements.[84] While allowing for distinctive ethnic expression, this separate development is a far cry from the diversity-in-unity expressed in the gospel (Ephesians 2:11–22; Galatians 3:28; Revelation 7:9). Durie predicts that by 2051 the ethnic Māori population will nearly double in size, reaching almost a million people, or 21 percent of the total population, and that by the same year, 33 percent of all children in the nation will be Māori.[85] Without neglecting their responsibilities to people of other ethnicities, the Pentecostal/Charismatic churches must, in their missionary endeavours to reach all people, consider strategies to reach and support a Māori ethnic populace rising in number. It will require intentionality on the part of leaders and congregations. Above all, it will require submission to the guidance and leadership of the holy spirit, upon whom we must depend to bring us into that unity and maturity in Christ that the Lord desires so much for his people.

Endnotes

1 J Mbiti, cited in P Jenkins, *The Next Christendom: The Coming of Global Christianity* (Oxford: Oxford University Press, 2000), 2.

2 D B Barrett and T M Johnson, 'Annual Statistical Table on Global Mission: 2004', in *International Bulletin of Missionary Research* 28.1 (January 2004): 24–5, cited in A A Anderson, 'Towards a Pentecostal Missiology for the Majority World', in *Asian Journal of Pentecostal Studies* 8.1 (2005): 29–47, 29.

3 A Anderson, 'Revising Pentecostal History in Global Perspective', in A Anderson and E Tang (eds), *Asian and Pentecostal: The Charismatic Face of Christianity in Asia* (Oxford/Baguio City: Regnum International/APTS Press, 2005), 151; Anderson, 'Towards a Pentecostal Missiology', 29.

4 A Anderson, *An Introduction to Pentecostalism* (Cambridge: Cambridge University Press, 2004), 281.

5 A Anderson, 'Introduction: World Pentecostalism at a Crossroads', in A H Anderson and W J Hollenweger (eds), *Pentecostals after a Century: Global Perspectives on a Movement in Transition* (Sheffield: Sheffield Academic Press, 1999), 25.

6 H Yung, 'Endued with Power: The Pentecostal-Charismatic Renewal and the Asian Church in the Twenty-First Century', in *Asian Journal of Pentecostal Studies (AJPS)* 6.1 (2003): 63–82, 73.

7 P Johnstone and J Mandryk, *Operation World* (Carlisle/Waynesboro: Paternoster/Lifestyle, 2001), 21; Anderson, *Introduction to Pentecostalism*, 103.

8 For example W Ma, 'When the Poor are Fired Up: The Role of Pneumatology in Pentecostal/Charismatic Mission', in V Kärkkäinen and J Moltmann (eds), *The Spirit in the World: Emerging Pentecostal Theologies in Global Contexts* (Grand Rapids: Eerdmans, 2009): 40–52, 40; Yung, 'Endued with Power'; A Anderson, 'The Origins of Pentecostalism and its Global Spread in the Early Twentieth Century', in *Transformations* 22.3 (July 2005): 175–85.

9 Pentecostal signs in Tamilnadu included tongues, interpretation of tongues, prophecy, dreams, visions and intense conviction of sin. Anderson, *Introduction to Pentecostalism*, 124; H Yung, 'Pentecostalism and the Asian Church', in Anderson and Tang, *Asian and Pentecostal*, 44.

10 Anderson, *Introduction to Pentecostalism*, 4. See also Anderson, 'The Origins of Pentecostalism'.

11 B Elsmore, *Like Them that Dream: The Maori and the Old Testament* (Auckland: Reed, 2000), 190.

12 See J M Henderson, *Ratana: The Man, the Church, the Political Movement* (Wellington: Reed/Polynesian Society, 1972), 31–6.

13 For example, the foretelling of the destruction of the bombing of London fifteen years before World War Two on 17 May 1924: 'I tell you all, the Angel of Death will visit this place, not a stone shall stand upon a stone …'; in K Newman, *Ratana Revisited: An Unfinished Legacy* (Auckland: Reed, 2006), 162.

14 Elsmore, *Like Them that Dream*, 191; for example Newman, *Ratana Revisited*, 72–3.

15 Newman notes that on the day of Pentecost, 31 May 1925, Rātana announced that it was an opportune time to establish a church, and that Rātana and a number of elders 'began speaking in a strange language', which many identify with Acts 2, which tells of the spirit descending upon the first Christian believers. Newman, *Ratana Revisited*, 162.

16 Anderson, 'Towards a Pentecostal Missiology', 30.

17 H Cox, *Fire from Heaven: The Rise of Pentecostal Spirituality and the Reshaping of Religion in the Twenty-First Century* (Cambridge: Da Capo Press, 1995), 259.

18 Evangelical Anglican Henry Venn was secretary of the British Church Missionary Society in the mid-nineteenth century, and a leading missionary statesman.

19 Anderson, *Introduction to Pentecostalism*, 210.

20 Anderson, 'Towards a Pentecostal Missiology', 46–7.

21 D Martin, cited in B Knowles, 'Pentecostalism and the Future of Christianity in the West: Reflections on a Conversation', in J Stenhouse and B Knowles (eds), *Christianity in the Post Secular West* (Hindmarsh: ATF Press, 2007): 177–208, 190.

22 D E Miller and T Yamamori, *Global Pentecostalism: The New Face of Christian Social Engagement* (Berkeley: University of California Press, 2007), 23.

23 Ma, 'When the Poor are Fired Up', 42.

24 Yung, 'Endued with Power', 71.

25 R Jaichandran and B D Madhav, 'Pentecostal Spirituality in a Postmodern World', in *AJPS* 6/1 (2003): 39–61, 42.

26 G B McGee, cited in Anderson, 'Towards a Pentecostal Missiology', 33.

27 A Anderson, 'The Gospel and Culture in Pentecostal Mission in the Third World', paper presented at the Ninth Conference of the European Pentecostal Charismatic Research

28 J Belich, *Paradise Reforged: A History of the New Zealanders – From the 1880s to the Year 2000* (Auckland: Allen Lane/Penguin, 2001), 473.
29 M King, *The Penguin History of New Zealand* (Auckland: Penguin, 2003), 470.
30 B Kernot, 'Maori Worldview and Spirituality', in *Stimulus* 6.2 (May 1998): 4–5.
31 M Marsden, 'God, Man and Universe: A Maori View', in M King (ed.), *Te Ao Hurihuri: Aspects of Maoritanga* (Auckland: Reed, 1992):117–137, 134.
32 E Shortland, *Maori Religion and Mythology* (London: Longmans, Green, 1882), 32–3; M Raureti, 'The Origins of the Ratana Movement', in M King (ed.), *Tihe Mauri Ora: Aspects of Maoritanga* (Wellington: Methuen, 1978):144–62, 148.
33 See Elsmore, *Like Them that Dream*.
34 B Haami, 'Tapu: a Pentecostal View', in *Stimulus* 6.2 (May 1998): 85–88, 86.
35 H Maxwell, 'Jubilee Reflections', in *Apostolic News* (July 1984): 3.
36 I G Clark, *Pentecost at the Ends of the Earth: The History of the Assemblies of God in New Zealand (1927–2003)* (Blenheim: Christian Road Ministries, 2007), 43.
37 B Knowles, *New Life: A History of the New Life Churches of New Zealand 1942–1979* (Dunedin: Third Millennium Publishing, 1999), 33.
38 Personal communication, Manu Pohio, former tumuaki, Māori and Pacific Island Council, ACTS/Apostolic Movement, 20 October 2010.
39 Personal communication, Kim Workman, director, Rethinking Crime and Punishment, 8 October 2009.
40 Personal communication, October 2009. Note that some names of those involved in personal communications referenced in this chapter have been omitted.
41 Personal communication, Lloyd Martin, 22 October 2009.
42 Personal communication, October 2010.
43 Personal communication, Kim Workman, 8 October 2009.
44 Personal communication, October 2009.
45 The *Te Hoe Nuku Roa* project measures the Māori cultural identity of a person, developing four cultural identity profiles: a secure identity, a positive identity, a notional identity and a compromised identity. See B Stevenson, 'Te Hoe Nuku Roa: A Measure of Māori Cultural Identity', in *He Pukenga Kōrero* 8.1 (2004): 37–45.
46 Personal communication, Glen Tupuhi, manager, strategic development human resources for Te Runanga o Kirikiriroa, 13 May 2010.
47 Clark, *Pentecost at the Ends of the Earth*, 238.
48 Knowles, *New Life*, 29–30.
49 Clark, *Pentecost at the Ends of the Earth*, 204.
50 P D Carew, 'Māori, Biculturalism and the Assemblies of God in New Zealand, 1970–2008', MA thesis, Victoria University of Wellington, 2009, 76; Apostolic Church New Zealand Census Information Summary Sheet, March 1993, 1; and March 2001, 1.
51 Carew, 'Māori, Biculturalism and the Assemblies of God', 115.
52 Personal communication, Peter Hira, former assistant superintendent of the Assemblies of God, 21 October, 2009. Hira speaks highly of the support for current superintendent Ken Harrison.
53 Clark, *Pentecost at the Ends of the Earth*, 238.
54 Carew, 'Māori, Biculturalism and the Assemblies of God', 131–3.
55 I Clark, cited in ibid, 89.
56 J E Worsfold, *The Origins of the Apostolic Church in Great Britain* (Wellington: Julian Literature Trust, 1991), 256.

57 J E Worsfold, *A History of the Charismatic Movements in New Zealand* (Bradford: Julian Literature Trust, 1974), 258.
58 Ibid, 268.
59 W L Worsfold, 'Subsequence, Prophecy and Church Order in the Apostolic Church, New Zealand', PhD thesis, Victoria University of Wellington, 2004, 252.
60 R Goulton, 'Release through Recognition, Respect and Righteousness', in *Te Reo Apotorika/Apostolic News*, March 1990: 1.
61 Worsfold, 'Subsequence, Prophecy and Church Order', 255.
62 L Martin, 'Counting the Cost of True Partnership', in *Reality* 65 (October/November 2004): 30.
63 Clark, *Pentecost at the Ends of the Earth*, 238.
64 Apostolic Church New Zealand Census Information Summary Sheet, March 2001, 1; personal communication, ACTS National Office, 2 June 2010.
65 Destiny Church, 'Our History': www.destinychurch.org.nz/index.php?option=com_content&view=article&id=48&Itemid=104 (accessed 4 January 2012).
66 Personal communication, Glen Tupuhi, 30 October 2008.
67 P Lineham, 'Among the Believers': www.massey.ac.nz/massey/about-massey/news/article.cfm?mnarticle=among-the-believers-05-04-2006 (accessed 4 January 2012).
68 P Lineham, 'Wanna be in my Gang?', in *New Zealand Listener* 195/3357 (11–17 September 2004): www.listener.co.nz/uncategorized/wanna-be-in-my-gang (accessed 4 January 2012).
69 J L Walton, *Watch This!: The Ethics and Aesthetics of Black Televangelism* (New York/London: New York University Press, 2009), 129–31 and 137.
70 B Tamaki, *Bishop Brian Tamaki: More than Meets the Eye* (Auckland: Tamaki Publications, 2006), 338–9.
71 Tamaki, cited in S Moetara, 'An Exploration of Notions of Maori Leadership and a Consideration of Their Contribution for Christian Leadership in the Church of Aotearoa-New Zealand Today', MTh dissertation, Laidlaw College, 2009, 51.
72 Lineham, 'Wanna be in my Gang?'
73 Lineham, cited in C Masters, 'Destiny "Latest in a Long Line"', in *New Zealand Herald*, 28 August 2004: www.nzherald.co.nz/section/1/story.cfm?c_id=1&objectid=3587622 (accessed 4 January 2012).
74 'Destiny's Brian Tamaki answers "cult" accusations', *Close UP – TV One*, Thursday, Oct 29, 2009; http://www.stuff.co.nz/national/3012558/Destinys-Brian-Tamaki-answers-cult-accusations [accessed 31 January 2012]; Garth George, "Tamaki"'s 700 'sons' swear oath of loyalty," in *NZ Herald* Thu 29 Oct, 2009;: http://www.nzherald.co.nz/nz/news/article.cfm?c_id=1&objectid=10605956 [accessed 31 January 2012].
75 S May, 'Accommodating Multiculturalism and Biculturalism: Implications for Language Policy', in P Spoonley, C Macpherson and D Pearson (eds), *Tangata Tangata: The Changing Ethnic Contours of New Zealand* (Southbank: Thomson/Dunmore Press, 2004), 250–1.
76 Department of Social Welfare, *Puao-te-Ata-Tu (Daybreak): The Report of the Ministerial Advisory Committee on a Māori Perspective for the Department of Social Welfare* (Wellington: Government Printer, 1988), 19.
77 D O'Sullivan, *Beyond Biculturalism: The Politics of an Indigenous Minority* (Wellington: Huia, 2007), 19.
78 Carew, 'Māori, Biculturalism and the Assemblies of God', 130.
79 Ibid, 131.

80 L Martin, *One Faith, Two Peoples: Communicating Across Cultures Within the Church*, 3rd edition (Paraparaumu: Salt Company Publishers, 2001), 39.
81 Anderson, 'Gospel and Culture', 3.
82 Personal communication, October 2009.
83 L Newbigin, *The Open Secret: An Introduction to the Theology of Mission*, revised edition (Grand Rapids: Eerdmans, 1999), 141.
84 Moetara, 'Notions of Maori Leadership', 10.
85 M Durie, *Ngā Kāhui Pou: Launching Māori Futures* (Wellington: Huia, 2003), 121–2.

Chapter Five
Māori Participation in the Assemblies of God

Philip Carew and Geoff Troughton

In 2007, the National Conference of the Assemblies of God in New Zealand commissioned Peter Hira, a senior pastor and former assistant superintendent, with the task of examining the problem of low Māori participation within the denomination. The perception of limited Māori involvement had existed for some time and been the cause of much perplexity. Other groups, like the Apostolic and Elim churches, and more recently Destiny Church, had demonstrated that Pentecostalism could be highly attractive to Māori. Furthermore, as the largest Pentecostal denomination in the world and one that emphasised cross-cultural mission, the Assemblies of God had a global reputation for building strong indigenous ministries.[1] While the New Zealand church was ethnically diverse, its apparent failure among Māori was a blot on that reputation. Discomfort about the situation became particularly obvious from the late 1980s, as bicultural ideals gained traction within New Zealand society.

The 2007 initiative clearly reflected growing sensitivity to these changes. It nevertheless raised significant questions about the extent of Māori participation in the Assemblies of God. This chapter addresses some of these by evaluating the denomination's history of engagement with Māori and identifying key factors that militated against high levels of Māori support. The analysis focuses on denominational structures and emphases, and highlights the role of dynamics internal to the Assemblies of God in undermining Māori participation.

Ethnic diversity in the Assemblies of God

Before addressing these dimensions it is worth assessing the known extent of Māori participation in the denomination and placing it in some perspective. Statistically, the best available sources come from the national Census and surveys of the Assemblies of God taken in 1992 and 2009.[2] According to the 1992 survey, Māori comprised just 7.1 percent of the Assemblies' population. By comparison, at this time nearly 25 percent of the Apostolic Church and 12.9 percent of the total New Zealand population were Māori.[3] The 2009 survey focused only on assemblies in the Wellington region, but its figure for Māori of 8.36 percent indicated a slightly higher proportion than the earlier survey.[4] If Wellington reflected the national situation then this suggests a slight increase, albeit at a similar rate to increases in the Māori population generally, since this had risen to 14 percent by 2006.[5]

This data suggests that Māori have not been entirely absent from the Assemblies of God during the last twenty years. Indeed, Māori may currently be more prominent in the assemblies on a week-to-week basis than in the mainline denominations, where Census affiliation is less likely to translate into active participation. Nevertheless, the perception of a weaker Māori presence than in other Pentecostal denominations or in proportion to their share of the population remains correct. Furthermore, there is only marginal evidence of growth.

The consistency of Māori participation belies the remarkable demographic transformations that have taken place within the Assemblies of God. The denomination has grown significantly since the 1990s, and experienced a concomitant increase in ethnic diversity. The 2006 Census indicated that its 15,300 adherents were nearly twice as numerous as the next largest Pentecostal denomination, and comprised about one-fifth of total Pentecostal affiliation. The church's own statistics put adherents at around 25,000. In terms of ethnic diversity, the Wellington survey indicates that Tongan, Fijian, Indian and Korean communities are all now present within the assemblies in higher proportions than their Census share of the population. Chinese representation has also increased substantially, though not at the rate of growth within the population at large.

The most significant demographic change is growth in the Samoan community. The formation of a Samoan Assemblies of God in 1926 in American Samoa laid the basis of a strong presence in the islands.[6] Migration to New Zealand in the 1960s led to the establishment of a Samoan stream within the local denomination from 1965. In 2005 there were ninety Samoan assemblies within the Assemblies of God in New Zealand, but in that year one-third of those seceded with Pastor Samani Pulepule to form the Samoan Assemblies of God in New Zealand Incorporated.[7] Despite this, Samoans were still the largest single ethnic group in the Assemblies of God in general, and accounted for over 34 percent of respondents in the Wellington survey. In 1992 the figure had been 23 percent.[8]

Irrespective of its causes, this spectacular increase had significant implications for the question of Māori participation. Combined with growing ethnic diversity in general, growth in Samoan numbers reinforced a characteristic commitment to multiculturalism. This ideology was a crucial factor in framing the church's responses as concerns about a lack of Māori participation increased during the latter decades of the twentieth century. The seeds of lower participation, however, had been sown in an earlier period.

Pentecostal origins and the Assemblies of God in New Zealand
The Assemblies of God traces its lineage back to the famous revival sparked by the ministry of William Seymour at Azusa Street, Los Angeles from 1906. The events at Seymour's Apostolic Faith Mission made a significant impact upon leaders in the Church of God in Christ. Despite being a largely African American denomination, the Church of God in Christ also included a network of white pastors, who later departed to form the Assemblies of God.[9] Commencement of the Assemblies of God in New Zealand in 1927 linked local Pentecostalism with this earlier history. The connections were largely nominal at first, and somewhat unexpected, for the earliest significant Pentecostal influences in New Zealand had come primarily from British sources.

The first local organisation, the Pentecostal Church of New Zealand, was formed during visits of the former Yorkshire plumber Smith Wigglesworth between 1922 and 1924.[10] But Wigglesworth ordained only one person, and drew up no constitution or statement of beliefs. This contributed to unrest over the new movement's government and direction. A short time later A C Valdez, another visiting speaker and a product of the Azusa Street revival, recommended adoption of the constitution and 'Statement of Fundamental Truths' of the Assemblies of God in the United States.[11] Not all Pentecostal churches agreed, but those that did approved an adapted constitution on 22 April 1927.[12] A New Zealand Assemblies of God had been created. The Pentecostal Church of New Zealand also continued, but was affected by further schism. Its remnant eventually joined with the Elim Church. Further Pentecostal groups emerged, including the Apostolic Church, which began locally in the 1930s, and the Indigenous Churches, later known as the New Life movement, in the 1940s and 1950s.[13]

Like other early Pentecostal churches, the Assemblies of God was primarily a spiritual renewal movement, and therefore drew many of its 'converts' from existing churches. The denomination grew slowly initially, with fellowships comprised largely of working class Pākehā, often led by inadequately supported pastors and meeting in makeshift facilities.[14] The strongest assemblies were in centres like Auckland, Wellington, Christchurch, New Plymouth and Palmerston North. Prior to the period of massive post-war urbanisation there is little evidence of contact between the church and Māori communities. This pattern persisted in the early post-war years, with some notable exceptions. Ray Bloomfield's Ellerslie-Tamaki Faith Mission affiliated with the Assemblies of God in 1954, while the Whāngārei assembly began the following year. These two new churches had markedly different impacts upon the Assemblies of God, but were significant in terms of their connection with Māori.

The Ellerslie-Tamaki Mission had a particularly extensive impact. Bloomfield attracted visitors from as far as Northland in search of healing, salvation and 'baptism in the holy spirit'. Bloomfield was soon introduced to Frank Houston, a former Salvation Army officer who claimed to have been healed of the effects of a nervous breakdown through his Pentecostal experience. Together, Bloomfield and Houston became leaders in a revival movement among Māori at Waiomio near Kawakawa in Northland, after Māori converts from the Ellerslie meetings invited the pair north in 1957. After initial suspicion, the physical healing of an elderly identity in the region paved the way for widespread acceptance. A local tohunga was reportedly one of the few who resisted the movement. The impact of events was such that others, including Noel Watson, Bruce Uren, Russell Ferguson and Malcolm and Bernice Tweed, were inspired to work in Northland among Māori for the Assemblies of God.

Despite this, engagement was limited during this period. Bloomfield and Houston apparently learnt a few Māori phrases, and accommodated certain protocols in their ministry. Nevertheless, their focus was broadly evangelistic, and the fact that Māori were the beneficiaries of their outreach was arguably incidental rather than the consequence of deliberate strategy. Their ministry emphasised strong preaching, signs and wonders, and distinctively Pentecostal forms of prayer, praise and worship that often proved appealing to Māori.[15] Crucially, however, Bloomfield and Houston did not attempt to develop Māori leadership or encourage reflection on issues of gospel and culture. Their failure to develop relationships with local marae and kaumātua also contrasted with the efforts of other Pentecostal denominations.[16]

Ultimately, the Waiomio revival did not nurture a significant Māori constituency over the longer term. The events were something of an aberration, and the denomination's presence among Māori waned as the initial revival broke down. A number of factors contributed to this, including conflict between Ferguson and Malcolm Tweed. Watson, who supervised the Northland work, also became involved in a 'questionable relationship' that undermined denominational support and the church's credibility in the community.

Events in Whāngārei in 1976 almost certainly had a more damaging impact. These took place at a time when race relations and the place of Māori culture within New Zealand society were being reevaluated. Developments like the repeal of the Tohunga Suppression Act in 1963, the Māori land march led by Whina Cooper in 1975 and the Treaty of Waitangi Act 1975 added urgency to these debates. They generated varied responses from within the Christian community. In May 1976, the *Northern Advocate* newspaper drew attention to one reaction in a front-page article entitled 'Petition calls for ban on Māoritanga "demon" lessons in schools'.[17] The campaign the article referred to was spearheaded by George Anderson, a member of the Whangarei Assemblies of God. Anderson was apparently so concerned about Māoritanga that he would not use ten-cent pieces because of the Māori designs on them. He reputedly once ripped up linoleum to see if there were any newspapers containing Māori images underneath. According to Graham Cruickshank, at that time a recently arrived member, strong preaching against Māori spirits and references to the cursing of the descendants of Ham featured regularly at the Whangarei Assemblies of God.[18] The pastor of the church, Geoff Lloyd, was under the 'covering' of Neville Johnson of the Auckland Assemblies of God, and both supported the petition.[19]

The original intention was to present signatures to the Minister of Education. The petition's three goals were to stop the teaching of Māoritanga in schools; to restrict the teaching of Māoritanga to such 'non-spiritual' aspects of the culture as fishing and agriculture; and to allow parents to withdraw their children from such classes. These suggestions generated considerable debate, subsequent articles and letters to the editor revealing deep hurt among Māori. Some were offended that the church had not talked with kaumātua before going public. Others noted that Māori had accepted Christianity in large numbers, and no longer attributed spiritual significance to aspects of the culture that concerned the petition's promoters. Some of these correspondents called on the church to trust Māori to be able to reconcile issues of faith and culture for themselves.[20]

Armstrong's petition was not universally supported within the Assemblies of God. Indeed, both the national executive and the Association of Pentecostal Churches distanced themselves from it.

Nevertheless, the episode was a disaster for the church. A protest group appeared in Whāngārei, which led to negative publicity. The local congregation was internally divided over the issue, and a number of Māori ended up leaving.[21] The church eventually apologised to the Māori community for the offence caused, while Lloyd ultimately left the Assemblies of God ministry. Significant damage had been done.

Māori and the Assemblies of God since the 1970s

By the 1970s, then, links with Māori were tenuous. No sustained or coordinated 'Māori work' had ever been sponsored; nor was there an obvious intention to cultivate any. Connections had been established in Northland, but then undermined. In other areas, however, the church was beginning to change. It grew rapidly during the early 1970s under the direction of a younger and more adventurous set of leaders like Houston, who had shifted to Lower Hutt, and Neville Johnson in Auckland. The Charismatic movement also made Pentecostalism more respectable and attractive, and the assemblies benefited from an influx of members from other denominations.

Numerical growth among Pākehā and Samoan migrants from the 1960s occupied the church's attention. It also deflected interest away from debates about Māori-Pākehā relations and biculturalism, which were becoming increasingly common elsewhere. Māori members within the church tended to have a low profile, and public discussion of issues pertaining to Māori was very limited. Between 1970 and 2008 just forty articles in the church's official publications (the *Evangel* and *Empowered*) contained any discernable reference to Māori. Only eleven of these were substantial in the sense that they directly addressed Māori-related issues or indicated significant Māori participation. Seven merely contained the picture or name of a Māori person without further comment.

A number of developments during the 1980s indicated growing awareness of the changing context in New Zealand and willingness to contemplate its implications. In 1985, Pastor Peter Hira (Tūhoe) was voted on to the executive. This was not cast as a culturally motivated development, but Hira was often thereafter responsible for initiating deliberation on matters of Māori culture.[22] There were a few other pastors of Māori descent within the movement, and women like Tui Cruickshank (Ngāti Kahungunu, Ngāpuhi, Ngāti Whātua) and Mina Acraman (Te Arawa) worked effectively with their husbands in pastoral roles. Few Māori, however, trained in the regional training centres in Auckland, Lower Hutt and Christchurch that were so crucial to the expansion of the Assemblies of God during this time.[23] Consequently, Hira carried much of the responsibility to be the denomination's 'Māori face'.

Other individuals also pressed the church to consider the needs of Māori, and to seek opportunities for ministry. Claire Chapman was one of the first women to pursue ordination through the Assemblies of God once that became possible in 1988. Early in their shared ministry, she and her husband Dan adopted a son, William, who was Māori. Chapman soon became conscious that many younger Māori did not understand the language of the 1952 version of the Māori Bible, and decided that a more contemporary version was needed.[24] After training with the Summer Institute of Linguistics she began the task, acting as administrator and theological overseer while her son did much of the translation. Struggling with limited resources, the pair approached the national executive seeking financial support. This was declined, though help in publicising the work was offered. Kem Price, an executive member at that time and the church's missions' coordinator, commented that he did not think a translation was necessary, since most Māori now spoke English.[25] Some leaders were concerned that the Chapmans lacked the ability to tackle the task, and worried about the theological implications of their translation decisions.[26] For her part, Chapman felt that the denomination's lack of support reflected its low priority on mission to Māori, and a preference for appealing to higher socio-economic groups at that time. The translation was never completed.[27]

Between 1988 and 1999 cross-cultural issues received greater attention than in any previous period. The denomination sponsored a 'National Conference on Maoridom' in 1988, at which more reflective attitudes were evident. Superintendent Jim Williams admitted that an 'unhealthy rejection of Māoritanga' existed within the movement, and that the movement needed to adopt culturally appropriate leadership training methods. Hira also spoke at this event, and commended the use of Māori protocol as good manners that created opportunities to share the gospel. Price reflected that churches were always planted and tended within the context of culture, and that European culture should not be forced upon Māori. Scriptural truth, however, was not to be compromised. All three men were on the executive at the time, and each acknowledged the importance of cultural awareness in the transmission of the gospel message, with the proviso that syncretism be avoided.[28] Evangelism was still clearly the primary consideration.

Strikingly, however, the strong emphasis on Māori culture at this initial conference was downplayed in subsequent events. In Hamilton in 1988 a local Assemblies of God seminar entitled 'Jesus, Christ to All Peoples' declared that 'true cultural identity is not found through cultural pursuits, but only found in pursuit of Christ', and that 'Christ is above every culture'.[29] Reports of the conference did not elaborate on the intended implications, or how these ideas might be implemented. Nevertheless, the minimising of culture as a factor in personal identity was notable given that the meeting was ostensibly designed as a forum for Māori to express their faith in a more culturally congenial context.

Further conferences on cultural issues followed. These invariably emphasised a multicultural philosophy, and encouraged cultural awareness rather than bicultural responsibility.[30] Suspicion about biculturalism and its political implications partly explains why the sesquicentennial of the Treaty of Waitangi in 1990 passed without comment in the *Evangel*, though the omission contrasted sharply with other churches' responses.[31] Nevertheless, the Rev. Lionel Stewart, superintendent of the Māori ministry department of the Baptist Church, spoke to the 'Culture and Evangelism Conference' at Ngāruawāhia in 1990. World evangelisation remained the church's priority, but events like these demonstrated growing appreciation of the limitations of a 'one size fits all' approach. Stewart emphasised that all Christians were culturally situated, while cautioning that all cultures and values should be evaluated in the light of scripture.[32]

This kind of teaching created more space for cultural difference. It did not lead to a dedicated mission to Māori, or a surge in Māori participation. In 1993, the *Evangel* reported that only 7 percent of Assemblies of God adherents were Māori.[33] This low proportion provoked some reflection, and was a contributing factor in Peter Hira initiating seminars on methods of outreach to Māori at the annual conferences in 1996 and 2000.[34] In recent years the national church has moved to acknowledge the particular significance of Māori culture in New Zealand. At a ceremonial or symbolic level, for example, the current general secretary Ken Harrison wears a korowai at national gatherings. New pastors are informed of the need to be familiar with Māori protocol at cultural events in which they participate, and are encouraged to read a book on tikanga.[35]

Some individual churches have also successfully fostered Māori participation at times. Māori pastors were often critical in this process. Mike Angel (Ngāpuhi) was pastor of the Picton assembly for a period during the 1980s. He persuaded the church to sing songs with verses in English and some in Māori, and had scripture texts in Māori displayed on the auditorium walls. Māori attended the church while he was there, but left when he did also. Remaining Pākehā took the texts down, seeing no reason to have something on the wall they did not understand.[36]

Interviews with leaders in the Assemblies of God suggest that congregations with significant Māori constituencies have typically taken deliberate steps to help cultivate engagement with Māori people and culture.[37] These include attempting to use Māori phrases correctly, greeting Māori members appropriately by publicly welcoming them into the community and acknowledging their presence in gatherings. Consultation with Māori on the best ways to honour their culture has also been important; practices like these have typically followed in the wake of advice offered by Māori to non-Māori pastors. Responses to consultation have resulted in diverse recommendations, ranging from extensive expectations to a firm preference for no 'special treatment'. The process of consultation itself seems to have been the critical factor, partly because that affirmed a sense of relationship, respect and inclusion.

In recent years, various practices have been encouraged within the church as these became more accepted in the wider community. Singing the national anthem now occurs regularly in some assemblies, often with at least one verse in Māori.[38] Some church leaders have encouraged the formation of Māori cultural performance groups within their congregations. In the early 2000s, a Māori group called 'Cloak of Praise' at Pakuranga Assemblies of God endeavoured to introduce a 'redemptive aspect to the culture' through music.[39] Some churches also hold cultural nights, which provide opportunities for Māori to perform along with other ethnic groups.

The increasingly cosmopolitan make-up of the Assemblies of God has been a crucial factor in the acceptance of greater diversity in cultural expression. Service formats have been affected, as has governance, to some extent. Ethnic groups have generally been supervised by the movement's regional overseers. While Samoans are the only group with representation on the executive council, others have appointed spokespeople who liaise with designated executive members. Developments like these have partly been motivated by a desire to avoid breakaway bodies forming along ethnic lines.[40] The gains for Māori have been rather limited, partly reflecting the limited pool of Māori workers and the small number of pastors with a particular interest in Māori culture.

Accounting for low rates of Māori participation
This overview has indicated that engagement with Māori culture and communities has been limited throughout the Assemblies of God's history. But why has there been such reticence in this regard, and why the persistence of relatively low levels of Māori participation? In short, low participation rates are partly a product of limited engagement, which has in turn been shaped by a combination of factors including ideological conviction, organisational structure and historical circumstance.

The post-missionary era origin of the Assemblies of God in New Zealand was one important practical factor. Quite simply, the denomination did not begin in the context of a specific mission to Māori, in the manner that the Anglican, Methodist and Catholic churches did. These churches built constituencies and developed resources for cultural engagement from their very earliest days. Moreover, their involvement in events at Waitangi in 1840, the inconsistency of their subsequent policy and the loss of their influence among Māori all framed their engagement with biculturalism when that became a priority later in the twentieth century.[41] By contrast, the assemblies arrived at a point when denominational loyalties had been established, and Māori churches like Rātana and Ringatū had also begun. Māori were recovering from numerical decline during the nineteenth century, but still represented only 5 percent of the population. They were therefore less visible, and in a sense the opportunities for the Assemblies of God were initially limited.

Historically, the denomination's urban origins and focus were related limiting factors. Analysis of representations at conferences and the location of churches shows that the denomination has always been overwhelmingly urban. Prior to World War Two this meant that Assemblies of God churches were generally based in areas where few Māori lived. This urban focus continued in the post-war era. By that time the denomination was largely European, and had not established a culture of engagement. This made it unlikely to attract newly urbanised Māori, who were often suspicious of Pākehā institutions.[42] Consequently, the church was left analysing the culture from a distance.

A third factor is simply that Māori have been neglected in terms of the church's missionary consciousness. The denomination's late beginning and urban focus did not make low rates of Māori participation inevitable. Indeed, the Apostolic Church began slightly later, but established a sizeable Māori constituency, through the deliberate efforts of influential members. Structures were established to support missionary outreach, leadership was developed and a strong community emerged. By contrast, the Assemblies of God never engaged with Māori communities in a sustained or deliberate fashion. In the early days of the movement, belief in the imminent return of Christ tended to discourage discriminating between 'lost sheep'. In more recent times, competition for 'market share' similarly discouraged concentration on minority groups that were perceived as requiring major investment. Church leaders with cross-cultural mission experience recognise that deliberate and comprehensive action is necessary to increase levels of Māori participation. This has clearly never occurred, and remains a curious lacuna.

A fourth factor has been the low priority placed on issues of social justice. Tensions between social justice concerns and conservative theology were older, but sharpened in the period during which Pentecostalism emerged in New Zealand. From its inception the Assemblies of God emphasised renewal, focusing on 'gospel preaching' and authentic spiritual experience. Suspicion about the impact of social justice on these central concerns undermined a potentially constructive basis for engagement with Māori. Debates about the Treaty of Waitangi, Treaty principles and bicultural ideals later in the twentieth century were shaped by frameworks of justice. The Assemblies of God tended to conceive of these as purely social and political issues, and disavowed any obligation for involvement with the state or in solving historically grounded social issues. A propensity to underplay the significance of social context, especially as it impacted upon Māori, also limited the forms of engagement that were possible, and eroded motivation. In a highly charged late twentieth-century environment, the approach did little to encourage new mission.

Denominational suspicion about social justice was primarily a matter of focus, though it also followed from views about the relative roles of church and state. Social justice was not a central priority in terms of the church's mission, but such matters were also perceived as belonging in the state's sphere of responsibility. It was not that the church was impervious to injustice, or for want of an activist mentality. The shape of Pentecostal activism, however, created further challenges. Observers of evangelical and Pentecostal Christianity often note that these forms tend to be characterised by a constant sense of urgency and preference for action over reflection.[43] This observation is particularly appropriate for the Pentecostal movement due to its emphasis on empowerment for witness and action.

Differences between Pākehā and Māori attitudes towards time, relationship and community have often proven difficult to negotiate.[44] Pākehā Pentecostal activism did not cohere well with Māori values in these areas, which provided an additional barrier to potential inclusion. This was particularly true in the period prior to Māori urbanisation, but not exclusively. In a wide-ranging reflection in 1990, Apostolic Pastor Ted Davis (Ngāpuhi) discussed the kind of attitude necessary for ministering to Māori in rural areas. He particularly emphasised the need to avoid imposing alien ideas of 'time' on the community, to demonstrate commitment by cooperating and participating fully in community life, and to avoid any suggestion of condescension. Davis explicitly linked existing attitudes to the exigencies of modern urban conditions. A relationship based on willingness to give time remained a central goal, yet it was also a profound obstacle for Pākehā Pentecostals.[45] A cultural bias toward activism need not have precluded Māori participation, but it exacerbated existing limitations.

Another crucial factor reinforcing this situation was the limited extent of Māori leadership within the denomination. This partly reflected a vicious cycle whereby the limited number of members begat a limited leadership pool. Yet the potential of Māori to generate strong leaders is well documented, and the experience of the Apostolic Church suggests that the problem arose partly from deficient strategy. For the Apostolic Church, development of indigenous Māori leadership was a clear priority. In time articulate and capable leaders emerged, including Manuel Renata, Manu Pohio and Brian Tamaki. Through a combination of personal charisma, their appeal to common cultural experience, and the freedom they were allowed to express themselves in Māori terms, leaders like these were able to attract Māori into the church.

Interestingly, insider observers like Graeme Cruickshank identify a comparable process within the Assemblies of God itself. Cruickshank and others ascribe much of the denomination's growth from the 1960s to the rise of New Zealand-born leadership.[46] Indeed, the ideal of indigenous leadership – that is, leadership emerging out of the local environment – is now an established principle in Assemblies of God policy globally. Initially, the movement's missionary strategy was minimal, and focused largely on spirit-led direction tuned by trial and error. Other principles were gradually adopted, and these invariably emphasised indigenous leadership. Thus, from the 1950s the Assemblies of God missiologist Melvin Hodges began propounding the 'three-self' strategy that Henry Venn had introduced to the Church Missionary Society in 1844.[47] Commitment to indigenous leadership training prompted the development of colleges such as Asia Pacific Theological Seminary in the Philippines. The New Zealand church has benefited from the Assemblies of God USA's work in Samoa, where indigenous leadership was promoted. To date, however, no comparable efforts to establish strong and effective Māori leadership have ever transpired.

One of the most important factors that militated against establishment of mission to Māori, and therefore weakened the prospects for Māori participation, was structural and philosophical. Specifically, the Assemblies of God's strong emphasis on local church autonomy was a barrier insofar as it limited the denomination's capacity for unified action. Originally rooted in early Pentecostalism's suspicion of institutions, and pastors' independent-mindedness, local autonomy made it difficult to secure collective commitment for anything except overseas missions. Even support for a national administrative office and mission-oriented agencies like Bible schools was always a challenge.

Thus, the denomination's emphasis on local church autonomy has been a double-edged sword. The drive and investment of committed local leaders facilitated the movement's global expansion, but initiatives were often focused on local growth rather than issues of national significance. Projects beyond the local church require the attention of individual activists, yet tremendous energy is necessary to obtain the accumulated support of fiercely independent and preoccupied congregations. By contrast, the Apostolic Church was historically more centrally governed. Centralisation facilitated the allocation of workers and resources to Māori ministry, while the national church also helped fund work. Though their structures are somewhat different, and practical congregationalism is now common, the same might also be said of the mainline churches. Centralised resources and strategies allow for more ambitious projects than most individual congregations attempt.

In recent decades the Assemblies of God's strong support for multiculturalism has, perhaps more than any other factor, proven a major impediment to the development of a strong Māori presence within the movement. Multiculturalism has been widely regarded as the most logical position for an ethnically diverse church. It has also been considered the most theologically defensible, and consistent with the church's emphasis on cross-cultural mission. Globally, the Assemblies of God has usually become the largest Pentecostal denomination wherever it has gone. That fact bolsters confidence in its multiculturalist policy.

In the New Zealand assemblies, multiculturalism has generally been correlated with ethnic diversity. In practice, the ideal has been expressed in the acceptance of self-initiating ethnic fellowships, along with recognition and occasional celebration of cultural diversity in particular events. Notions of power or resource redistribution have been less common. More negatively, multiculturalism has also been defined in terms of resistance to the preferential treatment implied by the idea of biculturalism, as well as its essentially political character.

These approaches have not helped increase the Assemblies of God's capacity to attract Māori. This is not because biculturalism is necessary per se, or provides any guarantee of Māori support. Rather, multiculturism reflects limitations in the existing model for addressing local conditions. On the one hand, the principle of self-initiating ethnic fellowships has inherent weaknesses. It implies that ethnic groups must strengthen themselves, which can reinforce the vicious circle. While there is no apparent opposition to Māori development, the initiative must come from Māori, and their numbers are now comparatively few. On the other hand, resistance to biculturalism has arguably diminished the denomination's confidence in taking initiatives, especially where these might be interpreted as political or indicative of 'special treatment'. Specifically Māori imperatives are downplayed when a multicultural lens is employed, as happened in the period when cultural issues were examined between 1988 and 1999. Such dynamics confirm old suspicions that multiculturalism undermines particular Māori claims. By avoiding 'the historical and social imperatives of the Māori situation', multiculturalism may effectively work in favour of the status quo.[48]

Conclusion

The Assemblies of God in New Zealand has not been as successful in fostering Māori participation in its churches as some other Pentecostal denominations. This reality continues to perplex the movement, and it seems likely that reflection on causes and cures will continue for some time yet. The situation is not, and was not, simply a product of denominational failings. More comprehensive evaluations will need to give further weight to Māori agency and choice, as well as to a broader range of social and cultural dynamics. Nevertheless, it seems clear that characteristic ideas, experiences and emphases have worked historically to limit the denomination's appeal, and contributed to lower rates of Māori participation.

In this respect it is tempting to look to the denomination's aversion to biculturalism as a leading explanatory factor. Given the significance of bicultural ideals within late twentieth-century New Zealand society, eschewal of biculturalism may well have placed the denomination in a marginal position and diminished its attractiveness to Māori. The experience of the mainline churches and others, however, suggests that this was not in itself the determining factor. Indeed, rejection of biculturalism was as much a symptom of disconnection with Māori as a cause. Rather, a complex range of interrelated factors contributed to low rates of Māori participation within the Assemblies of God. Lack of deliberate engagement with Māori culture and people was a primary one. Others included a combination of theological emphasis, historical circumstance, geographical location and the denomination's organisational structure. Whether new structures, priorities and conditions will emerge to change this situation yet remains to be seen.

Endnotes

1. For overviews of the history and ethos of the denomination, see E L Blumhofer, *Restoring the Faith: The Assemblies of God, Pentecostalism, and American Culture* (Urbana: University of Illinois Press, 1993); E L Blumhofer and A R Armstrong, 'Assemblies of God', in S M Burgess and E M van der Maas (eds), *International Dictionary of Pentecostal and Charismatic Movements* (Grand Rapids: Zondervan, 2002): 333–40.
2. For full survey details see *Evangel*, Autumn 1993: 7; P D Carew, 'Māori, Biculturalism and the Assemblies of God in New Zealand, 1970–2008', MA thesis, Victoria University of Wellington, 2009, 31–7.
3. *Apostolic News*, August 1992: 1.
4. Wellington region's ethnic profile is similar to that of the nation as a whole, though no claims are made for the representativeness of the region's religious geography.
5. The proportion of Māori and other non-Pasifika groups in Wellington may also be slightly inflated due to the lower rates of return by Samoan assemblies.
6. See T Pagaialii, *Pentecost 'to the Uttermost': A History of the Assemblies of God in Samoa* (Baguio: APTS Press, 2006).
7. Pulepule had been one of the most influential leaders in the Samoan assemblies in New Zealand since 1967. *Evangel*, October–November 1986: 16–18; *Evangel*, Summer 1991: 30–1.
8. Samoans made up 3.3 percent of the New Zealand population in 2006.
9. D J Rogers, 'The Assemblies of God and the Long Journey towards Racial Reconciliation', in *Assemblies of God [USA] Heritage* 28 (2008): 50–61.
10. J E Worsfold, *A History of the Charismatic Movements in New Zealand* (Bradford: Julian Literature Trust, 1974), 64–79 and 104–6; I G Clark, *Pentecost at the Ends of the Earth: The History of the Assemblies of God in New Zealand (1927–2003)* (Blenheim: Christian Road Ministries, 2007), 91–3.
11. Valdez had been conducting preaching tours in Australasia since September 1924. M Hutchinson, '"Second Founder": A C Valdez Sr and Australian Pentecostalism', in *Australasian Pentecostal Studies* 11 (2009): http://webjournals.alphacrucis.edu.au/journals/aps/issue-11/02-second-founder-a-c-valdez-sr-and-australian-pen (accessed 5 January 2012).
12. *Evangel*, October 1987: 8; Clark, *Pentecost at the Ends of the Earth*, 31–4; personal communication, Ken Harrison, 6 November 2008.
13. B Knowles, *New Life: A History of the New Life Churches in New Zealand 1942–1979* (Dunedin: Third Millennium, 1999).
14. *Evangel*, October 1987: 12.
15. *Apostolic News*, March 2001: 2.
16. Personal communication, Araiti Remuera, 20 February 2009.
17. *Northern Advocate*, 6 May 1976.
18. Personal communication, Graham Cruickshank, 25 February 2009.
19. The term 'covering' is used within Pentecostal churches to describe being under the authority, guidance or supervision of a senior leadership figure.
20. H Keretene, 'Hangi Pits for "Demon Petition" Organiser', in *Northern Advocate*, 14 May 1976; P W Pomare, 'Should it be "Tohungatanga"', in *Northern Advocate*, 15 May 1976.
21. 'Pro Maoritanga Group Formed', in *Northern Advocate*, 10 May 1976.
22. Clark, *Pentecost at the Ends of the Earth*, 192.
23. H Houston, *One Hundred Men* (Wellington: Hazel Houston, 1977), 3 and 11.

24 The 1952 version was the fourth revision of the original full translation published in 1868.
25 Personal communication, Claire Chapman, 2 February 2009.
26 Personal communications, Ken Harrison, 6 November 2008; Peter Hira, 14 May 2009; and Claire Chapman, 2 February 2009. For example, leaders specified that the word 'tapu', which Chapman associated with the concept of untouchability, was not to be used in their translation in relation to the Bible or the holy spirit.
27 Clark, *Pentecost at the Ends of the Earth*, 214–15.
28 *Evangel*, Winter 1988: 10.
29 Ibid: 11.
30 Ibid: 10 and 18.
31 For example, *Apostolic News*, March 1990.
32 *Evangel*, Autumn 1990: 5.
33 Ibid, Autumn 1993: 7.
34 Clark, *Pentecost at the Ends of the Earth,* 232; personal communication, Peter Hira, 21 July 2009.
35 Personal communication, Ken Harrison, 6 November 2008.
36 Personal communication, Ian Clark, 12 December 2008.
37 The following draws on interviews with Ken Harrison, 6 November 2008; members of Avalon Assemblies of God, 27 November 2008; Roy Brinck, 16 December 2008; Neil Hetrick, 23 January 2009; Owen Mounsey, 23 February 2009; Graham Cruickshank, 25 February 2009; and Denis and Mina Acraman, 5 June 2009.
38 Personal communications, Phil and Anthea Fairbrass, 27 November 2008; and Roy Brinck, 16 December 2008.
39 Interview with Ken Harrison, 6 November 2008.
40 Clark, *Pentecost at the Ends of the Earth*, 218 and 230.
41 Carew, 'Māori, Biculturalism and the Assemblies of God', 47–54.
42 P de Bres, 'Maori Religious Affiliation in a City Suburb', in H Kawharu (ed.), *Conflict and Compromise: Essays on the Maori since Colonisation* (Birkenhead: Reed, 2003): 144–66.
43 M A Noll, *The Scandal of the Evangelical Mind* (Grand Rapids: Eerdmans, 1994), 12.
44 For example, J Newton, *The Double Rainbow: James K. Baxter, Ngati Hau and the Jerusalem Commune* (Wellington: Victoria University Press, 2009), 192–3.
45 T Davis, 'A Country Practice', in *Apostolic News*, August 1990: 1.
46 Personal communication, Graham Cruickshank, 25 February 2009.
47 M L Hodges, *The Indigenous Church* (Springfield: Gospel Publishing House, 1953), 12 and 22; A Hastings, *Oxford History of the Christian Church: The Church in Africa 1450–1950* (New York: Oxford University Press, 1994), 294.
48 Department of Social Welfare, *Puao-te-Ata-Tu (Daybreak): The Report of the Ministerial Advisory Committee on a Māori Perspective for the Department of Social Welfare* (Wellington: Government Printer, 1988), 19.

Chapter Six

The Rise and Significance of the Destiny Church

Peter Lineham

Introduction

The excitement over the Destiny movement, the church and political party founded by Bishop Brian Tamaki, has subsided from its high in 2005, and so, probably, has the popularity of the church. Unfortunately the character of the church has been obscured by its controversial reputation. This chapter seeks to place Destiny within its context, and to provide a perspective that was absent in the furore surrounding its political campaign.

This chapter seeks in particular to understand the place of the Destiny movement within the Māori world and the tradition of Māori religious movements. Destiny Church also fits within broader trends of Pentecostalism and fundamentalism and moral debate within New Zealand and broader Western society. These aspects are relevant to Destiny's role within Māori society, and will also be explored, but much more could be said on them in their own right.

The moral right

The Destiny movement has primarily been interpreted as the flourishing of a new populist right-wing philosophy. It is an appealing interpretation. Dolores Janiewski and Paul Morris, in their study of the right-wing tradition of New Zealand politics, have suggested that often right-wing rhetoric has a religious veneer.[1] Typically this is a minor aspect in the New Zealand context, for religious factors have long been sidelined from politics, but in the United States the rhetoric of the right is normally based on moral alarm about the decadence of modern America, and on its seductive effects on personal moral values and the moral values of capitalism itself. This type of organisation typically combines economic conservatism and moral alarm. New Zealand has now some experience of right-wing think tanks. The Maxim Institute, for example, though more moderate than Destiny, initially modelled itself on American libertarian agencies. However, although Labour Party politician David Benson-Pope attacked Destiny and the Maxim Institute in 2004 as twin arms of a Nazi movement in New Zealand, there was in fact little congruence between the two.[2]

In the American context, the combination of right-wing economic policies and conservative moralism carries great resonance within the church. Some New Zealand churches seem to share the same outlook. There was widespread right-wing rhetoric within Pentecostalism in the 1980s. The Destiny attack on the fifth Labour Government's social legislation seems to reflect this stance. Does this explain the church and its policies? Certainly the economic policy of the Destiny Party, the church's political wing, in the 2005 election had a very similar emphasis to that of the ACT Party, extolling the shrivelling of the state, the reduction of welfare and tax breaks for married couples. Moreover, the exhortations of Bishop Tamaki on his television programme are usually towards taking personal responsibility for life. Church members are typically enthusiastic for moral and personal betterment, exemplified by Brian Tamaki and his family.

A further factor is their ardent defence of New Zealand as a Christian nation. This rhetoric is redolent of the politics of fundamentalist churches in the United States, with their concern that America is losing its godliness. In the Destiny case, worries over the involvement of the Labour Government in the 2006 InterFaith Forum led it to express concern at the risk to New Zealand. The statement released at that time insisted that the church was not against religious freedom but argued that such freedom could be maintained from the basis of a Christian country. The words of Brian Tamaki were quoted in the statement:

I endorse freedom of religious choice. But it is not necessary to deny our Christian heritage to host, cohabitate or fully function alongside those of different religious persuasions. Nor should we feel obliged to appease those who hold different religious views by minimising our faith. How can these values be passed on to the next generation if they cannot be openly advocated without fear of causing offence.

Christianity affirms the freedoms our Prime Minister is attempting to espouse in terms of religious diversity. However, she should be secure enough to make it very clear to foreign delegates that New Zealand has an established Christian religion. After all, many of these attending nations are fully secure in their religious identity![3]

The phrase that is most interesting in this statement is 'an established Christian religion'. There is no established church in New Zealand, yet the state has endorsed certain Christian practices – for example, prayer in Parliament and Bible education in schools, both of which have been the focus of campaigns for their continuance – and some Christians have sought to defend legislation on matters of personal morality, including homosexuality, prostitution and the right to smack a child. The writings of the Australian Pentecostal evangelist Col Stringer have had some influence in New Zealand conservative circles in recent years, and it would seem that Stringer's work on New Zealand as a Christian country widely circulates in these quarters.[4] Tamaki argued in 2005 that members of Parliament are entirely unrepresentative of the nominal Christianity of society, and this may be an important motivation for his politics. He argued that the fastest growing religion is the 'devilish stuff' of Islam with its evil fruits, and that this growth is due to the failure of Christians and the churches. He therefore insisted that it was time that the church came back into prominence.[5] He expressed profound outrage that the 'perverted leaders' of the nation bring offence to the church by defiling the Christian message in linking it with homosexuality.[6]

In 2003 Destiny New Zealand was established as a political party, and fielded a number of candidates in the 2005 general election.

Despite bold predictions that Destiny would rule New Zealand by 2008, the party received only 14,210 votes: some 0.62 percent of the popular vote. This figure is not a great deal higher than the 7000 church members, and suggests that democracy did not provide a groundswell for the Christian right at this election. Christian Heritage, casualties of its ex-leader's fall from grace (Graham Capill was jailed in 2005 for sex crimes against young girls), were even less successful, gaining 2821 votes (0.12 percent of the popular vote, compared to 1.4 percent in 2002). So Destiny did not even pick up the Christian Heritage share of the vote. Given the huge energy and expense it had invested in this campaign – with forty or so candidates standing, the costs to the church must have been around $100,000 or more – it was a costly electoral experiment.

In the 2008 election, the Destiny Party was relaunched as the Family Party, led by Richard Lewis and the former United Future MP, Paul Adams, after a fumbled attempt to work with other Christian political hopefuls in one wing of United Future. It did not do well. Overall it received 8176 votes or 0.35 percent of the popular vote (less than the vote for Legalise Cannabis). In 2010 the party advised the Electoral Commission that it was dissolving itself.[7]

Destiny politics have thus not made much of an impact. Its policies were not particularly distinctive, and where they were, they gained little traction. The New Zealand National Party and even the indigenous-based Māori Party leaned somewhat in the same direction. So the attempt to persuade voters to choose these policies fell flat both in 2005 and 2008. The Party leader, Richard Lewis, certainly felt this after the 2005 election:

> 'Obviously, there is intense disappointment at not having achieved our goal, but I am proud of our stand in politics for the things that really matter. We have a first-class organisation and our candidates performed admirably – we gave it our best shot,' said party leader, Richard Lewis.
>
> The Party has not made any decision as to whether it will contest the next General Election. 'We'll take a little time out

before considering our options and making a decision about the future of the party,' he added.[8]

This did not in any sense endanger the world of Destiny. At its heart the movement has always been more than a campaign for the moral right. While the movement dallied with these aspects, its leaders moved back into religious affairs. The essence of the movement was not in politics.

Pastor Tamaki made a prophecy in 2003 that Destiny would rule over the nation. It was after and probably because of this prophecy that the movement launched into politics. Its political strategy was nevertheless that of a traditional citizens' campaign. The prophetic tone of the church's political activism was from the outset at odds with its attempt to awaken broad moral outrage. The movement was much more inclined to an apocalyptic kingdom. They claimed that New Zealand should be under the governance of God, and that divine principles should shape the political and social order was a matter of belief in a deeply felt prophetic declaration. It was not a good basis on which to enter a political foray to win the votes of outsiders, and it always provoked suspicion from others. A political party linked to one church is at a particular disadvantage, and the Destiny Party could not but acknowledge its allegiance to Pastor Tamaki as its spiritual leader.

Pentecostalism

Less has been written on the Pentecostal character of Destiny. The origins of this new movement lie in the Apostolic Church, which had in the 1980s gathered a significant Māori support, but had struggled to hold it. The Apostolic Church had earlier hoped to revive the indigenous Rātana Church, initiating a visit to the Rātana temple by Derek Prince, the Pentecostal intellectual, in association with the Māori MP Whetu Tirikatene-Sullivan. The Apostolic Church had gained a significant Māori following over the years, although Māori members were often uncomfortable with the typically white character of the denomination. Māori awareness of the racist outlook of Pentecostals is vividly portrayed in Lloyd

Martin's description of a Bay of Plenty congregation that initially reached out to Māori and then excluded them.[9]

Brian Tamaki served as pastor of the Lake City congregation in Rotorua as it grew to be the second largest Apostolic congregation, comprising some 650 people. Then in March 1994 he split from it, complaining of a 10 percent levy by the national office.[10] He rejected the levy of $40,000 and claimed the property – the old theatre in which the church met. So his movement reflected a break-up of old traditions of Pentecostal conservatives. A number of Pentecostal churches subsequently seceded to join his new denomination. In 1997 Pastor Tamaki felt called to plant a church in Auckland, 'the largest Polynesian city in the world', and it commenced on 4 July 1998 as 'City Church, Auckland'. He controlled twenty churches by 2005, including one in Brisbane, thus justifying the name 'Destiny International', but the number had dropped to eleven by 2010, with the loss of the churches in Kaitāia, Thames, Te Puke, Gisborne, Napier, Taumarunui, Whanganui, Porirua and Dunedin.[11] The largest congregation took over a huge pharmaceutical warehouse at Allright Place, Mount Wellington in Auckland in 2001. Here a distinctive atmosphere is created from the outset by burly earphoned and suited Māori car park attendants. The services are colourful and high-tech, and the site also includes a gym, a school, a preschool and a space for a wide variety of programmes.[12]

Tamaki had been reared in a particular kind of Pentecostal theology. It was characteristic of New Zealand Pentecostalism in the 1960s and 1970s to envision a new movement that would bring revival in the last days before the end of the world. The outpouring of speaking in tongues and of healings was seen as evidence of a new age of the miraculous intervention of God before the appearance of Antichrist. The first Pentecostals formed a grass-roots exuberant and fervent movement, with a chaotic lack of structure.

Thirty years later, the end of the world and the great revival had not occurred, and Pentecostal churches were now competitive structures, highly controlled and highly structured. In Weberian terms, the prophets had been replaced by systems men. They employed church growth methods, television programmes and commercial strategies to promote their churches. It had become what one commentator calls 'religion as entertainment'.[13]

Meanwhile, mainstream Pentecostal theology switched from pre-millennial to kingdom theology. Prosperity teaching had long been part of Pentecostal teaching, but to some it now became a central theme, helping to build the funds of the powerful preachers. Destiny Church's statement of its core values bears this out. Its overall vision is to 'build the church', and its mission is to establish the kingdom. Its expansion of this vision indicates a number of interesting phrases, explaining its passions and priorities:

Foundation in Jesus Christ
Governing and Reformative
Powerful Unity
Return to Biblical Order
Radical Commitment
Covenant Relationships
Manifest Kingdom
Next Generation Minded
Uncompromising Biblical Truth[14]

Pentecostalism in recent years has developed and converged somewhat with broader fundamentalist movements, particularly in America. In some respects the category 'Pentecostal' is no longer coherent. The earlier tradition viewed itself as a movement of the poor.[15] More recent traditions have viewed it as a source of individual significance and identity; a kind of therapeutic movement.[16] But increasing awareness that Pentecostalism is a global group of associations has also led some to interpret it as a form of religion that has created a different form of cultural links than older forms of Christianity.

It is within these broader frameworks that the Destiny movement takes on a significance that most local observers have failed to recognise. It is back to the traditions of crude abrasive evangelism, exploiting contemporary media and benefiting from all publicity, negative or positive.[17] It pioneered local private religious televised services in March 2000 as 'Higher Ground' on TV1, losing its contract in 2004 and thereafter switching to the Prime channel.[18]

Tamaki's standing within the Pentecostal world is somewhat dubious. His sermon 'vipers of religion' attacked, without naming, a range of churches, including Pentecostals.[19] There have been attempts to maintain cordial relationships, but tensions were provoked when Destiny appointed a former Elim pastor, Ian Bilby, who was still under discipline from this denomination, as its head of training. At Christmas 2003, unnoticed by the media, Bilby was removed from this role. In more recent years the church has reduced the independence of its staff other than the senior pastor and his wife, and local pastors with particular skills do not remain long in the movement. The rifts created at that time remain, however, with caution about Destiny now widespread across the Pentecostal community. The very large Christian Life Centre in Auckland (since renamed Life Church), which had previously maintained public cordiality towards Destiny, distanced itself after Destiny broke its promises to keep a low profile in a 'family values' protest march by Pentecostals in March 2005 in Auckland. Only the more sectarian City Impact Church on the North Shore remained as an ally, although its decision to open a church in Sylvia Park in Auckland close to that of Destiny suggests that even that relationship is now strained.

Tamaki's movement has close links with one Pentecostal movement: the black Pentecostal tradition in America. This vast movement includes many people from poor backgrounds, and is characterised by passionate preaching and noisy worship. Tamaki heard of Bishop Eddie Long in 2002 and soon visited him. Long, in turn, visited Destiny in 2003 and became Tamaki's 'covering' or spiritual leader at that time.[20] Long is pastor of a 25,000-member church (New Birth Missionary Baptist Church) in Lithonia, Georgia and in Atlanta.[21] At the 2006 Labour Weekend conference Bishop T D Jakes, another fundamentalist black pastor, of the Potter's House (Dallas, Texas and beyond), which is noted for its social ministries, also participated.[22] These associations have been somewhat tarnished by recent allegations about Eddie Long's sexual predilection for young men, allegations that have extended to his companions on one of his visits to Destiny in New Zealand. Another American friend of Destiny was Martin Luther King's daughter, Bernice, who was closely associated with Eddie Long. She was invited to New Zealand by Tamaki to attack the way advocates of civil union drew on Martin Luther King's advocacy of equal civil rights.[23] All these elements suggest a blend of power and grand vision perhaps not quite as disturbing when one considers the community among whom Destiny makes its mark.

The alliance between Destiny Church and the black Pentecostals should not be viewed in isolation. In recent years black Pentecostalism has globalised, and in Latin America, the Philippines, South Korea and Africa, T D Jakes, Eddie Long and popular prosperity teachers like Kenneth Hagin and the late Derek Prince are familiar names. The growth of indigenous Pentecostalism in Africa has been particularly spectacular. Such churches emphasise spiritual forces and prosperity teaching. The Destiny movement inhabits this world much more comfortably than the world of slick western Pentecostalism.[24]

The use of episcopal titles is common among black Pentecostals, reflecting its roots in Methodism, which was episcopal from its beginnings in America. Moreover, the Apostolic Church, from which Destiny split, has apostles. This seems to lie behind the title 'bishop' adopted by Tamaki in 2005. At the time Bishop Brian was profiled in the following manner on the web page of Destiny Church:

> This God-appointed apostolic ministry is ushering in an era of restoration for the Church in New Zealand. As Church leaders, Bishop Brian and Pastor Hannah are demonstrating by purposeful design, what the glorious Church of Jesus Christ should look like, and what its influence in individual lives and the community should be. It is this clarity that has caused them to be sought after, both nationally and internationally as speakers and mentors.[25]

There is a 'totalitarian' side to Destiny that is assisted by its scale. The church can readily sustain a broad range of activities. These include the church's bilingual early childhood centre (Nga Tamariki Puawai), the Proton Bookshop, Proton Health & Fitness Centre and Destiny School. The church has had an impact within state schools in lower socio-economic areas through its mentoring programme. The school also clearly gives hope and meaning to men just out of prison and to women striving to survive in a rough world. It enforces smart suits and fine self-presentation, which give its members immense pride in their identification as members of Destiny.

Destiny has a significant appeal to young Polynesian people, which is reflected in the church's use of contemporary media. Members seem to speak a kind of 'gangsta rap', reflecting the ways in which black Americana has infiltrated the popular world.

Religious fundamentalism

Yet the church is more than this. Destiny is a very authoritarian movement. It espouses a bold religious fundamentalism, which has been an appealing formula in contemporary society. Secular journalists tend to discount this factor, unaware of the extent to which religion is a transformative influence in poorer parts of New Zealand society. Fundamentalism is effective as a religious grass-roots movement precisely because it defies the framework of modernity, using very contemporary methods to undermine contemporary values.

New Zealand has had a significant fundamentalist tradition. Its roots reflect Protestant suspicion of Anglicanism. Protestant dissent began as a search for a different range of values. There always was an aura of anti-clericalism in English society, which resented the social status and privilege of the church and the church rates that sustained it. The Puritan movement had created a strong sense of ardent biblicism as a counter to the institutional church, and when after 1660 this was pushed out of the church establishment, a tone of pride in exclusiveness and in possession of the truth and of a tight community of saints became a characteristic of one section of British society. Add to this the strand of a conversionist and evangelistic movement that emerged in Methodism during the eighteenth-century revival and an immense activist sense that the world could be transformed by effort, despite the objections of the establishment, and you have the makings of a deep part of English religion.

Yet this was not fundamentalism. Fundamentalism developed as these strands of populist Protestantism felt threatened by a new force; not the social superiority of old wealth but the contemporary cleverness of new knowledge. Fundamentalism was born when ordinary Protestants, especially lay people, set out to defend the church in the face of what they regarded as the pollution of modern ideas. Whereas a large and significant part of the old Puritanism embraced modernism as a great opportunity to develop Christianity, the fundamentalists protested the new biblical criticism and the ideas of evolution and sociology with 'the good old gospel'.

Tamaki's movement has the hallmarks of this kind of fundamentalism. It reflects backwoods defiance of the educated and the 'clever' that are thought to be in charge of New Zealand society. Its leaders passionately advocate religious knowledge above secular knowledge, defiantly challenging political and religious correctness. There is a powerful tone of defiance evident in these large Māori men in suits with their Bibles and their utter confidence that they have the truth. As one member blogged:

> MY LIFE WAS FULL OF DRUGS, ALCOHOL & VIOLENCE BEFORE I WENT TO DESTINY CHURCH. HMM..SHUCKS..LETS SEE MY SALVATION, GOD'S BLESSINGS, AWESOME PASTORS AND THE HAPPY LIFE I LIVE NOW?? OR MY DRUGGED UP, ALCOHOL FILLED & VIOLENT LIFE THAT WAS FULL OF NOTHING BUT DEPRESSION?? IT'S SO NOT A CULT THAT'S PRETTY SAD TO BE DUBBED THAT BUT- PEOPLE..JUST CHECK IT OUT OKAY. AN HOUR OF YOUR TIME ON A SUNDAY MORNING OR EVENING OR A LIFETIME IN HELL? YOU DECIDE.[26]

Tamaki in a number of interviews has exuded contempt for the educated elite, but he is not against education, only against the content of what is called 'knowledge' that seems to him to deny God's authority.

Sectarianism

Somewhat at odds with Tamaki's qualified endorsement of the value of secular education is the apparent sectarianism of the movement. The covenant ceremony that took place at the Labour Weekend Conference in 2009 provides ample evidence of this: it involved a covenant pledge of loyalty to Tamaki by adult male members of the church and covenant rings that Destiny men were expected to buy and wear.[27] The covenant document places loyalty to the church within an Old Testament framework of unique and specific loyalty to God. This exclusivism has led many to conclude that the movement is a 'cult'. It had long been featured on Mark Vrankovich's 'Cultwatch' website, but in 2010 the site elevated it to the status of a cult, on the basis of recent preaching by Tamaki.[28]

In his notable sermon in 2004, 'Vipers of Religion', Tamaki argued that 'the old order of religion is dead', and that in every generation God starts something new. He argued that the Christian church had embraced demonic forces, and therefore Christianity had lost its impact. As far as he was concerned, the old church was not only dead, it was also demonic, crushing life more effectively than the world does. He argued that the traditional church had allowed 'vipers' into its fold, and compromised on doctrines and values. He argued that you could lose your salvation through wrong doctrines, even though you had been baptised with water or baptised with the holy ghost. He scoffed that many sheepfolds (using a familiar biblical analogy) had been turned into goat farms. Only the churches with an appointed leader were ordained by God. Denominationalism as such simply cultivates vipers of religion, Tamaki said. Churches that use democratic principles reject the divine principle.

Tamaki's rejection of church boards seems to be a response to his experience in the Apostolic Church, although his particular sarcasm was focused on the Anglican, Catholic and Presbyterian churches and their problems over sexuality. Talking at an Auckland Christian leaders' meeting, he was also very critical of Baptists and Pentecostals who failed to stand against those who deny the power of demons and who accommodate their theology to the spirit of the age. As far as he was concerned, the sign of spiritual weakness was the loss of emphasis on tithing and deliverance ministries. Only an apostolic ministry could deal with demonic deceptions.

It has become clear over recent years that the relationship of Destiny Church with other evangelical and Pentecostal churches is a fractious one. VisionNet, the network of evangelical churches and organisations (now called the New Zealand Christian Network) laboured hard to improve these relationships, but it evidently found Destiny's exclusivism difficult to contain.

The church is very deliberate in retraining its members. When people join they go through a series of graduated classes. These begin with simple Christian instruction, but become more and more opaque to outsiders, even within the Christian community:

> Holy Spirit & Water Baptism.
> Christianity Explained.
> Water Baptism. (Practical)
> Tithes, Offerings, First Fruits.
> Evangelism.
> Bishop's Invitational Class.[29]

There is a prophetic element to the instruction: 'Several of the units deal with current revelation consistent with the teachings from our purpose and vision of Destiny Church',[30] the Destiny website advises. On the other hand, recent claims that Destiny has veered far apart from evangelical orthodoxy by denying the physical resurrection of Christ and by claiming that all believers would become divine seem to be based on a sloppy use of theological language, rather than a reconstruction of central Christian doctrines, judging by the pained reaction of the movement to Mark Vrankovich's allegations.[31]

The exclusivism of the church is therefore striking. A number of former members are very concerned about this:

I used to be a member of Destiny Church but I left over 5 years ago when Tamaki said he was the spiritual father, the shepherd (and that his sheep hear his voice) and the significant voice (where we were not permitted to listen to Radio Rhema or attend any other Christian ministry – this was considered 'spiritual adultery') of the church. That sounded like father, son and holy spirit to me – the *Bible* says people like this will come, and that they carry an anti-christ message.[32]

The teaching of the church is somewhat Gnostic at its core. A curious blend of Old Testament logic is hidden beneath the broadcast words of its teachers. Members generally possess great confidence that they have a grasp of the truth that other Christians lack. For example, here is a Destiny Church member on a blog site:

[You] need not compare us to the suicidal bombers now. also, everybody is right about how this nation is no more than the krishna, buddahs etc; because it is truly gods land and never truly belonged to any man.
P.Tamaki stands firm on the word of god and will give back this nation that everybody seems to suck, mainly because it is in the hands of the upright.
What do you mean there are also fellow brother/sister christians out there that don't believe our way is the way to go? Well, a few questions solely directed at any other christians that breeze past this.
Q)should god be the head or the tail?
Q)should god at least have his say?
Q)is he being heard?
Q)why not?
Q)how should we have approached this matter?
should we whom believe god should rule and reign march with pink shirts, singing bind us together? Why should we as christians (in general) watch these souls do what they want when they want however they want, especially when they without knowing it, depends on the church? Hmmm, and don't any one but any other existing christians respond to these questions. Please and thank you.[33]

This certainly suggests potential sectarian factors, and the tendency of Bishop Tamaki to scoff at the interpretations and actions of other Pentecostal leaders suggests the inherent sectarianism of the movement. Now this is no surprise. New Zealand has been the home of a significant number of sectarian movements, from the Exclusive Brethren to the Rangiora Pentecostal cult to the Centrepoint community. The Māori community has also had its share of such movements. Often these are focused on significant differences of social and economic status from the wider community.

A further aspect of this, the particular role given to Tamaki within the movement, was reinforced by his recognition as a bishop along with his symbolic adoption of the cloak of a rangatira. The origins of this go a long way back in the movement, for the Auckland trust document at the time of the purchase of the land in Allright Place declared: 'Brian Raymond Tamaki or his appointed successor as apostolic oversight of the church shall have absolute power of veto of any decision made by the Trust Board'.[34]

Perhaps this may be seen as less unusual when it is compared with Pasifika Pentecostal movements; the role of Destiny's leader and attitudes towards him seem entirely consistent with the role played by the leaders both of traditional and, particularly, new Pasifika religious movements, for example, the New Fellowship of Tonga.

Māori religious movement
Destiny stands in the tradition of Māori religious movements, including Ringatū, Rātana and many smaller groups. This is a distinctive category of religious movement in Aotearoa New Zealand. In this tradition indigenous churches are motivated by a vision for the future of the Māori people; this vision combines religion and politics, and is committed to transforming the condition of Māori people. Such churches are profoundly concerned at the depravity and decline of the Māori community, and feel a calling to restore Māori pride and identity by means of both religion and also political action. In so doing they awaken widespread fear and concern from the Pākehā community. This may sound like

a description of the Destiny Church and its political party. But it could serve equally well as a description of Rātana as it appeared to observers in the period 1922–1928.

Is it possible to place Destiny in the rich tradition of indigenous movements in Māori society? It is not a tradition that Pentecostalism has embraced. The caution of Pentecostal churches about ministry to Māori has been well documented. Philip Carew noted that although the Assemblies of God now has a very vigorous section of Pasifika congregations, there are no Māori congregations, and among the reasons for this is the sense of caution about Māori spirituality that features strongly in the rhetoric of New Zealand Pentecostal circles.[35] In Aotearoa many socio-political questions are raised by indigenous politics, and Pentecostalism has few tools to deal with them.

In these respects, Destiny is a very different type of Pentecostal church. Granted, Destiny does not restrict its membership to Māori, and is increasingly recruiting among Pacific Islanders; it even includes an Asian ministry.[36] Nevertheless the bulk of its members are Māori, and Pākehā pastors have not lasted long in the church (for example, Trevor and Campbell Bond). Moreover, although the church does not embrace the iwi agenda, it is supportive of justice under Te Tiriti o Waitangi. It may be seen as a Māori modernisation movement. Its members frequently scoff at other Māori, for example:

> OW THE MAJORITY OF YOU MAORI ARE STILL ON THE BENEFIT GETTING WASTED,ON BUD OR ALCOHOL OR WHATEVER YOU CAN GET YOUR HANDS ON. MAKING UP EXCUSES FOR YOUR SORRY OLD SELF TO REST IN THE PAST BECAUSE SOMETHING HAPPENED THAT WAS REALLY SAD, (OH NE -MIND). HOW DO I KNOW ? CAUSE I USED TO BE ONE THEREFORE 'IT TAKES ONE TO NO ONE'. AND THE MAORI IN DESTINY CAN USE THE HAKA IF THEY WANT BAYE. AT LEAST THEY HAVE CLEAN SIPITS [sic]. WAIRUA TAPU, IS MENTIONED

IN MAORI HYMNS!!!!! AYE AYE NOW WHAT U GOT M8..... YEAH BOI... DRUNKENS ON THE BLOODY BENEFIT TRYING TO BE GANGSTA, CAUSE DAD WAS ONE.....#### =UPOKOKOHUA BAK 2 YAS.BE SOMETHING THAT YOUR CHILDREN WILL NOT BE ASHAMED OF !!!!!!!1)????[37]

Destiny's relationship with Māori aspirations is interesting. Destiny attended the Waitangi Day ceremonies at Waitangi in 2006, and combined with the Rātana group, also new to Waitangi, in providing an alternative to the main church service. This raises the issue of Destiny and Rātana.

Keith Newman's research on Rātana has led to greater understanding of the nature of the religious appeal of that movement. Rātana appeals to Māori tradition, but it also challenges it.[38] Rātana began with a rediscovery of the power of healing in the strength of spiritual commitment. Each of these factors bears comparison with Destiny. Moreover, younger Rātana members seem to have responded somewhat to Tamaki (although the same is true of members of Te Hāhi Mihinare, the Anglican Māori Tikanga and the Latter-day Saints as well).

The first obvious point of comparison lies in the 'pentecostal' flavour of the two movements. Rātana's sense of vision, Rātana's mission of healing and Rātana's desire to break the power of the tohunga and develop a deeper Christian spirituality among Māori have real parallels in Tamaki's Pentecostal identity, his powerful appeal to Māori for transformation. I am informed that some Destiny pastors have been very active in miraculous and healing ministries.

Second, there is the role and status of the leader. Rātana himself came to occupy a very significant spiritual status as the mouthpiece of the divine to Māori people: the way God spoke to Māori. Shaped by notions from the nineteenth century that Māori were a kind of Israel, as espoused by such prophets as Te Ua Haumene, Te Kooti and Rua Kēnana, Rātana added a mana that came from his leadership, his organisational skills and prophetic insights. As a leader he was not immune from personal failures, but this never endangered his mana. Very similar things could be said of Tamaki, who makes much not only of his rough background, but also of his apostolic calling, insight and responsibility. This has become more pronounced in recent statements, which have urged Destiny members to treat him with special respect.[39] The ostentatious display of wealth is justified as the sign of a leader with a mandate from God. Carew in his research found that Tamaki was well aware of the mana of T W Rātana as the Māngai, the mouthpiece of God, and responded to this legacy by seeing himself as a latter-day māngai.[40] A further relevant characteristic of Tamaki is his respect for Kīngitanga, and his positive links with the late Māori Queen.[41] This comparison holds good for many other Māori movements as well, in which a prophetic or charismatic leader has navigated and guided the people through the desert and into the promised land.[42]

Third, the creation of a new select sectarian group is common to both groups. In Rātana's case these were the mōrehu: the people who had set aside their tribal identity and embraced a new identity in the movement. In Destiny, the members sign up to the tithe and submit to and purchase the covenant ring, thus committing themselves as new mōrehu.

Fourth, the blend of politics and religion has something in common. The Rātana movement's contest for the Māori seats was slow in its beginnings, but was seen as crucial if Māori were to rediscover their identity. For Destiny, the emergence of the secular Māori Party, with its strong advocacy of the principles of the Treaty of Waitangi, cost them a potential political justification. Like Rātana, Destiny makes a strong appeal to the principles of the Treaty, but the Māori Party has taken over much of that political ground.

Finally, both movements have produced modernised versions of Māori ritual, kapa haka and other cultural practices, although both have been critical of traditional Māori beliefs.

Where do these similarities stem from? In part, they are perhaps inevitable in any Māori Christian movement that is bound to offer Māori a new identity. In both cases, they stem from the endemic Māori struggle to find a secure place in Western capitalist society, although there are obviously huge differences between the rural Māori that Rātana reached out to and the urban Māori community that has flocked to Brian Tamaki. The development of a socially and politically active Christianity was a logical response in both cases.

On the other hand, Destiny has made no attempt to create a new theology of liberation. Tamaki was not raised in traditional ways. He does not speak te reo, and his story is a fairly ordinary one of a Waikato family: the mother had religious commitments, while the father's second home was the pub, and Tamaki in his youth focused on music and pig hunting. Both in Tamaki's family and his wife's family, the Pākehā parent did more to raise the children than the Māori parent.[43] Tamaki's focus is on improving Māori behaviour, not renewing the vision of Māori society.

Some have placed Destiny entirely in the category of Māori prophetic movements, given its blend of religion and politics. This does not seem completely adequate. Destiny seems a much more conventional church than most prophetic movements.[44] Alex Phillips' Mana Ariki Marae near Taumarunui is a more obvious example of a contemporary prophet movement, drawing on themes such as those of Rātana. Before his death in 2008 Phillips was widely recognised as a Māori prophet. His ministry was much less divisive than that of Tamaki, and rather less conventional. Tamaki has courted support from the Kīngitanga and Rātana, but the fundamentalist and populist aspects of Destiny have made this a fraught strategy. Yet when we see Destiny within a broader tradition of indigenous religious movements, we can understand that its offensiveness to Pākehā is not a handicap.

Indigenous Christian movements
A potential framework for analysing the Destiny Church may be a comparison with the indigenous traditions within African Christianity. In 1961, the great New Zealand scholar of religion Harold Turner, along with Bengt Sundkler, interpreted these new forms of church as embodying not syncretism but a cultural adjustment or 'Africanisation' of the faith.[45] This has provided the

basis for a rich reevaluation of indigenous Christian movements. Although it has led to extensive debate, most scholars use a framework that separates the indigenous sects into two primary theologies and structures: the Ethiopian on the one hand and the Zionist and Aladura traditions on the other.[46]

Ethiopian movements are tribalist and pan-African, and linked to black churches in the United States. The earliest examples were the Tembu tribal church (founded in 1884) and the Church of Africa (founded in 1889) in South Africa. Each resulted from a feeling that Africans were not permitted to take leadership in the churches, and the demand that Africa belong to the Africans. 'Ethiopia' – a biblical name, an ancient church and a state that had defeated the Italians in 1896 – summed up their hopes.[47]

Another Ethiopian-style movement emerged in West Africa under William Wade Harris of Liberia, who worked for the Methodists and the Episcopalians, but then founded a movement in the Ivory Coast that developed a sensational following.[48] Inspired by this, the Nigeria Native Baptist Church was established in 1888, the United African Methodist Church in 1917, and the Ijo Orile-Ede Adulawo Ti Kristi, the National Church of Christ, in 1919. Such movements rejected traditional African religious rituals and witchcraft, rejected the leadership of the traditional denominations, focused on miracles and developed their own purification rites.[49] Parallel movements have split the Anglican Church in Kenya, the Baptists in Cameroon and the Baptists in Ghana. Typically such churches are secessions from European denominations, and have developed political dimensions: for example, John Childembwe's Zulu rising in 1906.

There is a parallel between the Ethiopian traditions and Rātana's assertion of pan-tribal Māori leadership and his attempt to purify Māori of 'spiritism'. Some historians, including the Nigerian church historian S A Adewale, view Ethiopianism as 'purely a struggle for the re-discovery of African nationalism':

> It was for the emancipation and liberation of the Church in Nigeria from foreign political domination and ecclesiastical

bondage. It was a struggle for an independent African Church where the members could worship God in their own way to satisfy their spiritual needs and aspirations knowing full well that foreign agencies in the country could not effectively and adequately cope with the situation.[50]

Adawele is inclined to emphasise the political aspect, yet this is grounded in cultural factors. Thus the Nigeria movement was based on Yoruba culture and indigenous language and thought forms. The baptised were required to wear white for the annual communion service. Some of the movements have become more extreme and somewhat millennialist. One secession movement in Nigeria looked forward to an African saviour.

The political and cultural factors characteristic of the Ethiopian traditions deserve to be carefully measured in the New Zealand movements. Rātana certainly had a political role, but the movement demands more than political analysis. The model does not seem to fit Destiny so well, although some parallels can be drawn in terms of both its political and purificatory dimensions. So it makes sense to explore the other African independent religious tradition.

The Zionist and Aladura churches of Africa, in all their innumerable variety, have their origins in early Pentecostalism, focusing on prophets, healing and the return of Christ to reign. The South African movement has direct links with J A Dowie's Zion movement in Chicago, with its pre-Pentecostal emphasis on baptisms and the second coming. Dowie formed a branch of his church in South Africa in 1904, and through contact with early Pentecostals the Zion Christian Church was founded in 1910 by Ignatius Lekganyane. It had its own sacred city, and a spiritual hierarchy, but it also permitted some traditional spiritual practices. Zionist churches with innumerable variations have subsequently sprung up in many parts of Southern Africa. Zionist churches generally focus on prophecy, have strong leadership and look forward to a millennial future, and they often tolerate polygamy, encourage African modes of worship (for example, drumming), use divination and permit ancestor cults.[51] Variations of these movements are observable in East and Central Africa, one of the most striking of which is the Mutima Church in Zambia, which has its own saviour.

A somewhat parallel movement without the Zionist focus is the Aladura movement in Nigeria, which began in the 1920s. This prophetic movement destroyed African fetishes and adapted proverbial wisdom and ancestral traditions. It used healing rituals to protect people from witchcraft, and made these central to the practice of this form of Christianity. There were similar movements in Zaire and southern Africa.[52]

In the light of this concept, it is possible to also interpret various Asian movements as 'Zionist', including Uchimura Kanzo's Nonchurch movement in Japan, the Philippines Independent Church founded in 1902, and perhaps even Sun Myung Moon's Unification Church.

While Rātana has some parallels with this movement also, the Pentecostal values of Destiny and its American inspiration resonate with parallels to Zionism. The encouragement given to Māori traditions reflects the use made of indigenous traditions in Zionism and Aladura.[53] Like the Zionist and Ethiopian churches, Destiny identifies with black American religious values, and gives great respect to Eddie Long and T D Jakes, whose movements are an interesting blend of black traditions and Pentecostalism.[54]

There is a Zionist and a prophetic aspect to Rātana. The nineteenth-century traditions were a little different, but strongly prophetic and strongly Old Testament-related. But could not also Destiny be seen as a form of 'Ethiopianism'? Consider, in particular, Bishop Tamaki's status. This seems an odd combination of rangatira (the cope at his ordination was a Māori cloak) and ecclesiastical leader. In other words, the movement is blending selective aspects from different traditions into something that carries weight in its own community. Certainly the followers think so. The comments of one Destiny supporter, whose pen name was Whakapono (Belief), on a blog site show how this operates:

Firstly, what is a church?
It's a group of people that follow GOD'S WORD (the bible). So GOD SHOULD appoint a person he wants as a pastor/minister/bishop etc and that's the way it should be.
People on earth SHOULD NOT appoint, but decide if the mantle of God is on that man and follow him. There SHOULD NOT be a committee that decides what God is saying at the time. The man that has God's mantle/blessing on him should listen to what God is saying and preach.
This is how unity is created. Destiny church pasters [sic] are not self-appointed, but placed steadfast to serve for God.[55]

So the broader emphases of Destiny Church are seen by followers as subordinate to its special place in the appointment of God.

Broader issues

In post-colonial theory the concept of hybridity provides a clue to understanding these trends, for it suggests that effective 'native' agencies develop a blend of the tools of the coloniser, subaltern respect for the colonisers and creative use of new and old. Destiny is very effective in adapting black Pentecostalism at a time when many young Māori are profoundly influenced by popular media and draw on other aspects of black culture; for example, rap.

One commentator has written, 'the non-Western churches have heavily relied on the way of the western theology and their specific way of theologizing is in formation yet. In other words, the non-Western churches still express itself [sic] through the way of the Western theology. Generally speaking, the non-West knows the West better than itself.'[56] On the other hand, the gradual reduction in Christian exclusivism among mainstream theologians has created a space for a strong assertion of Christian uniqueness by others, and this approach seems part of the essence of Tamaki's discourse.[57]

For if Destiny creates a new 'black religious consciousness', it may indeed fashion a distinctive form of Christianity that has a massive impact on some parts of the Māori and Polynesian world. Some of this may not be particularly attractive to Pākehā onlookers, but the pattern of reshaping Christianity to fit its indigenous context is a trend that has an inherent interest, and one that will develop in spite of, or even on account of, middle-class Pākehā contempt and opposition.

Conclusion

This interpretation of Destiny Church has explained its origins, priorities and appeal from a number of angles. The church is a movement that holds together a number of contradictory elements. It is evangelical, Pentecostal and somewhat sectarian in familiar Western ways. It is a proto-political populist campaign. It is also an indigenous community, with marked similarities to earlier movements and indigenous religious movements in other parts of the world. It is a child of its time and a child of its heritage. It has embarked on a number of ventures, political, cultural, community-building and nationalist, not all of which have been successful. Its future may not be as striking as its early years, but it remains a very distinctive and contentious presence on the religious and the ethnic landscape. Although its Māori character would not satisfy the purists, it is a significant organisation within the Māori world.

Endnotes

1. D Janiewski and P Morris, *New Rights New Zealand: Myths, Moralities and Markets* (Auckland: Auckland University Press, 2005).
2. Radio New Zealand Newswire, 17 August 2004: 12:37. See M Mawson, 'Believing in Protest: The Liberal Ideal of Separation of Religion and Politics in Two Recent Religious Protests', in *New Zealand Sociology* 21.2 (2006): 196–214, particularly 205–10.
3. Destiny Church, 'Welcome to our Christian Country', 22 May 2007: www.destinychurch.org.nz/about-us-mainmenu-89/media-releases-mainmenu-75/51-welcome-to-our-christian-country (accessed 25 October 2010).
4. C Stringer, *New Zealand's Christian Heritage* (Robina, Queensland: Col Stringer Ministries, 2001).
5. B Tamaki, 'Vipers of Religion', audio sermon issued by Proton bookshop, 2004, (my transcription).
6. Ibid. See A Hardy, 'Destiny Breaks through Media Screens', in *Papers from the Trans-Tasman Research Symposium: 'Emerging Research in Media, Religion and Culture'* (Melbourne: RMIT Publishing, 2005): 40–56.
7. See B Edwards, 'Destiny Church's Family Party splits up': http://liberation.typepad.com/liberation/2010/03/destiny-churchs-family-party-splits-up.html (accessed 7 January 2012).

8 www.scoop.co.nz/stories/PO0509/S00221.htm (accessed 4 February 2012).
9 L Martin, *One Faith Two Peoples: Communicating across Cultures Within the Church* (Paraparaumu: Salt Company Publishers, 1991), 9–27.
10 L Worsfold, 'Subsequence, Prophecy and Church Order in the Apostolic Church, New Zealand', PhD thesis, Victoria University of Wellington, 2004, 247–8; 252–7. For Tamaki's interpretation of these events, see B Tamaki, *Bishop Brian Tamaki: More than Meets the Eye* (Auckland: Tamaki Publications, 2006), 151–5.
11 There are brief details of eleven churches in Destiny Church in *A Decade of Destiny: Destiny Church Celebrates* (Auckland: Destiny Church, 2008), [21–30]. The church commencements, from earliest to most recent with their original names, are: Lake City Church Rotorua, 1994, (City Church) Auckland, 1998, (Harbourside Church) Tauranga, 1999–2001, Brisbane, 2000, Nelson, 2001, Hamilton, 2002, Wellington, 2003, Whāngārei, 2003, Taranaki, 2004, Whakatāne (ex Apostolic), 2005, Christchurch, c. 2006.
12 Ibid, [11–12].
13 C K Robertson (ed.), *Religion as Entertainment* (New York: Peter Lang, 2002).
14 www.destinychurch.org.nz/about_visioncore.asp (accessed 23 September 2005). This URL is now out of date.
15 See R M Anderson, *Vision of the Disinherited: The Making of American Pentecostalism* (Oxford: Oxford University Press, 1979), which provoked extensive academic debate.
16 V Kärkkäinen, 'Pentecostal Theology of Mission in the Making', in *Journal of Beliefs and Values* 25.2 (2004): 167–76, 171.
17 See G Bond, 'Evangelistic Performance in New Zealand: The Word and What is not Said', PhD thesis, University of Canterbury, 2008 and Hardy, 'Destiny Breaks through Media Screens'.
18 Destiny Church, *A Decade of Destiny*, [10–11].
19 Tamaki, *More than Meets the Eye*, 192–3; audio file 28 June 2006.
20 Ibid, 322–4.
21 www.newbirth.org/history.htm (accessed 7 January 2012).
22 www.thepottershouse.org/BJ_about.html. See Tamaki, *More than Meets the Eye*, 365.
23 Tamaki, *More than Meets the Ey*, 325–30.
24 I owe this point to Paul Gifford. See P Gifford, 'Trajectories in African Christianity', in *International Journal for the Study of the Christian Church* 8.4 (2008): 275–89.
25 The quotation has now vanished from the Destiny web page, but is still used in part on http://www.streamingfaith.com/Destiny-Church-of-New-Zealand (accessed 4 February 2012).
26 www.kiwiblog.co.nz/archives/006835.html, written June–August 2004, (accessed 15 November 2004). Grammar original; URL out of date.
27 For details see G George, 'Tamaki's 700 "sons" swear oath of loyalty', in *New Zealand Herald*, 29 October 2009: www.nzherald.co.nz/nz/news/article.cfm?c_id=1&objectid=10605956&pnum=2 (accessed 7 January 2012).
28 M Vrankovich, 'Brian Tamaki's Destiny Church is Now a Cult': www.cultwatch.com/BrianTamaki.html (accessed 7 January 2012) (this entry changed somewhat between September 2010 and April 2011). Garth George in the *New Zealand Herald* echoed this verdict in 'Garth George: Destiny must be treated as a cult', 17 February 2011: www.nzherald.co.nz/news/article.cfm?c_id=466&objectid=10706749 (accessed 6 April 2011).
29 www.destinychurch.org.nz/ministries_training_institute.asp (accessed 23 September 2005). URL is out of date.

30 www.destinychurch.org.nz/calendar.asp (accessed 23 September 2005). URL is out of date.
31 See the revised version of Vrankovich, 'Brian Tamaki's Destiny Church is Now a Cult'. Tamaki appears to hold more of an Eastern Orthodox or Mormon view of the character of salvation than is common among Western and especially Pentecostal Christians.
32 www.cults.co.nz/d.php (accessed November 2010).
33 www.varsity.co.nz/discussions/posts.asp?id=619&page=5 (accessed 23 September 2005). Grammar and spelling original. URL is out of date.
34 Auckland trust deed, (6 (d)), 21 February 2000. See Charities Commission documents: www.register.charities.govt.nz/CharitiesRegister/CharitySummary.aspx?id=d819e26c-b68c-dc11-98a0-0015c5f3da29 (accessed 1 November 2009).
35 P D Carew, 'Māori, Biculturalism and the Assemblies of God in New Zealand, 1970–2008', MA thesis, Victoria University of Wellington, 2009, 112–31.
36 See Destiny Church, *A Decade of Destiny*, [5, 16].
37 www.kiwiblog.co.nz/2004/06/the_destiny_cult.html (accessed 7 January 2012); entry by 'Go On Ow' on 27 August 2004 (quoted verbatim, including punctuation, spelling, spacing and capitalisation).
38 See J M Henderson, *Ratana: The Man, the Church, the Political Movement* (Wellington: Reed/Polynesian Society, 1972) and K Newman, *Ratana Revisited: An Unfinished Legacy* (Auckland: Reed, 2006).
39 Particularly in the covenant document, which states 'Brian is the tangible expression of God and our call'. This document is extensively cited in TVNZ, 'Destiny's controversial covenant slammed': http://tvnz.co.nz/national-news/destiny-s-controversial-covenant-slammed-3101294 (accessed 7 January 2012) and in G George, 'Tamaki's 700 "sons" swear oath of loyalty'. I hold what purports to be the text of the covenant, and it parallels what is cited in these news reports.
40 Carew, 'Māori, Biculturalism and the Assemblies of God', 101.
41 Ibid, 99.
42 This point is made by 'Mamari' commenting on E Black, 'All grown up now: our very own evangelical cult, or something close to it': http://pundit.co.nz/content/all-grown-up-now-our-very-own-evangelical-cult-or-something-close-to-it (accessed May 2011).
43 Tamaki, *More than Meets the Eye*, 13–16.
44 See N Baker, 'Bishop Brian Tamaki – a Maori prophet?': http://nathanaelbaker.blogspot.com/2005/10/bishop-brian-tamaki-maori-prophet.html (accessed May 2011). For background see B Elsmore, *Mana from Heaven: A Century of Maori Prophets in New Zealand* (Tauranga: Moana Press, 1989).
45 H Turner, *African Independent Church, Volume 2: The Life and Faith of the Church of the Lord Aladura* (Oxford: Clarendon Press, 1967). See also D B Barrett, *Schism and Renewal in Africa: An Analysis of Six Thousand Contemporary Religious Movements* (Nairobi/Oxford: Oxford University Press, 1968) and a large literature, the most recent of which is D Venter (ed.), *Engaging Modernity: Methods and Cases for Studying African Independent Churches in South Africa* (Westport: Praeger, 2004). At page 13 this affirms the continuing acceptability of the framework of the African Independent Church.
46 See for general background, E Isichei, *A History of Christianity in Africa: From Antiquity to the Present* (Grand Rapids: Eerdmans, 1995), 4–11 and passim. For discussion of the categories, which uses an additional category of Apostolic churches, see Venter, *Engaging Modernity*, 18–20. Apostolic churches are those with more emphasis on prophecies and the authority of leaders.

47 Isichei, *A History of Christianity in Africa*, 125–7.
48 Ibid, 284–6, drawing on G Haliburton, *The Prophet Harris* (London: Prentice Hall, 1971).
49 D Chidester, *Christianity: A Global History* (London: HarperOne, 2000), 451–2.
50 S A Adewale, *The Religion of the Yoruba: A Phenomenological Analysis* (Ibadan: Department of Religious Studies, University of Ibadan, 1988), 9.
51 See Isichei, *A History of Christianity in Africa*, 229–30, 253–7.
52 Turner, *African Independent Church, Volume 2*: see in particular Turner's judgement in Epilogue, 370–2.
53 Venter, *Engaging Modernity*, 14 argues that there is a certain amount of overlap of categories among most African churches.
54 See C Young, '"Bishop" Eddie Long: Brian's Shepherd goes astray …???', 28 September 2010: http://gaynz.com/blog/redqueen/archives/941. URL is out of date.
55 www.varsity.co.nz/discussions/posts.asp?id=619&page=5 (accessed 23 September 2005). URL is out of date.
56 K S Ahn, 'Spring Lecture on the World Missionary Conference of Edinburgh 1910, 2010 Project': www.towards2010.org/downloads/t2010paper02kyoseongahn.pdf (accessed 6 April 2011). See also K S Ahn, 'From Mission to Church and Beyond: The Metamorphosis of Post-Edinburgh Christianity', in D A Kerr and K R Ross (eds), *Edinburgh 2010: Mission Then and Now* (Oxford: Regnum, 2009), 74–84.
57 See D Pratt, 'Exclusivism and Exclusivity: A Contemporary Theological Challenge', in *Pacifica* 20 (2007): 291–306.

Part II

Chapter Seven
Kaikatikīhama: 'Our Most Precious Resource'

Nathan Matthews

Introduction

Christianity has had a significant impact both on Māori religious belief and practice, but also on Māori culture itself. This chapter briefly traces the growth of the New Zealand Catholic Church in the nineteenth century, from its initial establishment under Bishop Pompallier through to the development of the diocese structure, particularly in regard to the development of the Wellington Diocese and the Marist Māori mission. The effects the New Zealand Wars had on this development are also explored. Finally the revival of the Marist Māori mission following the wars of the 1860s and 1870s is discussed. The wars led directly to the abandonment of the Māori mission for over two decades. The resultant bitterness and suspicion between settler and Māori severely retarded the growth of mission and development of the church within the Wellington Diocese. The role of the Māori kaikatikīhama (catechists) in the survival of the Catholic faith in Māori communities over that period and their support in the revival of the mission following the wars is discussed.

The New Zealand Catholic Church mission
The Roman Catholic mission to New Zealand officially began with the arrival of Bishop Jean-Baptiste Francois Pompallier at the Hokianga Harbour on 10 January 1838.[1] He was accompanied by Father Catherin Servant and Brother Michel, both of whom belonged to the Society of Mary. Although the Catholic Church

was a late arrival in comparison to its leading Protestant rivals, who had been in New Zealand since 1814, Bishop Pompallier was the first bishop of any denomination to reside permanently in New Zealand.[2]

The priests of the Society of Mary, the Marist Fathers, were originally assigned the responsibility of staffing the mission to the Western Pacific under the jurisdiction of Bishop Pompallier, and later were further instructed to accompany Bishop Viard to staff the newly formed Diocese of Wellington.[3] The Marists' initial brief and responsibility in New Zealand, and then in the Diocese of Wellington, was to minister and evangelise among Māori. However, as resources dwindled due to the rapidly increasing European settler population, the priorities of the church authorities changed. The role of the Marists in New Zealand also changed as they attempted to meet the needs of Māori and settler alike.

Throughout the first year of his residence in New Zealand, Pompallier and his staff travelled extensively around Northland preaching and conducting mass, in both Māori and English.[4] Interest in Catholicism was shown by Māori communities from the Hokianga, Mangakāhia and Mangonui, all having had prior contact with the Catholic faith through interaction with Catholic settlers.[5] This promising start led Pompallier and his companions to regard the prospects of their mission with enthusiasm and optimism.

Further priests and brothers arrived in 1839 to staff the Roman Catholic mission to New Zealand.[6] With the additional staff Pompallier began mission stations in Northland, and instituted the Bay of Islands station as the headquarters for the New Zealand mission. This was due to his observations of the large amount of traffic through the eastern port, in comparison to the Hokianga, and the navigability of the East Coast. The situation of the British Resident Captain James Busby at Waitangi also added to the appeal of the Bay of Islands.[7] As additional groups of missionaries arrived from Europe, Pompallier was able to extend steadily the influence of the mission southward.[8]

In 1841 Pompallier wrote the *Instructions pour les Travaux de la Mission* as a type of training manual for those working in the mission. It detailed Pompallier's philosophy for the evangelisation of Māori and its practical application within the New Zealand mission context. The ideas behind the *Instructions* bear some similarity to Samuel Marsden's Church Missionary Society view that the 'civilizing arts' and Christianity go hand in hand.[9] The *Instructions* contained two main themes. The first was that traditional Māori protocols and habits were to remain undisturbed so long as they were compatible with Catholic Church doctrine. The second explained the way in which Catholic missionaries were expected to behave during interaction with non-Catholic Christian missionaries and their teachings.[10]

In the *Instructions*, Pompallier subscribed to a gradualist approach regarding the introduction of Catholic morality to the Māori. He encouraged his missionaries to develop their relationship with Māori through gaining an understanding of Māori society, its practices and its rituals, and by showing kindness and setting a good example.[11] Unlike the Protestant approach, Pompallier recommended as little disturbance to Māori culture and lifestyle as possible, provided that custom was compatible with Catholic doctrine and practice.[12] He thought that the missionaries should build on the 'good things' already found in the Māori way of life and attempt to slowly change those habits that offended them or their Catholic views. The approach outlined in the *Instructions* were derived in the main from Pompallier's own beliefs regarding the best way to evangelise Māori, and were in fact quite enlightened for their time.[13]

With the signing of the Treaty of Waitangi in 1840 and the increase in organised European migration, settlements grew throughout New Zealand, and eventually some evolved into permanent towns. Port Nicholson (Wellington) began as a New Zealand Company settlement, and it was primarily through the efforts of one of its directors, Lord Henry Petrie, that the Catholic Church was initially established there.[14] Lord Petrie brought Father O'Reilly out from Ireland in 1843 to serve as his family chaplain, but O'Reilly was instead seconded into the New Zealand mission by Bishop Pompallier and given charge of Wellington. The following year Father Comte was sent to assist Father O'Reilly, and was assigned to care for the needs of the Māori living in the region.

By 1850 the European population in New Zealand had reached 22,000. This represented an increase of about 20,000 in only ten years. It reached 59,000 in 1858.[15] Many Catholic settlers were among this population increase. Their spiritual needs were tended to by the Māori missionaries, but soon the need for specialist European stations became apparent, particularly in the built-up areas of Auckland and Wellington. A European station was founded in Auckland in October 1842, with Father Petit-Jean as resident priest.[16] The number of Catholics, particularly Irish Catholics, greatly increased in the region with the advent of the government-funded fencible settlements of former British soldiers in Howick, Panmure, Ōtāhuhu and Onehunga, which were to act as a buffer against attack from the Māori living to the south of Auckland.[17] The non-Māori population continued to increase rapidly, due largely to the gold rushes in the South Island, so that by 1864 it was 171,000, and a decade later 255,000.[18]

Throughout Pompallier's tenure as bishop, the mission struggled with financial difficulties. While Pompallier was absent from New Zealand in 1842 retrieving the body of Father Peter Chanel, who had been killed on the island of Futuna the previous year, these financial difficulties increased. The situation was so drastic that the priests left in charge sent letters to Jean-Claude Colin, the superior of the Society of Mary in France, criticising the way in which Pompallier was managing the mission. This was the beginning of intense difficulties between Pompallier and the Marists, both in France and New Zealand. Pompallier's return to New Zealand in August 1842 saw a marked escalation in the controversy between the bishop and the Marists. Pompallier sent letters to Colin accusing him of interfering in the management of the mission, and also wrote to the Society for the Propagation of the Faith in Rome about the issue. Colin replied by accusing Pompallier of trying to gain control of the Oceania-based Marists, and broke any connection the bishop had with the Society of Mary. Despite this breakdown the missionary work continued.[19]

Following his consecration as bishop in 1846 Father Viard returned to New Zealand to assume the leadership of the mission in the absence of Bishop Pompallier, who was in Europe presenting his new plan for the mission.[20] The eventual outcome of Pompallier's trip was that New Zealand was divided into two dioceses, Auckland and Wellington (Port Nicholson).[21] Pompallier, with secular priests, maintained responsibility for the Auckland Diocese, while Viard, with the Marists, assumed management of the Wellington Diocese.

Diocese development

On 1 May 1850 Bishop Viard arrived in Wellington with his Marist staff to begin work in the new diocese. There were already good numbers of active Catholics in the diocese, through the work of various people in Wellington, Nelson and Akaroa and the Māori mission at Ōtaki. There was still much work to be done, however, in developing the rest of the South Island and large areas in the North Island like the Hawke's Bay, Whanganui and Wairarapa, which were part of the Diocese.[22] The responsibility of Viard and his staff included the town-based parishes as well as the mainly rural-orientated Māori missions. These Māori missions, and the people who comprised them, were a large focus of the society's effort, firstly in New Zealand generally, and then in the Wellington Diocese specifically.

The situation in the Wellington Diocese was to change drastically, both financially and demographically, in 1861 with the discovery of gold in Otago. There was a huge influx of people into the region as thousands of hopeful miners arrived to test their luck. A large number of these miners were Irish or Irish-Australian Catholics.[23] Gold was also discovered across the Southern Alps on the West Coast in 1864, and the resulting influx of miners hastened the development of the Catholic Church in this region also.[24] Expansion was also continuing in the Hawke's Bay, where Father Forest established a base at Meeanee and serviced both the Māori and European settlements in the region.[25]

In 1868 Bishop Viard visited Rome to discuss, among other things, the potential establishment of a third diocese. Agreement was reached between him and the Marist order, and it was decided that this diocese would be based in Dunedin.[26] Patrick Moran was appointed as its first bishop. New Zealand now had two Irish bishops in Moran and Croke, Bishop of Auckland, which reflected the demographic make-up of the New Zealand Catholic Church. As a result of the gold rushes and governmental immigration policies, a significant portion of the New Zealand population was now Irish. As a consequence, the New Zealand Catholic Church population began to take on the characteristics of an Irish church.[27]

Following the death of Viard in 1872, Francis Redwood was appointed bishop of Wellington.[28] Initial settlement was still occurring in many parts of the Wellington Diocese, and so the diocese remained in a period of development.[29] A notable event was the establishment of a Marist seminary at Meeanee in 1890, which gave the Society of Mary the opportunity to train priests in New Zealand, making them less reliant on those sent from Europe. In the 1880s discussion took place between the New Zealand bishops and their superiors in Rome regarding the establishment of a fourth diocese in New Zealand. On 13 May 1887 Father John Grimes became the first bishop of the new diocese of Christchurch, despite some opposition to the promotion of an English Marist to a diocese comprised mainly of Irish Catholics. The diocese was made up of Canterbury, Westland, south-west Nelson and the Chatham Islands. These areas had previously been part of the Diocese of Wellington.[30]

This positive development ended with the escalation in hostilities between Māori and the settler government that eventually resulted in the outbreak of the New Zealand Wars in 1860.[31] Although the New Zealand Wars in the Taranaki and Whanganui regions had disrupted the mission work of the church, there was still work to do in ministering to the Catholics among the British soldiers in these areas. The Catholic priests stationed there at this time tended to function primarily in the role of chaplains to the military.[32]

The Marist Māori mission

The Marist Māori mission in what was to become the Wellington Diocese began in 1844 when Father Jean-Baptiste Comte was stationed at Pukekaraka in Ōtaki. He initially experienced success, baptising local chiefs and employing the highly respected Hakaraia Rangikura as a catechist. By 1850 there were approximately 200 Māori Catholics in the area. Comte also worked hard to enhance the economic position of local Catholic Māori through the establishment of market gardens, a water mill and a schooner to transport goods to Wellington for sale. This led, however, to his resignation and return to France, as he struggled to reconcile his role in the commercial enterprises with his religious duty.[33]

The original mission to the Māori was very successful in its goal of baptising Māori and turning them to the Catholic faith. However, given the scant resources and huge distances involved, the maintenance of progress was generally difficult. This was exacerbated when the church turned away from its Māori communities, leaving them with little or no contact with clergy, as a consequence of the New Zealand Wars and racial conflicts of the 1860s. Many Māori Catholics were killed in these conflicts, and their churches and mission stations destroyed. In fact, due to the various wars and the resultant bitterness and suspicion between Māori and settlers, many Catholic Māori abandoned their faith altogether.[34] These conflicts consumed most of the North Island over a twenty-five year period, and had a significant negative impact on all of the Christian denominations, not just the Catholic mission. In the Church Missionary Society mission, for example, 'by 1860 almost all schools had closed and many missions [had been] deserted'.[35]

Added to these negative factors, Bishop Viard – and later, Archbishop Redwood – were more concerned with ministering to the ever-increasing Pākehā settler population than to the Māori.[36] There was also competition for resources from other Catholic missions based in the Pacific.[37]

The Māori mission in the Wellington Diocese during the 1870s and 1890s was based at the three primary mission stations: Pakipaki in the Hawke's Bay mission, Hiruhārama in the Whanganui mission and Pukekaraka in the Ōtaki mission. The effective abandonment of Māori in the diocese is illustrated by the fact that by 1871 Suzanne Aubert at Meeanee was the only full-time Māori missioner. In 1877 not one of the thirty-three Marist priests stationed in the diocese were working full time among Māori.[38] This meant that the maintenance of the faith among Māori was left to the various Māori catechists for a period lasting between fifteen and twenty-five years in most areas.

The Hawke's Bay mission

This was the situation in Hawkes Bay until 1879 and the arrival of Father Soulas from France to help staff the Māori mission in that area. His appointment was the beginning of a more concerted effort by the diocese to minister to Māori in the Hawke's Bay area, with the appointments of Fathers Melu and Lepretre and visits from Father Delach at his base in Ōtaki over the next twenty years.[39] Soulas began instruction from Aubert in the Māori language, and began to train new Māori catechists, to add to current catechists such as Raniera, Hoani Tokotoko and Hohepa Te Toko, who had sustained the work of the mission without any support from the bishops or clergy.[40] Sister Suzanne Aubert had transferred from Auckland to Hawke's Bay in 1871 due to her desire to work among Māori, and was the Māori missioner at Pakipaki in the absence of a priest.[41] There were approximately 120 Catholics among the Māori of the area; the largest concentration was to be found in Pakipaki.

The Whanganui (Hiruhārama) mission

As in the Hawke's Bay, the Whanganui region had largely been ignored following the early days of the Māori mission, despite the appeals during the 1870s of many Whanganui river chiefs and catechists, including Taiwhati, Werahiko, Atarea and Poma, to reestablish the mission.[42] This changed dramatically in 1883 with the appointments of Father Soulas, two Sisters of St Joseph of Nazareth – later to be replaced by the Third Order Regular of Mary – and Suzanne Aubert to Hiruhārama on the Whanganui River.[43] Suzanne Aubert, or Sister Mary Joseph, played an important role in the revival of the Māori mission within the diocese, firstly in the Hawke's Bay and later at Hiruhārama. Aubert was transferred to Hiruhārama because she was fluent in Māori, as well as being a capable nurse with a good medical knowledge.[44] In 1892 she became the first superior of the Daughters of our Lady of Compassion, formerly the Third Order Regular of Mary, based at Hiruhārama. The effect of the support that Aubert and her sisters gave to the Marist Māori missioners is noted by Tennant: 'The activities of the sisters were crucial to the success of the Marist mission, providing a vital element of female support absent from almost all the previous Catholic missionary efforts in New Zealand'.[45] The arrival of Father Soulas, together with Aubert and her sisters, and their achievements, produced a revival of interest in the Catholic faith among Māori; there were many new baptisms and the building of new churches in Māori communities.

The combination of the religious, educational and health services that the mission team provided is considered to have been an important factor in the success of the Whanganui mission during this period. This approach was one that was favoured by Marists in other parts of the Pacific, though it was not generally followed in New Zealand. Another notable factor was the continuing efforts of the various Māori catechists in the area who had worked for decades keeping the Catholic faith alive among Māori in the diocese. In fact, the strict religious observance by many Māori of Hiruhārama closely resembled that of a religious order.[46] In 1886 Father Cognet joined Soulas and the mission and was based at Rānana on the Whanganui River, which was home to many families that had long supported the Catholic faith.

The Ōtaki mission

In 1885 Father Melu was appointed to the Ōtaki mission; he was later joined for a short while by Father Cognet. The Ōtaki mission had not had a full-time priest since Comte in 1854. These two conducted the usual mission business of spreading the faith through baptism and the other sacraments, once again travelling extensively on horseback.[47] Of particular importance to Melu at this time was the building of churches in partnership with the Māori communities throughout the mission district; in this he achieved notable success.[48]

Melu and Delach, who began in 1893, also began to create some initiatives that were entirely new among mission practices in

New Zealand. Most notable of these were regular hui of Māori Catholics. The first was held in 1894 to mark the golden jubilee of the Ōtaki mission, and they continued into the twentieth century throughout the mission, organised by Delach in collaboration with leading Māori Catholics. These hui were used to bring together the many Catholic Māori groups from within the mission to discuss issues related to the faith and the ways Māori enacted the faith in their lives. They were seen as 'a central expression of Catholic Māori Mana'.[49]

Māori Catholic churches were opened throughout the Ōtaki mission, but perhaps more significant was the building of a wharenui (meeting house), opened in 1904, beside the presbytery at Pukekaraka. The wharenui was named 'Roma' to highlight its links to Rome and the Catholic Church, and the marae in front of it was named for the Virgin Mary, as was a second wharenui that was eventually built beside it.[50] These initiatives provided a combination of Māori and Catholic beliefs that allowed Māori to express their Catholic faith in a more Māori fashion: a unique idea at that particular time in the church's history, but one that harkened back to some of the ideas originally professed by Bishop Pompallier.[51] More importantly, these hui and the building of the marae and wharenui seemed to significantly encourage Māori participation and understanding in their faith, through the incorporation of some of their traditional cultural concepts and practice.[52]

Māori catechists

In the revival of the Māori mission that followed the New Zealand Wars, various Māori catechists played a significant role in the maintenance and continuation of Catholic religious observation in Māori communities in the Wellington Catholic Diocese. Despite this, they have remained largely invisible in diocesan and Catholic church histories of New Zealand.

The importance of Māori catechists to Māori mission was highlighted by Father Cognet, who stated: 'When these young people are clever and faithful, they render us invaluable services. They are our most precious resource and serve as levers to shake up the masses.'[53] The scarcity of staff and resources within the Māori mission meant that the role of the Māori catechists was significant. They often contributed immensely to the success, or lack thereof, of the mission.

Throughout the mission history there are examples of the support that Māori catechists gave during the period of limited contact with clergy. There are various examples of Māori, usually through their catechists, lobbying for the return of the church to their communities. Throughout the 1870s and 1880s various Whanganui chiefs approached the church to lobby for the return of the mission. Taiwhati, a chief of Hiruhārama, often visited the Marist base at Meeanee when travelling to trade sheep and mats in Hawke's Bay. While there he would approach Father Soulas about reviving the Whanganui mission.[54] In 1882 Taiwhati also met with Bishop Redwood in Palmerston North and presented his case for the recommencement of the mission. He was successful in gaining the bishop's assurance that he would send a priest to be based in Hiruhārama.[55] On the Whanganui River, Atarea, Poma and Werahiko of Kauaeroa, who were prominent catechists, also approached Father Soulas with a request for the permanent return of the mission to their region. The determination of Māori for the return of the mission to the Whanganui region can also be seen in the 1883 presentation of a petition signed by 150 Whanganui Māori to Father Soulas for submission to Bishop Redwood, requesting the appointment of a priest at Hiruhārama.[56]

Aside from lobbying for the return of the church, the catechists were also crucial in sustaining the faith during the absence of clergy. In the Hawke's Bay, Raniera, Hoani Tokotoko and Hohepa Te Toko sustained the faith in that region without any support from clergy for over a decade. The chief Puhara also kept his hapū adhering to the Catholic faith, despite having no visits or interaction with Catholic clergy for over two years. During this period he received regular visits from the Rev. Williams, who tried to persuade him to convert to the Anglican Church.[57]

Perhaps the most remarkable example of a catechist keeping the faith alive during the absence of contact with clergy is that of Werahiko from the Whanganui River Anglican village of Koroniti. He was an elderly catechist who, for fifteen years, rang the Catholic prayer bell morning and night, despite being the only person who ever responded. Upon the reestablishment of the mission in 1883 he became a prominent leader. Werahiko was extremely critical of those Māori customs he felt were in opposition of Catholic practices. Father Cognet recounts an incident at Koroniti in which Werahiko had a confrontation with a tohunga. The tohunga directed a mākutu (curse) at Werahiko that almost killed him. However, he was able to reverse the mākutu through the recitation of the rosary, and directed it back onto the tohunga, who died a few hours later. This incident was used by the Whanganui River catechists to assert the validity and mana of the Catholic faith.[58]

Even once the mission was reestablished, many villages within the mission would only see a priest a few times a year, due to the mission's vast geographical size and the time that it took to travel, on horseback and by boat. Therefore, it still fell to the Māori catechists to keep the faith alive among the people, by conducting regular weekday and Sunday prayers until such time as a priest returned to provide the sacraments.[59] Notable catechists at Hiruhārama included another Werahiko (Kauaeroa), who was a local chief and the head catechist at Hiruhārama, where he worked tirelessly for the Sisters of Compassion.[60] Te Menehera was the successor to Werahiko as the head catechist at Hiruhārama. He was also a staunch supporter of the mission, and had donated land for the Sisters of Compassion to build their base.[61] Mataroa was the head catechist at Hiruhārama for many years. He was extremely skilled in doctrine, and was always prepared to debate and argue with Māori of other denominations. His willingness to enter into a confrontation in defence of the Catholic faith, both verbally and, if necessary, physically, earned him the title of 'the fighting catechist'.[62]

Sources of concern to the Marists at this time were the various Māori prophets operating in the Taranaki and Whanganui regions. In 1886 Soulas and Cognet were invited by the influential Ngāti Ruanui prophet Raumati to visit his home of Whenuakura. Despite their suspicions of Māori prophets, they agreed to visit. Upon their arrival they were welcomed by the people of Whenuakura, and in his welcome speech Raumati declared his support for the Catholic faith and his belief that it was destined to spread throughout the Pacific. Due to his status and mana, Soulas and Cognet installed him as the 'great catechist' and itinerant preacher to all tribes of the diocese.[63] More often, however, the prophets were treated as hostile competition, and the priests used the catechists to dissuade people from attending the Māori prophets that often visited the area.[64]

This role of catechists as 'defenders of the faith' extended to contention with the other various Christian denominations. In fact New Zealand in the late nineteenth century was marked by the ongoing contest between the various Christian denominations for Māori adherents. A certain fluidity existed in which Māori often would change from one denomination to another, dependent on the contact (and thus influence) they had with a particular group of missionaries. For example, Ngāti Wairiki from Kauangaroa on the Whangaehu River were originally baptised into the Wesleyan faith and then changed to Anglican and again to Pai Mārire. Then, as their contact with local Catholic settlers increased, several of the families became Catholic.[65] As another example, in 1888 the Salvation Army established a presence in Peterehema, a village at the northern end of mainly Catholic Hiruhārama. The Marists believed that the only reason for their success was that the influential Māori catechists were in Whanganui at the Māori Land Court. Any long-term success for the Salvation Army was prevented when the elderly chief Poutini on his deathbed urged his people to return to Catholicism.[66] For the Catholic Church, who had a shortage of clergy and a complete absence of Māori clergy, this issue of Māori choosing to change faiths if contact was not maintained was a source of anxiety. The inability of the church to foster and develop Māori clergy, or systematically train catechists, severely limited its ability to evangelise Māori and to ensure the continued commitment of converted Māori.

In fact, thought was given to the creation of a school to train Māori catechists to assist in the work of the mission. However, due to a lack of personnel and resources, this was never established. Some potential catechists were sent to St Patrick's in Wellington and Sacred Heart College in Auckland in an attempt to create future catechists and Catholic leaders.[67] Despite this, no coherent structure or system was implemented to accelerate the creation of Māori catechists or clergy.

Despite the reliance on catechists to provide religious leadership in their respective villages, it seems that Father Soulas himself may not have been enthusiastic about the development of Māori clergy. An example of his reluctance is the case of Rure Te Manihera Keremeneta from Ngāti Hau, who wished to train as a Catholic priest. Soulas opposed the idea. As Bergin noted in 1986, there was 'a lack of concern for the development of a Catholic Māori priesthood'. This, he asserts, may have been a result of European paternalism, the belief that Māori were not able to serve as priests or the belief that Māori were heading for extinction.[68] Despite being denied the opportunity of entering the priesthood, Keremeneta continued as a catechist on the Whanganui River throughout his life. He was a committed believer and supporter of the Catholic faith who rarely missed daily mass and communion. In his young days he would climb down and then back up 1000 feet of steep hill country every day to attend mass.[69] His lifelong commitment to the faith and the high regard he was held in by Māori Catholics and Māori missioners suggests that he would have likely been an extremely successful priest, and in fact he lived his life with that level of spiritual commitment anyway.

This attitude contrasts starkly with that of the Protestant missionary groups who ordained Māori ministry. The CMS ordained their first Māori minister, Rota Waitoa, in 1853 and the second, Riwai Te Ahu, in 1855. Both men received training at St Stephen's School in Auckland, which had been established in 1844. Despite various obstacles and difficulties Protestants continued to ordain Māori at a steady – albeit slow – rate. By the end of the 1860s there were seventeen Māori ministers in the Anglican Church.[70] This progress far outshone the results produced by the Catholics by the same stage. Lange notes that there was a large gap between 'Polynesian culture and the nineteenth-century French catholic model of seminary formation' that hindered the Catholic aspirations of an indigenous clergy. Pompallier in the 1840s lamented the lack of missionary personnel and resources that would have allowed him to open more schools and a seminary.[71]

Not until the establishment of Hato Paora College in 1947 did the number of clergy increase significantly in the New Zealand Catholic Church. Hato Paora has contributed four of the country's seven Māori Catholic priests. The first, Father Robert Harwood, in 1964, was followed by Karaitiana Kingi, in 1969. The third, Max Mariu, in 1977, was followed later in the same year by Jack Smith, formerly Brother Sebastian.[72] About a decade later, a very important day for both Hato Paora and Māori Catholics arrived when in 1988 Father Takuira Max Mariu was ordained as the first Māori Catholic bishop.

Conclusion

The Catholic Church officially began in New Zealand with the arrival of Bishop Pompallier in 1838. He and a small band of Marist priests and brothers began to evangelise from their base in Northland, gradually extending their influence southward. Eventually, the mission was divided into the Auckland Diocese, under Pompallier, and the Wellington Diocese, under Bishop Viard and the Marist fathers. The Marists began to develop European parishes and a Māori mission with the diocese. The conflicts between Māori and settler of the 1860s, 1870s and some of the 1880s retarded this development, as the church effectively abandoned the Māori mission in favour of the European settlers. However, upon the completion of the wars there was a revival of the Māori mission, and the Marists renewed their focus on Māori communities.

During the period of abandonment Māori catechists within the diocese were instrumental in keeping the faith alive among Māori communities. They also continued to play a significant role once the mission was reinstituted, maintaining a Catholic Church presence in Māori communities and holding rival Christian faiths at bay in the absence of clergy between visits from missionaries. In fact, their mana and status often influenced the choice of religion and level of commitment to that religion within their communities. Despite existing in relative obscurity, the Catholic Māori catechists of the late nineteenth century contributed significantly to the development of the contemporary Māori religious landscape.

Endnotes

1. J Thomson, 'Some Reasons for the Failure of the Roman Catholic Mission to the Maoris 1838–1860', in *New Zealand Journal of History* 3.2 (1969): 166–74, 166.
2. E R Simmons, *A Brief History of the Catholic Church in New Zealand* (Auckland: Catholic Publication Centre, 1978), 11.
3. J Weir, 'Mission to Maori 1838–1870', in P Ewart (ed.), *Aspects of the apostolates of the Society of Mary in New Zealand since 1838: Assembled to commemorate the centenary of the establishment of the New Zealand Province of the Society of Mary, 1889–1989* (Wellington: Society of Mary, 1989), 4–5.
4. M King, *God's Farthest Outpost: A History of Catholics in New Zealand* (Auckland: Penguin, 1997), 49–52.
5. Simmons, *Brief History of the Catholic Church in New Zealand*, 13.
6. Ibid.
7. King, *God's Farthest Outpost*, 52.
8. J-B F Pompallier, *The Early History of the Catholic Church in Oceania* (Auckland: Brett, 1888), 77.
9. K Girdwood-Morgan, 'J-B.F. Pompallier's Instructions for Mission Work 1841', dissertation for diploma of social sciences, Massey University, Palmerston North, 1985, 3.
10. Ibid, 3–4.
11. Simmons, *Brief History of the Catholic Church in New Zealand*, 22.
12. Girdwood-Morgan, 'Pompallier's Instructions', 3.
13. E R Simmons, *Pompallier: Prince of Bishops* (Auckland: Catholic Publications Centre, 1984), 74.
14. Simmons, *History of the Catholic Church in New Zealand*, 31–2.
15. Ibid, 28.
16. Ibid, 29.
17. Ibid, 30.
18. M King, *The Penguin History of New Zealand* (Auckland: Penguin, 2003), 210.
19. Simmons, *History of the Catholic Church in New Zealand*, 18–21.
20. Ibid, 30.
21. Ibid, 35–8.
22. Ibid, 51.
23. Ibid, 55–6.
24. King, *God's Farthest Outpost*, 87.
25. Simmons, *History of the Catholic Church in New Zealand*, 57–8.
26. King, *God's Farthest Outpost*, 89.
27. Ibid, 93.
28. Ibid, 90.
29. Simmons, *History of the Catholic Church in New Zealand*, 78–82.
30. M O'Meeghan, 'Grimes, John Joseph 1842–1915', in C Orange (ed.), *Dictionary of New Zealand Biography Volume 2 (1870–1900)* (Wellington: Department of Internal Affairs, 1993), 179–80.
31. Simmons, *History of the Catholic Church in New Zealand*, 48.
32. Ibid, 59.
33. King, *God's Farthest Outpost*, 69–70.
34. P Bergin, 'Hoani Papita to Paora: The Marist Missions of Hiruharama and Otaki 1883 to 1914', MA thesis, University of Auckland, 1986, 1–2.

35 S Harman, 'The Struggle for Success: A Socio-Cultural Perspective on the French Marist Priests and their Māori Mission (1838–1867)', PhD thesis, University of Waikato, 2010, 283.
36 P Bergin, 'Education: the beginnings 1838–1889', in Ewart, *Aspects of the apostolates of the Society of Mary in New Zealand*, 30.
37 M Tennant, 'Aubert, Mary Joseph – Biography', from the *Dictionary of New Zealand Biography*, in *Te Ara – the Encyclopedia of New Zealand*: http://www.teara.govt.nz/en/biographies/2a18/1 (accessed 7 January 2012).
38 Bergin, 'Hoani Papita to Paora', 8.
39 Bergin, 'Education: the beginnings 1838–1889', 30–1.
40 Bergin, 'Hoani Papita to Paora', 9.
41 J Munro, *The Story of Suzanne Aubert* (Auckland: Auckland University Press/Bridget Williams Books, 1996), 80–96.
42 Bergin, 'Hoani Papita to Paora', 12.
43 Tennant, 'Aubert, Mary Joseph'.
44 Ibid.
45 Ibid.
46 Bergin, 'Hoani Papita to Paora', 17.
47 Bergin, 'Education: the beginnings 1838–1889', 35–7.
48 Bergin, 'Hoani Papita to Paora', 54–8.
49 Bergin, 'Education: the beginnings 1838–1889', 37–9.
50 Ibid, 37.
51 Ibid, 39.
52 Bergin, 'Hoani Papita to Paora', 117–19.
53 Ibid, 43.
54 Ibid, 12.
55 Ibid, 12.
56 Ibid, 13.
57 *Marist Messenger*, April 1931.
58 Bergin, 'Hoani Papita to Paora', 46–7.
59 Ibid, 43.
60 *Marist Messenger*, April 1931.
61 Ibid.
62 Ibid.
63 Bergin, 'Hoani Papita to Paora', 38–9.
64 Ibid, 75.
65 Ibid, 53.
66 Ibid, 77.
67 Ibid, 44.
68 Ibid, 85.
69 'Te Manihera Keremeneta', in *Zealandia*, 1959: 38–43.
70 R Lange, 'Ordained Ministry in Maori Christianity, 1853–1900', in *Journal of Religious History* 27.1 (February 2003): 47–66, 52–3.
71 Ibid, 56.
72 T Lawton, 'Whaia te Tika. Hato Paora College: The First Fifty Years', MA thesis, Massey University, Palmerston North, 1996, 116–17.

Chapter Eight

Representations of Māori in Presbyterian Children's Missionary Literature, 1909–1939

Hugh Morrison

Introduction

In July 1883 the editor of Otago and Southland's *New Zealand Missionary Record* lamented to his Presbyterian readers that 'it is a reproach upon the Presbyterian Church in this Province that she should be doing so little for the evangelisation of the original proprietors of the soil'.[1] There was a competitive note to this lament. The Synod of Otago and Southland, separated from the northern branch of the New Zealand Presbyterian Church between 1866 and 1901, was apparently falling behind its northern neighbour with respect to Māori missionary work. In an earlier comment the editor had noted that while southern churches annually contributed £50 'to aid in Missionary work among the Maoris in the North', this did not relieve them from responsibilities that lay closer to home.[2]

In late 1939 Presbyterian youngsters subscribing to *The Break of Day* magazine were exhorted to give generously to the annual children's missionary project Christmas present fund. The project for 1940 was to be the construction of a church building at Waikaremoana. This 'whare karakia' would be, wrote Deaconess Sister Kearney, a much-needed and 'suitable building in which we may serve and worship God'.[3] The children gave generously, donating just over £455 by early 1940.[4] To date this was the biggest sum of money donated in the thirty-year history of the fund, and came from children right around the dominion. Nearly sixty years on, then, the concerns expressed in 1883 that the church was not fulfilling its duty to tangata whenua had been answered. Furthermore, it was children who were deemed to be central to that response.

Up until World War Two, at least, Māori were still often cast in the role of missionary subjects. This partly resulted from the emergence of what historian Allan Davidson argues were two distinctive Christian streams in the colonial New Zealand context: the Māori missionary stream and the settler Pākehā stream.[5] The events of the mid- to late nineteenth century and the growing perception that Māori were a dying race in need of rescue served to reinforce missionary paternalism beyond 1900. A similar differentiated model is proposed by Helen May for understanding the histories of childhood in Aotearoa New Zealand; the 'indigenous Maori child' was clearly distinguished in popular perception and educational practice from the 'colonial Pakeha child' by 1900.[6] Settler children were important to the missionary ventures of New Zealand's Presbyterian churches: as supporters and as prospective adult missionaries. They inhabited a unique, but by no means exceptional, British-world colony in which this missionary vision was implemented both at home and abroad. Pākehā settler and Māori children within the Presbyterian Church potentially grew up in two different worlds, separated partly by distance, but also by culture and mentality. Therefore childhood is one important context within which religious differences might be examined.

In this chapter, I begin to unravel the ways in which images of Māori culture and Christianity were mediated to Presbyterian settler children between 1909 and 1939, specifically through the pages of the nationally dedicated children's missionary magazine *The Break of Day*. In these decades, Presbyterian actions and attitudes were typical of the other main Protestant churches both in New Zealand and the wider Anglo-American world. I ask questions of this material in terms of how far the imagery it contained supported or subverted the notion of difference. I approach these representations from two broad perspectives: a plain or face-value reading and a more complex and contextual reading.

Presbyterian children, missions and missionary literature

Overseas ('foreign') and domestic missions were an early priority for Presbyterians in Aotearoa New Zealand. In 1856 the Auckland Presbytery unanimously affirmed that Christian mission was a 'duty', an act both of 'obedience' and 'gratitude to God' and a task that was intrinsic to the church's 'spiritual welfare'.[7] By 1862 the New Hebrides (Vanuatu) had been identified as an appropriate 'field' to activate this missionary imperative, and a 'Committee on Foreign and Maori Missions' was established.[8] In 1866 the Presbyterian Church split over doctrinal differences, and existed as a bifurcated northern and southern church divided by the Waitaki River. The Otago-Southland Synod established a parallel committee, and by 1869 both Presbyterian branches had sent their first missionaries, albeit procured from Scotland. Over the next four decades the Presbyterian Church also established further missionary work in southern China and northern India. All three geographic regions became important for ongoing New Zealand Presbyterian identity.

Māori had always been included in the ambit of Presbyterian missionary thinking, prior to the church's overseas missionary involvement. The Rev. James Duncan, joined briefly by the Rev. John Inglis, began longer-term work in 1844 among Manawatū Māori, initially under the Reformed Presbyterian Church of Scotland. In Otago, the Rev. Thomas Burns itinerated in Māori settlements close to Dunedin, and the Rev. Alexander Blake was briefly employed at Ōtākou on the Otago Peninsula. More sustained work, associated with the Presbyterian Church, was carried out by the North German Missionary Society missionaries Johannes Wohlers, Abraham Honoré and Johannes Riemenschneider.[9] Yet all of these efforts were localised, ad hoc or faltering at best; the work of enthusiasts and their supporters. By 1867 the northern church had separated out its 'Foreign' and 'Māori' Missions Committees, but little progress was made. From the late 1860s the southern church effectively shifted its domestic missionary focus to the influx of Chinese migrants. By the 1890s the national church was also focused upon 'home missions' to the many rural communities established in areas opened up for farming and forestry. Therefore mission to Māori remained a priority more in principle than in practice. *The Break of Day*'s inception in 1909 and its subsequent systematic coverage of Presbyterian Māori mission work reflected a greater determination by the nationally united church, after 1901, to extend its ministry to Māori. This was primarily in the central and eastern North Island.

Presbyterian children's support for and involvement in missions was fostered early on in the colonial church's life, following a well-established trend for nineteenth-century British church-going youngsters.[10] By the early 1900s well-stocked Sunday schools had become important sites for missionary energies, pedagogy and socialisation.[11] Both the Presbyterian Women's Missionary Union and the Bible class movement added impetus to this juvenile and adolescent involvement. Childhood was, in the words of the Rev. Rutherford Waddell, a key time in which to inculcate 'wide sympathies' and the 'nobility of doing good'.[12] Global awareness and a self-sacrificing lifestyle went hand in hand.[13]

Missionary literature was the prime way by which images of and ideas about non-European peoples were mediated to Western children.[14] The ways in which Māori were represented to Presbyterian settler children illustrate this. This is a significant point to note, for inherent in this process were two specific ideas: the enduring mindset that continued to cast Māori as missionary subjects, and the notion that children's interest in missions should be both locally and globally focused. In the later nineteenth century this happened in a haphazard way through various Presbyterian periodicals. Between 1882 and 1885 the Rev. C Stuart Ross, an Australian minister living in New Zealand, edited a short-lived magazine titled the *New Zealand Missionary Record*. It was produced in Otago and aimed at an Otago/Southland audience of both Sunday school children and teachers.[15] A truly dedicated children's magazine did not properly appear until 1909, with the appearance of the first issue of *The Break of Day*. The magazine's founding editor, the Rev. James

Aitken, saw it through from its inception until his retirement from ministry in 1935. Content focused on both 'foreign' and 'domestic' missions. It was a more truly 'modern' print product in that it carried a balance of text, small engravings and many photographs. Between 1909 and 1920 monthly subscriptions to the magazine increased from just over 5000 to 9000; anecdotal evidence suggests continued modest growth.[16] By the 1930s the magazine was an important means by which Presbyterian children interacted with missionary material. Among other things it consistently featured an annual 'Christmas present' fund. Children were encouraged to save up their threepenny pieces and donate them to a nominated and well-advertised project. The results were then published, along with details about the projects' progress. Between 1909 and 1939 annual donations grew from £32 to £640 (Figure 1). An accumulated total of £8457 was collected by 1940. While most attention went to China and India, the church's Māori Mission was the recipient on five separate occasions (1913, 1919, 1928, 1932 and 1939), with the emphasis on mission infrastructure or medical equipment. There is no evidence to suggest that, in their giving, children thought the Māori Mission to be any less important. Their generosity was equally spread over projects at home and abroad.

Figure 1: **Contributions to** *The Break of Day* **Christmas present fund, 1909–1940**

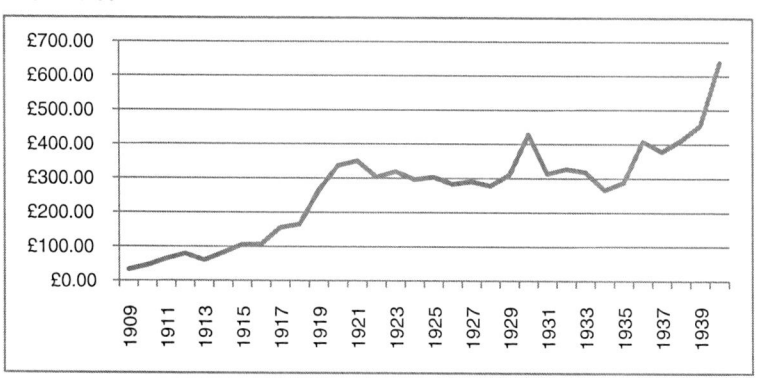

Source: Extracted from February issues of *The Break of Day*, 1909–1941. Archives Research Centre, Presbyterian Church of Aotearoa New Zealand.

The Break of Day presented Māori material in a range of ways, its focus squarely on communities in the central and eastern North Island. Children were typically engaged through stories, historical and geographical accounts, the retelling of legends, letters and reports from missionaries to the children, and many illustrations. A survey of this material immediately highlights the dissonance between our own world and that of the early decades of the twentieth century. Consequently it is all too easy to read the historical record in a reactionary and negative way. In light of this, my approach, using representative examples, is to suggest two possible readings of the material that might be fruitful for further discussion: a plain reading that identifies content and motifs, and a more nuanced reading that acknowledges ambiguities and context.

Representations of Māori: a plain reading

By the early 1900s language and sentiments were undeniably paternalistic and Eurocentric, reflecting the essentially 'European gaze' of The Break of Day. There was certainly greater care taken over details of people's or place names, and with respect to tikanga Māori than in similar publications of the late nineteenth century. It is also possible that Māori were depicted as being less distinctively 'other' and in a less condescending manner than (for example) Chinese or Indian people and cultures in the same pages. Likewise there was no attempt to depict Pākehā children dressed up as Māori, but a number of instances of children dressed in Indian and Japanese clothing.[17] Yet even by 1940 Māori were still generally depicted as exotic and 'other', inhabiting remote and foreign landscapes. There are, however, at least three broader motifs to consider: progress, difference and disadvantage.

The progressive motif contrasted the condition of Māori before and after the arrival of Christianity and, by implication, of Western civilisation. Even in the late 1800s settler children still read tales of Māori cannibalism and violence counterpoised against 'civilised' stories of peace and prosperity. Christianity and 'civilisation' were the key factors of change. While the more lurid images like cannibalism did not feature in The Break of Day, the broader narrative of progress endured over subsequent decades. In promoting the work of Sister Alison at Taumarunui, the Rev. George Budd depicted pre-European New Zealand as a 'land full of loveliness; full, too, of terror and horror'. After the arrival of Christianity the 'old things passed away, for the Light had come'.[18] This same rhetoric rejoiced at the passing of 'hauhauism' (the beliefs of the Pai Mārire religion), which was referred to as a 'delusion' with 'heathenish and Roman Catholic elements', now given up for 'the better way which Christ teaches us'. It also commended the transformation of one of Rua Kēnana's buildings at Maungapōhatu into a Sunday school.[19] In an account of Rua's tangi in 1937, Sister Olga felt compelled to voice regret that '[i]f only he had been captured for Christ at the commencement of his career he would have been a wonderful power for good'.[20] Her imagery was ironic, given his experience of literally being captured by so-called Christian Pākehā and the tragedy that followed his arrest in 1916, but her message was clear: Christianity was a potentially redeeming force of progress and betterment.

Difference was another obvious motif. For British or European children supporting missionary ventures, difference was a geographically distant phenomenon. For colonial Pākehā children, however, difference was at least potentially proximate. Differences were represented in all sorts of ways, but were often depicted graphically in illustrations, especially photographs. Warlike Māori as depicted in late nineteenth-century etchings no longer existed, but elements of Māori architecture, tikanga and clothing remained essentially different, especially in these illustrations. Staged images of women and children, especially, were less idealised or romanticised than in the late 1800s, but nevertheless were different.

Photographs also depicted Māori in rural terms with respect to domestic and economic activity. Here rurality was not so much domesticated as pioneering and primitive. Māori lived on the geographical and cultural margins. Their lives were eked out on the borderlands of both civilisation and the imagination. They inhabited a geographic space that, even in 1939, was still referred to as 'Maoriland'. Here Māori children and adults alike dressed

Teaching the Māori children at Ruatāhuna. *Auckland Weekly News*, P-A21.35-119. Archives Research Centre, Presbyterian Church of Aotearoa New Zealand.

differently (albeit in combinations of European clothing), conducted Christian worship outdoors or in architecturally different venues, lived communally and still utilised such modes of transport as horses and hand-hewn canoes.[21]

The difference motif went hand in hand with one of disadvantage. Many of the illustrations hinted at or implied a sense of physical or socio-economic deprivation. Many Pākehā child readers, especially those in urban areas, may have perceived a qualitative gulf between the way they and Māori children lived. Deprivation was a strong thread that ran through the letters written by Māori Mission deaconesses to *The Break of Day*. The rhetoric was well employed to gain children's sympathies and threepenny bits. Christianity and cleanliness were intertwined; a theme not uncommon in contemporary international constructions of Christian missions.[22] Māori were among many in the dominion who fitted into the category of the deserving poor;

requiring a salvation that was both spiritual and hygienic. This account by Sister Jessie in Nūhaka was typical:

> Let me describe one of the poorer homes, and you will understand how much a deaconess is needed to teach and help these people. Imagine a large unlined whare of one room with mud floor, a small door, and a sliding panel acting as window. On one side an open fireplace surrounded by pots and dishes, logs of wood, and buckets of water. On the other side the family sleeping place built a little off the ground, sloping from the wall to the centre of the floor – the rough boards covered with flax matting, and every variety of rug in readiness to act as night covering. That is one home … [Jesus] is waiting at their heart's door every day to give them new life, new thoughts, that will make them hate uncleanness and love only that which God loves. Just now their lives are like this whare – their minds shut in and dark, their time divided between eating and sleeping. The knowledge of God's love will be like a window into their souls, through which His light will shine giving new life, health and peace.[23]

More often than not this message was strongly gendered. It was 'Maori mothers' who lacked the knowledge to create a better lifestyle, thus needing 'someone to guide them'. That 'someone' was more often than not the 'lady missionary'.[24]

Representations of Māori: a more complex reading

The above discussion has revolved around both written and visual depictions of Māori in *The Break of Day* that reinforced notions of progress, difference and disadvantage. To take these exclusively at face value, or to view them as static over time, is to take a spurious historiographical position. In her discussion of the different worlds of New Zealand children, Helen May notes how visual representations of Māori children since the nineteenth century have discernibly changed according to modes of thinking or influential social, political and economic discourses.[25] Our 'plain' reading needs to be supplemented by a more nuanced reading of children's religious literature.

In the first instance the idea of 'progress' does not provide an altogether straightforward category for analysis of these texts. It is erroneous to argue that, predominantly, settler children were presented with the idea of Māori progress as being linear, consistent and irreversible. Māori adoption of Christianity, as understood by its Pākehā purveyors, was often the intended aim or ideal. Likewise, progressive assimilation through the appropriation of Pākehā values, English language and Western material culture was also important. But both goals were far from being fulfilled, according to Presbyterian children's literature. Children were told of classrooms, Sunday school groups and communities where English was the second language.[26] One deaconess recounted a tale of buying a horse for the mission at Maungapōhatu in the following terms: '"[K]apai for you this one", said the dusky Maori farmer. "He quiet, he not frightened, he not shy, you fall below him he not run. Kapai! He easily caught. By Gorry, he the one. He carry pack, pull the gig. Kapai for the pakeha wahine. You make the try," and the little pakeha wahine bought him.'[27] This account of the transactional dialogue served to reinforce prevailing cross-cultural stereotypes, and to underscore the message that progress was far from being attained.

There was, however, an additional element to the rhetoric around progress. Children were told on a number of occasions that progress for Māori had been severely compromised by at least two factors: Western vices and colonisation. Settlers had brought 'strong drink and bad habits' and disease, all of which had severely impacted upon Māori health and well-being. In 1913 Sister Margaret wrote that Pākehā children and adults 'forget that we took this land from the Maoris, and therefore ought to do what we can to help them'.[28] The Rev. Donald MacDiarmid, an ex-missionary in the Sudan and editor of *The Break of Day* after Aitken's retirement, wrote further in 1937 that:

The Maoris [sic] are a great race, and it is partly our fault that they are not much greater than they are. It is true that the coming of the white man to New Zealand brought some benefits to the Maoris by our civilisation, but at the same time we brought a lot of other things to New Zealand that have done terrible harm to the Maori race – strong drink and some diseases that were unknown in New Zealand in the olden days and many other things that the Maoris have little cause to thank us for.[29]

There was possibly an element of 'fatal impact' thinking here, mixed in with a 'Māori as victims' mentality.[30] It is evident, from other non-Māori content in *The Break of Day*, that there was a clear editorial intent to warn children off the perceived dangers of alcohol. In this case alleged alcohol abuse among Māori was as much an object lesson for children in general as it was a statement about Western colonisation. Yet it is clear that some of the realities of colonisation were being acknowledged, even if the implication was that Presbyterians needed to be the rescuers.

However, Māori were not always represented as completely passive. There were a number of instances in which Pākehā children were presented with exemplary and heroic Māori Christian individuals and stories worthy of emulation. The story of the girl martyr Tarore, and her fragment of Luke's gospel, was recounted at least twice in this vein.[31] Tarore, the story went, was a twelve-year-old girl who was killed as she slept with a copy of the gospel of Luke under her pillow. This gospel was central to the eventual rapprochement between the families of victim and perpetrator, and later was taken as far as Kapiti Island. Her story has been told many times through words and pictures; it was most recently published as a children's book by Joy Cowley. Tarore's grave can still be visited at Waharoa in the Waikato.[32] The versions printed in *The Break of Day* accentuated themes of forgiveness and the providence of God. One version, penned by the Rev. David Calder, Presbyterian minister and the Bible Society's general secretary from 1925,[33] differed in that it focused as much on the girl as on the gospel fragment that wound its way from Northland to Kapiti Island. In Calder's account Tarore, the child, was the conduit for adults' salvation. In turn Tarore, as a daughter, was faithful to both the gospel and to her father. In all respects she was a model child. Exemplary stories also focused on such individuals as Tamihana Te Rauparaha and Matene Te Whiwhi (whose stories were indirectly linked to that of Tarore's), Ruatara and the 'Taupō martyrs' Te Manihera and Kereopa.[34]

It is worth noting that such exemplary representations were often selective, potentially sanitised and moralistic in tone. Accounts of Tamihana Te Rauparaha, for example, stopped well short of his early involvement with the Kīngitanga or his contentious support for land sales.[35] Peka Hinau from Ruatāhuna was lauded in the 1930s as both a success story for the mission and as an exemplary Christian. The narrative emphasised certain elements: stricken by polio as a young child, prior to the Presbyterian Mission's arrival, Peka was subsequently 'found' by a deaconess, rehabilitated at Rotorua's public hospital and given a Christian education through the Mission. He eventually became the storekeeper/postmaster in Ruatāhuna and, in 1936, married Riporata in the Mission church.[36]

Biographical details of Peka Hinau's story stood alongside other messages that accentuated both the perceived impotence of traditional cosmology and the virtue of struggling through adversity. Peka Hinau's example, suggested James Aitken, reminded children that '[i]f we want – if we really want to be cheerful and useful, we must set about and try … And we must ask God to help us'.[37] Māori Christianity, then, could have a reflexive value for Pākehā Presbyterian children, even if the rhetoric was often in Western terms.

Thirdly, there are difficulties in using 'difference' as an exclusive way to frame our thinking about Presbyterian children's historical understandings of Māori society and culture. This is both a practical and a theoretical issue. At a practical level, it is apposite to ask whether children perceived difference to the extent that might be assumed and, if so, how. Up until World War One there were many rural districts that were still largely pioneering in terms of lifestyles and conditions. Life in many rural districts was tough and unsophisticated for Māori and Pākehā alike. For instance, the Rev. Clive Mortimer-Jones, Anglican home missionary priest in Northland, dramatically described what he saw as the dire physical and spiritual state of Pākehā settlements in the gum fields during the early 1900s.[38] Such descriptions were replicated by the many Anglican, Methodist and Presbyterian home missionaries deployed to rural areas in these decades. Rural readers of *The Break of Day* may not have perceived too great a difference between images of Māori and their own lifestyles. Evidence from *The Break of Day* also suggests that in some North Island rural districts Pākehā and Māori grew up side by side and, in some instances, may have attended Sunday school together. Busy Bee members in Ōpōtiki annually met up with and gave gifts to Māori children at the Tanatana mission school.[39] While such situations were probably exceptional rather than the norm, it is possible that difference was perceived more by children in the South Island or by children who lived more urbanised lives in the growing towns and cities, especially from the 1920s onwards.

Descriptions of another category of children also indicate a theoretical problem. Children reading *The Break of Day* in September 1909 learnt about 'large families of poor [non-Māori] boys and girls in our orphanages in Dunedin ... [who needed] lots of things you and I could easily spare [clothes, food and toys]'.[40] The notion of the 'other' has been popular in historical writing, especially since the seminal works on orientalism, culture and imperialism by Edward Said.[41] Race and culture have become commonly used categories by which scholars apply the notion of 'otherness' or difference to historical material. Colin Kidd has recently outlined ways in which race, scripture and ideology have combined to become influentially important in emerging expressions of Anglo-American Protestant Christianity. At the same time Kidd's work, and a recent essay by Brian Stanley, indicate the 'plastic' and changing nature of concepts of race by the 1920s.[42] Some historians have argued more specifically that religious or theological considerations complicate the issue. As

Geoffrey Oddie observes, in the context of nineteenth-century British evangelical Protestants in India, the 'most important polarity was not to be found in race or culture, but in the individual's morality and relationship with God ... [Therefore] "the other" was not only represented by Orientals, but also by less fortunate [British] country-men.'[43] Troy Boone further notes, in the same vein, that this way of thinking about the 'other' was an equally profound motivation behind Salvation Army missions to both the heathen of the British 'urban underworld' and the heathen in other parts of the world.[44]

To conclude that there were racial overtones in Presbyterian textual and pictorial representations for children seems inescapable. It is difficult, though, to know if these were intentional, unintentional or indeed a case of reading backwards from the present. The evidence is often decidedly ambiguous. For example, selective semi-fictional accounts in *The Break of Day* included such supposedly racist or derogatory references as 'Nigger' the blackbird (in a story on Māori children at Waikaremoana) and an 'ugly sister' (in a story from China).[45] There were quite strong parallels in these stories with a cycle of children's comic strips appearing at the same time in the New Zealand Anglican Board of Mission's magazine *The Reaper*.[46] There the imagery seems overtly stereotyped, paternalistic and condescending. But in both cases these were largely works of fiction, comprising fanciful and creative writing for youngsters, and in which images from nature and real life were readily interwoven. The contemporaneous gumnut babies' stories by Australian writer May Gibbs also come readily to mind in this context. Therefore it can be said that race was present as a category to be grappled with, but that this category may be seen as highly contentious or slippery.

In the context of this discussion, 'poor and needy' children – those perceived to be disadvantaged or different – were not just Māori. They were in all sectors of the dominion's population, both urban and rural. Presbyterian children, influenced by a prevailing evangelical logic, were called to care for all such people, irrespective of race or background. At the same time children continued to receive the message that there were differences between people that were both local and global, that these differences were predicated on a cluster of dualities that included race, and that it was Christianity that could potentially forge unities across differences. In this regard *The Break of Day* perhaps struck a note truer to its heart and intention when, in July 1913, it included the following photograph. The image is contrived and intriguing in terms of its structure; its caption, explicit message and very obvious ironies are all notable.

Discussion of race entails one final consideration: that representations of Māori were typical of prevailing Anglo-Christian mentalities, shaped by missionary thinking and apparatus and by imperial citizenship. In these senses Presbyterian children's

'Māori and Pākehā: All are one in Christ Jesus'. *The Break of Day*, July 1913, 8.

missionary literature was not at all exceptional. Methodist children, for example, read and viewed very similar material through their missionary magazine *The Lotu* and in targeted booklets like John Burton's *Brown Faces: A Missionary Book for Methodist Boys and Girls*.[47] The same was true for Canadian Methodist and Anglican children, who read similar literature.[48] All of these were inheritors of a century-old tradition fostered by British denominations and missionary societies that, from the early nineteenth century, quickly established juvenile missionary literature as a priority for engaging children's interest, imagination and energies. In doing so, they created a body of literature that, among many other things, served to shape knowledge of or attitudes towards the non-Western world. One historian has gone so far as to speculate that the 'formation of prejudice' was the most 'enduring legacy' of missionary societies among the young.[49] There are difficulties in applying this blanket observation to the whole period. By the 1930s New Zealand missionaries and church leaders, like their international counterparts, were beginning to develop a more diverse set of theological and political ideas about the non-Western world. Consequently, these ideas found their way into literary and pedagogical materials aimed at children. But Eurocentric attitudes prevailed, nonetheless. In the Canadian context, for example, it was still asserted in the late 1930s that Western Christians had the right to 'lead and instruct the indigenous and under-privileged races of this country' on the basis of superior religion, technology, history and culture.[50] Children's missionary literature throughout the British world simply reflected and maintained a long-lived confidence.

Conclusion

All of this serves to highlight the fact that, in any age, children and adults alike live within and negotiate their way between particular modes of thinking and living. This was no less true for early twentieth-century Pākehā Presbyterian children than it is today. Whether in school or Sunday school, Presbyterian children and settler children in general grew up learning to differentiate their 'world' from the 'worlds' of both indigenous Māori and other non-white societies beyond the colony's shores. They were 'part of the British family and could be proud of it'.⁵¹ Christianity held itself out as being able to break down such differences, but the lingering suspicion is that notions of cultural superiority predominated. Attitudes and imagery endured over successive decades; autonomy (including ordination) for Presbyterian Māori was not properly gained until the 1950s and 1960s. Evidence from Presbyterian missionary application records indicates that religious attitudes formed in childhood had a long legacy into adulthood.⁵² So the images presented to children over a number of decades possibly served to help create the conservative-minded adults who were relatively slow to move with respect to Māori ordination and autonomy within the Presbyterian Church of Aotearoa New Zealand.

If racism and the maintenance of prejudice were partly a legacy of this literature, then that needs to be acknowledged. At the same time, it is important to recognise that modes of thinking and living do change over time. Churches and state alike have engaged for the last three decades with a more determinedly bicultural journey in Aotearoa New Zealand. In educational circles, for example, bicultural elements and institutions are now commonplace, and middle New Zealand is often overly self-congratulatory about how much progress has been made. The rhetoric of *The Break of Day* inhabits an altogether other world when viewed from the present. Yet the journey is far from over, and the two worlds of tangata whenua and tauiwi are far from being reconciled on anywhere near equal terms. In light of the media furore over Hone Harawira in late 2009, for example, newspaper columnist Chris Trotter observed that 'New Zealand's official "bicultural" ideology enjoins its citizens to walk in two worlds with understanding and respect. But reality tells a very different story. Māori New Zealanders have no choice when it comes to walking in two worlds. Pākehā New Zealanders do – and most of us choose to stay in our own. It's enough to make a saint swear.'⁵³ If Christianity is one force that can potentially bring people together, and that would certainly be debated by many in this context, then the case of *The Break of Day* should remind us how easily Christianity and culture can be conflated, and how far we still have to travel on our bicultural journey.

Endnotes

1. 'Society for the Elevation of the Maoris in Otago', in *New Zealand Missionary Record* (NZMR), July 1883: 109.
2. 'Our Maori Population', in NZMR, May 1883: 92.
3. 'A Letter from Sister Kearney', in *Break of Day* (BD), November 1939: 4.
4. BD, February 1940: cover.
5. A K Davidson, 'The Interaction of Missionary and Colonial Christianity in Nineteenth Century New Zealand', in *Studies in World Christianity* 2.2 (1996): 145–66.
6. H May, 'Mapping some landscapes of colonial-global childhood', in *European Early Childhood Education Research Journal* 9.2 (2001): 5–20, 11.
7. Minute Book of the Presbytery of Auckland, 1856–1857 and 1869, 15 October 1856, MS 1501.P928, Box 1, Auckland Institute and Museum Library, Auckland.
8. *Proceedings of the General Assembly of the Presbyterian Church of New Zealand* (PCNZ PGA), 20 November 1861, 14; 25 November 1862, 22–3.
9. P Matheson, '1840–1870: The Settler Church', in Dennis McEldowney (ed.), *Presbyterians in Aotearoa, 1840–1990* (Wellington: Presbyterian Church of New Zealand, 1990), 38–9; J R Elder, *The History of the Presbyterian Church of New Zealand* (Christchurch: Presbyterian Bookroom, 1940), 93–5, 407 and 413; P Oettli, *God's Messenger: J.F. Riemenschneider and Racial Conflict in 19th Century New Zealand* (Wellington: Huia Publishers, 2008) 182-214, 223-33.
10. F K Prochaska, 'Little Vessels: Children in the Nineteenth-Century English Missionary Movement', in *Journal of Imperial and Commonwealth History* 6.2 (1978): 103–18; B Stanley, 'Missionary Regiments for Immanuel's Service: Juvenile Missionary Organization in English Sunday Schools, 1841–1865', in D Wood (ed.), *The Church and Childhood*, Studies in Church History Volume 31 (Oxford: Ecclesiastical History Society/Blackwell Publishers, 1994): 391–403.
11. D Keen, '"Feeding the Lambs": The Influence of Sunday Schools on the Socialization of Children in Otago and Southland, 1848–1901', PhD thesis, University of Otago, 1999, 290–3; G Troughton, 'Religion, Churches and Childhood in New Zealand, c.1900–1940', in *New Zealand Journal of History* 40.1 (2006): 39–56.
12. R Waddell, 'The Sabbath-school and Missions', in NZMR, February 1884: 44–9.
13. For a wider discussion see H Morrison, '"Little Vessels" or "Little Soldiers": New Zealand Protestant children, foreign missions, religious pedagogy and empire, c.1880s–1930's', in *Paedagogica Historica* 47.3 (2011): 303–21.
14. J Brooke, 'Providentialist Nationalism and Juvenile Mission Literature, 1840–1870', paper presented at the Henry Martyn Centre Research Seminar, Cambridge University, 2006: http://henrymartyn.dns-systems.net/media/documents/archive%20seminar%20papers%202003-2009/providentialist%20nationalism%20and%20juvenile%20mission%20literature%201840-1870.pdf (accessed 9 January 2012).
15. H Morrison, 'The "joy and heroism of doing good": *The New Zealand Missionary Record* and Late-Nineteenth-Century Protestant Children's Missionary Support', in *Journal of New Zealand Literature* 28.2 (2010): 158-182.
16. Extracted from the PCNZ PGA, 1909–1921.
17. BD, December 1910: 11; April 1911: 12.
18. Ibid, October 1913: 4.
19. Ibid, June 1909: 7–8; December 1921: 3.
20. Ibid, July 1937: 5.

21 Ibid, February 1909: 9; October 1914: 9; November 1924: 9; October 1910: 14; June 1911: 7; September 1936: 5; July 1937: 6; October 1939: 2.
22 M Jolly, '"To Save the Girls for Brighter and Better Lives": Presbyterian Missions and Women in the South of Vanuatu, 1848–1870', in *Journal of Pacific History* 26.1 (1991): 27–48; L Nyhagen Predelli, 'Sexual Control and the Remaking of Gender: The Attempt of Nineteenth-Century Protestant Norwegian Women to Export Western Domesticity to Madagascar', in *Journal of Women's History* 12.2 (2000): 81–103.
23 BD, July 1914: 5–6.
24 Ibid, October 1913: 5.
25 May, 'Mapping some landscapes of colonial-global childhood': 11–12.
26 BD, July 1937: 4.
27 Ibid, February 1929: 10.
28 Ibid, October 1913: 5 and 12.
29 'Our Maori Missions', in BD, July 1937: 1.
30 'Fatal impact' as a explanatory concept is most commonly linked, in the New Zealand context, with two now contested works: A Moorhead, *The Fatal Impact: An Account of the Invasion of the South Pacific 1767–1840* (Harmondsworth: Penguin, 1968) and H M Wright, *New Zealand, 1769–1840: Early Years of Western Contact* (Cambridge, Massachusetts: Harvard University Press, 1967).
31 'Tarore', in BD, June 1912: 8–9; 'The Story of Tarore', in BD, April 1930: 6–8 and May 1930: 6–7.
32 J Cowley, *Tarore and Her Book* (Wellington: Bible Society of New Zealand, 2009); New Zealand Bible Society, 'The Tarore Story': http://biblesociety.org.nz/the-tarore-story (accessed 9 January 2012); A Hedge, 'Pilgrimage around the Waikato': http://standrewcambridge.wordpress.com/2009/06/25/pilgrimage-around-the-waikato (accessed 9 January 2012)
33 P J Lineham, *Bible and Society: A Sesquicentennial History of the Bible Society in New Zealand* (Wellington: Bible Society in New Zealand, 1996), 128–9.
34 BD, July 1912: 3–4; August 1912: 4; and September 1912: 4–5.
35 S Oliver, 'Te Rauparaha, Tamihana – Biography', from the *Dictionary of New Zealand Biography*, in *Te Ara – the Encyclopedia of New Zealand*: www.teara.govt.nz/en/biographies/1t75/1 (accessed 9 January 2012).
36 'The Story of Peka Hinau', in BD, September 1936: 3–4. Story attributed to the Rev. John Laughton.
37 'Editorial', in BD, July 1933: 2.
38 Letter, Mortimer-Jones to Gladys, 21 May 1909, Mortimer-Jones Correspondence, KIN008/1/4, Kinder Memorial Library, St John's College, Auckland.
39 BD, September 1930: 16. 'Busy Bees' was a children's missionary support venture within the Presbyterian Church that was first begun by the daughters of an Invercargill minister in 1909.
40 Ibid, September 1909: 10.
41 E Said, *Orientalism* (New York: Vintage, 1979); E Said, *Culture and Imperialism* (New York: Knopf, 1993).
42 C Kidd, *The Forging of Races: Race and Scripture in the Protestant World, 1600–2000* (Cambridge: Cambridge University Press, 2006); B Stanley, 'From the "poor heathen" to "the glory and honour of all nations": Vocabularies of Race and Custom in Protestant Missions, 1844–1928', in *International Bulletin of Missionary Research* 34.1 (2010): 3–10.

43 G A Oddie, '"Orientalism" and British Protestant Missionary Constructions of India in the Nineteenth Century', in *South Asia* 17.2 (1994): 27–42, 29–30.
44 T Boone, 'Remaking "Lawless Lads and Licentious Girls": The Salvation Army and the Regeneration of Empire', in J C Hawley (ed.), *Christian Encounters with the Other* (New York: New York University Press, 1998): 103–21.
45 'One Little Bird that Talked', in BD, July 1912: 5; 'A Picnic in Maoriland', in BD, April 1930: 12–13.
46 *The Reaper*, 1930–1933.
47 J W Burton, *Brown Faces: A Missionary Book for Methodist Boys and Girls* (Melbourne: Methodist Missionary Society of Australasia, 1914(?)).
48 For example, *The Canadian Church Juvenile* (Anglican) and *The Sunbeam* (Methodist), specifically for children, and *The Missionary Outlook* (Methodist), with dedicated children's content.
49 Prochaska, 'Little Vessels': 110 and 113–14.
50 'Report of the Indian and Eskimo Residential School Commission', in *Proceedings of the General Synod*, Anglican Church of Canada, 1937, 422.
51 Morrison, '"Little Vessels" or "Little Soldiers"', 316.
52 'Presbyterian Missionary Candidates', Series 3, Presbyterian Church of New Zealand Foreign Missions Committee, GA0001, Archives Research Centre, Presbyterian Church of Aotearoa New Zealand, Dunedin.
53 C Trotter, 'Failure of bicultural ideal to "take" should worry Key', in *Otago Daily Times*, 13 November 2009, 9.

Chapter Nine

The Rise and Fall of Women Field Workers within the Presbyterian Māori Mission, 1907–1970

Lachy Paterson

From its arrival in New Zealand in the 1840s the Presbyterian Church provided missionaries to Māori, but until the late nineteenth century those efforts had been largely underfunded and a low priority for the church. Unlike the Anglican, Wesleyan Methodist and Roman Catholic churches, which had come to New Zealand as missionary endeavours, the Presbyterian Church was a settler church. Rev. James Duncan in the Foxton area was the only missioner to Māori from 1843 to 1870, followed by the semi-independent Rev. Honoré and Mr George Milson in the Whanganui, Rangitikei and Manawatū districts.[1] All experienced limited success.[2] The southern Presbyterian Church sponsored some missionary work to Māori, such as that of Rev. Wohlers on Ruapuke Island, but most of its missionary activity was devoted to foreign missions, or to the Chinese gold miners of Central Otago.[3] The Māori Mission, as a seriously organised venture, really began with the employment of Henry Fletcher as a missionary in Taupō in 1890.[4] However, it was Pākehā women who largely spearheaded the subsequent expansion of the Presbyterian mission into the remote Māori communities of the central North Island.

The Presbyterian Maori Mission Committee (PMMC) first employed women in 1907, and due to a conjuncture of factors discussed below women quickly became the mainstay of the

'The First Hut'. Nurse Euphemia Doull in her first hut at Matahi in the early 1920s. It was not unusual for the women who founded mission stations to be housed in rather substandard buildings. GAG/GA15 Maori Mission Committee 496/7 A-58-39. Archives Research Centre, Presbyterian Church of Aotearoa New Zealand.

Mission's workforce, employed as deaconesses, teachers, nurses and assistants. These women were sometimes provided with leadership opportunities not available to most women workers. For four decades, the mission would not have been able to operate had it not been for their efforts. The same was true for the church's foreign missionary projects. However, in the changing circumstances of the post-war years, the mission (which became Te Hinota Maori (THM) in the early 1950s) began to see women's services as less relevant. This chapter seeks to explain the rise of Pākehā women workers within the PMMC's mission stations,[5] their marginalisation and the eventual end to their employment in 1970.

Women as missionaries in the late Victorian and Edwardian eras

Increasing numbers of single women within the Protestant world were attracted to the mission field from the mid- to late nineteenth century, their involvement supported by widely held Victorian perceptions of intrinsic feminine qualities and roles. The heavily gendered world of that time saw women's 'innate' qualities as being morally superior to those of men, allowing them to take on more influential roles within the church, particularly in campaigns of moral regeneration and improvement.[6] These roles, of course, did not entail attacking the essential gender differences within the church and society of the time,[7] but seeking to improve society by infusing it with more feminine values.[8] Women were also seen as being particularly well suited to nurturing roles, such as nursing, teaching and proselytising women and children. As campaigners sought to improve either their own societies or those of other people, this 'women's work' became increasingly desirable. The normative and ideal role for women during this period was as wives and mothers, and spinsterhood was seen as unnatural or selfish.[9] But for women who were yet to marry, or who chose not to marry, employment within the church to undertake nurturing and useful roles was an acceptable and respectable option,[10] and preferable to other limited employment opportunities.

Two other commonly held late nineteenth-century beliefs also helped draw women to missionary work: first, the idea that women could cope with celibacy better than men, and second, Victorian ideals of personal heroism and sacrifice, which encouraged women to give up the comfortable lives they were accustomed to. Paid missionary work was only available to unmarried women, so women wanting to pursue this career were expected to remain celibate. As Olive Banks has argued, Victorians believed that women naturally had a low sexual drive; some even 'denied the existence of any natural sexual feeling in women at all'.[11] For some women who preferred celibacy to matrimony, missionary work was not only a suitable option but also a morally superior one.[12] If eschewing the pleasures of the marriage bed was not a heroic sacrifice for women, then many other aspects of missionary work could be. As Judith Rowbotham has stated, 'heroism was ... a quality of profound significance' for Victorians, although for women, this tended to be 'related to a more passive endurance and hardship'.[13] As single women became involved as missionary employees in the late nineteenth century,[14] their heroism and sacrifice were utilised in the literature of their parent bodies to inspire prospective missionary candidates and raise funds.

The perception that a need for church-sponsored 'women's work' existed, combined with the desire of women to undertake this work, saw a number of institutes established in Europe, North America and Australasia to train women as deaconesses: ordained women who could undertake some clerical duties.[15] Although the New Zealand Presbyterian Church's first deaconesses, employed for city congregational work, were trained overseas,[16] by 1904 the church had followed the overseas trend and established the

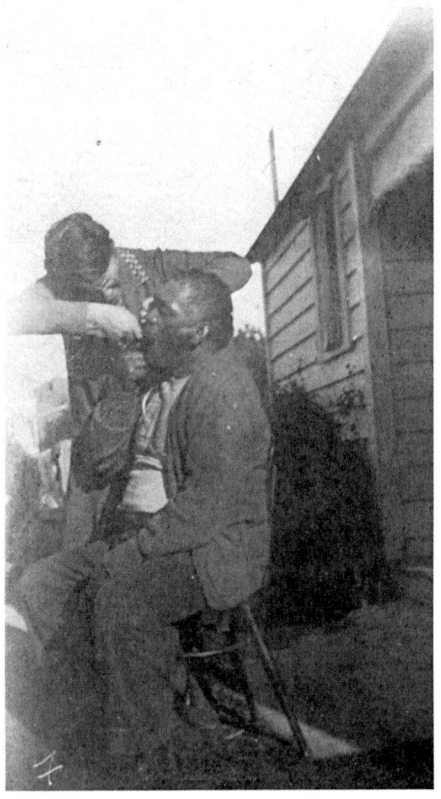

'The Missionary at Work'. Sister Annie Henry, also known as Hihita, was unusual in serving at just one mission station for her whole career, at Ruatāhuna from 1916 to 1948. Her many roles included running the post office, teaching, preaching, nursing, making coffins and pulling teeth. P-A21 Album 1, No. 54. Archives Research Centre, Presbyterian Church of Aotearoa New Zealand.

Presbyterian Women's Training Institute (later the Deaconess College) in Dunedin, offering a two-year course.[17] The course included training in two professions considered respectable for women, nursing and teaching,[18] as well as considerable theological material,[19] preparing women to become 'set apart as deaconesses' for work within either congregations, missions or institutions such as orphanages.[20]

The initial 'experiment'

In 1907 the PMMC engaged two deaconesses: Miss Jane Spence, known as Sister Alison, and Mrs Emare Poraumati.[21] The committee had subsidised Sister Alison's training at the Institute, although it was initially unsure whether she would become a field missionary or a teacher at the Māori girls' school at Turakina. Despite initial opposition from male missionaries, the PMMC undertook the 'experiment'[22] of employing Sister Alison under Rev. Fletcher at Taupō. Soon after, they employed Mrs Poraumati, a Te Arawa woman, who had worked at Tokaanu, also under the authority of Fletcher. Although she had not been formally trained at Dunedin, Emare Poraumati had previously worked among Māori for the Salvation Army.[23] Despite describing its employment of the deaconesses as an experiment, the PMMC was hardly being innovative from an international perspective.[24] Single American women had worked as missionaries to Native Americans from the 1820s.[25] Protestant women from Britain were employed in foreign missions from the 1860s – the first from New Zealand in 1876[26] – and in Canada and Australia women missionary workers were among indigenous peoples by the 1880s and 1890s respectively.[27]

Despite the precedents, the PMMC 'experiment' was hardly a success. Fletcher, offering cheap board to Sister Alison, expected her to largely assist his wife with household chores.[28] Sister Alison then boarded with native school teachers, but the two missionaries fell out over a number of issues. Sister Alison wanted to treat sick Māori in portable tents, but Fletcher quite rightly realised that if a Māori died in a tent or building, other sick Māori would refuse to be treated in that place.[29] Fletcher complained about an article in the Presbyterian magazine *Outlook* Sister Alison had written on the availability of medicines for Māori,[30] and generally did little to advance her work.[31] The PMMC, having received a number of letters from both complaining of each other, investigated. Despite Fletcher's assertion that Sister Alison was 'not the person I would choose for work among the Maori'[32] it moved Sister Alison to Tiroa, in the King Country, under the direction of the Taumarunui missionary Rev. Ward. Although always under the direction of a male missionary, Sister Alison remained a missionary in the Taumarunui area until her retirement in the 1940s, suggesting that her problems at Taupō concerned personalities rather than her abilities.

Mrs Poraumati was a keen evangelist, but less capable at looking after her own health or fulfilling the bureaucratic requirements of the Presbyterian Church. In the early twentieth century, Tokaanu, at the southern end of Lake Taupō, was very poor: if crops failed, the local Māori had little to eat, often leading to serious illness. Mrs Poraumati used all her energy to treat the sick and spent her salary on feeding the hungry, to the detriment of her own health. As she wrote to the PMMC, 'I feel very much ran [sic] down but while I stop here I cannot have proper rest I feel I must go out and help my people'.[33] The committee authorised a small fund for feeding the hungry, but Mrs Poraumati was unable to keep the receipts needed for reimbursement.[34] Her illnesses continued, and she resigned in 1909 after a review of missionary work in the Taupō region decided to close the Tokaanu station.

The benefits of female employment

Despite the less than auspicious start, there were compelling reasons for the PMMC to continue employing women as it expanded its operations. It appears that a disinclination among men to become involved in religious activity may have been both a national and even an international problem. In 1907 the *Outlook* reprinted a *Melbourne Messenger* article extolling the Presbyterian Brotherhood of America, and noted that in Australia, 'one of the most glaring defects in our Church life is that so few of the men of vigour and influence are taking any part in Christian work'.[35] Two years later, in an editorial entitled 'More Men Wanted', the *Outlook* suggested that 'the employment of sisters will not meet the city's wants nor answer the city's cry. What is being done for the men, old and young, who never darken a church's door? Practically nothing.'[36] It was difficult for the PMMC to attract trained men, especially as it was competing with the Home Mission[37] and the more glamorous Foreign Mission, as well as regular parish ministry. Women filled the vacuum.

Women were useful in opening up new mission fields: James Irwin suggests that women were able to enter areas that would have been barred to males,[38] especially in areas such as the Urewera and King Country, where the injustices of the nineteenth-century Land Wars and land confiscation were still felt keenly. The women's initial lack of mana meant that they did not threaten existing male hierarchies within Māori society. Their emphasis on visiting women and children within their homes and tending the sick, and in establishing schools, allowed them an entrance into tribal society without disrupting its politics. Sister Alison recorded:

> On my visits to Old Tiroa where there was a peculiar old meeting house I was allowed to take photographs, hold services, conduct burial rites and mix freely with a very conservative tribe. There were men here who could remember cannibalism, and had never worn complete European dress. They tolerated my ministrations because I was a woman who didn't matter much.[39]

However, it is clear that some women did matter. When a party of PMMC staff entered Maungapōhatu to establish John Laughton as the missionary there, Sister Annie, who had started the nearby Ruatāhuna mission a year earlier, accompanied them. As one of the party explained:

> There were some anxious moments on our arrival, since it was surmised that we might be agents of the police coming in to take their men away to the war. But a woman met us on the top in front of the meeting house, and then a girl named Polly recognised Sister Annie, and after that all was well, and we were made welcome.[40]

It would thus be an overstatement to suggest that women missionaries were totally without influence. Māori certainly appreciated their 'women's work', and this allowed them to establish mission stations where men may have found it more difficult.

Women workers were also cheap. Sacrifice was part of mission, and this included remuneration. As Irwin, a former employee, stated, the PMMC 'treated their missionaries shabbily, and shamelessly took advantage of their "call" to this mission field by paying them barely enough to cover the assorted requirements of life'.[41] This was true for both sexes, and in 1926 the matter was sufficiently pressing to concern the Presbyterian Women's Missionary Union, which at its conference recommended 'that no more Maori Mission workers should be appointed till the salaries of the present workers are increased'. This perturbed the PMMC convener, who reminded the committee that it had increased the salaries of the male missionaries: 'in his judgement the salaries of the Deaconesses with the perquisites they receive are quite adequate. However, it is manifestly impossible, even if it were necessary, at the present time to consider any further increase of salaries confronted as the Committee is with a shortage of revenue.'[42]

In 1926 the Revs Ward and Laughton were paid £300 yearly.[43] When a male divinity student was appointed to assist Rev. Laughton in Taupō in 1928, his salary was £230. In comparison, Molly Phairn, helping Sister Annie at Ruatāhuna in 1929, received only £100, and when she took over the running of the Matahi station in 1931, her salary was raised to a mere £120.[44] When the women missionaries' salaries are compared with similar female work being undertaken at the time, they still fall short. In 1921 the salaries of female native school teachers in the Nūhaka and Urewera mission areas ranged between £160 and £320, averaging £222. By 1929, the range was £190 to £345, averaging £274.[45] In 1921 the basic deaconess salary sat at £120, with annual £10 increments up to £160. In 1924 Miss Bruce, an assistant teacher at the Matahi Mission School, received just £70, although after complaining that this was insufficient to live on, the salary was raised to £100. By 1932 the now Sister Bruce was receiving the 'normal deaconess

Miss Milroy worked for many years as a teacher at the Kawerau Mission School, undertaking other missionary work outside of school hours that included working with women, for example in sewing instruction. This image was taken in 1949. Album P-A36 Album 2, No. 165. Archives Research Centre, Presbyterian Church of Aotearoa New Zealand.

salary' of £160.[46] The gender wage differential remained into the 1960s. In 1965 Miss Milroy, head of the Kawerau Mission School and Mission, received £555 per year, while Rev. Hawea made £900.[47] While it could be argued that the men had families to support, some of the women, notably Sisters Annie, Edith, Ross and Kearney, fostered or adopted Māori children.[48] Certainly Sister Kearney expressed anxiety to Rev. Laughton about her inability to afford the education she wanted for her adopted son.[49]

Notwithstanding the inferior wages, the attractions of mission work were sufficiently strong for women to join. For example, Sister Brown, a trained nurse who then graduated from the Presbyterian Women's Training Institute, wrote: 'I entered college, I believe, in obedience to a divine call, and in applying for this position I am endeavouring to follow God's will as far as I can see it'.[50] The religious call was sometimes inculcated from an early age. Mary Coombe, for example, explained:

Born into a Christian home, brought up in a family who loved and served the Church, I became a member of the Presbyterian Church in my eighteenth year. As a child in the Busy Bees, I became interested in the Missionary work of the Church. Bible Class and G.A. fostered my interest but it was [not] until I was at University that I felt called to offer myself for Maori Mission Work. I was accepted and was for almost three years at Waikaremoana as an Assistant. Wishing to take the Deaconess Training, I resigned and took the course at Deaconess College with the hope of returning to Maori work.[51]

The expansion of the mission offered other attractions. In 1914 the PMMC sent the second institute graduate, Jessie Alexander (Sister Jessie) to Nūhaka to win back Māori souls from Mormonism. This time, the deaconess worked directly under the PMMC and not a local male missionary: Sister Jessie was in charge of the station, assisted by Edith Walker and May Gardiner (later Sister Edith and Sister May). The female community was also sometimes bolstered by women native school teachers who boarded at the mission house, and in 1919 Sister Jessie's sister, Nurse Alexander, joined the mission to undertake medical work and thereby free the deaconesses for other duties. Thus, in addition to doing God's work, the missions offered women opportunities for leadership not readily available elsewhere,[52] as well as a lifestyle firmly situated within a feminine environment.

Race and gender in the mission stations

The period from 1914 to 1934 was a phase of intense expansion for the PMMC, spearheaded mainly by women, principally into the Urewera district and the Eastern Bay of Plenty. As Table 1 illustrates, the PMMC established fifteen new stations (including mission schools and a mission hospital) in just two decades, in addition to its existing stations at Taupō and Taumarunui. Apart from Maungapōhatu under John Laughton, women founded all the new stations; some established more than one station. In many cases, particularly in the Urewera, the stations were isolated, and

Table 1: New Presbyterian missions, schools and hospitals, 1914–1934

Station	Region	Founded	First head
Nūhaka	East Coast	1914	Sister Jessie Alexander
Ruatāhuna	Urewera	1917	Sister Annie Henry
Te Whāiti	Urewera	1917	Miss Eva Jack and Mrs Annie Gorrie
Maungapōhatu	Urewera	1918	Rev. John Laughton
Waiōhau	Urewera	1918	Miss Elsie Webber
Matahī	Urewera	1921	Nurse/Sister Euphemia Doull
Nūhaka Hospital	East Coast	1921	Nurse Lilian Alexander
Waikaremoana	Urewera	1921	Sister Jessie Alexander
Whakakī	East Coast	1922	Sister Edith Walker
Waimana	Urewera	1922	Sister Aileen Arthur
Te Teko	Eastern Bay of Plenty	1926	Sister Tiaki (Miss Jack)
Ōpōtiki	Eastern Bay of Plenty	1929	Sister Jessie Alexander
Kawerau	Eastern Bay of Plenty	1930	Mrs Annie Gorrie
Reporoa	Rotorua	1934	Miss M Wilson
Tokaanu	Taupō	1934	Sister Edith Walker

began in rather primitive conditions. Where a native school already existed, such as at Nūhaka, incoming missionaries might expect hospitality, but in Ruatāhuna, for example, Sister Annie's 'first house was a mere shelter of palings cut from bush trees', and she cooked outside on a camp oven.[53] Although women were largely responsible for establishing the new mission stations, as time went on male missionaries began to replace them, especially in the less isolated stations. For example, Sister Annie remained in charge of the remote Ruatāhuna station for thirty-one years before being replaced on her retirement by Rev. Madill in 1948. Similarly, relatively isolated Matahi and Waiōhau had a number of female heads for twenty-three and twenty-eight years respectively before being taken over by a male. In contrast, men were appointed to the less isolated stations of Te Teko and Ōpōtiki within five and six years respectively. When some women missionaries established stations they lived initially in raupō whare or tents, whereas male missionaries with their families wanted more comfortable manses to live in. By the early twentieth century the two original stations of Taupō and Taumarunui were no longer isolated Māori villages but towns with substantial Pākehā populations. When Rev. Fletcher resigned in 1925, Sister Jessie briefly took control of the Taupō station, but was soon after replaced by Rev. Laughton. Women missionaries took control two more times for brief periods, but the mission was largely managed by men. The charge of Taumarunui changed hands a number of times, in a succession of male missionaries.[54] It can thus be said that women missionaries, if they were not assistants to male missionaries, tended to predominate in the smaller, more remote mission stations.

Eileen Isabel Davidson served at Ruatāhuna from 1932 to 1937. She was ordained in 1937 as Sister Isabel, but married soon after. In this photograph she is giving a Sunday school lesson outside. P-A21 Album 1, No. 119. Archives Research Centre, Presbyterian Church of Aotearoa New Zealand.

Mrs Poraumati was a rare Māori face within the PMMC's mission staff. The Committee would have liked to have employed more Māori staff, especially because its Turakina Maori Girls' School was releasing a small cadre of educated girls each year. In 1914 the PMMC, with donations from Pākehā congregations, supported Miss Kirihaehae Iharaira, an ex-Turakina student, in her first year at the Training Institute.[55] However, after one year's training, the *Outlook* reported that '"Kiri" ... was compelled by her parents to contract a marriage in the interests of her tribe'. Nevertheless, the magazine was 'glad to learn that she is striving to do Christian work among her people at Mokai'.[56] It was many years before another Māori woman undertook the deaconess training, and then only one, Meri Kahukura, ever completed it; she served in the early 1960s in Wellington before having to relinquish her employment for marriage. Although a number of young Turakina women worked for short periods as assistants, practically all the PMMC's female employees were Pākehā.

From the 1920s the PMMC began employing Māori men. In 1928, a young Maungapōhatu man joined Laughton at Taupō with a view to training as a missionary.[57] However, despite a 'full confession and expression of repentance', he was unable to stick to the committee's strict anti-drinking rule, and resigned in 1932.[58] The committee had more luck with Hemi Potatau, a young convert from Nūhaka and Sister Edith's foster child from the age of fourteen. After his ordination as a minister in the early 1930s, he was based at Waimana to 'work the country between Te Onepu and Opotiki' from a motorcycle.[59] In terms of rank within the mission, gender trumped race. Although Māori women assistants were sometimes paid the most minimal wages,[60] there does not appear to have been any significant differences between the salaries of similarly qualified Māori and Pākehā men. Māori men earned more than Pākehā women and, if ordained, were their superiors.

From Table 2 it is clear that Pākehā women were the mainstay of rural mission work well into the 1950s, despite the fact that the numbers of Pākehā women employees shown here is boosted somewhat by the inclusion of trainees from the institute who were

Table 2: Presbyterian mission/synod field missionaries 1900–1960, by half-decade.

	1900s		1910s		1920s		1930s		1940s		1950s		1960
Pākehā men	2	3	3	5	4	5	8	6	8	12	9	6	4
Pākehā women	0	2	5	14	20	20	24	28	31	29	16	16	7
Māori men	0	0	0	1	1	1	3	2	1	4	5	8	10
Māori women	0	0	0	0	1	1	1	1	2	3	0	5	0

Source: Data derived from J G Laughton, *From Forest Trail to City Street: The Story of the Presbyterian Church Among the Maori People* (Christchurch: Presbyterian Bookroom, 1961).

gaining experience over their summer holidays. Female employment peaked in the late 1930s and 1940s and then declined from the 1950s, a trend matched by Pākehā male missionaries. In contrast, numbers of Māori men increased in the 1950s, until by 1960 they were the largest grouping within the synod's employees.

Although a number of Māori women gained employment, they worked, apart from the deaconess Meri Kahukura, only for short periods as assistants in the schools and missions. By 1965, the synod had eleven Māori ministers, and only two deaconesses engaged in parish work, at Waiohau and Wairoa. In 1969, the Waiohau and Kawerau stations were merged with Te Teko under a male Māori minister, effectively spelling the end of women as independent agents. This remained the state of affairs until 1970, when Miss Milroy was tragically killed in a car crash and Sister Ross resigned, thus ending Pākehā women's involvement in Presbyterian Māori missionary work.

One might suppose that the availability of more employment opportunities for middle-class Pākehā women in the immediate post-war period contributed to the decline in Pākehā field workers in the rural Presbyterian Māori missions, or that the idealism on which missionary and religious work fed lost its appeal in the aftermath of two world wars and a depression. On the contrary, as seen in Table 3, women graduates emerged from the Deaconess College at a greater proportion after World War Two than before: twenty-one deaconesses were ordained between 1950 and 1954. Thus it can be inferred that women still felt a call to religious work.[61] What is more striking,

Table 3: Ordained deaconesses undertaking rural work for the Presbyterian Māori Mission Committee/Synod

	1900s		1910s		1920s		1930s		1940s		1950s		1960–1962
Total ordained	0	12	13	5	12	8	12	10	14	16	21	18	6
Māori missions	0	1	1	2	6	4	10	3	5	5	2	0	0
Percentage in Māori missions	0	8.3	7.7	40	50	50	83	30	36	31	9.5	0	0

Source: Data derived from J D Salmond, *By Love Serve: The Story of the Order of Deaconesses of the Presbyterian Church of New Zealand* (Christchurch: Presbyterian Bookroom, 1962).

perhaps, is that the numbers of deaconesses who joined the Māori Mission's rural staff were strong from the late 1910s through the 1940s, and then dried up in the 1950s. From 1955 to 1959, only one newly ordained deaconess joined the Māori Synod staff, but as a city rather than a rural missionary. This indicates either that the Māori Mission was less desirable as a missionary calling for women than other roles, or that the Māori Synod chose not to employ women, or a combination of both.

Male attitudes to female workers

The end of World War Two ushered in a number of changes that impacted on the running of the Presbyterian Māori missions and the availability of work for Pākehā women workers. First, power had largely devolved to local male missionaries. Rev. Laughton had been appointed as superintendent of the missions in 1933, and in 1938 transferred to Whakatāne, 'where he would be free to devote his whole time to the guidance and the upbuilding of the whole work throughout the mission'.[62] Immediately after the war, an influx of Pākehā missionaries joined the missions, and although the number of Pākehā women employees always exceeded that of men, increasingly the men saw the women's contribution as less valuable. This is perhaps exemplified by the mission's decision to replace Sister Kearney at Waikaremoana in 1950. As the mission secretary wrote confidentially to her replacement, 'Without wishing to depreciate in any way Sister Kearney's significant work in Waikaremoana it is felt that the Maori work and the work amongst the Europeans living in the Hydro-Electric Scheme villages will provide much scope for a male worker and there are likely to be situations where a male worker would be able to give better service'.[63]

A letter from Jack Smith to the mission secretary in the same year further questioned:

> What is to be our future policy? Are we to continue with the situation where we are required to place two women workers in a station in view of the loneliness? Would it not be wiser to work out a policy of strengthening the work with more men? ... I fully appreciate what the women workers have done in the past but are we realistic enough in face of the present Maori situation? There are certain positions on our staff where women can be used, and indeed could only be used but we should map them out.[64]

In late 1950, a debate arose over the rights of the deaconesses within the Māori Mission to conduct the sacraments. In 1934 some deaconesses had been included on an official list of Presbyterian ministers entitled to conduct marriages. This led some deaconesses to believe that they also had the right to conduct the sacrament of baptism.[65] After the general assembly of 1950, at which Rev. Fred Robertson, a congregational minister, had spoken against this 'horrible thing', Sister Kearney wrote to the PMMC for clarification. By then, she was the only woman who claimed this 'right'.[66] The mission investigated the practice, and issued a circular instructing that 'in no case should the Sacrament of Baptism be administered by a Deaconess'.[67] It reassured the following assembly that, despite the misunderstanding, no deaconess had committed the greater offense of administering the Lord's supper.[68]

Despite the Presbyterian Church in 1965 for the first time ordaining a woman with full ministerial powers, an attitude of restricting women to 'women's work' persisted in the synod. Around 1965 a confidential document entitled 'Training of Women for Church Vocations in the Maori Synod' stated 'There does not appear to be a place for Deaconesses as ministers of the

Word <u>and</u> Sacraments in the Maori Synod', despite noting that male ministers had to visit parishes run by women to conduct the sacraments. Its reasoning was that despite 'the special contribution [women workers] have to make among the womenfolk, yet Maori men while tolerant in the matter do not respond particularly well to a woman's ministry'.[69] Thus ideas of differing gender roles were alive and well within the post-war church. A need for 'women's work' had been a justification for employing women in the 1900s (although cheapness and the lack of men were also relevant) and for women's part in the pre-war mission expansion. However, the ideas that women's abilities were or should be somehow restricted, and that as missionaries they were something less than men, became reasons to marginalise them as more male workers became available.

The indigenisation of the Māori Mission and Synod

The move to indigenise the Māori branch of the Presbyterian Church was a factor in the decrease of Pākehā employees, including women, from the 1950s. Within the settler world, home missionaries would typically go to new settlements, gather a congregation, build a church and establish a parish within the structure of the church. The mission stage, subsidised by donations, was meant to be temporary; new congregations would ideally gain the capability of funding the work of their own parish and beyond in this respect. It was thus seen as natural that the Māori Mission would evolve either into self-supporting congregations within the parent church or as a more autonomous structure, as had occurred in some overseas missions. It is clear that mission staff and Māori preferred a separate structure. In 1951 the Presbyterian Māori Synod/Te Hinota Māori came into being, gaining full presbyterial powers in 1955. According to Laughton, THM would meet the 'psychological needs' of Māori by providing a Māori space with a Māori leadership.[70]

As more Māori men became available to take ministry positions in the church, Pākehā women workers were sometimes designated as their assistants, in an arrangement not all were happy with. When the mission decided to replace Sister Kearney with Rev. Orange at Waikaremoana in 1950, Sister Kearney became an 'assistant' to Rev. Hemi Potatau at Taumarunui.[71] The relationship between Rev. Potatau and the deaconess began amicably enough. However, the following year Sister Kearney told Laughton that, with regard to a request to answer questions for *The Break of Day*, 'I think that Hemi is "pipped" because I was asked to do this'.[72] In turn, Sister Kearney was not above putting a spin on Potatau's activities. In 1951, she wrote to Laughton that Hemi had £126 from fundraising, suggesting 'I don't think any staff member should keep all that money lying around. I only hope it reaches you safely.' She then stated that Potatau was going to the general assembly as a representative of the Waikato Presbytery, adding 'Mr Muir told me that Hemi asked to be appointed'.[73]

By early 1954 the relationship had clearly deteriorated. Sister Kearney wrote to Laughton forwarding a letter from Rev. Smith, the acting superintendent in 1950, in which he had assured her that although Potatau would be the head, there would be a division of labour at Taumarunui. She noted that:

> There is no mention of me as working under Mr Potatau. I expected when I accepted the position here to be treated as an equal fellow worker. It never occurred to me that Mr Potatau would have the right to order my work once I was established in it. I can honestly say that I have done my utmost to work amicably with Mr & Mrs Potatau but I find that the less we see of each other the more we respect one another.

Sister Kearney stressed that she was 'not a Congregational Deaconess', and felt directly responsible to Rev. Laughton as the superintendent. 'This point should be made clear to Mr Potatau', she suggested.[74] Plagued with ill health, she resigned in early 1956.

Some deaconesses worked well with Māori ministers, and disputes between Pākehā men and women also occurred, but it is also possible to surmise that some Pākehā women who had been used to roles superior to Māori within the church hierarchy felt increasingly insecure in the new indigenising structure.

Although Rev. Laughton, who had effectively run the mission for the previous two decades, served the first two terms as the moderator of THM, the future role of Pākehā workers, including women, within the new structure was naturally problematic. In 1957 the joint committee of the PMMC and THM discussed the 'future policy re Pakeha ministers and deaconesses' and whether 'prospective pakeha field workers' would be accepted into the synod's staff. The issue was referred to the synod: Laughton informed the committee that 'Pakehas would be welcomed on the staff of the Maori Synod as co-workers'.[75] However, his tone strongly suggested that Pākehā would not be seen as the natural leaders of THM, and perhaps could even become peripheral. Ten years later, when there were only 'one minister and three deaconesses on the staff who are pakeha', the synod reported to the National Council of Churches that 'it is considered desirable that the majority of ministers should be Maoris, but non-Maoris are not excluded from serving on the staff if it is considered that they have a contribution to offer in our particular situation'. At a time when 'integration' was still the government's race relations policy, the report stated that 'there is no desire to separate from Europeans, but at the present juncture Maori and Pakeha needs are not identical and therefore must be met in different ways'.[76] Although acknowledging the Pākehā mainstream belief in assimilation or integration, THM saw itself as a Māori organisation. Naturally such a church would have limited room for Pākehā workers, including women, ministering to its people.

The effects of Māori urban migration

Up until the end of the Second World War, the mission's focus had been primarily in rural areas, where the vast majority of Māori lived. However, large numbers of Māori began to shift to towns and cities as the economy boomed, the most rapid growth occurring in the two decades after the war's end. The Department of Māori Affairs actively encouraged Māori migration, targeting young individuals and families. This led the PMMC to reconsider its focus, particularly with regard to single young people. It established hostels in Whakatāne and Auckland, and set up new missions in Auckland, Wellington, Wairoa, Whakatāne and Rotorua, all magnets for migrants from the mission's traditional areas. The mission, and later the synod, also closed some of the more remote stations, and consolidated Waiohau, Te Teko and Kawerau into the single parish of Putauaki.

As noted above, the Pākehā male missionaries tended to gravitate to missions in the larger centres, whereas women workers predominated in the more remote stations. Māori urban migration and the synod's responses to it naturally impacted most on the women who had initiated and run the rural missions. In 1968 Sister Hercus, the principal of the Deaconess College, wrote to the synod enquiring about employment possibilities for her students and 'if there is any defined policy for expansion which could include the service a deaconess could give'.[77] A Breward, the synod's secretary, informed her that 'if I interpret the mind of the Synod correctly, I would say that the possibility is fairly remote, because the Synod's policy is not to employ any more deaconesses'.[78] He wrote back soon after to inform her that he had been wrong, but, although there might be openings for city work, 'with more ministers available for ordinary parish work, and with some of our smaller and more remote stations closing down, there will not be the

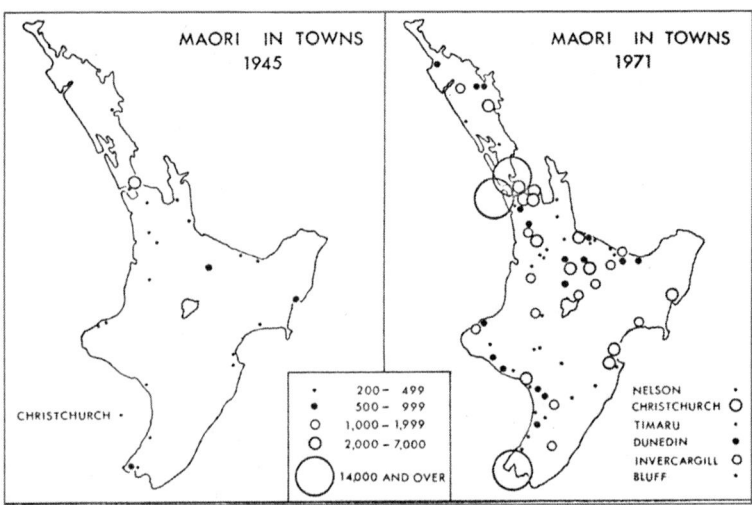

A C Walsh and G Rice, *Cultural Interaction: New Zealand since 1911, South Africa, 1919–1961* (Wellington: Reed, 1975).

openings for Deaconesses to take charge of the parishes and schools that there used to be'.[79]

It is likely that Sister Hercus passed on this discouraging news when discussing options with her graduates. However, THM had not given up completely on employing women. The following year the new secretary, Mac Temara, wrote to Sister Hercus to 'enquire whether any Deaconess would consider Maori parish work'. He reiterated that the mission was now focusing on city work, where 'the conditions should at least be more favourable than those of a few years ago, when many sacrifices had to be made by our staff because of isolation and poor conditions in the country'.[80] There was just one graduate in 1969, who decided not to take a position with THM.[81] Less than a year later, the synod employed no women in its parishes whatsoever.

Conclusion

In 1907, the PMMC wished to expand its field operations from its two existing male missionaries at Taupō and Taumarunui, and employed two women missionaries as deaconesses. The mission's 'experiment' in hiring women followed a wider, international trend within the Protestant world of women undertaking 'women's work', such as teaching, nursing and communicating the gospel to women and children. Although the PMMC would perhaps have preferred more male missionary workers, women, who otherwise had limited employment opportunities, were readily available. They were also cheap, and often could enter into Māori communities with more ease than men. Missionary work appealed to idealistic religious women, especially those who did not relish the existing norm of married life and who cherished opportunities of leadership denied most women of the time. Between 1907 and 1970 the PMMC employed over 100 women, comprising about two-thirds of its total staff. When the PMMC was most active in expanding its mission into the isolated rural Māori communities in Nūhaka, the Urewera and the Eastern Bay of Plenty, it was women who were primarily responsible for ensuring its goals were met.

Despite the success and ubiquity of women missionaries, they became increasingly marginal to the mission's requirements after the Second World War. This was due to a number of reasons. The number of Māori and Pākehā males making themselves available for mission service increased, thereby reducing the opportunities available for women, especially in heading mission stations. It appears also that some male missionaries, despite historical evidence to the contrary, considered women workers to have lesser capabilities, and therefore provided fewer opportunities for them. Because the majority of women workers were Pākehā, their place with the Māori Synod became less straightforward as the synod sought to become more responsive to Māori needs and aspirations through a policy of indigenisation. A natural growth of Māori ministers slowly squeezed Pākehā workers, including women, out of the church. The changing demographic face of Māori further caused the demise of opportunities for Pākehā women field workers. In the past, women had tended to staff the mission's schools and remoter stations. As Māori migrated to the towns and cities, the synod increasingly concentrated its efforts into urban areas, and these positions contracted. Although the number of women training as deaconesses was consistent into the 1960s, from 1950 only two ordained women joined THM's staff. Certainly the new synod had no positive news to impart in 1968 to the principal of the Deaconess College, and when in 1969 it sought to hire a new deaconess it was unsuccessful. Pākehā women thus had less than seven decades' work within the Presbyterian Church's Māori field. What had first begun as an experiment became the mainstay of the PMMC, but faded away as both Māori society and the space for the Māori church transformed in the post-war years.

Endnotes

1 P Matheson, '1840–1870: The Settler Church', in D McEldowney (ed.), *Presbyterians in Aotearoa 1840–1990* (Wellington: Presbyterian Church of New Zealand, 1990), 38–9; J Dickson, *History of the Presbyterian Church of New Zealand* (Dunedin: NZ Bible, Tract, & Book Society, 1899), 45; J R Elder, *The History of the Presbyterian Church of New Zealand* (Christchurch: Presbyterian Bookroom, 1940), 34 and 246. Honoré also worked for the Presbyterian Church in Otago: see Elder, *History of the Presbyterian Church*, 93–4.

2 J Laughton, *From Forest Trail to City Street: The Story of the Presbyterian Church Among the Maori People* (Christchurch: Presbyterian Bookroom, 1961), 7–9.
3 J Collie, *The Story of the Otago Free Church Settlement 1848–1948* (Christchurch: Presbyterian Bookroom, 1948), 156–70.
4 Laughton, *From Forest Trail to City Street*, 9.
5 The PMMC also employed women at Turakina Maori Girls' School, at its two farm schools at Manunui and Te Whaiti and at hostels at Whakatāne and Auckland, as well as for administration and other work. The term 'field worker' here refers to those employed at missions and parishes in Māori villages and in smaller towns, and the three mission schools at Tanatana, Onepū and Matahi.
6 O Banks, *Faces of Feminism: A Study of Feminism as a Social Movement* (Oxford: Martin Robertson, 1981), 7; T O Beidelman, 'Altruism and Domesticity: Images of Missionizing Women among the Church Missionary Society in Nineteenth-Century East Africa', in M T Huber and N C Lutkehau (eds), *Gendered Missions: Women and Men in Missionary Discourse and Practice* (Ann Arbor: University of Michigan Press, 1999):113–43, 124.
7 J Godden, 'Containment and Control: Presbyterian Women and the Missionary Impulse in New South Wales, 1891–1914', in *Women's History Review* 6.1 (1997): 75–93, 77.
8 Banks, *Faces of Feminism*, 91.
9 S Coney, *Standing in the Sunshine: A History of New Zealand Women Since They Won the Vote* (Auckland: Viking, 1993), 15.
10 S C Coleman, '"Come over and help us": White Women, Reform and the Missionary Endeavour in India 1876–1920', MA thesis, University of Canterbury, 2002, 49–50.
11 Banks, *Faces of Feminism*, 71. See also Beidelman, 'Altruism and Domesticity', 124.
12 Banks, *Faces of Feminism*, 71.
13 J Rowbotham, '"Soldiers of Christ?" Images of Female Missionaries in Late Nineteenth-Century Britain: Issues of Heroism and Martyrdom', in *Gender and History* 12.1 (2000): 82–106, 84.
14 Certainly wives of missionaries were active in the mission field from the beginning, but single women were not employed until the 1880s. See E Stock, *The History of the Church Missionary Society: Its Environment, Its Men and Its Work* (London: Church Missionary Society, 1899), 368.
15 K Piercy, 'Patient and Enduring Love: The Deaconess Movement, 1900–1920', in J Stenhouse and J Thomson (eds), *Building God's Own Country: Historical Essays on Religions in New Zealand* (Dunedin: Otago University Press, 2004): 196–208, 197. Other Protestant denominations in New Zealand also established deaconess orders. For example, see M Tennant, 'Pakeha Deaconesses and the New Zealand Methodist Mission to Maori, 1893–1940', in *Journal of Religious History* 23.3 (1999): 309–26.
16 'Waddell, Mrs Christabel', in Register of New Zealand Presbyterian Church Ministers, Deaconesses & Missionaries from 1840: www.archives.presbyterian.org.nz/Page207.htm (accessed 13 November 2007); J D Salmond, *By Love Serve: The Story of the Order of Deaconesses of the Presbyterian Church of New Zealand* (Christchurch: Presbyterian Bookroom, 1962), 11–13.
17 Salmond, *By Love Serve*, 15.
18 Coney, *Standing in the Sunshine*, 208; Coleman, '"Come over and help us"', 76.
19 For example, see *Proceedings of the General Assembly of the Presbyterian Church of New Zealand* (PCNZ PGA), November 1905, 123–4.
20 Ibid, November 1902, 193.

21 'Poraumati' was also occasionally spelled as 'Poroumati' and 'Paraumati'.
22 The PMMC used this term several times. For example, see letter, Ryburn (PMMC convenor) to J Spence, 17 July 1906, PCNZ/GA (1 of 2) Maori Missions Committee/ Subject, File. Convener's Correspondence, Outward c. 1908 AD 1/4, PMMC Outward (1908), Archives Research Centre, Presbyterian Church of Aotearoa New Zealand Archive (ARC-PCANZ), Dunedin. Interestingly, when the Lundon sisters ran the Lower Waihou Native School in the late 1870s, their appointment was also seen as an 'experiment'. See J Barrington, *Separate but Equal?: Māori Schools and the Crown 1867–1969* (Wellington: Victoria University Press, 2008), 31.
23 Mrs Poraumati's service in the Salvation Army was noted in both her testimonials, from Rev. F Bennett, (Anglican) Maori Mission, Rotorua, 18 February 1907, and S J Brent, Brent's Bathgate House, Rotorua, 20 February 1907, PCNZ/GA (1 of 2) Maori Missions Committee/Subject, File. Convener's Correspondence, Inward c. 1907 AD 1/4, PMMC Inward (1907), ARC-PCANZ, Dunedin.
24 Not all missionary societies welcomed such moves, but by the end of the nineteenth century women workers were employed in increasing numbers in British and American-run missions. This coincided with a number of factors: better education for girls; improved infrastructure within colonies, which made missionary work less isolated; a belief that there was a 'surplus' of woman who would not be marrying; as well as the belief that only women could evangelise certain groups of women, such as those in Hindu and Muslim societies. See E Prevost, 'Assessing Women, Gender and Empire in Britain's Nineteenth Century Protestant Missionary Movement', in *History Compass* 7.3 (2009): 765–99, 767; Huber and Lutkehau, 'Introduction', in *Gendered Missions*, 9; P Williams, '"The Missing Link": The Recruitment of Women Missionaries in some English Evangelical Missionary Societies in the Nineteenth Century', in F Bowie, D Kirkwood and S Ardener (eds), *Women and Missions: Past and Present: Anthropological and Historical Perceptions* (Providence: Berg, 1993): 43–69, 56; and C Swaisland, 'Wanted – Earnest, Self-Sacrificing Women for Service in South Africa: Nineteenth century recruitment of Single Women to Protestant Missions', in Bowie, Kirkwood and Ardener, *Women and Missions:*, 56 and 70–83.
25 D Robert, *American Women in Mission: A Social History of Their Thought and Practice* (Macon: Mercer University Press, 1996), 107–8.
26 A Johnston, *Missionary Writing and Empire, 1800–1860* (Cambridge: Cambridge University Press, 2003), 7.
27 R Gagan, 'Gender, Work, and Zeal: Women Missionaries in Canada and Abroad', in *Labour/Le Travail* (Spring 2004): www.historycooperative.org/journals/llt/53/gagan. html (accessed 25 May 2010); A O'Brien, *God's Willing Workers: Women and Religion in Australia* (Sydney: University of New South Wales Press, 2005), 122.
28 Letter, J Spence to Ryburn, 13 May 1907, PCNZ/GA (1 of 2) Maori Missions Committee/Subject, File. Convener's Correspondence, Inward c. 1907, AD 1/4, PMMC Inward (1907), ARC-PCANZ, Dunedin. Fletcher's expectations may have been more acceptable in earlier times, but by the twentieth century there was a greater expectation that trained women would be more than mere helpmeets. See Prevost, 'Assessing Women, Gender and Empire', 768. Clashes between trained women and established male missionaries also occurred elsewhere. See L Early, 'Women's Work for Women: The Life of a Methodist Missionary Sister in the Solomon Islands 1924–42', BA Hons thesis, University of Otago, 1990, 33–4; R Gillett, 'Helpmeets and Handmaidens: The Role of Women in Mission Discourse', BA Hons thesis, University of Otago, 1998, 57–76; J Haggis, 'Ironies of Emancipation: Changing Configurations of

"Women's Work" in the "Mission of Sisterhood" to Indian Women', in *Feminist Review* 65 (2000): 108–26, cited in H Morrison, 'Antipodeans Abroad: Trends and Issues in the Writing of New Zealand Mission History', in *Journal of Religious History* 30.1 (2006): 77–93, 84.

29 Letters, Fletcher to Ryburn, 20 August 1907; 24 August 1907; 27 August 1907, PMMC Inward (1907), ARC-PCANZ, Dunedin.

30 See *Outlook*, 27 April 1907, 8; letter, Fletcher to Ryburn, 20 May 1907, PMMC Inward (1907), ARC-PCANZ, Dunedin.

31 Letter, Ryburn to Ward, 8 October 1907, PMMC Outward (1907), ARC-PCANZ, Dunedin.

32 Letter, Fletcher to Ryburn, 24 August 1907, PMMC Inward (1907), ARC-PCANZ, Dunedin.

33 Letter, Mrs Poraumati to Ryburn, 10 September 1908, PMMC Inward (1908), ARC-PCANZ, Dunedin.

34 Letter, Fletcher to Ryburn, 19 August 1908, PMMC Inward (1908), ARC-PCANZ, Dunedin.

35 *Outlook*, 25 May 1907, 21.

36 Ibid, 27 February 1909, 21. The 'Laymen's Missionary Movement' from America was briefly successful in garnering male interest in missions in 1910. See H Morrison, '"It is Our Bounden Duty": The Emergence of the New Zealand Protestant Missionary Movement 1868–1926', PhD thesis, Massey University, 2004, 96 and 121.

37 The Presbyterian Home Mission's role was to proselytise in the new settlements being established, and to establish congregations so that parishes could be formed.

38 J Irwin, 'The Rise and Fall of a Vision: Maori in the Midst of Pakeha in the Presbyterian Church of New Zealand', PhD thesis, Victoria University of Wellington, 1994, 103.

39 Salmond, *By Love Serve*, 31–2.

40 *Outlook*, 6 August 1918, 6.

41 Irwin, 'The Rise and Fall of a Vision', 2.

42 PMMC Minute Book, 6 December 1926, Te Aka Puaho Archive (TAPA), Ohope.

43 Ibid, 11 August 1926, TAPA.

44 Ibid, 24 October 1928, 22 April 1929 and 5 October 1931, TAPA.

45 *Appendices to the Journal of the House of Representatives*, 1922, E3.

46 PMMC Minute Book, 20 December 1924, 17 July 1925 and 29 November 1932, TAPA.

47 Letter, Kirk (secretary) to L Sparks (New Zealand Presbyterian Bible Classes), 25 January 1965, Bible Class Unions 1963–70 File, TAPA; letter, Kirk (secretary) to Rev. Rothwell (convener, Women's Work Committee), 20 September 1965, Assembly-General 1964–67 File, TAPA.

48 Sister Annie adopted Pekahina Wharekura and Rata Rawiri, Sister Edith brought up Hemi Potatau, Sister Ross adopted Ron Tuka and Gwen Lewis, and Sister Kearney cared for a boy by the name of Iki.

49 Letter, Sister Kearney to Laughton, 18 January 1949, Janet Kearney File, TAPA.

50 Letter, Sister Brown to Turner (secretary), 9 October 1957, Sister D J Brown file, TAPA.

51 Letter, M Coombe to Smith, 24 August 1951, miscellaneous files, TAPA.

52 Some opportunities existed for female leadership within the native schools system. Despite a preference for married men as head teachers, in 1900 eight of sixty-five heads of native schools were women. See Barrington, *Separate but Equal?*, 58.

53 Salmond, *By Love Serve*, 32, 36.

54 Data derived from Laughton, *From Forest Trail to City Street*.

55 *Outlook*, 3 February 1914, 21.
56 Ibid, 24 November 1914, 12.
57 PMMC Minute Book, 25 July 1928, TAPA.
58 Ibid, 15 February 1932 and 31 October 1932, TAPA.
59 Ibid, 29 November 1932, TAPA.
60 For example, When Miss Minnie Macauley, recently a student at Turakina Girls' School, was appointed as assistant teacher to Matahi Mission School, her salary was 'at the rate of fifteen shillings per week which will be paid to Nurse Doull for her board, & in addition £15 per annum'. Ibid, 20 December 1924, TAPA.
61 Hugh Morrison notes a general increase of New Zealanders undertaking overseas missionary work from 1945 into the 1960s. See Morrison, 'Antipodeans Abroad', 90.
62 Laughton, *From Forest Trail to City Street*, 38.
63 Letter, secretary, PMMC to Rev. Orange, 1 June 1950 (marked confidential), Staff, Rev. A J E Orange File, TAPA.
64 Letter, Rev. Smith to PMMC, 14 November 1950, Smith Papers, TAPA.
65 PCNZ PGA, 1951, 125.
66 Letter, Sister Kearney to Laughton, 18 November 1950, Janet Kearney File, TAPA; see also PCNZ PGA, 1950, 60.
67 Circular to deaconesses, 8 December 1950, Circulars to Staff to 31 December 1962 File, TAPA; Letter, PMMC to Sister Kearney, 21 November 1950, Janet Kearney File, TAPA.
68 PCNZ PGA, 1951, 125.
69 'Training Women for Church Vocations in Maori Synod' (n.d., c. 1965), Women's Work Committee 1963-8 File, TAPA.
70 Laughton, *From Forest Trail to City Street*, 47–52.
71 Letter, Secretary to Rev. Orange, 1 June 1950, Staff, Rev. A J E Orange File, TAPA.
72 Letter, Sister Kearney to Laughton, 17 July 1951, Janet Kearney File, TAPA.
73 Letter, Sister Kearney to Laughton, 17 October 1951, Janet Kearney File, TAPA.
74 Letter, Sister Kearney to Laughton, 1 March 1954, Janet Kearney File, TAPA.
75 Joint committee minutes, 22 August 1957 and 14 November 1957, TAPA.
76 'Consultation on Maori Work, Maori Section N.C.C.', Te Hinota Maori 1963–70 File, TAPA.
77 Letter, Sister H Hercus, Deaconess College, to synod, 4 July 1968, Deaconess College, Students' Salary Regulations 1963–9 File, TAPA.
78 Letter, A Breward (secretary) to Sister H Hercus, Deaconess College, 8 July 1968, Deaconess College, Students' Salary Regulations 1963–9 File, TAPA.
79 Letter, A Breward (secretary) to Sister H Hercus, Deaconess College, 8 October 1968, Deaconess College, Students' Salary Regulations 1963–9 File, TAPA.
80 Letter, M Temara (secretary) to Sister H Hercus, Deaconess College, 22 August 1969, Deaconess College, Students' Salary Regulations 1963–9 File, TAPA.
81 Letter, Rev. Madill, Women's Work Committee to synod, 2 October 1969, Association of Presbyterian Women 1967–70 File, TAPA.

Chapter Ten
Hihita me ngā Tamariki o te Kohu

Hone Te Rire[1]

Introduction

Annie Henry was born on 25 July 1879 at the 'The Narrows', near Riverton in the South Island of New Zealand, the daughter of Francis Henry, a sawmiller, and Catherine McKillop. She was an amazing person, and is the centrepiece of this chapter. As a young girl Annie attended Oraki School and then Riverton District High School,[2] and after a short period there moved to the North Island to stay with a brother, devoting her time to Sunday school teaching and church-based youth work.[3] In 1913 Annie was appointed the first matron of the Manunui Maori Boys' Agricultural College, established by the Presbyterian Church near Taumarunui, and in 1915 began studies at the Presbyterian Women's Training Institute (PWTI) in Dunedin. In her first year at PWTI Annie declined a posting to North India in favour of continuing her vision to become a deaconess. Her studies at PWTI included learning te reo Māori, as well as church history and pastoral care. On successful completion of the course on 24 November 1916 Sister Annie was ordained a deaconess at St John's Church in Wellington. Two weeks later she joined the staff of the Māori Mission committee of the Presbyterian Church of New Zealand, and then in 1917 along with her good friend Miss Abigail Monfries accepted an appointment to Ruatāhuna as a teacher.[4] So begins the story of this amazing and wonderful woman, Sister Annie Henry, known as 'Hihita' (Sister).[5]

The chapter begins with the life of Hihita at Ruatāhuna; in particular, her life with the children she taught, cared for and

Sister Annie Henry, Sister Isabel, Tawhare and others, Ruatāhuna, c. 1949. Photographer unknown. Sister Annie Henry Collection, 1/2-030853: F. Alexander Turnbull Library, Wellington (reproduced with permission).

nurtured. Then we walk with Hihita as she enters into the vast unknown of the Tūhoe homelands.[6] Next, the chapter introduces stories and recollections from children who had a close association with Hihita, of the life they had with her. These stories form the nexus of this chapter, as some have never before been told. The final part of the chapter summarises those recollections and gazes into the lives of these children after Hihita's death, in particular how their past has informed their future.

Hihita ('I love Sister')

A tall, strong woman, Hihita was well suited physically and temperamentally to her task as a missionary of God. Practical skills, fluency in Māori and empathy for people enabled Hihita to devote her entire working life to the Māori people known as the Tūhoe. Ruatāhuna in the 1900s was 76 miles from the closest doctor in Rotorua, and 20 miles from the nearest telephone. The Urewera was wild, untouched and remote. Sister Annie and her friend Abigail

Monfries overcame the hardship of remote life by focusing on their mission for God: caring for the people. As the only permanent resident Pākehā for many years, Hihita not only taught and gave pastoral care; she was also 'doctor, midwife, nurse, dentist, lawyer, carpenter, plumber, policewoman and social worker'.[7] Sister was a 'jack of all trades'. It was during the 1918 influenza epidemic that her skills and selfless care for the people were noticed by Tūhoe. Hihita nursed many Tūhoe children back to better health without, it is said, any loss of life.[8]

Once a road was put through to Ruatāhuna, the church purchased a car for Hihita, but even then she preferred to walk. Hihita became close to those she loved most, the children, and for many years she nurtured them as if they were her own, later adopting two local Māori boys, Peka Wharekura and Rata Rawiri. Stories and accounts of these two boys will be covered later in this chapter.

Hihita had grown up in a world far removed from the wild interior of the Urewera Ranges, but she was an adventurous sort who relished a new challenge and never turned away an opportunity to seek new adventures. The experiences in Ruatāhuna tested her resolve and commitment, and many times she came close to giving in. One night rats visited while Hihita and Miss Monfries slept in their three-roomed earthen floor whare (house) at Oputao.[9] Along with her frightened friend, she was ready to pack up and head home, but in the morning they vacated the whare and found alternative accommodation.[10] This was one of many experiences that recall the character of a person who was driven by the desire to serve others.

Hihita was an upright person, and was never afraid to question the motives of the koroua (elders) when she thought it was necessary. Sister was also one of a few Pākehā women who were allowed to speak in traditional Māori settings, such as at hui (meetings) on marae. In Tūhoe society the elders were never questioned; people did what they were told. So Hihita's intrusions were somewhat startling for the old men of Tūhoe, who at times were unsure of her motives. Another who questioned her motives was Rua Kēnana, who in 1918 returned to his beloved homeland and the remnants of his community at Maungapōhatu. Sister thought Rua a kind and gentle man, and they became good friends. Rua even allowed Hihita to enter the sacred courthouse, Hiona,[11] at Maungapōhatu; their relationship would last until Rua's death in 1938.

Hihita received many gifts from friends, including a takawai (calabash) said to have been brought to Aotearoa from Hawaiki 600 years earlier on the Mataatua canoe, an iron pot from Captain Cook's *Endeavour* and an electric clock originally made for King George VI but given to Hihita after the royal tour was cancelled in November 1948. In 1929 Hihita was made a justice of the peace; in 1937 she was awarded the King George VI coronation medal, and she was honoured with an MBE in 1951 in recognition of services to the community.

The encounter with Tūhoe

In February 1917, at the age of thirty-seven, Sister Annie was appointed missionary to Tūhoe of Ruatāhuna. The Presbyterian Church had recently opened a school and begun educating children and young adults. Hihita's journey to Tūhoe was undertaken at a time when 'there was much resentment towards Pākehā among Tūhoe, especially after the arrest of Rua Kēnana and the shooting of his son, Toko, during the mêlée at Maungapōhatu in 1916'.[12] When she arrived in the district, Hihita was told that she was mad even thinking of going into the area, because it was not only dangerous but practically impossible.[13] On arrival in the Urewera, Hihita and Miss Monfries' first contact with Tūhoe was with Makurata and Paitini Wi Tapeka, who were living at Heipipi. Paitini had fought with Te Kooti, and was a survivor of the battle of Orakau in 1864. He was also an informant of Elsdon Best (Te Peehi) who had contributed to one of Best's books, *Tuhoe: Children of the Mist*. The presence of Sister and Miss Monfries created much excitement when they arrived at Ruatāhuna; some took to the bush in shock at seeing a Pākehā woman for the first time. They thought they were seeing a kēhua (ghost). John Hoani Laughton Mahia[14] remembers as a child seeing Hihita for the first time. He recollects:

I was a young child when I first met Hihita. I was leaning on the fence of the farm when she came riding along. I got such a fright and thought, "Aue, he kehua" [a ghost]. I jumped the fence and "Ka tere au ki te oma ki roto i te ngahere. Tino mataku ai au ki te kehua." [I ran fast to the bush. I was very afraid of this ghost.][15]

Despite the excitement for both parties, strong relationships were cemented from the outset, and this placed Hihita in good stead for the challenging times ahead. Despite the arduous conditions of the region, both Hihita and Abigail Monfries forged ahead in their quest to service the needs of a desperate people in times that were mentally and physically tough.

The late Mona Riini, past moderator of Te Aka Puaho, accounts for some of Hihita's time in Ruatāhuna. She notes that Hihita's parents and friends, upon hearing of her journey to the Urewera, had said to her, 'You must be out of your mind. Those natives will kill you and eat you.' Mona Riini continues:

> These were words spoken to a lady, whose family was worried about her safety. But she felt she had to go, she must accept this calling, a call from God, the Great Creator.
>
> She was Sister Annie Henry, who came to Ruatahuna ... the land of Tuhoe, Children of the Mist, nestled in the bush cleared valley, surrounded by bush clad hills and by the Huiarau ranges.
>
> This was many years before I was born, but because she was there at my birth and during my childhood, and because she made such an impact on many people's lives, I have felt the urge to reveal to all, some of the work of this great woman. Some of the information that I write was given by my parents and by relatives, some by Sister herself, and some comes from my own experience of her.[16]

Undeterred by any warnings, Hihita and Miss Monfries set off. They made the two-day journey to Ngā Tamariki o te Kohu (the children of the mist) initially by a vehicle driven by Rev. Henry

Fletcher, senior missionary in Taupō, then by horse-drawn buggy, and then on foot. Presbyterian minister Rev. John G Laughton of Maungapōhatu, with help from local Māori, had built a school at Ruatāhuna for both teachers in preparation for their first class. Up to seventy children between the ages of five and seventeen were taught at their school; a separate night school was set aside for the adults.

Over the years and out of the goodness of her heart Hihita adopted two local boys. One was Pekahina Wharekura, a tipuna of mine[17] and father of Sam (Hamiora) Wharekura, who is currently training to be an amorangi (minister) for Te Aka Puaho.[18] The other was Rata Rawiri, who unfortunately died at the young age of eighteen years. Hihita's love for children was unsurpassed, and throughout her years in Ruatāhuna she taught, cared for and took in many of the local children as her own. Many of those children remember Hihita fondly, telling stories about her as a person with high standards, a devoted teacher and a mother. I see her more as the latter.

Hihita retired in 1948 to Ohope, until sickness obliged her removal to Whakatāne Hospital. There she received frequent visits from her children, who continued to seek her advice. Sadly, Hihita died at Whakatāne on 29 July 1971, aged ninety-two. She was buried, at her request, at Ruatāhuna. The services held throughout the district commemorated her contribution to Tūhoe.

He hokinga mahara – the memories

This section is comprised of a collection of memories and stories told by the children I call here Ngā Tamariki o te Kohu. Although this is a generic term used to describe the Tūhoe of the Urewera, I use the term to describe the children who were nurtured by Hihita. This section relates the stories and lived experiences of these tamariki (children). We walk with them as they remember their life with Hihita.

The journey begins with a well-known Tūhoe Māori mental health worker, artist and father, Wairere Tame Iti.[19] Tame was born in 1956 in the heart of Tūhoeland and raised by his parents,

Hukarere Turuwhenua and Te Purewa Biddle. He knew Hihita well. Tame is a freedom fighter, a warrior of God, a child of the mist. We started our interview with Tame's memories of Hihita:

> I met Hihita, our māhita[20] at Ohope. I grew up around the knowledge of this kuia Pākehā, although I was a mischief-maker, and did not listen. I learnt a lot from Hihita. Our kuia and koroua encouraged us to follow the pathway of the church. Hihita had good listening skills. She was a person who was adept at writing and spoke in two languages, Pākehā and the language of Tūhoe. This was good, as we walked the journey of knowledge and spirit with Hihita.
>
> Hihita was always the highlight of the day. We went to the Ringatū sabbath on Saturday and then to the Pākehā service on Sunday. This was never a problem to us, as we were comfortable in both churches. Hihita was viewed by some as being a person who should be feared, a person of awe, but I never looked at Hihita that way. She was a person I admired for her strength and courage, and love for others no matter who the person was. My mother was Hukarere Turuwhenua, whose father was Teuaua Turuwhenua. They both left the Ringatū church to become Presbyterian. The Hāhi Pākehā was strong at Piripari, Tataiahape, Tanatana and Waimana. Our whānau was also strong in the Presbyterian church, along with whānau such as the Noemas, Riinis, Te Purewas and others.

I asked Tame if he had a view about how Tūhoe felt after the events at Maungapōhatu in 1916. Rua Kēnana had been arrested by the police and his son Toko had been shot before Hihita arrived in the Urewera. Tame responded:

> Our koroua, Te Makarini Temara, spoke to us about what occurred at Maungapōhatu, especially about this koroua, Wititi. The anger was still with this koroua when Hihita arrived to the Urewera. Wititi was one of the tamariki who was hiding in the scrub at Maungapōhatu and saw all that happened; his memory was vivid and he recalled everything. The people of

Tūhoe were not angry at the Pākehā; they were angry at te ture (the law). Hoani Laughton assisted with discussing and settling the issues with those at Ruatāhuna. The Hāhi Perehipitiriana, through the works of Hihita and Hoani Laughton, were able to settle the dust of contention with those at Ruatāhuna and Maungapōhatu. Hihita and Hoani could speak the language of Tūhoe, and so a good communication link was established between Tūhoe and the Haahi. Through the prophetic statement of Te Kooti, 'ko tēnei te tira haramai nei' ('this is the group who are coming'), Hihita and Laughton were seen as the people who brought the good news of the gospel and the new ways to Tūhoe.

In 1945 Hihita retired to Whakatāne, but the children never left her side. They were always visiting and checking on her. Tame recalls that:

> Hihita's strength and love for her children never wavered, although she was aged; she never slowed and never forgot her children. Hihita moved to Whakatāne to retire, where it was warmer, which was good for her old and weary bones. I was not present at Hihita's tangihanga, as I had left home and gone elsewhere. It is a huge honour that Tūhoe had taken Hihita home to Ruatāhuna to be buried among her people; this is an honour and a moment that only the old people would understand, because it was their way.[21]

Tame currently works for the Tūhoe Hauora in Rūātoki[22] as a mental health worker, and is still very active as a warrior of Tūhoe tino rangatiratanga (self-determination). Tame is a warrior of God carrying the emblems of peace and goodwill to all mankind; he is one of Hihita's children of the mist.

The next person I introduce is Rev. Hariata Haumate, a full-time minister of Te Aka Puaho. Hariata is based at Te Kākano o Te Aroha, and serves the people of Wellington, the Wairarapa and the Horowhenua.[23] Our discussions took place at her son's home in Tāneatua.[24] Rev. Haumate was born and raised in Ruatāhuna, and as a young child she knew Hihita intimately. Her memories of Hihita are boundless, and as we traversed the journey back in time together I could see her eyes light up as if she were back in the times of those now passed on. She shares her memories with us:

> My first impression of Hihita was when I saw this Pākehā kuia wearing a white-laced hat, a navy blue dress with white-laced collars and high-heeled shoes. She was a beautiful, wonderful sight in my eyes. Hihita was an inspiration to me because I would say to myself, 'one day I want to be like you, I want to be strong in the faith like you'. This was my Hihita. She was always gentle; I never saw her angry towards others. I can recall her saying, 'Don't do that'. I can also remember the songs she taught us, like 'Wide, wide as the Ocean', 'I am H-A-P-P-Y', 'Jesus loves me this I know' and 'Hear the Pennies Dropping' (the sound of the coins jingling as they were put into the container at offering time). These were the stories that meant a lot to me, as well as the love of God that Hihita instilled in me.

In the 1920s the Presbyterian Church provided Sister Annie with a car so that she was able to visit the families in Ruatāhuna.[25] Most times Hihita preferred to walk or travel on a horse. Hariata particularly remembers some humorous adventures concerning Hihita's car:

> One day we saw her car coming towards Uwhiarae Marae at Ruatāhuna. Here we were, a bunch of dirty, snot-nosed children all lined up by the roadside. When the car stopped we piled onto Hihita's car. Hihita said to us, 'The big ones can walk to Mataatua Marae'; we replied, 'No, Hihita, we want to hop on your car'. Well, what a sight: there we were on her car, hands and feet hanging out everywhere. 'We want to sit in your car, sister', we would say. Hihita said to us big ones, 'Shouldn't you get off and walk?' We would say, 'No, Hihita, we want to hop on your car'. This did not bother Hihita. Here she was, singing away merrily as the car meandered down the road, 'Jesus loves me this I know …' Arriving at Mataatua Marae our

relations would look at us in astonishment, counting us as we got off the car, saying, 'How did you all fit on Hihita's car?' It was a novelty to us, a hard-case thing to watch; here is this car packed with snot-nosed kids and a Pākehā woman driving the car cheerfully singing away. We were her children of the mist and she treated us as such.

Hariata talked about the relationship of the Presbyterian Church to the Ringatū Church. The Ringatū were strong in Ruatāhuna and Maungapōhatu because of the influence of Te Kooti and, more recently, Rua Kēnana. Hihita viewed the old ways, which the Ringatū held on to, as bad for Māori, but never discouraged the people from following them. William Bird, inspector of native schools, in a letter to Miss Anna Kirkwood, supported this view when he said, 'The most remarkable feature of her work, in my opinion, was her mode of attack. She made no frontal attack on their customs or their beliefs, their superstitions, but she quietly showed by her work among them that she possessed a more desirable way of life.'[26] In response Hariata adds:

> The Ringatū and the Presbyterians were strong at Ruatāhuna and Maungapōhatu. Our family attended both church services. On Saturday was the Ringatū service and on Sunday the Presbyterian. We were able to blend the two churches together; it wasn't difficult for us during those times. I also recall the sports days, an event that involved the whole community. We would help Hihita prepare the marae, set the tables, gather food, and set and cook the hangi. It was because of Hihita that these community events occurred; it brought everyone, young and old together. Ruatāhuna would be packed with people on our sports days; Pākehā and people from other communities would be present.
>
> Church services that were run by Hihita were always packed, and unless people were sick the pews were never empty. The old people admired Hihita's work and always supported her. I recall Hihita unselfishly helping a girl when she was in labour;

it was in the middle of the night, pouring with rain, cold and muddy, but Hihita went to her aid. I know the values and the spirit taught by Hihita are still alive in Ruatāhuna to this day. For example, the koroua know how to bake bread because of Hihita. Having said that, Hihita was not afraid to talk to the elders if need be. The old people would say to her, 'E Hihita, tau ki raro' ['Sister, sit down']. I knew Hihita as a strong person who was not afraid to share her opinions with the old people, but she loved and respected them dearly, as they did her.

We always went to Hihita's place, and our parents and old people always knew where we were. Hihita had an open-door policy to us all. I remember when Hihita was sick the ambulance arrived for her. We all cried; we cried for our kuia. Our old people were also sad that Hihita had gone from Ruatāhuna. Peka was also sad, but we knew the move was good for her health. It was not cold at Whakatāne and she was closer to the hospital, doctors and nurses.

I visited Hihita at Whakātane hospital before she died, where she said to me, 'when I die take me back to Ruatāhuna'. I remember that talk vividly, and there were others that heard this as well. I went to her tangihanga at Te Maungārongo Marae at Ohope. When Hihita first met my future husband she said to him, 'You look after my mokopuna'. Hihita was present at my marriage, where she gave us a dinner set as a gift. I saw with my own eyes the love of Hihita for the old people, the children and everybody. Hihita is a person strong in the faith, and truly believes in the power of prayer. She lies peacefully in our urupā at Ruatāhuna next to her boys, Rata and Peka.

If it were not for Hihita I would not be here now talking about her; she gave me the faith, and because of her I am who I am. She gave me the desire to be a servant of God. Because of Hihita I am strong in the faith. She was a strong and determined woman who prepared us well to walk into the new world. Her spirit is still alive at Ruatāhuna, and her spirit will never die.[27]

The next person to share memories is Sam (Hamiora) Wharekura, the son of Hihita's whāngai (adopted son), Peka Wharekura. Sam's father is the topic of this interview. Sam lives in a quiet suburb of Rotorua, attends the Rotorua Parish of Saint Columba, and is training to become an amorangi minister. Sam explained to me:

> Peka Wharekura, my father, was born with a disability: his hands and feet were bent backwards and he crawled about on his hands and knees. Upon seeing my father this way Hihita enquired to those at Ruatāhuna, 'who does this child belong to?' I know now that it was because of Hihita that my father became a great person and respected in the community. He became the postmaster at the Ruatāhuna Post Office, a minister of the Presbyterian Church, and a leader of the marae. He was knowledgeable in reading the scriptures, and he was able to walk upright. Hihita did these things for my father. Dad did well at school, excelling at mathematics, which held him in good stead as the postmaster. I know that because of Hihita and his time at St Stephens College Dad achieved academically. Hihita was a patient and wonderful person to Dad and all the children of Ruatāhuna. I recall my dad telling us that Hihita looked after a small child who was hiding in the bush because no one wanted this child. Everyone was too frightened to go into the bush, but it was no problem to Hihita.
>
> My father was alive when Hihita died. Everything my father told us about Hihita was good. She was the doctor, nurse, mother, counsellor, everything. I recall my older brother talking about a time when someone got into Hihita's bag.
>
> One day at a church service Hihita told the children about the story of David and Goliath and how David slew Goliath with his sling and stone. She said to the children, 'I will throw this stone at the person who got into my bag'. Of course she was joking, but, as she pretended to throw the stone, a child in the group ducked to avoid the stone. Hihita immediately knew this was the child who got into her bag.

Hihita did not scold this child but instead gave the child love and some corrective counselling. This is what Hihita was like; she gave love to her children no matter what, she never scolded them, instead showering them with love. These are the things I remember about Hihita.[28]

The next person I interviewed was Ms Georgina Horiana Koia Hayes, known affectionately as Aunty Bunny. Horiana lives in Whakatāne in the Eastern Bay of Plenty region, and is in training to be an amorangi minister for Te Aka Puaho. Aunty Bunny takes her second name from Horiana Te Kauru, wife of the Rev. J G (Hoani) Laughton of Maungapōhatu. Aunty Bunny remembers Hihita well:

> It was in 1948 when I was just eight years old that Hihita came to take Sunday services and Sunday school at our home. Until then Mr Laughton had taken our Sunday church services. We lived on a farm and to get to our home you had to walk through four paddocks. In the winter the paddocks were wet, muddy, thick and boggy with mud through the gateways. Hihita came most Sundays, even when it was wet and cold. She came with her kit of songs, hymns, pictures and memory cards. She always came in her Sunday best, and always wore stockings and heeled shoes even on wet days.
>
> We were a family of eight with very little money. Hihita often brought books and sometimes shoes from the mission house. Sister had an unusual singing voice, but she always sang with passion. Today it is not only those stories I remember but that unusual voice. Many times I hear that voice when I need uplifting. Songs like:
>
> > Jesus, Saviour, pilot me
> > Over life's tempestuous sea;
> > Unknown waves before me roll,
> > Hiding rock and treacherous shoal.
> > …
> > May I hear Thee say to me,
> > 'Fear not, I will pilot thee'.

And when we lost our granddaughter at age fourteen in a motorbike accident I asked God many questions. As I listened for his answer it was a hymn that Hihita taught us, 'Whither Pilgrims', that I kept hearing:

> Tell me, pilgrims, what you hope for
> In the better land?
> Spotless robes and crowns of glory
> From a Saviour's hand.

What a beautiful picture and words that brought me a deep inner peace. Then there is the hymn:

> Lead, kindly Light, amid th'encircling gloom,
> Lead Thou me on!
> The night is dark, and I am far from home;
> Lead Thou me on!

Words as an eight-year-old I found unusual and did not fully understand. But listening to stories of Hihita and her mission work in the Urewera area I think those words would have been a comfort to her in that land far from home, amongst the Māori people who had never seen a white woman before. So today I thank Sister Annie and Mr Laughton for sowing those seeds in my life all those years ago.[29]

Horiana's recollections describe Hihita as a person who loved to share the gospel. Spreading God's word and prayer was Hihita's primary focus, and as Horiana describes in her memoirs, nothing was an obstacle. Rain, hail or snow Hihita would serve her people. Hihita is described in Horiana's story as a kind and loving person, especially to the children of the mist.

There are many others I would have interviewed but for the space constraints of this chapter. I acknowledge them and hope one day to gather their stories and recollections as well. The stories of those that are not included in this chapter will be the topic of further research, as I intend to publish a book about the children nurtured by Hihita.

Life after Hihita

An excerpt from the late Mona Riini describes Riini's experiences of and thoughts about Hihita long after Hihita had passed away. It tells of love for a woman who gave hope and love to a community of Māori who had been suppressed by the scourges of post-colonialism and the dictates of Pākehā supremacy. Sister was, in the eyes of these children, an angel sent by God to care for them. Mona Riini says:

> Kāhore e wareware i a mātau, i ahau rawa atu, ngā waiata, ngā hīmene a Hihita. Ki tōku whakaaro, nā Hihita i rui te purapura Karaitiana ki Ruatāhuna. Ahakoa anō te kaha o te hāhi Ringatū ko tēnei te mea ātaahua ki a mātau. I tēnei rā, kua tipu, kua puāwai ētahi o aua purapura, arā, kua minita ētahi, kua kaumātua ētahi, ā, kei roto ētahi i ngā hāhi Karaitiana hou o tēnei ao. Nā Hihita i tīmata te Hinota Māori mō te Hāhi Perehipitiriana.
>
> None of us, including myself, will ever forget the songs and choruses Sister taught us. I believe that she sowed the seeds of Christianity in Ruatāhuna. Although the Ringatū Church had many adherents, hers was more appealing to us. Today the fruits of the seeds she sowed flourish. Some of the men are ordained ministers, some are elders of the Church (Presbyterian) and a great many have joined recent Christian groups. She started the first Synod Group.[30]

Tame Iti said that Hihita left an indelible mark on his life from the first time he met her as a kura māhita (schoolteacher) at Maungapōhatu. Tame explained, 'Hihita was knowledgeable and used all the skills of a teacher to show us (children) how to count, write, sing and read books. She was marvellous and nurtured us.'

Rev. Haumate mentioned that because of Hihita she became closer to God, and that she is a better person today because of Hihita. The importance of prayer and love for people were values that she learnt from Hihita. These values have held Rev. Haumate in good stead as a minister, and as a matriarch of her whānau.

Horiana Hayes describes that it was the seeds or good values sown by Hihita that made her a better person. She is able to stand tall with pride, and to weather the storms of adversity no matter the challenges of life.

Hamiora Wharekura describes Hihita as a person who was good; a person who unselfishly gave to others. Hihita cared for those that others rejected, and adopted those who were bereft of love.

Conclusion

Sister Annie Henry came from Riverton in the deep south of the South Island, a place far removed from the rugged homelands of the Tūhoe where she worked as a Māori Mission worker for the Presbyterian Church. Hihita was an enigma who captivated the hearts and minds of the children she took into her arms. By the accounts of her given by those who knew her well, Hihita was a person who loved and cared for the health and well-being of the children. The children who are referred to in this chapter as 'Ngā Tamariki o te Kohu' remember Hihita vividly, from her initial arrival in Ruatāhuna in 1917 to the time she passed away in 1971.

There is a common theme that weaves the children's stories together, and that is Hihita's love for them and her love for God. These two values permanently imbued the children with confidence in themselves, high self-esteem and the ability to serve others. Hihita gave hope to these children, who were struggling in their world prior to her arrival, where hopelessness would have been their future. Many of the children have done well with their lives, while some found life challenging, and others have gone to join their Hihita. One of the informants described the experience of Hihita as something that changed the community of Ruatāhuna, and said that her wairua is still alive in that remote community. Hihita lived by the deaconesses' motto, 'Amore servite', which means 'By love serve', and it is this motto that the children she served live by today.

Endnotes

1 I would like to thank the many people with whom I have worked in a variety of ways since beginning this paper. I begin with paying compliments to my wife and children, whose enduring support enabled me to complete this article. The many long nights and times away from home were quietly suffered, and so my thanks and gratitude are boundless and without end. I am most grateful to the koroua and kuia of Tūhoe who assisted me

with this paper. Indeed I must also pay tribute to Rev. Te Ahorangi Wayne Te Kaawa for his assistance and help, and also give my many thanks to the moderator of Te Aka Puaho, Ms Millie Te Kaawa, for her wisdom and guidance. I would also like to record my gratitude to Rev. Hariata Haumate, Mr Hamiora Wharekura, Mr Wairere Tame Iti and Ms Horiana Hayes for their heartfelt generosity and time in contributing towards this article. I acknowledge the others I would have interviewed but for the space constraints of this article. I would also like to thank Ms Yvonne Wilkie and Ms Jane Bloore of the Knox College Archives Research Centre for their assistance and contribution. I hope that my footnotes provide due acknowledgement for other contributions. Finally I would like to acknowledge and offer my sincere gratitude to Te Aka Puaho for their enduring assistance and guidance in helping me with the journey I embarked on.

Heoi, e aku rangatira, e kore e mimiti te puna o te mihi me te aroha noa o tō tātou Ariki ki a koutou, otirā ki a tātou katoa. Kia tau iho ngā manaakitanga o te Āriki ki runga i a tātou i ngā wā katoa. Heoi te mihi.

2 J D Salmond, *By Love Serve: The Story of the Order of Deaconesses of the Presbyterian Church of New Zealand* (Christchurch: Presbyterian Bookroom, 1962), 36.
3 The name of Sister Annie's brother could not be found by the time this chapter went to print.
4 M Riini, 'Te Whaea Hihita', in *Te Ao Hou* 70 (1972): 8–12.
5 'Hihita' was the name given to Sister Annie by Tūhoe. It is a transliteration of 'Sister'. However, the children interpreted it as 'I love Sister': 'Hihita and Hoani: Missionaries in Tuhoeland' (exhibition at Whakatane Museum & Gallery, 2008).
6 Salmond, *By Love Serve*, 35–6.
7 James Veitch. 'Henry, Annie – Biography', from the Dictionary of New Zealand Biography. Te Ara – the Encyclopedia of New Zealand, updated 1 September 2010: http://www.teara.govt.nz/en/biographies/3h16/1 (accessed 16 January 2012).
8 Personal communication, Rev. Te Ahorangi Wayne R M Te Kaawa, 18 February 2010.
9 Oputao is a marae at Ruatāhuna: www.naumaiplace.com (accessed 20 June 2010).
10 'Hihita and Hoani'.
11 A description and photo of the round house can be found in J Binney, G Chaplin and C Wallace (eds), *Mihaia: The Prophet Rua Kenana and His Community at Maungapohatu* (Auckland: Auckland University Press, 1979), 47.
12 Veitch, 'Henry, Annie – Biography'.
13 Riini, 'Te Whaea Hihita', 8.
14 John Mahia was named after the Rev. J G Laughton.
15 Original in te reo Māori, translated by the author.
16 Riini, 'Te Whaea Hihita', 8.
17 A term of endearment used to describe one's ancestors or great-grandparents.
18 'Te Aka Puaho', meaning 'the glowing vine', was the name given by Hohepa Kereopa of Waimana in 1996 to the Presbyterian Māori Synod.
19 Personal communication, Tame Iti, Whakatāne, 29 March 2010. Interview given in te reo Māori, translated by the author.
20 A Māori term for schoolteacher that, literally translated, means 'master'.
21 Personal communication, Tame Iti.
22 Rūātoki is located 30 kilometres south of Whakatāne in the Eastern Bay of Plenty.
23 Te Kakano o Te Aroha is a parish of Te Aka Puaho and is located at 136 Randwick Road, Moera, Lower Hutt.
24 Tāneatua is located in the Eastern Bay of Plenty, approximately 20 kilometres south of Whakatāne.

25 Veitch, 'Henry, Annie – Biography'.
26 Letters held at the Presbyterian Archives Research Centre, Knox College, Dunedin.
27 Personal communication, Rev. Hariata Haumate. Interview given in te reo Māori, translated by the author.
28 Personal communication, Sam (Hamiora) Wharekura. Interview given in te reo Māori, translated by the author.
29 Personal communication, Georgina Horiana Koia Hayes.
30 Riini, 'Te Whaea Hihita', 10–11.

Chapter Eleven
The Subversive Theology of Rua Kēnana

Murray Rae

In 1906–1907 the ethnographer Elsdon Best wrote in his monumental study *Tuhoe: The Children of the Mist* that at the turn of the century the Tūhoe people didn't have much use for Christianity.[1] Apparently, however, the 'Christianity' for which Tūhoe had little use was the institutional forms of Pākehā Christian faith, for, later in the same volume, Best writes: 'The Maori of the present day is keenly religious. He seems to take much interest in his peculiar brand of Christianity, and is fond of attending numerous services. Among the Tuhoe people, who have evolved a ritual termed by them Ringa tu, based on the Scriptures, two or more services are held each day.'[2]

There had been Anglican missionary activity among Tūhoe during the 1830s and 1840s and some Roman Catholic presence about the same time, but it had not flourished, and had largely been abandoned by the mid-1860s. The missionary endeavours of the Presbyterian Church, which would eventually establish an enduring presence among the Tūhoe people, had not yet begun. And yet, as Best somewhat condescendingly observes, there was a brand of Christianity, substantially adapted to Māori sensibilities and ambitions, that had gained a significant following among Tūhoe. The story of Ringa tū, later Ringatū, begins with its founder, the charismatic leader Te Kooti Arikirangi Te Turuki (c. 1832–1893). There is a rich tapestry of tradition, both oral and written, surrounding the figure of Te Kooti. Much of it serves to account for and legitimate the prophetic authority claimed by Te Kooti, and testifies to the divine appointment of Te Kooti to lead his people out of the oppression they were suffering at the hands of the European settlers. Te Kooti himself came to prominence when in 1866 he was unjustly accused of collaborating with the Pai Mārire movement and, along with many members of Pai Mārire, was deported without trial to a penal settlement on Wharekauri, the Chatham Islands.[3] During an illness suffered at Wharekauri, Te Kooti experienced a vision in which, like Moses, he was appointed by God to lead his people from captivity. As Bronwyn Elsmore tells the story, Te Kooti 'attested that the "Spirit of God" spoke to him, appointing him to a special position and task: "Arise, God has sent me to bring you to life to make known his name to his people who are in captivity in this place so that they may know that Jehovah drove them out into this land ...."'[4] And further:

> Fear not because thy cry hath reached unto God, and God hath heard the crying, hearken I will strengthen thee and will cause thee to know the things whereof I have spoken unto your forefathers, to Abraham to Isaac to Jacob and all their children down to David, man's knowledge is from writing and cometh from without only, as for mine it is from within and cannot be seen by another, thou must tell my words and make them known to my people, it is only my words that thou must speak.[5]

Te Kooti's familiarity with the Old Testament, from which he took inspiration, was developed through his schooling at the Anglican mission at Whakatō in Poverty Bay from 1850 to 1853.[6] He is known also to have studied the Old Testament when held in captivity at Wharekauri, concentrating especially on the books of Joshua and Judges and the imprecatory psalms,[7] texts that fuelled his militaristic conception of the divine deliverance that he had been called upon to lead. Identification with Israel's plight and divine calling became commonplace among Māori in the nineteenth century, not simply because of parallels in their circumstances – oppression by foreign power – but also because of a conviction that they were descended from the Israelites, and that God had now chosen them to be his people, the new 'children of Jehovah'. The original hymn of the Ringatū faith was the 'Lamentation of Jeremiah', which describes the pain and suffering of Israel. The hymn concludes with the lines, 'Our own lands have been taken by strangers, but you will always be my Father for ever'.[8] Further inspiration was drawn from Jeremiah 31:16–17, a text used by Te Kooti at the first service that he led on Wharekauri: 'Thus saith the Lord; Refrain thy voice from weeping, and thine eyes from tears: for thy work shall be rewarded, saith the Lord; and they shall come again from the land of the enemy. And there is hope in thine end, saith the Lord, that thy children shall come again to their own border.'[9]

Imprisonment on Wharekauri – his captivity and exile – undoubtedly heightened Te Kooti's sense that Israel's story had become his own. He appears to have had little difficulty in convincing his fellow prisoners of his divine appointment, and together they captured a supply ship and made their escape back to the mainland in 1868. Although Te Kooti anticipated trouble on his return, his goal was to make his way peacefully to Tauranga, a village on the eastern shore of Lake Taupō. It was there, he had predicted while still on Wharekauri, that the tabernacle for the ark would be. The tabernacle was to be set up as a precursor to the exiles returning to Canaan, their promised land.[10] Te Kooti's party of escapees was watched, of course, but they were to be allowed to make their way towards Lake Taupō if only they would give up their arms. This Te Kooti refused to do. Wi Pere, one of the messengers sent to convey the offer, reported that Te Kooti 'replied angrily that he would not listen to me, that the Almighty was directing his actions'.[11] That refusal of acquiescence was Te Kooti's Rubicon. There was little prospect now of avoiding conflict. Te Kooti's party were tracked by Māori forces, and his own men determined to defend themselves. Te Kooti said, 'I expected this after my refusal to surrender our arms and selves again to the Government. … The taniwha lies across our path, and we must kill it or ourselves be killed.'[12]

Te Kooti's party of supporters was thus established as a fugitive people, seeking a return to their land but hounded by the government. Te Kooti was convinced, and cultivated the belief among his people, that God was on their side, promising a return to the land, and sanctioning their engagement in war. Eria Raukura, one of Te Kooti's followers, and a chief source of information about the period, reported Te Kooti's frequent appeal to Old Testament precedent, including, for example, a sermon on the text of Exodus 14:30–1: 'Thus the Lord saved Israel that day out of the hand of the Egyptians; and Israel saw the Egyptians dead upon the sea shore. And Israel saw that great work which the Lord did upon the Egyptians: and the people feared the Lord, and believed the Lord, and his servant Moses.'[13]

Te Kooti's story continues in this vein. Divine warrant and guidance were claimed as the basis for resistance to government oppression and the quest for freedom and self-governance. As Bronwyn Elsmore reports, 'the people of the new prophet believed that their cause was a just one, and that God was behind them supporting and protecting their campaigns'.[14] Texts from the Old Testament provided ample justification in Te Kooti's mind for the pursuit of God's purposes with the weapons of war. According to William Greenwood, Joshua 23:5–6 was one such text that provided a mandate for the forceful reclamation of Māori land:

> And the Lord your God, he shall expel them from before you, and drive them from out of your sight; and ye shall possess their land, as the Lord your God has promised unto you. Be ye therefore very courageous to keep and to do all that is written in the book of the law of Moses, that ye turn not aside therefrom to the right hand or the left.[15]

Many Maori who had links to the military were killed by Te Kooti, as were Europeans who were living on land that had been taken from Te Kooti during his exile on Wharekauri. Te Kooti's militaristic pursuit of justice gained him considerable notoriety, but he took refuge from the authorities in the heavily forested hills of the Urewera that are the Tūhoe homelands, and succeeded again and again in evading the government forces sent to apprehend him. Te Kooti's flight to the Tūhoe territory of the Urewera gained him a following among Tūhoe but also led to their suffering under the efforts of the military to starve Te Kooti out. Resentment of the Crown was thus considerably strengthened among Tūhoe in the latter half of the nineteenth century, and fuelled by confiscations of Tūhoe land beginning in 1866.[16]

Eventually, however, Te Kooti set aside the sword and determined to seek justice through the law. The determination to live peacefully thereafter left a lasting impression upon people of the Ringatū faith. Stories are told of an incident at Makaraka in which Te Kooti thrust either a gun or a sword into the ground, indicating that it would be needed no more. A version of the story is told by Ned Brown, who emphasises Te Kooti's words:

> He said, 'There'll be no more wars by the Māori people with the Europeans: the last will be with me. This is a promise from God to us.' Then he poked the sword in the ground. He took his hand off it, and the sword started going down, right into the ground – on its own accord. ... At the crossroads at Mākaraka: that's where that sword is.[17]

There was also a reconciliation with Te Hāhi Matua, the Anglican Church, in which Te Kooti had been raised.[18] Nevertheless it was the Old Testament scriptures that continued to provide the inspiration for Te Kooti. His people were reliving Israel's story; they were still in captivity and thus were still seeking liberation. Perhaps Te Kooti had begun his career as a religious leader under the impression that he would be the great deliverer, but, while he enjoyed some success, as time passed he began to prophesy that there would be one who would come after him who would be the new prophet of the people. His successor, Te Kooti said, would come from the people of Tūhoe.[19] 'There will be a child who will turn upright the canoe and he will unite the people through the Gospel.'[20] As he lay dying at Ohiwa in 1891, Te Kooti prophesied further: 'In twice seven years, a man shall arise in the mountains to succeed me. He shall be unmistakeable here.' It was this mantle of Te Kooti that Rua Kēnana claimed to inherit. Te Kooti's prophesy may be compared to that of John the Baptist, who foretold the one coming after him who would baptise with the holy spirit and with fire. Rua saw Te Kooti as the forerunner and himself as the promised messiah who would deliver the people from their bondage. At Pakowhai in 1906, Rua explained that he was 'the second Christ':

> He ... had a messenger, a John the Baptist in the person of Te Kooti. He reminded his audience that Christ took three years to be born and indeed, it took him [Rua] three years to be recognized. ... The people were now living in bondage and he had come to deliver them. ... Rua went on to say that Adam had two children – Cain and Abel – Cain being the Pakeha and Abel the Maori. And so it was today that the Pakeha continues to attack the Maori.[21]

Not all of Te Kooti's followers accepted Rua's claims. Some saw him as the fulfilment of other sayings of Te Kooti that foretold dissension and division among the people. But Rua saw himself as the one who would usher in an era of prosperity and peace. Asserting the prerogative of Te Kooti's expected successor, Rua removed from the Ringatū liturgy the penultimate prayer, the Pōkaikaha, a prayer for deliverance from confusion, doubt and sorrow, and replaced it with Maungārongo, a prayer of peace, thus claiming that the struggle and sorrow that had marked Te Kooti's era had been replaced by a time of lasting peace, attributable to the coming of the messiah.

Alongside actions such as these, indicating Rua's assumption of prophetic mana and authority, numerous stories are told of incidents that were understood by Rua's followers to authenticate his claims to be Te Kooti's promised successor. Among them is the story of Te Kooti's diamond, allegedly hidden atop Maungapōhatu, the sacred mountain of Tūhoe that lies in the heart of the Urewera.[22] In about 1905, Rua, responding to an angelic visitation, climbed the sacred mountain with his wife Pinepine. As they ascended the mountain they were guided by a woman who appeared before them. She was Whaitiri, ancestress of Tuhoe. Then the figure of Christ appeared beside her, and it was revealed to them where the diamond lay. The disclosure to Rua of the location of Te Kooti's diamond and his visionary experiences on the mountaintop confirmed for many that Rua was the rightful successor to Te Kooti and that the God of the Bible had anointed him to be the leader of his people.

There were other claimants to Te Kooti's mantle: notably Wi Wereta of Tokomaru, and a little later Wi Raepuku of Ohana. Each of them, including Rua, asserted their claims to be the rightful successor by retracing the steps of Te Kooti and visiting the places associated with him.[23] It was Rua, however, who secured the blessing of Eria Raukura, who Te Kooti himself had baptised in 1881 and who was the major tohunga of the Ringatū. Judith Binney reports that in 1906, Eria baptised Rua as the messiah before a great crowd of people.[24] Rua also received endorsement from Te Hurinui Apanui, the leading Ngāti Awa chief, who was considered to be the paramount figure of the Mataatua tribes.[25] The endorsement of these leading figures certainly gave great impetus to Rua's leadership, but he did not enjoy universal support, even among his own iwi. Claiming biblical precedent, however, that reality could easily be interpreted in favour of his claims to prophetic status. Jesus himself encountered opposition and, after rejection in Nazareth, said to his disciples, 'Prophets are not without honour, except in their hometown, and among their own kin, and in their own house' (Mark 6:4).

Having secured among many his claim to be Te Kooti's successor, Rua proceeded to interpret that succession in messianic terms. In line with Jewish expectations that the messiah would assume the throne of David, Rua established his own claim to kingship. That claim was advanced through two incidents at Gisborne. The first was a visit to Rongopai, a Ringatū house of worship that had been built for Te Kooti but which – on account of his fugitive status – he had never been able to visit. A tapu had been placed on the house, preventing anyone from entering it, but in 1906 Rua went into the house. In stories told of the incident, 'it is said that Christ and Te Turuki [Te Kooti] greeted him as the King who would fulfil the prophecies'.[26]

The second incident took place during a trip to Gisborne in 1906. Rua announced that King Edward was coming to Gisborne.

Rua would meet him there and, with a box full of precious stones, he would buy back the land occupied by Pākehā throughout the country and the Pākehā would leave. Rua and his party waited three days on the wharf at Gisborne anticipating the king's arrival. On the third day, perhaps deliberately chosen on account of its biblical resonances, Rua announced that he was to be their king, the one for whom they had been waiting. 'Here I am', he said, 'with all my people'.[27]

Rua's claims to divine appointment and authority were repeated in various forms. At times he simply identified himself with Jesus Christ. He is said to have told the story of the New Testament using a series of pictures laid out on the floor. He would pause at each of the portraits of Jesus and say, 'I am that fella'.[28] At other times he claimed that God the Father had two sons, and that he was the second son, the brother of Jesus Christ. Just as there was a Messiah for Pākehā, Rua said, so he was the messiah for Māori. Repeated – apparently miraculous – provisions of food, claims to be able to walk on water, wounds resembling those of Christ and predictions of his own resurrection reinforced his messianic credentials. On one occasion, Rua took his followers down to the water's edge and said to them, 'do you believe that I can walk on water?' On hearing the enthusiastic shouts of assent, Rua responded, 'then I have no need to prove it to you'. Rua's identification of himself with Jesus appears to have lessened somewhat over the years, perhaps because of the closer relationship he developed with the more orthodox Christian view represented by John Laughton and by subsequent representatives of the Presbyterian mission who established a school and then services of Presbyterian worship among the people of Rua's community.

Sometimes Rua's claims to divine authority appealed to the spirit, rather than to Christ. He claimed that he was the mouthpiece of the holy spirit, and at other times that he was himself the holy spirit. The trinity, he said, consisted of 'God, Christ and Rua'.[29] Rua's theological claims are clearly drawn from a New Testament framework, but the Old Testament was an even more important influence upon his theological vision. Like Te Kooti before him, Rua saw his own story as a continuation of God's deliverance of Israel from bondage, and the progress of Rua's prophetic leadership appears to consist in a deliberate reenactment of Israel's story.[30] The community he gathered about him, for example, were called the Iharaira, the Israelites; he encouraged them to grow long hair after the fashion of the Nazarites identified in Numbers 6:4, and proclaimed himself to be their king. Following predictions of a coming flood of judgement, he encouraged his followers to leave the lowlands, and led them in an Exodus-like migration to Maungapōhatu, where he established Te Hiruhārama Hou, the New Jerusalem, a house for his own habitation with proportions loosely based on Solomon's temple. He lived there with his seven wives, a number justified by the vision of Isaiah 4:1: 'Seven women shall take hold of one man in that day, saying, "We will eat our own bread and wear our own clothes; just let us be called by your name."' The largest and most distinctive building at Maungapōhatu was a council house that Rua called Hiona, Zion. Isaiah 2:3 provides an apt summary of the mandate that Rua was claiming:

> Many people shall come and say,
> 'Come let us go up to the mountain of the Lord,
> to the house of the God of Jacob;
> that he may teach us his ways
> and that we may walk in his paths'.
> For out of Zion shall go forth instruction,
> And the word of the Lord from Jerusalem.

Rua's ascent of the sacred mountain of Maungapōhatu and the visionary experiences he had there were comparable to those of Moses on Mount Sinai. He and Pinepine were led down from the mountain by a rainbow, the biblical sign of a new covenant and further confirmation that Rua had been chosen by God. Building further upon the Mosaic precedent, Rua instituted a strictly observed law among his community, commendable especially for its insistence upon high standards of hygiene and the prohibition of alcohol.[31] He kept a large Bible that he called 'the covenant' and housed it in an ark, following the pattern of the covenant given to Israel. He gathered about him twelve disciples called Rīwaiti, the Levites, in a dual allusion to the twelve tribes of Israel and the twelve disciples of Jesus. Bronwyn Elsmore observes that, 'The move back to Maungapōhatu under Rua was a symbolic return of the people to their homeland. This ancestral land he called "Peura", Beulah, a poetic name for Israel in its future restored condition.'[32] Again drawing from the book of Isaiah Rua adopted for himself the name Hephzibah, rendered in Māori as Hepetipa, which refers to the daughter of Zion and means 'My delight is in her' (Isaiah 62:4). The adoption of the name constituted a further claim upon the mantle of Te Kooti, for in a statement made in 1885 Te Kooti had appealed to the same passage, declaring that in the coming age of peace the land formerly known as Reneti Hawira would be called Beulah, and 'you' would be called Hephzibah.[33] The following year Te Kooti had offered a further 'promise', again drawn from the Bible: 'I shall restore the remnant of the people created by my hand. I shall drive away the wicked, and I shall restore the boundaries of Reneti Hawira. There are two meanings of this statement and both are completed. One is the gospel and that it is completed, and also his anger towards the world.'[34]

The restoration of a remnant was, repeatedly in the Old Testament, a sign of God's enduring faithfulness to his people and the continuation of his purposes after disaster, divine anger and judgement. 1 Kings 19:18, for instance, refers to God's retention of 7000 in Israel, of 'all the knees that have not bowed to Baal, and every mouth that has not kissed him'. In his letter to the Romans (11:5), St Paul takes the incident as precedent for God's choosing a remnant in Paul's own time to continue his covenant purposes. Rua could see himself in this same tradition as the leader of a faithful remnant, set apart to be the agent of God's salvific and restorative purpose for Māori.

Throughout his career as prophet and leader of his people Rua drew upon his extensive knowledge of the Bible in order to show both that the biblical story applied with powerful force to his own times and that its fulfilment, for Māori at least, was being worked out through him. We come now to the question: how are we to assess Rua's theology? I ask the question as a Christian theologian: as one committed to what we might call 'orthodox Christian faith' but who is willing to acknowledge nevertheless that the proclamation of the biblical message must be renewed again and again as it is addressed to and articulated from within the particularities of time and place, of changing social and political circumstances, and of diverse languages and cultures. The importance of an indigenous expression of Christian faith has long been recognised in the church's mission among Māori in New Zealand. The Rev. J G Laughton, who spent many years working alongside Rua, wrote, in his account of 'the Presbyterian Church among the Māori People':

> The missionary work of the whole Church throughout the world has been revolutionised by the recognition that the Kingdom of God is never securely established among any people until it has been made indigenous by handing over its leadership to the native Church. The following statement contained in the report of Te Hinota Māori [the Māori Synod of the Presbyterian Church] became the focus for deliberations of the Conference: 'We believe that the situation in the Maori section of the Church is exactly the same as in the work of the Church among other races overseas, that is that only when the fullest expression is given to native leadership within the Church does the Church become indigenous and of the soil and people and cease to be foreign'.[35]

Despite his respect for and long-standing friendship with Rua, however, Laughton was certain that the indigenous interpretation of biblical faith established by Te Kooti and carried on by Rua was misguided and constituted a hindrance to the propagation of the gospel among Tūhoe. In Laughton's report to the Presbyterian General Assembly in 1926, written from Maungapōhatu, he wrote:

> These people were all nominally Christian prior to Te Kooti rising. ... When Te Kooti led forth his revolt it was necessary for him to break all hold of the missionaries over his people. He did not lead them back to the old ancestral gods to champion their cause in battle, but what he did do was to take Jehovah

and install Him in the empty ancient shrines. What I mean is this: He did not lead his people back to worship idols, but, retaining the name of our God, he reverted to a largely heathen conception of deity. ... They substituted a ritual taken from the Scriptures for the ancient incantations to their gods, but still those scriptural passages were recited exactly as were the old incantations, missing if not entirely, almost entirely, the Christian conception of communion with God.[36]

Later in the same report, Laughton continued:

We have a people who nominally worship the same God as we do, but whose whole conception of Him and of how He is to be worshipped, and of the true meaning of religion is of that darkness which His name is meant to dispel. ... I sometimes think it would be easier to carry the Gospel to people who were altogether outside the pale of Christendom, than to people who think they are just all right, when, in reality, they are all wrong.[37]

It is worth noting a further factor identified by Laughton as a major hindrance to the propagation of the gospel among Māori. 'Our inconsistency as a Christian nation', Laughton wrote, 'is a serious handicap to the promulgation of the Gospel'. The Māori:

... expects that if we are a Christian nation, we shall nationally act in a Christian manner. Moreover, he expects the individual to be typical of the whole, and so when he contemplates how he has been wronged by us as a people in such things as unfair confiscations of land during the Maori War ... he thinks Christianity is a humbug.[38]

Two themes emerge from Laughton's assessment that deserve further consideration: first, the claim that in respect of Christianity, the people are 'all wrong', and second, the observation that when Māori contemplate how they have been wronged by a purportedly Christian nation, they think 'Christianity is a humbug'. In what follows I shall argue that with respect to the wrongs promulgated by the 'Christian nation', Rua's interpretation of biblical faith was not 'all wrong'. Indeed, Rua's prophetic resistance to the wrongs inflicted upon his people can claim a legitimate basis in Christian scripture.

We have seen the degree to which Rua rooted his theology very deeply in the scriptures that were brought to Aotearoa by Pākehā settlers, by the very same race of people who had confiscated Tūhoe land, who had imprisoned Te Kooti the prophet, who had imposed great suffering upon Tūhoe and who, in time, would arrest and imprison Rua himself. One might have thought, and Laughton certainly suspected, that a people harassed in this way would be disinclined to believe in the God proclaimed by their oppressors. But matters are not so simple. It might be argued that in some respects at least Rua understood the God proclaimed by the Pākehā better than some Pākehā did themselves. There are numerous ways in which Rua demonstrated his belief that the God made known through the Bible was not a Pākehā God and could not be interpreted as providing divine sanction for all of the Pākehā ways.

Much is revealed in the name chosen by Rua for his community: Te Iharaira, the Israelites. Three things in particular, I suggest, are implied by Rua's identification with Israel. First, there was a deliberate identification with those in bondage, with those subjected to slavery in Egypt but eventually delivered by God. That deliberate identification began with Te Kooti but was continued by Rua. Māori are not the only oppressed peoples to have taken up this theme from the Bible presented to them by their oppressors. It is the dominant theme of the 'liberation theology' that came to prominence among the poor and oppressed in Latin America in the 1970s and 1980s, but which is also to be found in the spirituals written and sung by black slaves in America. In defiance and in lament, the biblical tones rang out: 'Go down Moses, way down in Egypt's land. Tell ol' Pharaoh, to let my people go.' Among many writers who testify to the identification of slaves with Israel's religious heritage, Gayraud S Wilmore writes:

> … the preeminent relevance of the Old Testament for blacks, as many of the most famous spirituals bear witness, was found in the story of the Exodus. The Egyptian captivity of the people

of Israel, their miraculous deliverance from the hands of the pharaohs, and their eventual possession of the land promised by God to their ancestors – this was the inspiration to which the black believer so often turned in the dark night of the soul.[39]

Wilmore continues, '[w]henever the Judeo-Christian tradition is made known to an oppressed people, the scenario of election, captivity and liberation in the Old Testament seems to have a special appeal'.[40] There can be little doubt, I suggest, that in this matter the oppressed have heard the message of the Bible more faithfully than have their oppressors.[41]

Second, the name chosen by Rua for his people distances the Iharaira from those who called themselves Christian. In the New Testament, made available to Māori in their own language before the books of the Old Testament, a sharp distinction is sometimes drawn between Jew and Christian. There is evidence that some Māori started calling themselves Jews, ngā Tiu, or ngā Hūrai, precisely to make clear that they were not to be counted with the Pākehā Christians.[42]

Third, the identification of Māori with Israel carried a subtle message that they were God's chosen people now. In the Old Testament, God sided with Israel in giving them a land; Rua was clearly suggesting that the name 'Iharaira' identified in his own time the rightful inhabitants of the land. There is probably merit in Bronwyn Elsmore's suggestion that Rua's name must have influenced his sense of divine appointment.[43] Rua (two) and Kēnana (Canaan) alludes to a second Canaan, a second land promised by God; this time to the people gathered under the leadership of Rua.

What are we to make of Rua's elevated claims about his own identity: his claims to be the messiah or the spirit or sometimes the mouthpiece of the holy spirit? It is difficult to know precisely what Rua intended in making these claims, but they signal, at least, a subversion of Pākehā claims to authority over Māori. God does not need a Pākehā intermediary in order to communicate his purposes to Māori. God can establish among Māori themselves a sufficient means for the communication of his word. Māori are not below

Pākehā in the divine ordering of things. They are equal before God, and God communicates directly to and through both peoples. The equality of Māori and Pākehā was asserted in the motto inscribed upon Rua's flag: 'Kotahi te ture mo ngā iwi a rua' ('There is one law for the two peoples'). Rua no doubt intended with this slogan to hold the government to account by its own law, but he may also have had in mind the divine law: a law superior to any made by the government and carrying ultimate authority.

Rua's denial of Pākehā lordship and of Pākehā kāwanatanga (government) is evident in numerous practices of his community and in many of the incidents of their history. In 1927, for instance, when the community and its buildings at Maungapōhatu had begun to decline and had been struck by the ravages of a typhoid epidemic, Rua issued a new series of millenarian prophecies in which the sacred mountain was again to be the place of refuge from the wrath to come. The buildings in poor repair were demolished and new ones were built in their place. Judith Binney reports:

> The village was carefully laid out with the two main streets and the houses grouped geometrically along them. Irene Paulger [the Pākehā teacher at the school at Maungapōhatu] was quite clear that Rua had an underlying purpose in his actions. The Health Department doctors, who had lived at Maungapohatu during the typhoid epidemic, had talked to him about the poor houses and the general lack of sanitation. They had recommended that new homes should be built, with two rooms and outside lavatories. Rua, she believed, had no intention of complying openly with these suggestions and instead chose a more indirect path. 'At a meeting of his people, Rua prophesied that the end of the world would come. ... First would come a bombardment of stars, and after everything else had fallen from the heavens then God himself would appear. His people were told that the only way in which they could save themselves was to build houses (after the method described to Rua by the Health Department) with tin roofs, and on the night of the end of the world, the people were to remain indoors. There was a frantic

rush to build the new dwellings, the outdoor conveniences etc. before the time prophesied. This was done ... a new, clean, more sanitary village had been built.'[44]

The recommended end of improved conditions for Rua's community had been achieved, but Pākehā authority had been subverted in favour of divine authority channelled through Rua himself.

Recognising the subversive effect of Rua's actions, not just in 1927 but throughout his years of charismatic leadership, the government had made several attempts to strip Rua of his mana and the esteem in which he was held by the Iharaira. The Tohunga Suppression Act of 1907 was the government's first strike: a piece of legislation drawn up precisely to counter Rua. The immediate cause of the Act was Rua's withdrawal of Māori children from the 'native schools'. The children would have no need of English language, Rua contended. He claimed later that at the schools the children had learned only European vices.[45] He proposed instead that an education would be provided for them at Maungapōhatu, where they would not be exposed to Pākehā 'evils'.[46]

Then in 1909, a campaign against Rua charged him with selling alcohol without a licence, an offence for which Rua served three months in jail.[47] Far from stripping him of his mana, however, the arrest and imprisonment were interpreted by his followers, with Rua's encouragement, as the inevitable persecution and suffering inflicted on the messiah. It is important to note that the actions taken against Rua were not simply a matter of Pākehā against Māori. The Tohunga Suppression Act was promoted in Parliament by two Māori MPs, James Carroll and Apirana Ngata. The opposition could thus be interpreted by Rua as the antagonism of state power, rather than simply of Pākehā, toward God's appointed prophet or messiah.

Government and police disquiet at the flourishing of Rua's settlement continued. Allegations of sedition were made against him, and in 1916 the old charges relating to illicit sale of alcohol were revived as an excuse to suppress this. The allegations referred to Rua's consistent proclamation of a future for Māori freed from the strictures of colonial governance, but the more immediate basis was Rua's opposition to the enlisting of Tūhoe men to serve as soldiers in the First World War. In both cases Rua's actions and pronouncements were perceived as a threat to New Zealand security and the rule of law. That perception, along with the remoteness of Rua's settlement, which was accessible only by foot or on horseback, fuelled considerable speculation about the magnitude and nature of the threat: 'By early 1916, rumours were spreading all over the country that Rua was arming his followers. He was said to possess a machine gun and to favour a German victory' in the war in Europe.[48] In response to the rumours, Rua invited a minister of the Crown to visit the community at Maungapōhatu 'so that he could see for himself its peaceful nature'.[49] Rua said, 'I want to draw your attention to the fact that the policemen have lied throughout. They said that I had machine guns and cannons when I did not.'[50] The invitation to the minister was not taken up. Instead, seventy armed police raided Maungapōhatu, arrested Rua and killed two members of the community. Rua was tried and imprisoned.

In opposing the draft of Tūhoe men to serve in the First World War, Rua was denying to the Crown the exercise of absolute authority. The Crown was not Lord and could not demand that his people should take up arms. Notably, the pacifist principles evident here were drawn from the Christian scriptures. This, I suggest, is highly commendable theology. There is a sense in which all biblical faith is seditious, simply because it proclaims a lordship other than, and superior to, that of the state. Rua appears to have learned that lesson well, precisely through reading the scriptures brought to Aotearoa by the race that now oppressed his people. The God testified to in Christian scripture typically sides with the oppressed, and proclaims good news to the poor and release to the captives.[51] He stands in judgement over the unjust wielding of political power, and, in the case of Israel at least, associates liberation from oppressive political powers with the provision of land. It is not difficult to see why Rua, in the context of illegal land confiscations and a government intent on subduing Tūhoe claims to sovereignty, sought to reenact the story of divine liberation and of Israel's settlement in the promised land. Of course, if God was truly to be found on the side of the oppressed, then, repeating the pattern of biblical history once more, it was clear that God would send a leader, a prophet, a messiah, to be the agent of this salvation. Rua's claim that he was God's chosen one followed reasonably enough in Rua's mind from the conviction that God was at work again among those who were oppressed and deprived of their land.

Let me conclude by drawing a further comparison with the faith of black slaves in America. There is evidence that white slave owners were reluctant initially to promote Christian faith among their slaves, for fear, apparently, that they might read the Bible and learn there of the equality of all people before God and of God's deliverance of the Israelites from slavery in Egypt. When, in time, the slaves did begin to get hold of such ideas, the slave owners started to promote Christianity with particular emphasis on Paul's injunction that slaves should be obedient to their masters. An important theological question thus arises: is the word of God to be conceived as an instrument of political control, serving the interests of the powerful, or is it more properly understood as a word that subverts and challenges all human pretensions to lordship?

Rua appears to have taken the latter view. God sides with the oppressed – against oppressive power. Whatever else about Rua's theology might be open to question, that insight, it seems to me, is not.

Endnotes

1 E Best, *Tuhoe: Children of the Mist*, 4th edition (Auckland: Reed, 1996), 1: 564.
2 Ibid, 1: 1029.
3 Considerable uncertainty surrounds the events leading to Te Kooti's arrest and detainment. Judith Binney gives an extensive account of the varying evidence in *Redemption Songs: A Life of the Nineteenth-century Maori Leader Te Kooti Arikirangi Te Turuki* (Auckland: Auckland University Press/Bridget Williams Books, 1995), chapter 2.
4 B Elsmore, *Mana From Heaven: A Century of Maori Prophets in New Zealand*, 2nd edition (Auckland: Reed, 1999), 201.
5 Cited in ibid.
6 Binney, *Redemption Songs*, 17.
7 Elsmore, *Mana From Heaven*, 201.
8 Binney, *Redemption Songs*, 66.
9 Ibid.

10 Ibid, 93.
11 Cited in ibid, 94.
12 Cited in ibid, 95. 'Taniwha' means a water monster, or sometimes a powerful person representing a threat.
13 Eria Raukura's report is found in ibid, 98.
14 Elsmore, *Mana From Heaven*, 207.
15 W Greenwood, 'The Upraised Hand, or the Spiritual Significance of the Rise of the Ringatu Faith', in *Journal of the Polynesian Society* 51 (1942): 1–80, 25.
16 For a full account of the confiscations see J Binney, *Encircled Lands: Te Urewera 1820–1921* (Wellington: Bridget Williams Books, 2009), especially chapter 5.
17 Cited in Binney, *Redemption Songs*, 506.
18 Elsmore, *Mana From Heaven*, 208–9.
19 J Binney, G Chaplin and C Wallace (eds), *Mihaia: The Prophet Rua Kenana and his Community at Maungapohatu* (Auckland: Auckland University Press, 1979), 16.
20 From the prophecies of the elders of the land published in *Te Whetū Marama o Te Kotahitanga*, 29 August–5 September 1931, 9, cited in Binney, Chaplin and Wallace, *Mihaia*, 17.
21 *Te Pipiwharauroa*, C (1906), 6 (trans. M Penfold), cited in Binney, Chaplin and Wallace, *Mihaia*, 29.
22 The following account is drawn from Judith Binney's record of the story. See Binney, Chaplin and Wallace, *Mihaia*, 20 and a more extensive version in Binney, *Redemption Songs*, 506–9.
23 Brief accounts of the journeys of the respective claimants can be found in Binney, *Redemption Songs*, 513–16.
24 Binney, Chaplin and Wallace, *Mihaia*, 20.
25 Ibid, 21.
26 Ibid, 27.
27 Cited in ibid, 30.
28 The story is recounted in ibid, 73.
29 Again, see ibid, for these references, especially 49.
30 A suggestion made also by Binney in *Redemption Songs*, 298.
31 This prohibition was relaxed in the later years of the community.
32 B Elsmore, *Like Them That Dream: The Maori and the Old Testament* (Auckland: Reed, 1985), 184.
33 Reported in Binney, *Redemption Songs*, 356.
34 Cited in ibid.
35 J G Laughton, *From Forest Trail to City Street: The Story of the Presbyterian Church Among the Maori People* (Christchurch: Presbyterian Bookroom, 1961), 49. The conference referred to was a conference on Māori missions called by the 1951 General Assembly of the Presbyterian Church and which met in Fielding, 16–18 September 1952. It is worth noting that in Laughton's report to the Presbyterian General Assembly in 1926, he complained that the effort to establish an indigenous religion was a hindrance rather than an aid to the acceptance of the gospel among Māori. That complaint was directed against the leadership provided by Te Kooti and Rua. See *Proceedings of the General Assembly of the Presbyterian Church of New Zealand* (PCNZ PGA), 1926, 77.
36 PCNZ PGA, 1926, 75–6.
37 Ibid, 76.
38 Ibid, 77–8.

39 G S Wilmore, *Black Religion and Black Radicalism: An Interpretation of the Religious History of Afro-American People*, 2nd edition (Maryknoll, New York: Orbis, 1983), 37.
40 Ibid.
41 For a detailed account of Māori identification with the themes of the Old Testament, see Elsmore, *Like Them That Dream*. Chapter 20, 182–9, offers an account of Rua and the Ihiraira.
42 Elsmore provides a number of examples in *Mana From Heaven*. See 100–3, 121, 125–30, 198 and 200.
43 See ibid, 308.
44 Binney, Chaplin and Wallace, *Mihaia*, 156–8.
45 *New Zealand Herald*, 20 April 2008, cited in ibid, 34.
46 Binney, Chaplin and Wallace, *Mihiaia*, 34.
47 Rua's repeated attempts to obtain a licence so that he could regulate the sale of alcohol among his community and thus curb excessive drinking had been denied by the authorities.
48 Binney, Chaplin and Wallace, *Mihaia*, 82.
49 Ibid, 88.
50 *Auckland Star*, 15 July 1916, as cited in ibid.
51 Such revolutionary actions constitute the content of the ministry of Jesus, announced in Nazareth when Jesus quoted from the scroll of Isaiah. See Luke 4: 16–21.

Chapter Twelve

Rātana, the Prophet: Mā te wā – the Sign of the Broken Watch

Keith Newman

Mā te wā. Is it simply 'see you later', as the TV presenter says when she signs off? Maybe 'we'll wait and see' is a more appropriate rendering, or better still 'there is a right time and place for everything'. It's a term Māori prophet, healer and political visionary Tahupotiki Wiremu Rātana used a lot. It was like he had a peculiar relationship with time.

Rātana's uncanny perceptiveness earned him national and international respect. Often when people were fussing and debating over critical issues he would remain quietly in the background, waiting for the right moment to settle the matter. Like a good musician, his timing was impeccable. Perhaps Ecclesiastes 3:1 nails it: 'To every thing there is a season, and a time to every purpose under heaven'. Another scriptural intangible might be the often flippantly quipped: 'And we know that all things work together for good to them that love God, to them who are called according to his purpose'.[1] Both challenge our perceptions of time.

My foray into writing the story of Rātana was a reluctant one; at first it felt like I was poking my nose into other people's business, and there was no shortage of people telling me so. As a writer, however, my curiosity was piqued, and I sensed an important part of New Zealand's colourful history was being neglected. The Rātana legacy is still strongly guarded today; many know snippets but are short on fact or detail, and those who do know are often reluctant to share. There is, however, an attractive drawing power when curiosity is heightened, and by serendipity or coincidence

Paula Novak, *Ratana the Prophet*, 2005.

we are rewarded with a surreal education. Add patience to the mix and over time, possibly because we are now attuned to our subject, an intangible synchronicity – an aligning of parallel but unrelated events – can produce a sense of moment or meaning that has all the hallmarks of the spiritual.

This was my experience during twenty years' researching and writing *Ratana Revisited* for Reed in 2006 and the less athletic follow-up *Ratana the Prophet* for Penguin in 2009. Every time I was about to give up, new sources were revealed, or a flow of information came my way that I might not have recognised or appreciated unless I had been at that particular crossroads. This sidereal way of seeing things takes us into the realm of that most misunderstood of individuals – the prophet – and is in part why I entitled this essay 'Mā te Wā – the Sign of the Broken Watch'.

In September 2009 I received an email from Debbie Martin, curator of the twentieth-century New Zealand history exhibition planned for Te Papa Museum in Wellington in October 2010. Among the storylines she was developing was that of the Rātana–Labour alliance, particularly the gifting of symbolic objects by Rātana to Prime Minister Michael Joseph Savage in 1936. Among the Savage memorabilia placed in glass cases inside his mausoleum were documents, personal effects, gifts and Māori artefacts. Debbie wanted to know whether a broken watch they had discovered could be the same one given to the then prime minister by T W Rātana.

A fortuitous meeting

Shortly after his election as the first Rātana MP, Eruera Tirikatene had been looking for a political partner for Rātana: someone who could be trusted and was true to Christian principles. It was Tirikatene who first tabled in Parliament the Treaty of Waitangi, described by some as the nation's founding document. He arranged the meeting between Mickey Savage and Rātana in Parliament Buildings on 22 April 1936. In a symbolic act Rātana placed before Savage a waka (canoe), actually a kūmara (some records say a potato) with three huia feathers in it. The huia, which signified chiefly mana and the heritage of Māori, was already rare at the turn of the century but rapidly descended into extinction through introduced predators and opportunists, particularly after a visit by King George in 1901, when its feathers became a fashion statement.[2] The kūmara represented the land that had been taken from Rātana's people, so they could no longer plant their food.

Next Rātana produced a greenstone tiki, saying 'This represents the power, richness and nobility of the Māori people which I place in your hands. Yes, greenstone represents the power and authority of the Māori people which in this day and age has been lost to them through European laws.' He then handed Savage his grandfather's broken gold watch and chain. Te Rātana had been loyal to the government, but 'As it happens, this tewa itikoura (watch) has no glass. My ancestor had no money to replace the glass, and it so happens I haven't any money either to replace the glass. I give these objects into your hands.'

Rātana also presented Savage with the moon and star emblem of the Rātana movement, symbolic of the 40,000 people who had signed his covenant and petition seeking to have the promises of the Treaty of Waitangi honoured, saying 'I hand this over to your safe keeping and care, that you may be their father in justice in the physical works.' He added, 'May you never forget your responsibilities to the Māori people, for when you forget this, your government will fall.' If Savage would fix the problems presented to him by introducing new laws and helping to save the Māori people, he would earn the right to wear the huia feather, the sign of the ariki, the paramount chief of Māoridom.[3]

Reluctant prophet

Rātana, whose name incidentally translates to 'lantern', was a reluctant prophet standing at an important crossroads in New Zealand's evolution as a nation. In some ways he was the kaitiaki or caretaker of ancient things, shedding new light on the powerful cultural and spiritual shift that occurred when Māori first encountered the gospel story; a relationship that lost focus somewhere between the Land Wars of the 1860s and Rātana's extraordinary rise to prominence between the two world wars.

To many it appeared Rātana carried the mantle of the Māori prophetic tradition that in some cases predated the arrival of Europeans, and certainly gained new expression in the decades after

Samuel Marsden's first Christian sermon at Oihi Bay in the Bay of Islands on Christmas Day 1814. While the missionaries were still landlocked in the Far North by Hongi Hika's musket wars, former Māori slaves, who had learned at the missionary schools and often been released as a consequence of the Christian message, took the rongo pai (good news) back to their own tribes. From around 1836 the message that all were equal under one God, that forgiveness was the antidote to utu (revenge) and that peace was preferable to the endless tribal wars that seemed to plague Māoridom spread rapidly across the length and breadth of the country.

Inevitably the Bible stories, particularly those relating to the Old Testament prophets and heroes of the faith, and an awareness that their customs and practices and land issues were similar to those of ancient Israel, aroused the Māori imagination. As colonial promises of shared governance, including the protection of Māori land, customs and rights provided for in the Treaty of Waitangi, were increasingly betrayed, a new militancy emerged. Māori in some parts of the country demanded a voice in their own temporal and spiritual affairs, which often mixed ancient and modern belief systems. Several Māori prophets,[4] typically having learned at and even taught at the various Wesleyan or Church Missionary Society/Anglican mission schools, initiated various responses to the Crown's escalating land acquisitions. The fact that many of the missionaries they had come to trust, including the Anglican Bishop Selwyn, had been seen acting as chaplains to the troops during the 1860s helped to alienate some Māori from the missionary churches. After confiscations in the Waikato, Tauranga and Taranaki and the last stand at Parihaka, colonisation was deemed an unstoppable force, and Māori were increasingly scattered and dispossessed. All the while, though, there remained an undercurrent of faith that one day someone would come who would again stand firm on the two texts still deemed so important to the future of Māoridom, the Bible and the Treaty. Northern prophet and founder of the Kotahitanga movement Aperahama Taonui was among those who gave voice to such hopes when he spoke out in 1863, reflecting on his original request for the Treaty of Waitangi to be signed outside Busby's

Treaty House over a Māori cloak rather than the Union Jack: 'And you, Ngapuhi, who won't listen, well the person who will live in this house with all its customs and habits shall be a spider. The day is coming when you will see a man carrying his two books, the Bible and the Treaty of Waitangi. Listen to him.'[5]

If you could step back and get a God's-eye view you might see the roads of history converging on Rātana's time and space. He was raised on the borders between the major tribes of the lower North Island, and proved to be the perfect pan-tribal bridge-builder and logical inheritor of the mantle of the Kotahitanga (unity) political and Maramatanga (enlightenment) spiritual movements. Moving along one of those roads was the warrior-prophet Te Kooti, whose Old Testament experience saw him railing against his wrongful arrest and Chatham Island imprisonment, and on his escape rampaging across the central North Island at the end of the Land Wars. In his wiser, more temperate New Testament phase, as he moved from law to grace, he was following a dream of peaceful coexistence. He was looking for a successor to the great Māori prophetic lineage: someone who could unite the people and bring them into a new spirituality, based around the one God of Christianity.

At the mouth of the Whanganui River in January 1893, Te Kooti told a local Ngāti Apa elder, the 'promised one' would come from beneath his 'armpit'; that is, from that area. He stated: 'a garden of many flowers shall come forth from out of the mouth of the Whangaehu River, and its fragrance will be dispersed throughout the four winds of the country'. Later in that year, just before he died, Te Kooti elaborated on a long-standing prophecy about certain stars signifying the rise of the next great Māori leader. 'From Kati Kati to Cape Runaway there will be one child. If he arrives within six years there will be great tribulation. If his advent does not take place in that time, in 26 years he will rise from the west and will unite the people.'[6]

Rangitikei chief Te Kere and Wairarapa prophet Pōtangaroa had both prophesied the coming of a new movement to unite the Māori people. Before his death Te Kere erected a wooden cross on Tikanga, a distinctly carved house beside the Rangitikei River, located in Ngāti Raukawa territory close to the borders of Rangitane and Ngāti Apa. Te Kere said the person the cross fell on would continue his prophetic tradition. When the cross toppled it struck Atareta Mere Rikiriki Kawana Ropiha. She had been raised by the Rātana or Ngahina family, as they were then known, and later in life was recognised as a prophetess with a healing gift. She was based at Parewanui Marae. She had founded a non-denominational Māori church, Te Hāhi o te Wairua Tapu (the Church of the Holy Spirit). Her spiritual home became the Parewanui church building Wheriko (Jericho), built by the missionary Rev. Richard Taylor in 1862. Her movement was based on Christian scriptures and principles, with a strong emphasis on the role of the holy spirit, the unity of Māori under one God and the importance of the Treaty of Waitangi.

She had prophesied: 'The time is near when a young man will rise in my place; when he comes there will be weeping and gnashing of teeth; when he comes the true and the false will never survive together, neither with righteous and the unrighteous, nor doctrines that are of God and the doctrines of man and the Devil.'[7] Mere Rikiriki was impressed by the intuition of Rātana Ngahina, who believed his grandson Tahupotiki Wiremu Rātana was destined for much higher things than labouring on the farm and adding to the profits of the local tavern. Events confirming her choice would occur just twenty-six years after Te Kooti's very specific prophecy.

Rātana's empowering vision

A series of challenging incidents and a sense that destiny was overshadowing him kept drawing Rātana away from the pub and his role as champion wheat-stacker and local bookie. On the afternoon of 8 November 1918, three days before the end of the First World War, Rātana was standing on the veranda of his farmhouse when he saw a cloud coming toward him from the ocean.

It was dark on the outside but the centre was pure white, and at the back was a bright glowing colour like a flame. When it was directly over him it 'broke open' and he was overwhelmed by its presence. It was then that he saw highways, roads and pathways from all over the world leading to his house. As if in a trance, he walked into the kitchen, jumped onto the table and exclaimed: 'Peace be unto you all, for I am the Holy Spirit that speaks unto you all. Straighten yourselves. Repent.'[8] His daughter Maata ran to get the family Bible, but her father explained his message was in the Bible, and threw the book on the mantelpiece. In doing so an old clock belonging to his grandfather fell and broke on the stone hearth. There was concern at the damage, but Rātana responded that 'the time had come for the clock to finish its work and that everything that was in the clock was in his heart'. He said 'if you wish, this clock shall ring at 5 o'clock', and then threw the pieces in the fire. The story, according to his own words, is that a Pākehā visitor quickly retrieved the pieces from the fire, and when it was sitting on the hearth again, it rang on the fifth hour.[9] The timing was perfect.

Two days after his vision Rātana began moving everything out of the house – all the furniture, food and ornaments – until all that was left was a large pile of clothes on the bare floor in one room. He gave his immediate family water and took them on a long walk across the rugged farm landscape throughout the night. The next day, Rātana's family moved in with a neighbour while he continued his cleansing process, and then he sent word to his mother and family to leave the township of Pātea, as a voice had told him a disaster was about to strike. His mother and nephew followed his advice; those who did not died within days, including most of those who had owned the clothing Rātana had piled on the floor of the now-barren family home.[10] The 'Spanish flu' spread like a plague in two virulent waves, leaving 8573 people throughout the country dead. The mate urutā (death cold) claimed over 2000 Māori lives.[11] Rātana himself had a slight attack, but his family suffered severely – among the twenty-one grandchildren of Rātana Ngahina only his two sisters remained, leaving Wiremu Rātana the sole male heir to the family farm. He had acted just in the nick of time.

Over the succeeding weeks Rātana had a number of visions, including a pivotal message that was to further shape his mission. The holy spirit spoke to him explaining that he had been called to unite Māori under Ihoa o ngā Mano (Jehovah of the Thousands) to heal the people and turn them from their fears and superstitions.[12]

From 1920 onwards people flocked to the Rātana family farm seeking prayer and guidance. He told them to believe in the father, son and holy spirit, and prayed in the name of Jesus. He never laid hands on anyone. Over time thousands were healed, and crutches, walking sticks, glasses, wheelchairs and other items, including tapu objects given by tohunga and surrendered by those making a Christian commitment, piled up and were eventually stored away in the 'jailhouse' or Whare Māori building at Rātana Pā.

A world tour and war prophecies

While touring the country, lifting curses, healing people and encouraging unity under one God, Rātana also conducted thorough research into injustices and breaches of the Treaty of Waitangi. He gathered up signatures from two-thirds of Māoridom, and when the New Zealand government rejected his petition, he took it to London. In 1924, he and a party of forty musicians, cultural performers and elders visited the United Kingdom, ostensibly to have the Treaty acknowledged by the Crown and the British Parliament. Here too, however, he was rejected. Again he found himself slipping into an uncanny mode of knowing.

On 17 May 1924 the party were looking around Westminster Abbey, and as they crossed Westminster Bridge, Rātana stopped in the middle and proclaimed: 'As I stand on this bridge and look all around me, I tell you all, the Angel of Death will visit this place, not a stone shall stand upon a stone and the inhabitants of these houses will live under the ground.' He is also reported to have said: 'When all your castles [stone houses] are destroyed in time to come, then will the carpenters, the blacksmiths and the shoemakers be in power, and I will be the government.'[13] Some say that in describing the destruction of the stone buildings and referring to a prophecy of King Tāwhiao's,[14] Rātana foresaw the Luftwaffe bombings of London, which reduced the buildings around Westminster to rubble, and the subsequent election of Labour governments in both England and New Zealand.

Dejected and with a broken heart, Rātana took his people on the final part of their journey, to Japan. On the way he prophesied that he would reveal 'hidden things' to the Japanese people, after which a great war or blaze would come.[15] He and his people were hosted by Bishop Juji Nakada, who, alongside Oswald Chambers, had cofounded the Oriental Mission Society. Rātana and Nakada became great friends, and much was shared. They even exchanged national costumes, and presided over a spiritual marriage between their nations and the literal marriage of Rātana's daughter and Nakada's son to their respective partners (Nakada performed the marriage of Rātana's daughter and Rātana the marriage of Nakada's son).

Initially all the major Christian denominations supported 'the Māori miracle man', even allowing some of their own ministers to remain with him as they clamoured to be part of the great Māori revival. Rātana didn't want to form a separate church, and had frequently urged his people to stay within their own denominations. However, Catholics, Anglicans and other denominations were pressuring him to commit to their particular Christian persuasion, and all the while pin-pricking him about his theology. There was quite a controversy raging about his alleged elevation of the holy angels and use of the term 'māngai', which simply means mouthpiece, spokesperson or one who broadcasts the word of God. A lasting friend and advisor proved to be superintendent of the Methodist Māori Mission, 'Father' Arthur J Seamer, who helped draw up the Christian-based Rātana Creed.

Rātana scolded several followers who had formed a separate church while he had been away in England in 1924, and had it annulled. During a Christmas 1924 hui at Rātana Pā, he attempted to reach a consensus with the various churches over allegations of heresy. After several days of debate there seemed to be widespread agreement, but just as Father Seamer was about to summarise, contention once more entered in, when an Anglican and a Ringatū minister began contending over what role the established churches should take. Rātana and Seamer agreed the mood of the meeting had been lost. Rātana feared his people would be divided, saying 'I can't address them after that! The church has too many voices and the people are divided. We must go our own way!' The Rātana Church of New Zealand was officially registered on 15 July 1925.[16]

Within two and a half years the pride of the Rātana faith, Te Temepara Tapu o Ihoa (the Sacred Temple of Jehovah), had fulfilled Rātana's vision of 'a magnificent temple' at Rātana Pā, representing the mana and symbolism of his ministry and conveying 'something greater and nobler than what can be seen by the human eye'.[17] Rātana's connection with the Japanese people, the prophecies he made in Japan, the official opening of the Rātana Temple by Juji Nakada, Nakada's provision of a large clock mechanism for the lawn and Rātana's prophecies about thousands of Asians and Japanese coming to New Zealand are worthy of a book in themselves.[18]

Potangaroa's prophecy

On 14 April 1928, 144 people from Rātana Pā made the journey to Te Oreore Marae at Masterton to expose the 'Mauri stone' that had been placed in the meeting house on 16 March 1881 by the prophet Pōtangaroa. Several tohunga had died in the attempt to remove the stone, and children who had touched the marble statue above it had also died or become ill. A petition signed by 500 people from the Ngāti Kahungunu iwi had invited Rātana to come and cleanse the site.

In the late 1800s Te Pōtangaroa and Rangitikei prophet and master carver Te Kere had planned to build a large carved house, but after an argument Te Kere withdrew. When the building was completed, Pōtangaroa was at the height of his influence, and had recently converted to Christianity. Before he died, he made predictions about the coming of a new Māori church: 'There is a religious denomination coming for us; perhaps it will come from there, perhaps it will emerge here. Secondly, let the churches into the house – there will be a time when a religion will emerge for you and I and the Māori people.' He predicted a number of signs that over the next forty years would inform Wairarapa Māori when this would be. Over the years several movements claimed the prophecy pointed to them, but nothing definitively fulfilled the prophecy until Rātana was called to this location forty-seven years later, in 1928.[19]

Once the descendants of Pōtangaroa were in complete agreement about the removal of the stone and the spiritual cleansing, Rātana confirmed this was 'the most powerful of curses throughout the country'. He declared he had come to this place with the purpose of uniting 'the fish' (Te Ika a Māui – the North Island), as there were representatives from all parts of the country present: 'It has been nine years now since I have called for the whole country to unite under the protection of Ihoa o nga Mano. Yet there are some who still remain aloof, outside watching this revelation with curiosity.' Rātana said the elders, who had previously had a strong foundation of truth based in Jehovah, had added their own mixture of sorcery, and their faith had become defiled. He challenged the priests, sorcerers and intellectuals who he said had twisted or dismissed the truths of Jehovah, and urged the people to come together in one waka, that they might be in unity in paddling towards a quick recovery.

Inside the meeting house Rātana and a number of young men lifted the marble statue and carried it outside. Rātana began sawing through the floorboards where the statue had stood, and reached in to lift out a large glass bottle sealed with wax. This disintegrated, revealing a sheepskin with writing on it, coins and the remains of three skeletons. The writing on the folded sheepskin had faded, but underneath it Rātana found what he had come for: a 100-pound greenstone slab, which was lifted through the hole in the floor. As soon as Rātana began to touch the objects, 'a heaviness' came over him, so he prayed for extra strength and protection. The three skeletal remains, according to Rātana, had been placed there as food for the pounamu (greenstone), and the karakia (incantations, charms or spells) of the elders of the time had invoked a powerful force, which had backfired on Pōtangaroa's descendants. It is said Rātana slept for fifteen hours after his ordeal, but his actions in removing the stone increased his mana in the eyes of Wairarapa Māori, and many joined his movement. The statue, which was moved outside, is still there today, with a plaque commemorating Rātana's success at removing the stone and the curse.[20]

In the mid-1980s, Regan Pōtangaroa, a highly respected civil engineer and a direct descendant of the prophet Pōtangaroa, saved the Rātana movement hundreds of thousands of dollars when he came up with a low-cost 'foundational rocking system' to stabilise the Rātana Temple from the impact of earthquakes. The movement had planned to approve a million-dollar structural protection process; the money saved by the Wairarapa prophet's great-grandson was now freed up for other restoration work. It was during this time that Regan Pōtangaroa first learned about the deep links between his family and the Rātana movement; he came to consider his efforts in stabilising the Rātana Temple as payback for Rātana removing the curse at Te Oreore Marae sixty years previously.[21] The hands of time had aligned once more, adding further richness to the Rātana legacy.

The Mount of Olives prophecy

One of the names given to Rātana Pā is Hiruhārama Hou (New Jerusalem) – the promised land of the Book of Revelation. As one turns off the main highway midway between Palmerston North and Whanganui toward the tiny village, there is a dip in the road known as Te Moana Whero (the Red Sea). In other words, one has to go through the Red Sea to get to the promised land. The hill, as one heads down into the first gully from the turn-off into Rātana Pā, is known as Maunga Oriwa (the Mount of Olives). On 11 November 1936, Rātana was speaking to his followers, the mōrehu (the scattered remnant of believers), about the history of the farming scheme he had organised, when he began to prophesy:

> You have all heard and are familiar with the word that says: 'Night time has passed, the new break of dawn draws near', there is a day unfolding when you will see two towers standing on the Mount of Olives, and at that time you will see a woman rising up from the Labour Party who will become prime minister, and then you will know you are at the doorway, not nearing it, but actually at the doorway. ... [22]

It is certainly curious that today Telecom and Vodafone cellphone towers stand in that field, and that Helen Clark became New Zealand's first elected woman prime minister in 1999 as head of the Labour government. Obviously Rātana, who seems to have a fairly good track record of 'knowing the times', was trying to tell us something that went way beyond any party political affiliation.

In Rātana's pan-tribal political model, his body was split into ngā koata e whā (the four quarters), which not only represented his plan to capture all four Māori seats in Parliament but also had a great spiritual significance.

In his spiritual overview the northern tribes were seen as guardians of the birthplace of Christianity, where the holy Bible was first made available to Māori and the gospel preached. It was here Māori independence was first declared and the Treaty of Waitangi signed. Rātana related the north to his role as Piri Wiri Tua – the treaty campaigner, the ploughman turning over the topsoil to expose the deeper red soil of the nation – as he pushed through to the other side in his social and political works.[23]

The South Island or Te Waipounamu tribes he saw as guardians of greenstone and gold, representing spiritual and economic power or mauri and associated with his son Te Omeka.

The West Coast tribes were seen as guardians of the blood spilt upon Waitara and the tragedy at Parihaka, where the Crown was seen to have provoked civil war through its invasions. This area, associated with Rātana's son Te Arepa, included Mt Taranaki and Te Rere o Kapunui (the waterfall of the prophets), where Rātana often received inspiration.

The East Coast tribes were viewed as guardians of the first rays of the sun, and associated with Rātana's third son Hamuera. This area represented the door or gateway to the future, and retained special significance in the Rātana prophetic understanding. Rātana often referred to the East Coast from Wairarapa to Te Māhia as his 'father and mother', because the people had been eager to accept the Bible and support the independence movement and the Treaty of Waitangi. Christianity had caught on like wildfire down this coast, from Tauranga to Gisborne and through Hawke's Bay, after

Māori slaves freed from Northland brought the gospel to their own people, often well before the missionaries visited.

The memorial arch at the Rātana Temple gates, which Rātana opened in July 1935, states: 'Te Arepa – the beginning, Te Omeka the end, Hamuera the last full stop. Therefore, this treasured memorial now stands revealed, from now on the Spirit will do its work and you shall know its fruits.' According to Rātana tradition the era of Hamuera, the youngest son, is the 'full stop' on the works of men and the beginning or doorway (te tatau) of the Kororia Hareruia (Glory Hallelujah) era, when Ihoa (Jehovah) would make his purposes known to the faithful mōrehu.[24] Rātana was determined to leave the people with a deep sense that the mission he had begun did not end with him, and that a doorway to a new era would be opened to them after a time of fire and great darkness.

The passing of the prophet

Rātana the miracle worker and passionate advocate for the political and spiritual unification of the Māori people took his final breath at 10 a.m. on Monday, 18 September 1939, aged sixty-six. A large crowd, including Prime Minister Michael Joseph Savage, several members of Parliament and about 3000 faithful gathered for the tangi, which lasted a week. Even his old nemesis, long-standing East Coast politician and reformer Sir Apirana Ngata, made a gracious speech to commemorate the passing of the man he had often criticised and challenged in the public arena:

> Farewell, my friend. For your way was not an easy one to walk but you had intentions to run off because people like you who are prophets can see things coming before they reach us. You see the fire burning on the other side, this is why I said … your body is a different body unlike the body of others because your body is the body of a prophet.[25]

As Rātana's spirit passed on to be with his creator, Germany moved in to bomb Warsaw and bring the world into the second great global conflict of the twentieth century. By the time of his death, 100 years after the signing of the Treaty of Waitangi, the followers of T W Rātana had grown to become New Zealand's largest and most influential Māori religious community. Rātana remains the most successful faith healer this country has seen: he challenged the old superstitions, gave Māori a unique church they could call their own and spearheaded a political movement that even today holds considerable influence. Rātana accurately predicted a time when ngā koata e whā, the four quarters of his body, would be in Parliament to return the Treaty of Waitangi to prominence. However, he also foresaw a time when the promises made by the politicians of his time and those made by his own people to protect his spiritual legacy would be neglected.

Rātana's political partner and friend, Prime Minister Michael Joseph Savage, followed him to the grave on 27 March 1940 after a long illness. Although individual Rātana members of Parliament doggedly persisted in pushing through significant changes that benefitted Māori over many years, the potential impact of that historic relationship was systematically undermined by party politics. While Rātana held the Labour government in power through several critical elections, its members were never elevated to any role beyond junior ministers, and had little direct responsibility even for Māori affairs.

Today many in the Rātana movement still cling to the coat-tails of the seventy-six-year-old symbolic alliance between two visionary Christian gentlemen, Rātana and Savage, who foresaw Māori taking a pivotal part in the future governance of this nation. At the 2010 Rātana celebrations, Prime Minister John Key, his National Party colleagues and their unlikely Māori Party allies were graciously welcomed onto the marae and their efforts on behalf of Māori applauded. Labour leader Phil Goff, like a defeated warrior rattling old grievances, perhaps in an attempt to stir a corpse to life, was given a telling off by Rātana elders for his party's failure to meet Māori aspirations during its last terms in power. A challenge from Rātana to place its members high on the Labour Party list, where they were more likely to succeed in the next elections, was rejected, almost confirming that any such 'alliance' was a spent force.[26]

Today the Rātana movement continues to have a strong political influence but its future vitality and influence may well have more to do with training up young people to take their place in society and in its role at the spiritual intersection of New Zealand history, where Rātana stood ninety years previously as a sentinel; a rallying point re-visioning the words of the old Māori prophets and mixing them with gospel-infused revelations of his own. Today he is still a 'finger' pointing to a brighter future, where Māori are no longer second-class citizens in their own land.

Several times Rātana called forth the prophecies of East Coast prophet Arama Toiroa,[27] Te Kooti, King Tāwhiao and others, saying their prognostications relating to the future of Māoridom were now in the palm of his hand.[28] He also spoke as the kaitiaki of the physical boundaries of this land, stating 'the foreshore is my boundary'.[29] Was this egotism and arrogance, or part of a broader drama that Rātana took part in for a time? Most of Rātana's followers understood such revelation as coming from Te Māngai (the mouthpiece), as Rātana was overshadowed by the wairua tapu (holy spirit). These were the times when his followers felt reassured that Ihoa had not forgotten them.

In 2009 I was asked whether I thought the broken watch found in Michael Joseph Savage's mausoleum might be the same one that had belonged to Rātana's grandfather. The only description I could provide was that the watch was old and gold, had a chain and had no glass on the front. I asked Whetu Tirakatene-Sullivan, whose father Eruera Tirikatene had been present when these symbolic gifts were placed on the table in April 1936. 'Who could ever know?', she said, but like me she was excited at the possibility. In October 2010, just ahead of the opening of 'Slice of Heaven: 20th Century Aotearoa' at Te Papa, I rang the curator Debbie Martin to see if the identity had been confirmed. She revealed with some disappointment that a photograph had been located confirming the watch had actually belonged to Savage's grandfather.

In some ways that just adds to the mystery about what happened to the curiously famous Rātana timepiece. Stretching the symbolism, you might be tempted to say perhaps time failed both men, who died within months of each other before their visions were completed. Some say Rātana's broken timepiece represented the broken promises of the Treaty of Waitangi; particularly the misuse of land laws that allowed the confiscation of so much Māori land in the 1860s and beyond. Perhaps it suggested that time couldn't move on until these matters were addressed.

Some talk of Rātana's third-generation prophecies, as if the same spirit that empowered him will again move mightily among the mōrehu at a specific time, while others suggest that spiritual influence is a general principle of inheritance, intended to inspire each succeeding generation to expand his legacy. In accepting the mantle placed on him through the visions of the Māori prophets, Rātana once said: 'in one of my hands is the Bible; in the other the Treaty of Waitangi. If the spiritual side is attended to, all will be well on the physical side.'[30]

I have been criticised for not being more analytical in my books by dissecting Rātana's so-called healing and prophecies in the light of modern psychological and medical knowledge, and for allowing stories of his miracle-working power to go unchallenged.

Today few talk about the humanitarian Christian origins and principles of the Treaty of Waitangi,[31] and many reject the Bible as being God's 'word' to the generations and are embarrassed at the possibility of the supernatural or the miraculous. They mock any concept of a divine purpose, destiny or morality, suggesting everything can be explained by time and chance, leaving earth's inhabitants as accidental tourists caught in the eternal struggle for survival. Clever atheists and humanists, and even some theologians, seem evangelistically determined to dismiss the creator as 'natural forces' at best, and to demote Christ to no more than a gifted man. I think Rātana would have been horrified at the new 'intellectual' tohunga who have rationalised and sterilised our spiritual history, replacing the miraculous with the mundane in their attempt to sever that tightly woven three-fold cord of faith, hope and love.[32]

Broken watches, broken promises, broken connections and broken history? Who am I to try and put a modern sceptical framework around this great man and his life? All I know is that

Rātana believed the holy spirit's power was available to all believers, and that there was a special measure for Māori. Perhaps it is the role of the prophet to look around the corner of time, to see the ideal of how things could be, to deliver insights on how to put things right and to assist with restoration, reconciliation and renewal. So what is the sign of the broken watch; is it still a symbol of outstanding issues and legal mechanisms that failed Māori, or have the hands begun to move again? For this writer, some things must remain a matter of faith, particularly when dealing with 'prophets' who seem to have an uncanny ability to deliver challenging messages from a realm beyond our usual perceptions. Rātana was a man for his time. He stood in the gap like a timepiece, one hand pointing to the past and another to the future. Perhaps he is still the kaituki (time-keeper) at the head of the waka urging us all to 'pull, pull, pull' together in unity and common purpose under one God, honouring both the Bible and the Treaty of Waitangi. The alternative is that we just keep going round in circles. Perhaps it's time to take a compass reading, reclaim our 'spiritual history', and synchronise our watches. Mā te wā?

Endnotes

1 Romans 8:28.
2 N Olliver, 'Nga Huia' (2002): www.nzbirds.com/birds/huia.html (accessed 17 January 2012).
3 R N Love, 'Policies of frustration: the growth of Maori politics; the Ratana/Labour era', PhD thesis, Victoria University of Wellington, 1977, 296–7, citing the records of the meeting recorded by P K Paikea and comparing them with *Te Whetū Marama o te Kotahitanga* (newsletters published by the Rātana Church from 1924) and 'Nga Akoranga' (internal study notes in four bound volumes (*Tahi, Rua, Toru, Wha*), produced by past secretaries and elders of the Rātana Church in 1982 and revised in 1987; copies held by the author). Love also interviewed Jim Henderson, who spoke personally to E T Tirikatene about the meeting.
4 Including Te Ruki Kawiti in the Far North; Te Ua Haumene, founder of the Paimārire (Hauhau) and Tītokowaru in Taranaki; Tāwhiao Te Wherowhero in the Waikato; Te Kooti Arikirangi, who founded the Ringatū movement, in the Bay of Plenty; Aperahama Taonui in the Far North; Hipa Te Maiharoa in the South Island; and Te Whiti o Rongomai and Tohu Kākahi at Parihaka. See also B Elsmore, *Mana From Heaven: A Century of Māori Prophets in New Zealand*, 2nd edition (Auckland: Reed, 1999) and K Newman, *Bible & Treaty: Missionaries Among the Māori – A New Perspective* (Auckland: Penguin, 2010).

5 'Nga Akoranga' (*Wha*); see also J Binney, 'Taonui, Aperahama – Biography', from the *Dictionary of New Zealand Biography*, in *Te Ara – the Encyclopedia of New Zealand*: www.teara.govt.nz/en/biographies/2t7/1 (accessed 17 January 2012).

6 'Nga Akoranga' (*Wha*); J Binney, *Redemption Songs: A Life of the Nineteenth-century Maori Leader Te Kooti Arikirangi Te Turuki* (Auckland: Auckland University Press/Bridget Williams Books, 1997), 458; and D Young, *Woven by Water: Histories from the Whanganui River* (Wellington: Huia, 1998).

7 Interviews with elders who knew Mere Rikiriki, supervised by her great-grandson, Morgan Kawana, in an unpublished document (c. 1985) held in the Uri Whakatupuranga Archive at Rātana Pā. Also citing D Young, 'Mere Rikiriki', in C Macdonald, M Penfold and B Williams (eds), *The Book of New Zealand Women: Ko Kui ma te Kaupapa* (Wellington: Bridget Williams Books, 1991), 568–70; and Young, *Woven by Water*, 175–7.

8 T W Ratana in an interview with his secretary Pita Moko in 1920 ('Nga Akoranga' (*Tahi*); also retold in 'Te Rongo Pai Hou a T.W. Ratana', Sheet 8–9, Volume One, Rātana Pā, 1930–1940). The latter reference is to a collection of unpublished documents in te reo, collated in bound form and held at Rātana Pā.

9 Eyewitness account from Maata Hura, cited in Love, 'Policies of Frustration', 191; also Moko, interview with Rātana in 'Nga Akoranga' (*Tahi*) and in 'Te Rongo Pai Hou'.

10 Maata Hura, cited in Love, 'Policies of Frustration', 192–3.

11 G W Rice, *Black November: The 1918 Influenza Pandemic in New Zealand*, revised edition (Christchurch: Canterbury University Press, 2005), 159–61.

12 Moko, interview with Rātana, in 'Nga Akoranga' (*Tahi*) and in 'Te Rongo Pai Hou'.

13 *Te Whetū Marama*, 10 March 1924; 'Te Rongo Pai Hou'.

14 Tawhiao's prophecy referred to bringing the common people together and was made in 1892 in meetings relating to establishing a Māori parliament. See Michael King, *Te Puea* (Auckland: Sceptre, 1987) 24.

15 H Tokouru Rātana, 'World Tour Journal 1924', Uri Whakatupuranga Ratana Archive, Rātana Pā, 69.

16 J M Henderson, *Ratana: The Man, the Church, the Political Movement* (Wellington: Reed/Polynesian Society, 1972), 45–6.

17 'Nga Akoranga'.

18 See K Newman, *Ratana Revisited: An Unfinished Legacy* (Auckland: Reed, 2006) and K Newman, *Ratana the Prophet* (Auckland: Penguin, 2009).

19 A Ballara and K Cairns, 'Te Potangaroa, Paora – Biography', from the *Dictionary of New Zealand Biography*, in *Te Ara – the Encyclopedia of New Zealand*: www.teara.govt.nz/en/biographies/1t57/1 (accessed 18 January 2012).

20 Ibid; 'Nga Akoranga' (*Wha*) and *Te Whetū Marama*, 21 April 1928. See also Elsmore, *Mana From Heaven*, 246–55.

21 Personal communications, Wayne Johnson (Rātana Church legal advisor) and Regan Potangaroa.

22 *Te Whetū Marama*, 28 November–5 December 1936.

23 'Nga Akoranga' (*Toru*), 34–6; *Te Whetū Marama*, 7 July and 13 October 1928.

24 *Te Whetū Marama*, 12 January–23 February and July–August 1935.

25 Ibid, September 1939. (photostat)

26 'Labour needs to look past Ratana pact', in *New Zealand Herald*, 26 January 2010: www.nzherald.co.nz/nz/news/article.cfm?c_id=1&objectid=10622239 (accessed 18 January 2012).

27 'Te ingoa o to ratou Atua, ko Tama i Rorokutia, he Atua pai, otira, ka ngaro anō te tangata.' ('The name of their new God will be "The Son Who was Killed", a good God, however the people will still be oppressed.') Toiroa made this prophecy about a new religion in 1766, three years before Captain Cook arrived. Binney, *Redemption Songs*, 11–29.
28 *Te Whetū Marama*, 28 October 1933; 'Nga Akoranga' (*Toru*), 105–6.
29 On Rātana's sixty-second birthday, 25 January 1935 (*Te Whetū Marama*, 12 January–23 February 1935), reminding the people of a similar statement he made in 1928.
30 Love, 'Policies of frustration', 242; 'Nga Akoranga' (*Toru*), 23.
31 Newman, *Bible & Treaty*, 140–4.
32 1 Corinthians 13:13.

Chapter Thirteen

Translating the Gospel in the Māori Art Tradition: The Works of Hapai Winiata

Bernard Kernot[1]

The Māori artistic tradition responded in various ways to the Christian message from a very early stage in its encounter with Christianity, judging by two small ceremonial paddles in the British Museum dating from 1823. The pommel of one carries a naturalistic male figure, while its companion piece features a female figure. Each paddle has a serpent winding down the shaft to the blade, strongly suggesting an Adam and Eve motif.

Dating from a little later is a Māori Madonna said to have been carved for a Catholic church near Rotorua in 1845.[2] By the 1840s the various missionary churches had become significant patrons of the artistic tradition, including its architecture, and came to assert a significant influence on its development that continues to the present day.

This paper examines the work and vision of one notable tohunga whakairo (carver), Hapai Winiata, who went on to become the Anglican Assistant Bishop of Wellington in 1987.

Background

Huia Hapai Winiata (1926–2004), of Ngāti Raukawa descent, was the eldest of seven children born into a devout Anglican household adjacent to the family marae at Hokio, near Levin in the Horowhenua district. He, of all his siblings, showed a marked sensibility in religious matters that began at an early age. In an interview with his sister Margaret recorded in 1999 he spoke of his early religious upbringing:

> Miss Kenworthy came to teach us Bible Stories. She was a kind woman. She was the one who made things about God easy to understand. Once a month Paora Temuera took the service. He was a lovely caring man. We were sent outside when Communion started, but I used to look through the window. I saw the grown-ups holding their hands out and I wanted that. I got confirmed in a Church hall in Levin, then I knew I could have Communion.[3]

In his mature years he remained closely associated with the church, first as a lay reader and then offering himself for the ministry. There is no record of him ever distancing himself from the church, or of a sudden conversion. To the contrary, his life seems to have entailed a steady maturing of faith and spirituality in the Mihinare[4] tradition, nurtured by Māori clergy from Rangiātea Church in Ōtaki.

By whakapapa Hapai affiliated to both the Ngāti Pareraukawa and Ngāti Parewahawaha sections of Ngāti Raukawa, and it was through his connection with Ngāti Parewahawaha that he was introduced to the Māori carving tradition. When he took up the invitation to work on the Parewahawaha meeting house he was farming family land at Ōhakea. He was well integrated into both the Māori and Pākehā communities around Bulls, even joining the Masonic Lodge.[5] Working on the Parewahawaha meeting house was his first encounter with the more esoteric side of Māori tradition and its spirituality.

The carving tradition had always been an essentially religious activity. Its subject matter represented the sacred domains of mythology and ancestors, and the craft was regulated by the institution of tapu in a complex system of prohibitions and restrictions. By the end of the nineteenth century the religious character of the tradition had been eroded by various colonial influences, which included Christianity and commercial tourism. This process, described as secularisation by Neich,[6] was hastened further in the revival of Māori architectural arts initiated by Sir Apirana Ngata in the early/mid-twentieth century. The senior tutor at Ngata's School of Māori Arts and Crafts in Rotorua, Eramiha Kapua, dispensed with tapu restrictions for the students, fearing they were more at risk from a poorly understood initiation into the tapu traditions than from never having been initiated.

This really marked a significant break with the old tradition, opening the way for a more politically conscious Māori art. Ngata had even introduced carved figures to ornament the Anglican churches and chapels built under his direction. Nevertheless, something of the old order still inhered in the art, and some of the carvers trained in Ngata's school were later to reintroduce the tapu foundation of whakairo rākau (wood carving).[7]

Hapai was fortunate in that the overseer on the Parewahawaha project, and his tutor, was Henare Toka. Toka had been a foundation student at the School of Māori Arts and Crafts and may well have been uncomfortable himself working in tapu environments. According to Hapai, Toka made two big concessions for the project. The first was teaching the carvers not to identify the figures until they went into the house and were named, at which point they would become tapu. The second was having the tapu lifted off the entire project so that men and women could work together in the same space.[8] Hapai would later try to introduce both these practices in subsequent projects, with partial success.

Throughout most of the twentieth century Ngāti Raukawa as a tribe suffered a steady erosion of culture and language, until this was arrested and reversed in the 1970s by the 'Whakatupuranga Rua Mano'[9] programme and the opening of Te Wānanga o Raukawa in Ōtaki.[10] It was in this environment of cultural decline that Hapai grew up. Living adjacent to the marae he would have been aware of family and tribal connections and marae ceremonial procedures, but also of a knowledge and language possessed by elders that was not passed down to him. On the other hand, the church was an ever-present reality that filled much of the cultural vacuum of his upbringing.

Attitudes

Hapai's attitudes towards what he perceived as traditional culture reflected his upbringing. In a series of interviews between 1975 and 1978[11] he often challenged the relevance of tradition to his generation, which he believed had lost the knowledge of the old ways, and he felt he should not be bound by traditions he did not understand.

He was also critical of those who put too much emphasis on the past at the expense of the present: a criticism he applied to his own craft. Carving, he believed, should be relevant to the present as well as the past, and should be able to engage the creative imagination of craftsmen, which may entail breaking with convention. Indeed creativity, imagination and innovation were recurring themes in his conversations, and he believed the creative spark had a divine source. According to his daughter, he saw his carving as a means of spiritual growth.

Hapai's basic postulate was that Christianity had transformed Māori society and culture, so the old ways were no longer binding if they did not share in that transformation. 'We are a new people', he once told me, 'with new blood and a new culture'. This led him to an interpretation of tribal history in which Christianity was seen as 'the greatest event in Māori history'. His presentation of tribal history in Ngatokowaru II asserts this two-testament vision by demarcating pre-Christian and Christian phases.

Of all the traditions pertaining to carving, Hapai was least comfortable with tapu, and could not work under strict tapu conditions. Alma Winiata, his daughter, records: 'He admitted that he couldn't handle total tapu restrictions; he wanted freedom to do things that made him comfortable. They included being able to take chisels home, blowing on his carvings if he wished to. Dad wasn't saying that he didn't have any respect for these areas. It only meant that he couldn't work with them.'[12]

Ngatokowaru II

Planning the replacement of their old and unadorned house known as Ngatokowaru was the business of Ngāti Pareraukawa whānau as a whole and not of the carver alone. The whānau had to decide on the conceptual theme of the house, which ancestors were to be included, and where they would be placed, as well as suitable tukutuku and kōwhaiwhai patterns to decorate walls and rafters. There were some among the whānau who were strongly traditionalist in all things to do with marae, while others, like Hapai, were more relaxed. As the master carver, Hapai urged the whānau to allow him to be free to innovate and develop his particular interpretation of whānau history, and requested working conditions that were free of tapu and its restrictions. Debates were fierce, and extended over many meetings. At one meeting he said he cried and left the meeting because he realised he had pushed the whānau too far, but in the end they choose the house he wanted. On the issue of tapu he won some concessions. He was able to take his tools off-site and use them for other tasks, and he could blow on his wood shavings, but food and women were not permitted in the building area.

Neich's argument that removing tapu restrictions at the School of Māori Arts and Crafts secularised the craft could not be sustained in the case of Ngatokowaru II. While such restrictions were partly suspended here, Hapai regarded the activity as essentially religious. He simply substituted Christian prayers for traditional karakia that were performed at critical stages of a project. He also had recourse to prayer when difficulties arose in the course of the project. Alma Winiata records a dramatic moment when a technical problem in the carving of the maihi (barge-boards) was resolved after prayer in the middle of the night.

Ngatokowaru II is a fully carved and decorated wharenui (meeting house) modelled closely on Parewahawaha at Bulls. The forty or so ancestor figures are conventional in form, representing ancestors selected by the community, and placed in the building according to traditional criteria. These ancestors make whakapapa (genealogical) links to other tribes. Through them traditional tribal history is preserved.

However, within the house another kind of story – a salvation history – is woven into the fabric of whānau history. This is most apparent on the rear wall, which is redolent of Christian imagery.

This wall was planned as the reference point for ministers conducting religious services, and is decorated with a purapura whetū (star) pattern that makes a direct visual reference to the great Rangiātea Church at Ōtaki. Two windows that pierce it are emblazoned with large red crosses. A pair of poupou (wall post) figures represents the Church Missionary Society missionary Octavius Hadfield, as bishop, and the Catholic priest Delachienne.[13] Two other poupou represent the chiefs Matene Te Whiwhi and Tamihana Te Rauparaha, who were instrumental in bringing Hadfield to the district in 1839.[14] Tamihana is also formally recognised in the Anglican Church as missionary to the South Island, and is commemorated in the Church calendar on May 18.[15]

Each of these chiefs is presented carrying a symbol of rank: a ceremonial toki poutangata (adze) in the case of Tamihana and a patu (club) for Matene. In each case a cross is superimposed over the emblem, and in the centre of each cross is a weeping eye representing the love of Christ. Hapai explained that it was the acceptance of that love that had transformed Māori life. These tūpuna (ancestors) were appropriate for that wall, as they stood at the threshold of the Christian era and actively promoted it.

Another reference to Rangiatea is to be found on the poupou featuring the ancestor Wehiwehi. He is presented carrying a basket with a superimposed cross. Ngāti Wehiwehi, a sub-tribe of Ngāti Raukawa, are the guardians of the sacred soil from the shrine of the priestly island of Ra'iatea in Tahiti, brought here on the Tainui canoe and subsequently laid under the altar of Rangiātea. In local tradition the original Rangiātea (that is, Ra'iatea) was located in the highest heaven and was the source of spiritual power.

Another ancestral figure symbolic of the new faith is the tekoteko at the apex of the barge boards representing Te Whatanui. This nineteenth-century warrior chief led Ngāti Raukawa in their migration to the Kapiti Coast in the 1820s, and his life spanned pre-Christian and Christian eras. The tekoteko recalls his act of mercy in giving refuge to the remnants of the Muaūpoko tribe when he symbolically shielded one of them with his cloak. He is presented naturalistically, draped in his cloak, holding a weapon but with a smiling countenance. Hapai felt a conventionally defiant pose would have been inappropriate in view of Te Whatanui's conversion to Christianity.

In all these figures the carver has imaginatively introduced a new iconography to tell the Christian story of his people. In another series of four poupou and a feature mural on a side wall he was more innovative and controversial.[16] The mural, he explained, was an abstract representation of modern man struggling in a concrete jungle to achieve wholeness in harmony with nature. It was inspired by the view Hapai had of One Tree Hill in Auckland while at St John's College. The tree stood out for him as an image of freedom in nature; below the hill was the concrete jungle of modern urban life. It was a personal reflection on contemporary life rather than traditional history. The stylisation of figures was derived from the work of Cliff Whiting and John Bevan Ford, two modernist Māori artists.[17]

Representation of tribal and whānau history is continued in a series of eight tukutuku panels, which Hapai designed with his wife Emma; these move from front to rear of the house in narrative sequence. They begin with a mythological reference to 'the works of Māui', and pass through sequences of tribal history down to contemporary times. The critical point in this sequence is marked by the panel entitled 'Te Rongo pai' (the Good News), again stressing the arrival of Christianity as the critical juncture in tribal and whānau history.

Kōwhaiwhai patterns that adorn the house interior were designed by the late Martin Winiata, brother of the carver. These too are innovative and imaginative. They carry such names as 'Whakapapa', 'Rangimarie', 'Huarahi o te Ora' and 'Whakarongo ki te Reo o Nga Tupuna', which make links between traditional tribal and Christian values.

Two dominant themes stand out in the decoration of Ngatokowaru. The first is that of unity, which sees the whānau incorporated within Ngāti Raukawa iwi and extends outwards to include all the iwi of Aotearoa, through the representation of tribal and canoe ancestors. This reflects the whakapapa structure of traditional history. Ultimately, with the inclusion of Pākehā missionaries, Ngatokowaru II embraces diverse cultures and religions.

The second theme is the narrative of whānau and tribal history from mythological times to the present day, with a critical division of the story into pre-Christian and Christian eras, which Hapai referred to as the old and the new testaments of tribal history.

St Michael's Church

Ngatokowaru II is a traditional meeting house that nevertheless takes on some of the functions and character of a church. Hapai's next major project was to build a church that would take on some of the functions and character of a meeting house, most importantly as a place where people could bring their dead for the rites of the tangihanga. He undertook this project while he was pastor of the Rangitikei-Manawatū Māori Pastorate in Palmerston North. The church, St Michael's, was opened in 1982.

In planning the building to be able to accommodate cultural activities associated with marae, Hapai was showing a pastoral commitment to the cultural needs of Māori people in Palmerston

St Michael's Church, Palmerston North. Photograph by Kamila Skapa.

North. Many of them were migrants from other tribal areas and had no means of satisfying the important social and cultural obligations that give Māori life its vitality. This sensitivity on Hapai's part no doubt sprang from his upbringing on the family marae at Hokio and his later association with Ngāti Parewahawaha at Bulls.

Unlike at Ngatokowaru II, where Hapai's opponents were able to exercise some control over his proposals, there was no opposition at St Michael's, and the carving and tukutuku teams of men and women worked together without restrictions, as they had done on Parewahawaha. As pastor and master carver, Hapai had a free rein in the conceptual design of the building.

Assisting him with the carving were Calvin Kereama and Dean Flavell and students of the Tu Tangata carving school, while his wife Emma supervised the tukutuku work and Ralph Flavell designed the kōwhaiwhai patterns. Much of the construction work was undertaken by volunteers from many sections of the Palmerston North community. All of these aspects accorded well with the ecumenical outlook of the pastor. The commemorative booklet produced on the church's completion acknowledges that its purpose was reflected in the way cultural and denominational barriers had been transcended in the cooperative effort of many people.[18]

All carved work is on the exterior of the building, on the façade and porch, and no named ancestors are represented. Each of the six conventional figures on the pair of amo (side posts that support the maihi), carved by guest carvers, represents regional styles that embrace 'all of Aotearoa'. A set of eight poupou figures on the porch represent Christian values, as well as the bishoprics of Aotearoa and Wellington. One poupou has a figure bearing a patu overlaid with a cross with the weeping eye motif that featured in Ngatokowaru II. Here the figure 'represents the ancestors of the Māori people who put aside the weapons of war and took hold of the Gospel of Christ'.[19]

The long running-boards of the maihi and paepae (beam across the front of a meeting house) offered Hapai the opportunity to develop his narrative skills in presenting multi-layered stories with

Mana Māori and Christianity

Weeping eye figure, St Michael's Church. Photograph by Kamila Skapa.

Weeping eye figure: detail. Photograph by Kamila Skapa.

Maihi, St Michael's Church. Photograph by Kamila Skapa.

Christian themes. On the maihi are represented the Manawatū and Rangitikei Rivers[20] flowing from their mountain sources near the apex. Places of worship, as well as Māori and Pākehā communities within the pastorate, are indicated along the banks. The rivers reach the ocean at the raparapa (lower end of the maihi), where a figure is shown fishing. This figure may be given multiple interpretations, including Māui fishing up the North Island, Peter as Christ's fisherman and all Christians called to be fishers for Christ.

This straightforward narrative gets hooked into another allegorical story that begins at the paepae, which, as it progresses, deepens the spiritual meaning of the rivers and mountains. The paepae depicts three figures, representing the traveller (Everyman), the forces of evil and the forces of good. The traveller, scarred in the struggle with evil but rescued by the good forces, continues his life's journey up the amo and emerges, still scarred, at the lower end of the maihi. Here he encounters a follower of Christ, one of the 'fish' netted in the raparapa, who shows the traveller aroha. These two manaia figures now form an intertwining frieze moving up the maihi, as the scarred traveller is first introduced to the word of

Raparapa, St Michael's Church. Photograph by Kamila Skapa.

God, and then starts drinking from the rivers, which have become the 'spiritual waters of life' referred to in John 4:14. He is restored to wholeness and the two eventually arrive at the mountains at the top of the maihi, which now stand for the abode of God. In the mountains a light represents the burning bush of Moses,[21] reminding those about to enter the house they are on holy ground.

The kōruru at the apex of the maihi takes the form of a canoe prow, representing the church as the ship of Christ, just as the metal cross surmounting it as a tekoteko is the symbol of Christ. The canoe also has other levels of meaning: it stands for all New Zealanders who as migrants are joined together in building a new country, as well as spiritual voyages of discovery 'into the world of partnership within Christ'.[22]

In a similar way the pare (lintel) over the door is a fusion of traditional and non-traditional forms in an extraordinarily complex set of meanings. In summary, they highlight the eternal nature of God (in the takarangi spiral), Christ's death (in a stylised crucifix), the church (in this case Anglican, with coats of arms and emblems)

Pare, St Michael's Church. Photograph by Kamila Skapa.

and the peaceful coming together in Christ of Māori and Pākehā (in an innovative koru-based figure).

Inside, the decoration is carried entirely by kōwhaiwhai and tukutuku patterns. Both carry graphic paradigms of Christian values and gospel events, such as Te Kakenga (the Ascension), which is the theme of the ridge pole. The symbolic heart of the building, and the focal point of all the artistry, is the sanctuary. The exterior carvings are envisaged as flowing upwards to the canoe of Christ, and are then carried along the ridge pole to the sanctuary. In a similar way the interior artworks flow up through the heke (rafters) to the ridge pole and on to the sanctuary. As the commemorative booklet has it: 'This movement of the art forms is symbolic of the philosophy of the building, which places Christ at the centre of life'.[23]

In the history of Māori church buildings the marae-church is a relatively recent development.[24] The concept appears to have had its genesis with the opening of Te Unga Waka Catholic Marae in Auckland in the 1960s. In 1975 the kaumātua of the newly formed Anglican Māngere Mission laid plans for a marae-church. Building

Te Kakenga (the Ascension) design, St Michael's Church. Photograph by Kamila Skapa.

began in 1980, but proceeded only as funds became available. It was not dedicated until 1998, as 'Te Karaiti Te Pou Herenga Waka'.[25] Of interest here is the fact that Hapai was at St John's College from 1974 to 1976, and very likely was aware of the Māngere project; he brought the idea to Palmerston North when he was appointed to the Rangitikei-Manawatū Māori Pastorate in 1977. He himself was not very forthcoming on the matter, merely saying: 'It began as a thought; it began as a dream and then became a challenge.'[26]

Wherever the thought came from, Hapai wasted little time bringing it to fruition. In May 1981 a special general meeting of the pastorate resolved to go ahead with the building, and twelve months later it was officially opened, becoming an early example of the marae-church model.

St Michael's follows neither the style of the early Church Missionary Society churches exemplified by Rangiātea nor the churches built in the Ngata era. The early churches, from the 1840s to the 1860s, were very large, able to comfortably accommodate congregations of 700 (Rangiātea) to 1200 (Kaupapa). Although their Māori builders had never before attempted to raise buildings

Tukutuku panels in the sanctuary, St Michael's Church. Photograph by Kamila Skapa.

on such a scale, they generally adhered to Māori architectural principles, though clad in gothic exteriors.[27] They were mostly uncarved,[28] but the interiors were decorated with kōwhaiwhai and tukutuku designs. The Ngata churches are essentially gothic buildings overlaid with the decorative arts that Ngata was promoting through the School of Arts and Crafts in Rotorua to give them a Māori character. With a few notable exceptions, there was little that was specifically Christian in these decorations.

St Michael's differs from both of these models. It has the façade and some of the features of a modern meeting house, but was designed primarily as a church: a holy place where liturgical worship takes precedence over all other activities. The slightly raised sanctuary at the rear with its altar and furnishings draws the eye, and is given further emphasis by the steeple that rises above and illuminates it. Within the steeple the east window has a poutama design in red and gold, while the west window has a central red cross radiating golden rays. The architectural form and artistic detail therefore seek to bring together two cultural traditions that in their blending find a transcending unity. This is as Hapai intended, as he made clear in a confessional statement at the church's opening:

> What is the kaupapa of this building? I believe it is expressed in the structure and the art forms, whether they be whakairo, tukutuku, kōwhaiwhai, panelling or steeple. In the art forms we tell a story of our people and build the whole around Christ. Within the steeple we see the Cross and the poutama design blending together. All these forms embrace what is good and beautiful in both our cultures. It is a blending, a growing, a sharing together in Christ. Together great things have been achieved and we stand united in His name as the tangata whenua and say – 'I am, because I belong to Christ'. This is the kaupapa: this is the foundation on which the Church of Saint Michael has been built.[29]

Discussion

Hapai's statement is positive towards culture, and he accepts all cultures while firmly embracing his own Māori heritage. We see it in the underlying imagery of his thought: the whanaungatanga of tribal society is replaced by the whanaungatanga of Christ: all believers are referred to as 'tangata whenua' at St Michael's. In another metaphorical application of Māori terms, Hapai once observed that the church had a spiritual whakapapa through bishops and baptism back to Christ.[30] We see this concept reflected also in Hapai's marae-focused activities and in his practice as a tohunga whakairo. On the other hand, he was discerning in what he recognised as valid tradition. In particular, he dispensed with tapu and its restrictions on his projects, substituting a Christian spirituality. More generally, he sought to make his art relevant to his generation and to his Christian faith.

This same faith also shaped and defined his bicultural vision, the first graphic expression of which was in a side window he designed for Parewahawaha that depicts the arrival of a missionary family off the sailing ship and being welcomed ashore by a Māori family. The theme reappears in Ngatokowaru II, where he included Pākehā missionaries among the tūpuna figures of the whare. It is most fully developed in St Michael's, where the art and architecture of both cultures find a unity in the sanctuary, which carries the words 'Ko Ahau te Aranga mai me te Ora' ('I am the Resurrection and the Life'). The Māori art works are no longer concerned with tribal history but 'have been used to depict the Christian faith in ways that are meaningful to both Māori and Pākehā'.[31] Just as the art works find their unity in Christ, so too does the worshipping community, regardless of cultural background – all are tangata whenua in St Michael's. This is a departure from the ethos of the traditional marae, which is based upon the kinship bonds of a family group. St Michael's is based upon the family of Jesus Christ.

As one who appears always to have walked at the boundaries of two cultures, it is not surprising that Hapai's vision is inclusive rather than exclusive, and that in both his art and his pastoral ministry he should reach out to make connections between the cultures. His images of Christ's tears of love (surely the leitmotif of his artistry) are his unique symbol of reconciliation of all in Christ: Christ with humanity; tribe with tribe; Māori with Pākehā. St Michael's is itself a monument to such a reconciliation, as a Māori church serving a Māori community yet opening itself out to the wider world in its art works that are meaningful to both Māori and Pākehā.

Not all Christian Māori share Hapai's bicultural vision. Some see it as a blurring of cultural boundaries, or worse, as a denial of cultural identity and integrity.[32] A number of Māori theologians have put more emphasis on traditional culture and its spirituality, finding within this the source of an authentic Māori Christianity. The late Rev. Māori Marsden was raised in the northern traditions passed down to him through Te Wānanga o te Tai Tokerau.[33] His theological and philosophical reflections on their deeper meanings led him to appreciate that much of the Māori world view could be made compatible with the Christian faith.[34]

Another Māori theologian, Father Henare Tate, has also looked to his indigenous northern traditions as a foundation on which to base an authentic Christian Māori spirituality. His theology attempts to redefine and transform the meaning and practice of tapu and mana into an inculturated Māori Catholicism.[35] He expressed his thoughts in a striking metaphor: 'The challenge of the present and immediate future is to rediscover that lost spirituality, and to graft onto the kauri tree the buds and shoots of Christianity. Then there will be a stronger tree. Its roots will reach deeper into the native soil and its branches will reach even higher into the heavens.'[36]

Both Tate and Marsden operate in what Stephen Bevans calls 'the anthropological model' of contextual theology. The primary concern of this model 'is the establishment or preservation of cultural identity by a person of Christian faith'.[37] The model asserts God's presence in all cultures, and the practitioner looks for 'God's revelation and self-manifestation within the values, relational patterns and concerns of a culture'.[38] Its inspiration lies with St Justin Martyr and his idea of 'the seeds of the Word'. Justin taught that the seed-bearing word had been planted in the heart of every culture, but only in Christ is to be found the fullness of the truth.[39] Tapu and mana are examples of such seeds that must now be brought to the fullness of the truth in Christ.

Hapai followed a very different theological path. It is glimpsed in H Richard Niebuhr's 'conversionist' model, in which Christ is preeminently the transformer of culture.[40] However, more recent models are closer to his position.[41] Bevans identified five models in contextual theology. His 'translation model', derived from Charles Kraft, is of particular interest. Its essence lies in the supra-cultural message of the Bible being 'translated' into the meaning systems of particular cultures in order to transform them. It is serious about culture, but holds that the biblical message must always take priority. Where there is an incompatibility between message and culture, it is culture that must give way. 'The emphasis is on Christian identity being more important than, though not exclusive of, cultural identity.'[42]

Hapai sums up his own theology in his interpretation of the famous whakatauki (proverb) of his Ngāti Raukawa people: 'E kore au e ngaro, te kakano i ruia mai i Rangiātea' ('I will never be lost, the seed planted here from Rangiatea'). The seed sown from Rangiātea, he explained, referred not only to the people but also their spirituality. With the adoption of Christianity he believed Rangiātea became identified with the new seed of the gospel,[43] and he saw himself as the new seed replacing the old. Here the message has trumped the culture, and conversion has led to a new life in Christ and a new identity as Māori Christians.

Conclusion

The world view, spirituality and identity that Winiata brought to the carving tradition had been shaped in the Mihinare tradition in which he was raised. It is within the context of that tradition that his art is to be interpreted.

With his chisel he translated the gospel message of a loving, redeeming Christ into the ancient craft of whakairo rākau. He no longer felt constrained by the customary conventions of the craft, as his daring artistic innovations, his new way of thinking tribal history and his substitution of a traditional spirituality all testify. His works are undoubtedly controversial, but they followed a 'theology of translation' first introduced by the Church Missionary Society missionaries in the nineteenth century.

Endnotes

1 I am deeply indebted to the family of Hapai Winiata; in particular to his daughter Alma Winiata-Kenny and his sister Margaret Rangimakaora Davis, both of whom made available their own research on Hapai, completed as course work for Te Wānanga o Raukawa. I am also indebted to Dame Joan Metge, Dr Phyllis Mossman, Rev. Peter Stuart and Fr Philip Cody for their helpful comments on the original paper and its various drafts, though I take full responsibility for the text. The vestry of St Michael's has been most cooperative in allowing access for photography. My thanks go to Kamila Skapa for the photography.
2 R Neich, *Carved Histories: Rotorua Ngāti Tarāwhai Woodcarving* (Auckland: Auckland University Press, 2001), 196–7.
3 M R Davis, unpublished typescript, 1999, held privately.
4 Māori Anglican, derived from the Church Missionary Society.
5 A Winiata, unpublished typescript, 2001, 2–4, held privately.
6 Neich, *Carved Histories*, 76.
7 Ibid, 78–9; D Brown, *Māori Architecture: From Fale to Wharenui and Beyond* (Auckland: Raupo, 2009), 105.
8 Personal communications, 19 January and 11 May 1978; Winiata, unpublished typescript, 5–6.
9 'Generation Two Thousand', a cultural renewal project for Ngāti Raukawa young people.

10 For a description of Māori cultural life in Ōtaki in 1941, see E and P Beaglehole, *Some Modern Maoris* (Wellington: New Zealand Council for Educational Research, 1946). For a general review of Māori life and culture in the mid-twentieth century see J Metge, *The Maoris of New Zealand: Rautahi* (London: Routledge & Kegan Paul, 1976), especially 48–52.
11 Personal communications, 30 November 1975, 14 January 1976, 17 March and 20 August 1977 and 19 January and 11 May 1978.
12 Winiata, unpublished typescript, 7.
13 Fr Delachienne was more familiarly known as Fr Delach. He served in the Ōtaki Marist Mission from 1893 to 1914. M O'Meeghan, 'The French Marist Maori Mission', in J Dunmore (ed.), *The French and the Maori* (Waikanae: Heritage Press, 1992), 64.
14 W H Oliver, 'Te Whiwhi, Henare Matene – Biography', from the *Dictionary of New Zealand Biography*, in *Te Ara – the Encyclopedia of New Zealand*: www.teara.govt.nz/en/biographies/1t89/1 (accessed 18 January 2012).
15 Church of the Province of New Zealand, *A New Zealand Prayer Book: He Karakia Mihinare o Aotearoa* (London: Collins, 1989), 18.
16 B Kernot, 'An Artist in His Time', in J Huntsman (ed.), *Future Directions in the Study of the Arts of Oceania* (Auckland: Polynesian Society, c. 1981): 157–69, 164.
17 Personal communication, 19 January 1978. Alma Winiata records that two works he completed about 1989 were influenced by Henry Moore.
18 H Winiata, *The Dedication of St Michael's Church: A Commemorative Booklet 5 June 1982* (Palmerston North: privately published, 1982), 5.
19 Ibid, 11. Hapai said he first used this motif in a poupou he carved for St John's College as a gesture of appreciation.
20 These are the major waterways within the pastorate.
21 Exodus 3:2.
22 Winiata, *Commemorative Booklet*, 10.
23 Ibid, 17.
24 A 'marae-church' is a church modelled on the meeting house and observing some of the functions of the marae. Ringatū services have traditionally been held in meeting houses that, to the best of the writer's knowledge, are not primarily dedicated to liturgical services.
25 J Metge, 'Te Karaiti Te Pou Herenga Waka', unpublished notes, 1, held privately.
26 Winiata, *Commemorative Booklet*, front cover.
27 R A Sundt, 'On the Erection of Maori Churches in the Mid 19th Century: Eyewitness Testimonies From Kaupapa and Otaki', in *Journal of the Polynesian Society* 108.1 (1999): 7–17. See also Brown, *Māori Architecture*, 42–8.
28 The exception was at Manutuke, where William Williams allowed carved poupou, apparently misunderstanding the significance of the manaia figures. See Brown, *Māori Architecture*, 47–8.
29 Winiata, *Commemorative Booklet*, front cover.
30 Personal communication, 11 May 1978.
31 Winiata, *Commemorative Booklet*, 1.
32 This has been argued most forcefully by the late Rev. Maori Marsden in his essay 'God, Man and Universe: A Māori View': 'As a person brought up within the culture, who has absorbed the values and attitudes of the Māori, my approach to Māori things is largely subjective. The charge of lacking objectivity does not concern me; the so-called objectivity some insist on is simply a form of arid abstraction, a model or a map. It is not

the same thing as the taste of reality.' Republished in Te A C Royal (ed.), *The Woven Universe: Selected Writings of Rev. Maori Marsden* (Ōtaki: Estate of Rev. Maori Marsden, 2003), 2.

33 Te Wānanga o Te Tai Tokerau appears to have been founded in the early 1850s by the hapū of Te Tai Tokerau in order to preserve their history, tikanga and traditions, which were under threat mainly as a result of missionary teaching. See ibid, xxx-xxxii.

34 Ibid.

35 H Tate, 'Stepping Into Māori Spirituality', in H Bergin and S Smith (eds), *Spirituality in Aotearoa New Zealand: Catholic Voices* (Auckland: Accent Publications, 2002): 38–53.

36 Pa Henare (Henare Tate), *Tamatea Motuti* (Auckland: NZ Forest Products, 1987), 30.

37 S Bevans, *Models of Contextual Theology* (Maryknoll, New York: Orbis, 1998), 47.

38 Ibid, 49.

39 Ibid, 47. See also A Shorter, *Toward a Theology of Inculturation* (Maryknoll, New York: Orbis, 1988), 76–7.

40 H R Niebuhr, *Christ and Culture* (San Francisco: Harper & Row, 1975), 190–229.

41 C H Kraft, *Christianity in Culture: A Study in Dynamic Biblical Theologizing in Cross-Cultural Perspective* (Maryknoll, New York: Orbis, 1988); Bevans, *Models of Contextual Theology*. One might point out in passing that Marsden was strongly influenced by Kraft in developing his analysis of a Māori world view. It is particularly evident in his discussion paper 'Kaitiakitanga: A Definitive Introduction to the Holistic Worldview of the Māori', in Royal, *The Woven Universe*, 54–72. Compare Kraft, *Christianity in Culture*, 53–60.

42 Bevans, *Models of Contextual Theology*, 35.

43 Winiata, *Commemorative Booklet*, 13.

Contributors

Philip Carew is a commerce teacher at Naenae College in Wellington, a multicultural school committed to addressing issues of Māori and Pasifika student achievement. A commitment to working out his faith in terms of social justice was a catalyst to Philip undertaking a masters research project into the way his denomination, the Assemblies of God New Zealand, has addressed issues of biculturalism in comparison to other denominational groups.

Dr Harold Hill is a retired Salvation Army officer who served in Zimbabwe and New Zealand and teaches Salvation Army history part-time for Booth College, Sydney College of Divinity. He has published *The Twelve Steps Workshop* (2001, 2011) and *Leadership in the Salvation Army: A Case Study in Clericalisation* (2007) and edited *Te Ope Whakaora: The Army that Brings Life: A Collection of Documents on the Salvation Army and Maori 1884–2007* (2007).

Dr Robert Joseph completed a doctorate in law in 2006 and is now a member of the Faculty of Law at the University of Waikato. His research interests include the realisation of the Treaty of Waitangi rights and responsibilities; the interface of traditional Māori knowledge systems and Western science; the internal self-determination rights and responsibilities of indigenous institutions; Canadian and North American indigenous studies; treaty processes and post-settlement development; dispute resolution processes, particularly with respect to resolving disputes between different cultures; and Māori and indigenous peoples' governance in settler nation-states. He is currently writing a biography of his paternal tūpuna (ancestors) who fought at the famous 1864 Battle of Ōrākau during the Waikato Wars.

Bernard Kernot retired in 1996. He was formerly a senior lecturer in Māori studies and anthropology at Victoria University of Wellington. He also held honorary and part-time positions at Te Wānanga o Raukawa (1984–1994) and the Wellington Catholic Education Centre (1997–2009). He has published extensively on Māori art, religion and spirituality.

Dr Brett Knowles is a retired senior lecturer in church history. He has held academic positions at the University of Otago, Sydney College of Divinity and Sekolah Tinggi Teologi Tawangmangu (Tawangmangu Theological College) in Indonesia. He has published a history of the New Life Churches of New Zealand, as well as a number of articles on New Zealand Pentecostalism. He has also edited and co-edited publications for the Department of Theology and Religion and the Department of History at the University of Otago.

Associate Professor Peter Lineham is associate professor of history in the School of History, Philosophy and Classics and also the regional director for the College of Humanities and Social Sciences at Massey University's Albany campus. He has written extensively on the religious history of New Zealand, including recent articles on revivalism, Judaism, church attendance patterns and the Anglican diocese of Auckland. He is also a media commentator on matters of religion and culture in New Zealand.

Dr Nathan Matthews is a senior lecturer in the Department of Māori and Multicultural Education in the College of Education at Massey University. He was previously a lecturer in Māori studies at the University of Otago, where he completed a doctorate that examined Māori Catholic secondary education. He is currently involved in research related to Māori Catholicism, the Māori performing arts and Māori leadership.

Rev. Simon Moetara is a lecturer in theology and biblical studies at Vision College New Zealand and an adjunct lecturer for Laidlaw College. He is also a teaching pastor at Vision Church Eastside in Hamilton. He is of Te Roroa descent.

Dr Hugh Morrison is a senior lecturer in the College of Education at the University of Otago and a research associate in the History Department at the University of Waikato. His research interests include Protestant missions; New Zealand religious history and historiography; and children, missions and empire. He is co-editor (with Geoffrey Troughton) of *The Spirit of the Past: Essays on Christianity in New Zealand History* (2011), and has recently contributed a chapter to a history of the Auckland Anglican Diocese.

Keith Newman is a published author, freelance journalist and producer working in print media and radio. He is author of *Ratana Revisited: An Unfinished Legacy* (2006), *Ratana the Prophet* (2009), *Connecting the Clouds: The Internet in New Zealand* (2008) and *Bible & Treaty: Missionaries Among the Māori – A New Perspective* (2010).

Dr Lachy Paterson is a senior lecturer in Te Tumu: School of Māori, Pacific and Indigenous Studies at the University of Otago, with research interests in Māori language print culture and Māori history. His publications include a study on mid-nineteenth-century Māori-language newspapers, *Colonial Discourses: Niupepa Māori 1855–1863* (2006) and, co-edited with James Watson, *A Great New Zealand Prime Minister?: Reappraising William Ferguson Massey* (2011). He is currently researching the deaconesses and other women workers of the Presbyterian Māori Mission.

Professor Murray Rae is head of the Department of Theology and Religion at the University of Otago, where he teaches theology and ethics. His research interests include Māori engagements with Christianity, theology and architecture, the work of Søren Kierkegaard, Christian responses to war and violence and theological hermeneutics. His recent publications include: *God of Salvation*, co-edited with Ivor Davidson (2011), *Kierkegaard and Theology* (2010), *Christian Doctrine*, co-edited with Stephen Holmes and Lindsey Hall (2010), and *History and Hermeneutics* (2005).

Rev. Wayne Te Kaawa is the moderator of Te Aka Puaho, the Māori Synod of the Presbyterian Church of Aotearoa New Zealand. He is also te ahorangi of the Wānanga a Rangi, the ministry training centre of the Māori Synod, and a researcher and writer on the history of Māori interaction with the Presbyterian Church. His most recent publication is *Hihita and Hoani: Missionaries in Tuhoeland* (2008).

Hone Te Rire (Ngāti Tūwharetoa, Tūhoe, Te Whakatōhea and Tuhourangi) is a curriculum designer at Te Wānanga o Aotearoa, having previously worked for six years at Te Wānanga o Raukawa as a senior academic and manager of its master of management programme. A recent graduate of the University of Otago, Hone's thesis report was centered on indigeneity and religion. He is an amorangi minister of Te Aka Puaho, the Māori Synod of the Presbyterian Church of Aotearoa New Zealand.

Dr Geoffrey Troughton is a lecturer in religious studies at Victoria University of Wellington, where he teaches courses on religion in New Zealand, Christianity, secularism and interactions of religion and politics. His previous publications and current research focus on New Zealand religious and social history, and the history of Christianity.

Glossary

Te Aka Puaho	Presbyterian Māori Synod
Aladura	Nigerian religion associated with Pentecostal-like practices
amo	upright boards that support the maihi of a wharenui, often carved
amorangi	minister of Te Aka Puaho
ariki	paramount chief
hāhi, haahi	church (institution)
Te Hāhi Matua, Te Hāhi Mihinare	Anglican Church; Church of England
haka	vigorous posture dance
hāngī	earth oven; food cooked in hāngī
hāpati	sabbath
hapū	kin grouping; clan; sub-tribe
Hauhau	see Pai Mārire
heke	rafters of a wharenui
Hihita	deaconess; 'Sister': often used specifically for Sister Annie Henry
hīkoi	march, generally of some distance, undertaken as a means of protest
hīnau	native tree
Te Hīnota Māori	Presbyterian Māori Synod, now more generally known as Te Aka Puaho
Hoani Laughton	Rev. John G Laughton
Huarahi o te Ora	lit. Pathway of Life
hui	meeting; gathering
Iharaira	Israelites; followers of Rua Kēnana
Ihoa o ngā Mano	Jehovah of the Thousands
Te Ika a Māui	North Island of New Zealand
iwi	tribal grouping

291

kai	food
kāinga/kāika	Māori settlement
kaitiaki	guardian
kapa haka	Māori performing arts group
kapai, ka pai	lit. it is good
karakia	prayer; incantation
kaumātua	elder, elders
kaupapa	principle, purpose
kawariki	edible plant
kawenata	covenant
kēhua	ghost
Kīngitanga	Māori King Movement
ngā koata e whā	lit. the four quarters; the four Māori parliamentary seats
kōrero	talk
koroua	old man; male kaumātua
korowai	feather cloak
koru	motif in whakairo and kōwhaiwhai, based on immature fern frond
kōruru	carving depicting a human face placed at the apex of the maihi, below the tekoteko of a wharenui
Kotahitanga	Māori autonomy movement
kōwhaiwhai	painted patterns on the rafters of a wharenui, generally utilising koru motifs
kuia	old woman; female kaumātua
kūmara	sweet potato
mahita/kura mahita	schoolteacher
māhoe	native tree
maihi	barge-boards on a wharenui, often carved
mākutu	witchcraft; curse
mana	power and authority; charisma; intregity; prestige; numinosity
mana Māori	(aspirations for) Māori autonomy
manaia	flat carving of human face viewed from the side
māngai	mouthpiece (of God)
Māoritanga	Māori culture and way of life
marae	the area in front of a wharenui where formal oratory takes place; a complex comprising the meeting house together with surrounding land and buildings; tribal base of a Māori hapū or other grouping
Māramatanga	Māori spiritual movement

matakite	seer
mātauranga	knowledge
mate urutā	epidemic
mauri	spiritual life-force (of a person, place or resource)
Mihinare/Mihingare	Anglican; Church of England
mokopuna	grandchild; descendant
mōrehu	Followers of T W Rātana (lit. remnant)
Te Ope Whakaora	Salvation Army
pā	Māori settlement
pae/paepae	low beam across the front of a wharenui; the place where speakers of the host side sit at times of formal marae-based oratory
Pai Mārire	religion founded in Taranaki in the early 1860s by Te Ua Haumene; both the religion and followers were also known as Hauhau
Papa/Papatūānuku	earth-mother of the Māori creation myth
pare	door lintel of a wharenui, often carved
patatē	small forest tree
patu	hand club made of stone, wood or bone
Perehipitiriana	Presbyterian
Piri Wiri Tua	political role assumed by T W Rātana
piupiu	traditional kilt made of processed flax leaves, now commonly worn by kapa haka performers
pounamu	greenstone; green jade
poupou	vertical carved wooden slabs depicting ancestral figures placed on the interior walls of wharenui
poutama	staircase motif (on tukutuku panels)
purapura whetū	star motif (on tukutuku panels)
rangatira	chief; leader
Rangi/Ranginui	sky-father of the Māori creation myth
rangimārie	peace
raparapa	the outside ends of the maihi in a wharenui, often carved
raupatu	land confiscations
raupō	bulrush reeds
rengarenga	New Zealand spinach
te reo (Māori)	Māori language
Te Rongo Pai	the Good News; gospels
taha Māori	the Māori perspective; the Māori side: an education programme for schools initiated in the 1980s to recognise the place of Māori within New Zealand

takarangi	spiral motif
tamaiti	child
tamariki	children
Ngā Tamariki o te Kohu	Ngāi Tuhoe; lit. Children of the Mist
tangata whenua	indigenous people; hosts
tangihanga/tangi	funeral; Māori funeral rituals
taonga	valued possession
tapu	spiritual restriction(s); sacred; restricted
tauiwi	stranger; non-Māori
tekoteko	carved figure (generally an ancestor) at the apex of the maihi of a wharenui, above the kōruru
Te Temepara Tapu o Ihoa	lit. The Sacred Temple of Jehovah: Rātana Church Temple at Rātana Pā
tika	correct, appropriate
tikanga	customs; practices; norms
Tikanga	three governance streams of the Anglican Church, representing Pākehā, Māori and Pacific Islanders
tiki	heitiki; flat carved greenstone figure worn as a pendant
tino rangatiratanga	Māori indigenous rights guaranteed under Article 2 of the Treaty of Waitangi
Te Tiriti o Waitangi	Treaty of Waitangi
tohunga	expert; priest; specialist; spiritual healer
tohunga matakite	seer
toki poutangata	ceremonial adze
tongi	prophetic statement
tukutuku	woven wall panels, placed between poupou on the interior walls of a wharenui
tupuna/tūpuna	ancestor/ancestors
upokokōhua	boiled head (an extreme insult)
urupā	Māori cemetery
utu	reciprocity; revenge
wahine	woman
wairua	spirit; spiritual side
waka	canoe
Te Wānanga o Raukawa	Ngāti Raukawa tribal university based at Ōtaki
whakaari	prophetic statement
whakairo (rākau)	carving (of wood)
whakapapa	descent lines; genealogy

Glossary

Te Whakapapa o te Whakapono	Lineages of Faith research group
Whakarongo ki te Reo o Ngā Tūpuna	lit. Listen to the Voice of the Ancestors
whakataukī	proverb; saying
Whakatupuranga Rua Mano	Generation 2000, a cultural renewal project for Ngāti Raukawa young people
whānau	extended family group
whanaungatanga	familial relationship
whare	house
whare karakia	church building
Te Whare Māori	lit. the Māori House; a specially built house at Rātana Pā
Wharekauri	Chatham Island
wharenui	meeting house on a marae

Bibliography

Archival sources
Archives, Historical Department of the Church of Jesus Christ of Latter-day Saints, Salt Lake City, Utah
Archives, Home of Sisters of Compassion, Wellington (AHSC)
Mortimer-Jones Correspondence, KIN008/1/4, Kinder Memorial Library, St John's College, Auckland
New Zealand Mormon Church History Centre, Temple View, Hamilton
Presbyterian Church of Aotearoa New Zealand Archives (ARC-PCANZ), Dunedin
Salvation Army Archives, Wellington
Te Aka Puaho Archive (TAPA), Ohope
Uri Whakatupuranga Rātana Archive, Rātana Pā

Church periodicals
All the World
Apostolic News
Deseret News
Evangel
Home and Foreign Missionary Record
Marist Messenger
New Zealand Missionary Record
Outlook
Te Whetu Marama o te Kotahitanga
The Break of Day
The Reaper
The Victory
The War Cry
Zealandia

Other newspapers and periodicals
Auckland Star
New Zealand Herald
New Zealand Listener
Northern Advocate
Otago Daily Times
Otago Witness
Te Ao Hou
Te Pipiwharauroa
Wairarapa Standard

Primary sources
Church of Jesus Christ of Latter-day Saints. *Manuscript History of the New Zealand Mission, Volume 1* (Salt Lake City, Utah: Church of Jesus Christ of Latter-day Saints, 1883)
Church of Jesus Christ of Latter-day Saints. *The Mormon Temple* (Hamilton: Church of Jesus Christ of Latter-day Saints, 1958)
Church of the Province of New Zealand. *A New Zealand Prayer Book: He Karakia Mihinare o Aotearoa* (London: Collins, 1989)
Department of Social Welfare. *Puao-te-Ata-Tu (Daybreak): The Report of the Ministerial Advisory Committee on a Māori Perspective for the Department of Social Welfare* (Wellington: Government Printer, 1988)
Department of Statistics. *2001 Census of Population and Dwellings*
Department of Statistics. *2006 Census of Population and Dwellings*
Destiny Church. 'Our History': www.destinychurch.org.nz/index.php?option=com_content&view=article&id=48&itemid=104 (accessed 4 January 2012)
——. *A Decade of Destiny: Destiny Church Celebrates* (Auckland: Destiny Church, 2008)
——. 'Protocols and Requirements between Spiritual Father & His Spiritual Sons', October 2009
Minute Book of the Presbytery of Auckland, 1856–1857 and 1869, 15 October 1856, MS 1501.P928, Box 1, Auckland Institute and Museum Library, Auckland
Proceedings of the Diocesan Synod of the District of Wellington, First Session of the Ninth Synod, October 1881
Proceedings of the General Assembly of the Presbyterian Church of New Zealand (PCNZ PGA), various years
Proceedings of the General Synod, Anglican Church of Canada, 1937

Other sources

Adewale, S A. *The Religion of the Yoruba: A Phenomenological Analysis* (Ibadan: Department of Religious Studies, University of Ibadan, 1988)

Ahn, K S. 'From Mission to Church and Beyond: The Metamorphosis of Post-Edinburgh Christianity', in D A Kerr and K R Ross (eds), *Edinburgh 2010: Mission Then and Now* (Oxford: Regnum, 2009): 74–84

――― ―――. 'Spring Lecture on the World Missionary Conference of Edinburgh 1910, 2010 Project': www.towards2010.org/downloads/t2010paper02kyoseongahn.pdf (accessed 6 April 2011)

Amaru, W. 'Karaitaina Tuteketenui Amaru', unpublished manuscript, n.d.

Anderson, A A. 'Introduction: World Pentecostalism at a Crossroads', in A Anderson and W J Hollenweger (eds), *Pentecostals after a Century: Global Perspectives on a Movement in Transition* (Sheffield: Sheffield Academic Press, 1999)

――― ―――. 'The Gospel and Culture in Pentecostal Mission in the Third World', paper presented at the Ninth Conference of the European Pentecostal Charismatic Research Association, Missions Academy, University of Hamburg, Germany, July 1999: www.epcra.ch/papers_pdf/hamburg/anderson_1999.pdf (accessed 4 January 2012).

――― ―――. *An Introduction to Pentecostalism* (Cambridge: Cambridge University Press, 2004)

――― ―――. 'The Origins of Pentecostalism and its Global Spread in the Early Twentieth Century', in *Transformations* 22.3 (July 2005): 175–85

――― ―――. 'Towards a Pentecostal Missiology for the Majority World', in *Asian Journal of Pentecostal Studies* 8.1 (2005): 29–47

Anderson, A A and E Tang (eds). 'Revising Pentecostal History in Global Perspective', in *Asian and Pentecostal: The Charismatic Face of Christianity in Asia* (Oxford/Baguio City: Regnum International/APTS Press, 2005)

Anderson, C. 'Labors among the Maoris', in *The New Zealand Mission*, 18 February 1885

Anderson, R M. *Vision of the Disinherited: The Making of American Pentecostalism* (Oxford: Oxford University Press, 1979)

Ballantyne, T. 'Christianity, Colonialism and Cross-Cultural Communication', in J Stenhouse and G A Wood (eds), *Christianity, Modernity and Culture* (Adelaide: ATF Press, 2005), 23–57

Ballara, A. 'Te Hapuku', in Department of Internal Affairs, *The People of Many Peaks; The Māori Biographies from the Dictionary of New Zealand Biography, Volume 1, 1769–1869* (Wellington: Bridget Williams Books, 1991)

――― ―――. 'Hamiora Mangakahia', in Department of Internal Affairs, *The Turbulent Years 1870– 1900: The Māori Biographies from the Dictionary of*

New Zealand Biography, Volume 2 (Wellington: Bridget Williams Books, 1994)

Ballara, A and K Cairns. 'Te Potangaroa, Paora – Biography', from the *Dictionary of New Zealand Biography* in *Te Ara – the Encyclopedia of New Zealand*: www.teara.govt.nz/en/biographies/1t57/1 (accessed 18 January 2012).

Ballara, A and P Sciascia, 'Te Atua, Henare – Biography', from the *Dictionary of New Zealand Biography*, in *Te Ara – the Encyclopedia of New Zealand*: www.teara.govt.nz/en/biographies/3t12/1 (accessed 4 January 2012)

Banks, O. *Faces of Feminism: A Study of Feminism as a Social Movement* (Oxford: Martin Robertson, 1981)

Barker, I. 'The Connexion: The Mormon Church and the Maori People', MA thesis, Victoria University of Wellington, 1967

Barrett, D B. *Schism and Renewal in Africa: An Analysis of Six Thousand Contemporary Religious Movements* (Nairobi/Oxford: Oxford University Press, 1968)

Barrett, D B and T M Johnson, 'Annual Statistical Table on Global Mission: 2004', in *International Bulletin of Missionary Research* 28.1 (January 2004): 24–5

Barrington, J. *Separate but Equal?: Māori Schools and the Crown 1867–1969* (Wellington: Victoria University Press, 2008)

Beaglehole, E and P. *Some Modern Maoris* (Wellington: New Zealand Council for Educational Research, 1946)

Beidelman, T O. 'Altruism and Domesticity: Images of Missionizing Women among the Church Missionary Society in Nineteenth-Century East Africa', in M T Huber and N C Lutkehau (eds), *Gendered Missions: Women and Men in Missionary Discourse and Practice* (Ann Arbor: University of Michigan Press, 1999): 113–43

Belich, J. *Paradise Reforged: A History of the New Zealanders – From the 1880s to the Year 2000* (Auckland: Allen Lane/Penguin, 2001)

Bennion, A. *Matthew Cowley Speaks* (Salt Lake City, Utah: Deseret Book Company, 1954)

Bergin, P. 'Hoani Papita to Paora: The Marist Missions of Hiruharama and Otaki 1883 to 1914', MA thesis, University of Auckland, 1986

—— ——. 'Education: the beginnings 1838–1889', in P Ewart (ed.), *Aspects of the apostolates of the Society of Mary in New Zealand since 1838: Assembled to commemorate the centenary of the establishment of the New Zealand Province of the Society of Mary, 1889–1989* (Wellington: Society of Mary, 1989)

Best, E. *Tuhoe: Children of the Mist*, 4th edition (Auckland: Reed, 1996)

Bevans, S. *Models of Contextual Theology* (Maryknoll, New York: Orbis, 1998)

Binney, J. 'Te Kooti Arikirangi Te Turuki', in A Ballara (ed.), *The People of Many Peaks; The Māori Biographies from the Dictionary of New Zealand Biography, Volume 1, 1769–1869* (Wellington: Bridget Williams Books, 1991): 194–201

———— ————. *Redemption Songs: A Life of the Nineteenth-century Maori Leader Te Kooti Arikirangi Te Turuki* (Auckland: Auckland University Press/Bridget Williams Books, 1997)

———— ————. *Encircled Lands: Te Urewera 1820–1921* (Wellington: Bridget Williams Books, 2009)

———— ————. 'Taonui, Aperahama – Biography', from the *Dictionary of New Zealand Biography* in *Te Ara – the Encyclopedia of New Zealand*: www.teara.govt.nz/en/biographies/2t7/1 (accessed 17 January 2012)

Binney, J, G Chaplin and C Wallace (eds), *Mihaia: The Prophet Rua Kenana and his Community at Maungapohatu* (Auckland: Auckland University Press, 1979)

Blumhofer, E L. *Restoring the Faith: The Assemblies of God, Pentecostalism, and American Culture* (Urbana: University of Illinois Press, 1993)

Blumhofer, E L and A R Armstrong. 'Assemblies of God', in S M Burgess and E M van der Maas (eds), *International Dictionary of Pentecostal and Charismatic Movements* (Grand Rapids: Zondervan, 2002): 333–40

Bolton, B. *Booth's Drum: The Salvation Army in Australia 1880–1980* (Sydney: Hodder & Stoughton, 1980)

Bond, G. 'Evangelistic Performance in New Zealand: The Word and What is not Said', PhD thesis, University of Canterbury, 2008

Boone, T. 'Remaking "Lawless Lads and Licentious Girls": The Salvation Army and the Regeneration of Empire', in J C Hawley (ed.), *Christian Encounters with the Other* (New York: New York University Press, 1998): 103–21

Bradwell, C R. *Fight the Good Fight* (Wellington: Reed, 1982)

———— ————. 'Moore, George – Biography', from the *Dictionary of New Zealand Biography*, in *Te Ara – the Encyclopedia of New Zealand*: www.teara.govt.nz/en/biographies/3m58/1/1 (accessed 3 January 2012)

Britsch, R L. 'Māori Traditions and the Mormon Church', in *New Era* (June 1981): 38

———— ————. *Unto the Islands of the Sea: A History of the Latter-day Saints in the Pacific* (Salt Lake City, Utah: Deseret Books, 1986)

Brooke, J. 'Providentialist Nationalism and Juvenile Mission Literature, 1840–1870', paper presented at the Henry Martyn Centre Research Seminar, Cambridge University, 2006: http://henrymartyn.dnssystems.net/media/documents/archive%20seminar%20papers%2020032009/providentialist%20nationalism%20and%20juvenile%20mission%20literature%201840–1870.pdf (accessed 9 January 2012).

Brooking, T W H. *And Captain of Their Souls: Cargill & the Otago Colonists* (Dunedin: Otago Heritage Books, 1984)

Brown, D. *Māori Architecture: From Fale to Wharenui and Beyond* (Auckland: Raupo, 2009)

Buck, P. *The Coming of the Maori* (Wellington: Whitcombe & Tombs/Maori Purposes Fund Board, 1962)

Budd, G. *The Story of Maori Missions: Being Five Studies* (Auckland: Presbyterian Women's Missionary Union, 1939)

Burton, J W. *Brown Faces: A Missionary Book for Methodist Boys and Girls* (Melbourne: Methodist Missionary Society of Australasia, 1914(?))

Carew, P D. 'Māori, Biculturalism and the Assemblies of God in New Zealand, 1970–2008', MA thesis, Victoria University of Wellington, 2009

Chidester, D. *Christianity: A Global History* (London: HarperOne, 2000)

Chitham, K (ed). *Hihita and Hoani: Missionaries in Tuhoeland* (Whakatāne: Whakatāne District Museum & Gallery, 2008)

Clark, I G. *Pentecost at the Ends of the Earth: The History of the Assemblies of God in New Zealand (1927–2003)* (Blenheim: Christian Road Ministries, 2007)

Coleman, S C. '"Come over and help us": White Women, Reform and the Missionary Endeavour in India 1876–1920', MA thesis, University of Canterbury, 2002

Collie, J. *The Story of the Otago Free Church Settlement 1848–1948* (Christchurch: Presbyterian Bookroom, 1948)

Coney, S. *Standing in the Sunshine: A History of New Zealand Women Since They Won the Vote* (Auckland: Viking, 1993)

Cowley, J. *Tarore and Her Book* (Wellington: Bible Society of New Zealand, 2009)

Cowley, M. 'Maori Chief Predicts Coming of L.D.S. Missionaries', in *Improvement Era* 53 (September 1950), 697

Cox, H. *Fire from Heaven: The Rise of Pentecostal Spirituality and the Reshaping of Religion in the Twenty-First Century* (Cambridge: Da Capo Press, 1995)

Cresswell, I. *Canoe on the River*, first published in *The War Cry* in installments in 1971 and reprinted in H Hill (ed.), *Te Ope Whakaora, The Army that brings Life: A collection of documents on the Salvation Army and Maori 1884–2007* (Wellington: Flag Publications, 2007)

Davidson, A. *Christianity in Aotearoa: A History of Church and Society in New Zealand* (Wellington: Education for Ministry Network, 1990)

———. 'The Interaction of Missionary and Colonial Christianity in Nineteenth Century New Zealand', in *Studies in World Christianity* 2.2 (1996): 145–66

Davis, R. 'The Maori Temple or Whare Wananga', in *Te Karere* (August 1953), 275–7

de Bres, P. 'Maori Religious Affiliation in a City Suburb', in H Kawharu (ed.), *Conflict and Compromise: Essays on the Maori since Colonisation* (Birkenhead: Reed, 2003): 144–66

Dickson, J. *History of the Presbyterian Church of New Zealand* (Dunedin: NZ Bible, Tract, & Book Society, 1899)

Duffy, A E. 'Te Haahi o te Ruuri Tuawhitu o Ihowa', BA research essay, Victoria University of Wellington, 1973

Dunford, A R (ed.). 'Missionary Journals of Oliver Cowdery Dunford & Ida Ann Osmond Dunford, 1889–1892' (Hamilton: New Zealand Mormon Church History Centre).

Durie, M. *Ngā Kāhui Pou: Launching Māori Futures* (Wellington: Huia, 2003)

Early, L. 'Women's Work for Women: The Life of a Methodist Missionary Sister in the Solomon Islands 1924–42', BA Hons thesis, University of Otago, 1990

Eason, A M. 'Christianity in a Colonial Age: Salvation Army Foreign Missions from Britain to India and South Africa, 1882–1929', PhD thesis, University of Calgary, 2005

Elder, J R. *The History of the Presbyterian Church of New Zealand* (Christchurch: Presbyterian Bookroom, 1940)

Elsmore, B. *Mana from Heaven: A Century of Maori Prophets in New Zealand* (Tauranga: Moana Press, 1989; 2nd edition Auckland: Reed, 1999)

—— ——. *Like Them that Dream: The Maori and the Old Testament* (Auckland: Reed, 1985; 2nd edition 2000)

Errington, J. *Linguistics in a Colonial World: A Story of Language, Meaning, and Power* (Oxford: Blackwell, 2008)

Gagan, R. 'Gender, Work, and Zeal: Women Missionaries in Canada and Abroad', in *Labour/Le Travail* (Spring 2004): www.historycooperative.org/journals/llt/53/gagan.html (accessed 25 May 2010)

Gibson, W W. *The Rev. James Duncan: First Presbyterian Missionary to the Maori* (Auckland: Presbyterian Historical Society, 1975)

Gifford, P. 'Trajectories in African Christianity', in *International Journal for the Study of the Christian Church* 8.4 (2008): 275–89

Gillett, R. 'Helpmeets and Handmaidens: The Role of Women in Mission Discourse', BA Hons thesis, University of Otago, 1998

Girdwood-Morgan, K. 'J-B.F. Pompallier's Instructions for Mission Work 1841', dissertation for diploma of social sciences, Massey University, Palmerston North, 1985

Godden, J. 'Containment and Control: Presbyterian Women and the Missionary Impulse in New South Wales, 1891–1914', in *Women's History Review* 6.1 (1997): 75–93

Gorst, J. *The Maori King; or, the Story of our Quarrel with the Natives of New Zealand* (London/Cambridge: Macmillan, 1864)

Goulton, R. 'Release through Recognition, Respect and Righteousness', in *Te Reo Apotorika/Apostolic News* (March 1990): 1

Grace, J Te H. *Tuwharetoa: The History of the Maori People of the Taupo District* (Wellington: Reed, 1959)

Greenwood, A. 'Mission Journal for 1883', unpublished manuscript, 1883
——— ———. 'My New Zealand Mission', in *Juvenile Instructor* 20 (1885), 222
Greenwood, W. 'The Upraised Hand, or the Spiritual Significance of the Rise of the Ringatu Faith', in *Journal of the Polynesian Society* 51 (1942): 1–80
Gunderson, L. 'That long looked for something that we before lacked', unpublished manuscript, Kia Ngawari Trust, Hamilton, n.d.
Haami, B. 'Tapu: a Pentecostal View', in *Stimulus* 6.2 (May 1998): 85–88
Haggis, J. 'Ironies of Emancipation: Changing Configurations of "Women's Work" in the "Mission of Sisterhood" to Indian Women', in *Feminist Review* 65 (2000): 108–26
Haliburton, G. *The Prophet Harris* (London: Prentice Hall, 1971)
Hardy, A. 'Destiny Breaks through Media Screens', in *Papers from the Trans-Tasman Research Symposium: 'Emerging Research in Media, Religion and Culture'* (Melbourne: RMIT Publishing, 2005): 40–56
Harman, S. 'The Struggle for Success: A Socio-Cultural Perspective on the French Marist Priests and their Māori Mission (1838–1867)', PhD thesis, University of Waikato, 2010
Hastings, A. *Oxford History of the Christian Church: The Church in Africa 1450–1950* (New York: Oxford University Press, 1994)
Head, L. 'Wiremu Tamihana and the *Mana* of Christianity', in J Stenhouse and G A Wood (eds), *Christianity, Modernity and Culture* (Adelaide: ATF Press, 2005), 58–86
Henderson, J M. *Ratana: The Man, the Church, the Political Movement* (Wellington: Reed/Polynesian Society, 1963 and 1972)
Hippolite, J. 'Wetekia Ruruku Elkington 1879–1957', in C MacDonald, M Penfold and B Williams (eds), *The Book of New Zealand Women: Ko Kui ma te Kaupapa* (Wellington: Bridget Williams Books, 1991), 205–7
Hodges, M L. *The Indigenous Church* (Springfield: Gospel Publishing House, 1953)
Hodgson, F. *None Shall Excel Thee: The Life and Journals of William Michael Bromley* (Yorba Linda, California: Shumway Family History Services, 1990)
Holman, J P. *Best of Both Worlds: The Story of Elsdon Best and Tutakangahau* (Auckland: Penguin, 2010)
Houston, H. *One Hundred Men* (Wellington: Hazel Houston, 1977)
Huber, M T and N C Lutkehau (eds). *Gendered Missions: Women and Men in Missionary Discourse and Practice* (Ann Arbor: University of Michigan Press, 1999)
Hunt, B. *Zion in New Zealand: A History of the Church of Jesus Christ of Latter-day Saints in New Zealand 1854–1977*, 2nd edition (Temple View: Church College of New Zealand, 1977)
Hutchinson, M. '"Second Founder": A C Valdez Sr and Australian Pentecostalism', in *Australasian Pentecostal Studies* 11 (2009): http://webjournals.alphacrucis.

edu.au/journals/aps/issue-11/02-second-founder-a-c-valdez-sr-and-australian-pen (accessed 5 January 2012)

Hutson, J. *As For Me and My House: A Salute to Early Gisborne Salvation Army Families 1886–1952* (Wellington: Flag Publications, 2004)

Hwa, Y. 'Endued with Power: The Pentecostal-Charismatic Renewal and the Asian Church in the Twenty-First Century', in *Asian Journal of Pentecostal Studies* 6.1 (2003), 63–82

Irwin, J. 'The Rise and Fall of a Vision: Maori in the midst of Pakeha in the Presbyterian Church of New Zealand', PhD thesis, Victoria University of Wellington, 1994

Isichei, E. *A History of Christianity in Africa: From Antiquity to the Present* (Grand Rapids: Eerdmans, 1995)

Jaichandran, R and B D Madhav. 'Pentecostal Spirituality in a Postmodern World', in *Asian Journal of Pentecostal Studies* 6.1 (2003): 39–61

Janiewski, D and P Morris. *New Rights New Zealand: Myths, Moralities and Markets* (Auckland: Auckland University Press, 2005

Jenkins, P. *The Next Christendom: The Coming of Global Christianity* (Oxford: Oxford University Press, 2000)

Jensen A (ed.). *Church Chronology* (Salt Lake City, Utah: Deseret News, 1914)

Johnston, A. *Missionary Writing and Empire, 1800–1860* (Cambridge: Cambridge University Press, 2003)

Johnstone, P and J Mandryk. *Operation World* (Carlisle/Waynesboro: Paternoster/Lifestyle, 2001)

Jolly, M. '"To Save the Girls for Brighter and Better Lives": Presbyterian Missions and Women in the South of Vanuatu, 1848–1870', in *Journal of Pacific History* 26.1 (1991): 27–48

Jones, P Te H. *King Pōtatau: An Account of the Life of Pōtatau Te Wherowhero: The First Māori King* (Auckland: Polynesian Society, 1959)

Jones, P Te H and A Ngata. *Nga Moteatea*, Part One (Wellington: Polynesian Society, 1945–1957)

Kärkkäinen, V. 'Pentecostal Theology of Mission in the Making', in *Journal of Beliefs and Values* 25.2 (2004): 167–76

Keen, D. '"Feeding the Lambs": The Influence of Sunday Schools on the Socialization of Children in Otago and Southland, 1848–1901', PhD thesis, University of Otago, 1999

Kernot, B. 'An Artist in His Time', in J Hunstman (ed.), *Future Directions in the Study of the Arts of Oceania* (Auckland: Polynesian Society, c. 1981): 157–69

—— ——.'Maori Worldview and Spirituality', in *Stimulus* 6.2 (May 1998): 4–5

Kidd, C. *The Forging of Races: Race and Scripture in the Protestant World, 1600–2000* (Cambridge: Cambridge University Press, 2006)

Kimball, S W (ed.). 'The Book is Translated', in *New Zealand Church History* (Hamilton: New Zealand Division Seminary & Institute Department, 1974)

King, M. *Te Puea: A Biography* (Auckland: Hodder & Stoughton, 1977)

——— ———. *God's Farthest Outpost: A History of Catholics in New Zealand* (Auckland: Penguin, 1997)

——— ———. *The Penguin History of New Zealand* (Auckland: Penguin, 2003)

Kirkwood, C. *Te Arikinui and the Millennium of Waikato* (Hamilton: Turongo House, 2001)

Knowles, B. *New Life: A History of the New Life Churches of New Zealand 1942–1979* (Dunedin: Third Millennium Publishing, 1999)

——— ———. 'Pentecostalism and the Future of Christianity in the West: Reflections on a Conversation', in J Stenhouse and B Knowles (eds), *Christianity in the Post Secular West* (Hindmarsh: ATF Press, 2007): 177–208

Kraft, C H. *Christianity in Culture: A Study in Dynamic Biblical Theologizing in Cross-Cultural Perspective* (Maryknoll, New York: Orbis, 1988)

Lambert, G (ed.). *Gems of Reminiscence*, 17th Faith Promoting Series (Salt Lake City, Utah: George C Lambert, 1915)

Lange, L. 'Ordained Ministry in Maori Christianity, 1853–1900', in *Journal of Religious History* 27.1 (February 2003): 47–66

Laughton, J G. *From Forest Trail to City Street: The Story of the Presbyterian Church Among the Maori People* (Christchurch: Presbyterian Bookroom, 1961)

Lawton, T. 'Whaia te Tika. Hato Paora College: The First Fifty Years', MA thesis, Massey University, Palmerston North, 1996

Lee, M S and M S Peterson (eds). *History of William Thomas Stewart* (Provo, Utah: Grant Stevenson, 1972)

Lineham, P. *Bible and Society: A Sesquicentennial History of the Bible Society in New Zealand* (Wellington: Bible Society in New Zealand, 1996)

Love, R N. 'Policies of frustration: the growth of Maori politics; the Ratana/Labour era', PhD thesis, Victoria University of Wellington, 1977

Ma, W. 'When the Poor are Fired Up: The Role of Pneumatology in Pentecostal/Charismatic Mission', in V Kärkkäinen and J Moltmann (eds), *The Spirit in the World: Emerging Pentecostal Theologies in Global Contexts* (Grand Rapids: Eerdmans, 2009): 40–52

MacFarlane, R. *The History of Henare Haeata Ngakuku* (privately held by the Haeata whānau, Masterton)

Mahuta, R. 'Tawhiao's Visions', presentation, Centre for Māori Studies and Research, University of Waikato, 20 June 1990

Marsden, M. 'God, Man and Universe: A Maori View', in M King (ed.), *Te Ao Hurihuri: Aspects of Maoritanga* (Auckland: Reed, 1992): 117–37. Also published in Te A C Royal (ed.), *The Woven Universe: Selected Writings of Rev. Maori Marsden* (Ōtaki: Estate of Rev. Maori Marsden, 2003)

—— ——. 'Kaitiakitanga: A Definitive Introduction to the Holistic Worldview of the Māori', in Te A C Royal (ed.), *The Woven Universe: Selected Writings of Rev. Maori Marsden* (Ōtaki: Estate of Rev. Maori Marsden, 2003)

Marsh, P K. 'Church History in the Tamaki Branch', unpublished manuscript, Church College of New Zealand Manuscript Archives, Hamilton, n.d.

Martin, L. *One Faith, Two Peoples: Communicating Across Cultures Within the Church*, 3rd edition (Paraparaumu: Salt Company Publishers, 2001)

—— ——.'Counting the Cost of True Partnership', in *Reality* 65 (October/November 2004): 30

Matheson, P. '1840–1870: The Settler Church', in D McEldowney (ed.), *Presbyterians in Aotearoa, 1840–1990* (Wellington: Presbyterian Church of New Zealand, 1990), 15–42

Maunsell, E S. Report to the Native Department, 25 April 1886, in *Appendices to the Journal of the House of Representatives*, 1886, G-1

Mawson, M. 'Believing in Protest: The Liberal Ideal of Separation of Religion and Politics in Two Recent Religious Protests', in *New Zealand Sociology* 21.2 (2006): 196–214

Maxwell, H. 'Jubilee Reflections', in *Apostolic News* (July 1984): 3

May, H. 'Mapping some landscapes of colonial-global childhood', in *European Early Childhood Education Research Journal* 9.2 (2001): 5–20

May, S. 'Accommodating Multiculturalism and Biculturalism: Implications for Language Policy', in P Spoonley, C Macpherson and D Pearson (eds), *Tangata Tangata: The Changing Ethnic Contours of New Zealand* (Southbank: Thomson/Dunmore Press, 2004)

Meha, S. 'A Challenge Met', in G Rudd (ed.), *New Zealand: A Short Collection of Items of History to add to our Memories and Appreciation* (Salt Lake City, Utah: privately published, 1993 with additions in 2007)

—— ——. 'A Condensed History of the Church of Jesus Christ of Latter-day Saints in New Zealand', unpublished manuscript, New Zealand Mormon Church History Centre, Temple View, Hamilton, n.d.

Metge, J. *The Maoris of New Zealand: Rautahi* (London: Routledge & Kegan Paul, 1976)

—— ——. 'Te Karaiti Te Pou Herenga Waka', unpublished notes, 1, held privately

Miller, D E and T Yamamori. *Global Pentecostalism: The New Face of Christian Social Engagement* (Berkeley: University of California Press, 2007)

Mitchell, H and J Mitchell. *Te Tau Ihu o Te Waka: A History of Maori of Nelson and Marlborough: Volume II: Te Ara Hou – The New Society* (Wellington: Huia, 2007)

Moetara, S. 'An Exploration of Notions of Maori Leadership and a Consideration of Their Contribution for Christian Leadership in the Church of Aotearoa-New Zealand Today', MTh dissertation, Laidlaw College, 2009

Moorhead, A. *The Fatal Impact: An Account of the Invasion of the South Pacific 1767–1840* (Harmondsworth: Penguin, 1968)

Morrison, H. '"It is Our Bounden Duty": The Emergence of the New Zealand Protestant Missionary Movement 1868–1926', PhD thesis, Massey University, 2004

—— ——. 'Antipodeans Abroad: Trends and Issues in the Writing of New Zealand Mission History', in *Journal of Religious History* 30.1 (2006): 77–93

—— ——. '"Little Vessels" or "Little Soldiers": New Zealand Protestant children, foreign missions, religious pedagogy and empire, c. 1880s–1930s', in *Paedagogica Historica* 47.3 (2011): 303–21

Munro, J. *The Story of Suzanne Aubert* (Auckland: Auckland University Press/ Bridget Williams Books, 1996)

Neich, R. *Carved Histories: Rotorua Ngāti Tarāwhai Woodcarving* (Auckland: Auckland University Press, 2001)

Newbigin, L. *The Open Secret: An Introduction to the Theology of Mission*, revised edition (Grand Rapids: Eerdmans, 1999)

Newman, K. *Ratana Revisited: An Unfinished Legacy* (Auckland: Reed, 2006)

—— ——. *Ratana the Prophet* (Auckland: Penguin, 2009)

—— ——. *Bible & Treaty: Missionaries Among the Māori – A New Perspective* (Auckland: Penguin, 2010)

Newton, J. *The Double Rainbow: James K. Baxter, Ngati Hau and the Jerusalem Commune* (Wellington: Victoria University Press, 2009)

Niebuhr, R. *Christ and Culture* (San Francisco: Harper & Row, 1975)

Noll, M A. *The Scandal of the Evangelical Mind* (Grand Rapids: Eerdmans, 1994)

Nyhagen Predelli, L. 'Sexual Control and the Remaking of Gender: The Attempt of Nineteenth-Century Protestant Norwegian Women to Export Western Domesticity to Madagascar', in *Journal of Women's History* 12.2 (2000): 81–103

Oddie, G A. '"Orientalism" and British Protestant Missionary Constructions of India in the Nineteenth Century', in *South Asia* 17.2 (1994): 27–42

Oliver, S. 'Te Rauparaha, Tamihana – Biography', from the *Dictionary of New Zealand Biography*, in *Te Ara – the Encyclopedia of New Zealand*: www.teara.govt.nz/en/biographies/1t75/1 (accessed 9 January 2012)

Oliver, W H. 'Te Whiwhi, Henare Matene – Biography', from the *Dictionary of New Zealand Biography*, in *Te Ara – the Encyclopedia of New Zealand*: www.teara.govt.nz/en/biographies/1t89/1 (accessed 18 January 2012)

Olliver, N. 'Nga Huia' (2002): www.nzbirds.com/birds/huia.html (accessed 17 January 2012)

Olsen, N P. 'New Zealand: Our Māori Home', in *Improvement Era* 35 (May 1932): 446

O'Brien, A. *God's Willing Workers: Women and Religion in Australia* (Sydney: University of New South Wales Press, 2005)

O'Meeghan, M. 'The French Marist Maori Mission', in J Dunmore (ed.), *The French and the Maori* (Waikanae: Heritage Press, 1992)

—— ——. 'Grimes, John Joseph 1842–1915', in C Orange (ed.), *Dictionary of New Zealand Biography Volume 2 (1870–1900)* (Wellington: Department of Internal Affairs, 1993): 179– 80

O'Sullivan, D. *Beyond Biculturalism: The Politics of an Indigenous Minority* (Wellington: Huia, 2007)

Pagaialii, T. *Pentecost 'to the Uttermost': A History of the Assemblies of God in Samoa* (Baguio: APTS Press, 2006)

Parsonson, G S. 'Duncan, James 1813–1907', in *Dictionary of New Zealand Biography, Volume One 1769–1869* (Wellington: Ministry of Culture and Heritage, 1990), 114–15

Patete, A. 'Patete, Haimona – Biography', from the *Dictionary of New Zealand Biography*, in *Te Ara – the Encyclopedia of New Zealand*: www.teara.govt.nz/en/biographies/3p14/1 (accessed 4 January 2012)

Piercy, K. 'Patient and Enduring Love: The Deaconess Movement, 1900–1920', in J Stenhouse and J Thomson (eds), *Building God's Own Country: Historical Essays on Religions in New Zealand* (Dunedin: Otago University Press, 2004): 196–208

Pompallier, J-B F. *The Early History of the Catholic Church in Oceania* (Auckland: Brett, 1888)

Potangaroa, P (trans. J Rimene). 'The Prophecies of Paora Potangaroa, 4 April 1881', unpublished manuscript, New Zealand Mormon Church History Centre, Temple View, Hamilton, n.d.

Pratt, D. 'Exclusivism and Exclusivity: A Contemporary Theological Challenge', in *Pacifica* 20 (2007): 291–306

Prevost, E. 'Assessing Women, Gender and Empire in Britain's Nineteenth Century Protestant Missionary Movement', in *History Compass* 7.3 (2009): 765–99

Prochaska, F K. 'Little Vessels: Children in the Nineteenth-Century English Missionary Movement', in *Journal of Imperial and Commonwealth History* 6.2 (1978): 103–18

Pybus, T A (ed. A W Reed). *Maori and Missionary: Early Christian Missions in the South Island of New Zealand* (Wellington: Reed, 1954)

Raureti, M. 'The Origins of the Ratana Movement', in M King (ed.), *Tihe Mauri Ora: Aspects of Maoritanga* (Wellington: Methuen, 1978): 144–62

Rice, G W. *Black November: The 1918 Influenza Pandemic in New Zealand*, revised edition (Christchurch: Canterbury University Press, 2005)
Robert, D. *American Women in Mission: A Social History of Their Thought and Practice* (Macon: Mercer University Press, 1996)
Robertson, C K (ed.). *Religion as Entertainment* (New York: Peter Lang, 2002)
Rogers, D J. 'The Assemblies of God and the Long Journey towards Racial Reconciliation', in *Assemblies of God [USA] Heritage* 28 (2008): 50–61
Rowbotham, J. '"Soldiers of Christ?" Images of Female Missionaries in Late Nineteenth-Century Britain: Issues of Heroism and Martyrdom', in *Gender and History* 12.1 (2000): 82–106
Rudd, G (ed.). 'Ephraim Magleby: He Came to Serve', in *New Zealand: A Short Collection of Items of History to add to our Memories and Appreciation* (Salt Lake City, Utah: privately published, 1993 with additions in 2007)
Said, E. *Orientalism* (New York: Vintage, 1979)
—— ——. *Culture and Imperialism* (New York: Knopf, 1993)
Salmond, J D. *By Love Serve: The Story of the Order of Deaconesses of the Presbyterian Church of New Zealand* (Christchurch: Presbyterian Bookroom, 1962)
Schwimmer, E G. *The World of the Maori* (Wellington: Reed, 1966)
Shorter, A. *Toward a Theology of Inculturation* (Maryknoll, New York: Orbis, 1988)
Shortland, E. *Maori Religion and Mythology* (London: Longmans, Green, 1882)
Simmons, E R. *A Brief History of the Catholic Church in New Zealand* (Auckland: Catholic Publication Centre, 1978)
—— ——. *Pompallier: Prince of Bishops* (Auckland: Catholic Publications Centre, 1984)
Sinclair, K. *A History of New Zealand* (Harmondsworth, Middlesex: Penguin, 1959)
Smith, M K. 'Maori Missions – A New Wave: Baptist, Brethren, Salvation Army and the United Maori Mission 1880–1950', MA thesis, Auckland University, 1985
Smith, S P. *The Lore of the Whare Wananga* (New Plymouth: Avery, 1913)
Stanley, B. 'Missionary Regiments for Immanuel's Service: Juvenile Missionary Organization in English Sunday Schools, 1841–1865', in D Wood (ed.), *The Church and Childhood*, Studies in Church History 31 (Oxford: Ecclesiastical History Society/Blackwell Publishers, 1994): 391–403
—— ——. 'From the "poor heathen" to "the glory and honour of all nations": Vocabularies of Race and Custom in Protestant Missions, 1844–1928', in *International Bulletin of Missionary Research* 34.1 (2010): 3–10
Stevenson, B. 'Te Hoe Nuku Roa: A Measure of Māori Cultural Identity', in *He Pukenga Kōrero* 8.1 (2004): 37–45
Stock, E. *The History of the Church Missionary Society: Its Environment, Its Men and Its Work* (London: Church Missionary Society, 1899)

Stringer, C. *New Zealand's Christian Heritage* (Robina, Queensland: Col Stringer Ministries, 2001)

Sundt, R A. 'On the Erection of Maori Churches in the Mid 19th Century: Eyewitness Testimonies From Kaupapa and Otaki', in *Journal of the Polynesian Society* 108.1 (1999): 7–17

Swaisland, C. 'Wanted – Earnest, Self-Sacrificing Women for Service in South Africa: Nineteenth century recruitment of Single Women to Protestant Missions', in F Bowie, D Kirkwood and S Ardener (eds), *Women and Missions: Past and Present: Anthropological and Historical Perceptions* (Providence: Berg, 1993): 70–83

Tamaki, B. 'Vipers of Religion', audio sermon issued by Proton bookshop, 2004

—— ——. *Bishop Brian Tamaki: More than Meets the Eye* (Auckland: Tamaki Publications, 2006)

Tate, H. *Tamatea Motuti* (Auckland: NZ Forest Products, 1987)

—— ——. 'Stepping Into Māori Spirituality', in H Bergin and S Smith (eds), *Spirituality in Aotearoa New Zealand: Catholic Voices* (Auckland: Accent Publications, 2002): 38–53.

Tennant, M. 'Aubert, Mary Joseph – Biography', from the *Dictionary of New Zealand Biography*, in *Te Ara – the Encyclopedia of New Zealand*: http://www.teara.govt.nz/en/biographies/2a18/1 (accessed 7 January 2012)

—— ——. 'Pakeha Deaconesses and the New Zealand Methodist Mission to Maori, 1893–1940', in *Journal of Religious History* 23.3 (1999): 309–26

Thomson, J. 'Some Reasons for the Failure of the Roman Catholic Mission to the Maoris 1838–1860', in *New Zealand Journal of History* 3.2 (1969): 166–74

Troughton, G. 'Religion, Churches and Childhood in New Zealand, c.1900–1940', in *New Zealand Journal of History* 40.1 (2006): 39–56

Tucker, F B. *Muktifauj, or, Forty years with the Salvation Army in India and Ceylon* (London: Marshall Brothers, 1923)

Turner, H. *African Independent Church, Volume 2: The Life and Faith of the Church of the Lord Aladura* (Oxford: Clarendon Press, 1967)

Underwood, G. 'Mormonism and Shaping Maori Religious Identity', in G Underwood (ed.), *Explorations in Mormon Pacific History* (Provo, Utah: Brigham Young University Press, 2000)

Veitch, J. 'Henry, Annie – Biography', from the *Dictionary of New Zealand Biography* in *Te Ara – the Encyclopedia of New Zealand*: www.teara.govt.nz/en/biographies/3h16/1 (accessed 16 January 2012)

Venter, D (ed). *Engaging Modernity: Methods and Cases for Studying African Independent Churches in South Africa* (Westport: Praeger, 2004)

Waddell, R. 'The Sabbath-school and Missions', in *New Zealand Missionary Record* (February 1884): 44–9

Walton, J L. *Watch This!: The Ethics and Aesthetics of Black Televangelism* (New York/London: New York University Press, 2009)

Warner, T. *Bonds That Make Us Free: Healing Our Relationships, Coming to Ourselves* (Salt Lake City, Utah: Shadow Mountain Press, 2001)

Weir, J. 'Mission to Maori 1838–1870', in P Ewart (ed.), *Aspects of the apostolates of the Society of Mary in New Zealand since 1838: Assembled to commemorate the centenary of the establishment of the New Zealand Province of the Society of Mary, 1889–1989* (Wellington: Society of Mary, 1989)

Whaanga, H. 'A Maori Prophet', in *Juvenile Instructor* 37 (1902): 152–3

Whaanga, M T. 'On the Rock Our Fathers Planted', unpublished manuscript, 8 September 2010

Williams, P. '"The Missing Link": The Recruitment of Women Missionaries in some English Evangelical Missionary Societies in the Nineteenth Century', in F Bowie, D Kirkwood and S Ardener (eds), *Women and Missions: Past and Present: Anthropological and Historical Perceptions* (Providence: Berg, 1993): 43–69

Williams, W. *East Coast (N.Z.) Historical Records* (Anglican Church, 1895)

Wilmore, G S. *Black Religion and Black Radicalism: An Interpretation of the Religious History of Afro-American People*, 2nd edition (Maryknoll, New York: Orbis, 1983)

Wilson, J. *The History of Hawke's Bay* (Wellington: Reed, 1939)

Winiata, H. *The Dedication of St Michael's Church: A Commemorative Booklet 5 June 1982* (Palmerston North: privately published, 1982)

Worsfold, J E. *A History of the Charismatic Movements in New Zealand* (Bradford: Julian Literature Trust, 1974)

—— ——. *The Origins of the Apostolic Church in Great Britain* (Wellington: Julian Literature Trust, 1991)

Worsfold, W L. 'Subsequence, Prophecy and Church Order in the Apostolic Church, New Zealand', PhD thesis, Victoria University of Wellington, 2004

Wright, H M. *New Zealand, 1769–1840: Early Years of Western Contact* (Cambridge, Massachusetts: Harvard University Press, 1967)

Young, D. 'Mere Rikiriki', in C MacDonald, M Penfold and B Williams (eds), *The Book of New Zealand Women: Ko Kui ma te Kaupapa* (Wellington: Bridget Williams Books, 1991): 568–70

—— ——. *Woven by Water: Histories from the Whanganui River* (Wellington: Huia, 1998)

Index

Entries in **bold** are references to figures, tables or illustrations.

A

Aaronic priesthood 66
Acraman, Mina 98
ACTS Churches (formerly Apostolic Church)
 episcopal titles in 119
 faith healing in 77
 Māori leadership in 81–2, 85, 104
 Māori ministry of 105–6
 and origins of Destiny Church 115
Adams, Frederick 32
Adams, Paul 114
Aitken, James 162–3
Aladura movement 132
alcohol
 impact on Māori of 15, 168–9
 Rua's prohibition of 231, 242n47
Allsworth, Rev. Ralph Joshua 11
Alston, Agnes 25
Amaru, Karaitiana Tuketenui 53
Anderson, Charles 65
Anderson, George 96
Angel, Mike 100
Anglican Church
 artisan missionaries of 18
 children's literature of 174
 commemoration of missionaries 270
 fundamentalist opposition to 120
 Māori carvings in 267
 Māori clergy in 154
 Te Kooti and 227
 and Tūhoe 223
 Winiata and 266
Anglican Mangere Mission 277
Apostolic Church, *see* ACTS Churches
Armstrong, Alexander ('Kaha') 26, 29, 31–2
Aroolappen, John Christian 74
Assemblies of God
 ethnic diversity in 92–3, 101, 106
 faith healing in 77
 impact on Māori 79–80
 leadership in 104–5
 Māori involvement in 91, 97, 100–1, 126
 and Māoritanga ix–x, 96–9
 origins of 93–5, 102–3
 and social justice 103
 urban strength of 102
Aterea, Hori 28–9
Aubert, Suzanne 24–5, 41, 147–9
Auckland, Catholic Church in 144
Azusa Street revival 74, 93–4

313

B

Bailey, Reuben   26, 28
Bain, Kate   26
Baker, Mr and Mrs   15, 17
Baptist Church   24, 99
Batt, George   47–8
Bay of Plenty, Salvation Army in   23, 29, 31
Bell, Colin and Doreen   33
Bell, Donald   23
Bennett, Bishop   39
Best, Elsdon   208, 223
Bible
   importance to Pentecostals   78, 85
   supra-cultural message of   282
   in te reo Māori   98
biculturalism
   and Assemblies of God   99, 106–7
   contemporary resistance to   175
   in Pentecostal churches   79–80, 84
   in Salvation Army   26, 39–41
   in Winiata's work   280–1
Bilby, Ian   118
Bird, William   214
Blake, Alexander   16, 161
Blincoe, Bessie   31
Bloomfield, Ray   79, 94–5
Booth, William   27, 37, 42n24
The Break of Day
   Christmas present fund   **163**
   criticism of colonialism in   168–9
   founding of   162–3
   imagery of the Other in   170–3
   and Māori missions   159–60, 162
   representations of Māori in   164–7
   Sister Kearney in   196
   story of Tarore in   169–70
Brethren   24, 125
Breward, A.   198
Bridge Pā, *see* Korongata

Bromley, William   45–6
Brown, Henare and Nani   33
Brown Faces   174
Budd, George   4, 18, 165
Burns, Thomas   14, 18, 161
Burrows, Eva   34
Burton, Fred   32–3
Busby, James   142, 247
Busy Bees   171, 177n39, 188

C

Calder, David   169–70
Canada, Eurocentrism in   174
cannibalism   164, 185
Capill, Graham   114
Cargill, William   14–15, 19
Carroll, James   238
Chanel, Peter   144
Chapman, Claire   98
childhood
   Christian ideas of   162
   formation of attitudes in   174–5
   Māori and Pākehā histories of   160, 167
   in pioneer rural areas   170–1
children's literature, Māori in   x
Chinese migrants   92–3, 162, 179
Christchurch, Catholic Church in   146
Christian churches, competition for Māori adherents   153
Christian Heritage Party   114
Christianity
   beginnings of among Māori   247, 256–7
   and cleanliness   166
   colonial forms of   75, 85–6, 234
   global centre of gravity   73
   indigenous African traditions of   129–32

indigenous leadership in 38,
104–5, 233
main denominations in
New Zealand 46
Māori and Pākehā streams of 160
Māori culture and ix, 43, 265,
268, 281–2
and pacifism 239
place of Rātana movement in 252
and race 171–2, 175
tohunga under 47
traditional accounts of influence
vii–viii, 164–5
and Tūhoe 223
in Winiata's work 269–71, 275–7,
280, 283
Church College of New Zealand
(Mormon) 66
Church Missionary Society (CMS)
on the civilizing arts 143
early churches 278–9
Henry Venn in 105
Māori ministers in 154
and New Zealand Wars 147
at Parewanui 10
and translation theology 283
Church of Africa 130
City Impact Church 118
Clark, Helen 256
Clark, Ian 80
Cognet, Father 149–50, 152–3
Colin, Jean-Claude 144
Comte, Jean-Baptiste 143, 146–7, 149
Conference of Churches of Aotearoa
New Zealand 34–5
contextual theology 282
Coombe, Mary 187–8
Cooper, Whina 96
Cowley, Matthew 56–8
Cox, Thomas 66
Cross, Rex and Glenys 33

Cruden, James and Janet 33
Cruickshank, Graham 96, 104–5
Cruickshank, Tui 98

D

Daughters of our Lady of Compassion
149
Davis, Ted 104
de Blois, Henry 25
Delach, Father 148–50
Delachienne, Father 270
Destiny Church
and African Christianity 132
core values of 117
as fundamentalist movement 120–2
as Māori religious movement 91,
125–7, 129, 133–4
moral stance of 83
origins of 82, 116
as Pentecostal movement 115–16,
118–19
political philosophy of 111–13
sectarianism of 122–5
social projects of 120
Destiny Party 112, 114–15
Doull, Euphemia **180**, 204n60
Doull, James 13, 19
Dowie, J. A. 131
Duncan, James **5**
Māori mission of 7–8, 18, 161, 179
at Parewanui 10
and Henry Fletcher 12
Dunford, Oliver Cowdery 45

E

East Coast
Anglican Church in 33
Salvation Army in 32
Edwards, Lizzie 25

Elim Church   78, 94
Elkington, John   65
Elkington, Weikia Ruruku   64–5
Ellerslie–Tamaki Mission   95
episcopal titles   119
Estill, W.   29
Ethiopian movements   130–1
evangelists, itinerant   78–9
exodus motif   xii, 14, 226, 235

F

Fairbrother, Basil and Mavyis   32–3
faith healing
  in Pentecostal movement   116
  in pre-European religion   77
  by Rātana   251, 258
Family Party   114
Ferguson, Russell   95
Ferris, John   62–3
Flavell, Dean and Ralph   273
Flaxmere   36
Fletcher, Henry   10–13, 20, 179, 183–4, 190, 209–10
Forest, Father   145
Foxton   6, 8, 36
Free Presbyterian Church of Scotland   13–14
Full Gospel churches   77
fundamentalism   111, 118, 120–1, 129

G

Gilfillan murders   6, 20n8
Gilliard, Alfred   38
Gisborne
  Mormon Church in   51
  Salvation Army in   38
Gnosticism   124
Goff, Phil   258

Goffin, Dean   34
gold rush   145
Gore Browne, Governor   7
Goulton, Ron   81
Grace, Laurence   10
Greenway, Alfred   81
Greenwood, Alma   50–1, 59
Grey, George   8, 29
Grey, Wini   25, 29
Grimes, John   146
Groesbeck, Joseph   64

H

Hadfield, Octavius   7–8, 270
Haerewaho   5
Hamilton, Salvation Army in   36
Harris, William Wade   130
Harrison, Ken   100
Harwood, Robert   155
Hato Paora College   155
Haumate, Hariata   212–14, 219
Hawke's Bay
  Catholic Church in   145, 147–8, 151
  Mormon Church in   60
Hay, James   32
Hayes, Georgina (Aunty Bunny)   217, 219–20
Hinau, Peka   170
Hinckley, Ira   50–1
Hira, Peter   80, 91, 97–100
Hirini, Mavis   35
Hiruhārama (Jerusalem)   11–12, 23–5, 41, 147–9, 151–3
Hiruhārama School   11
Hodderville   42n24
Hodges, Melvin   105
Hokitika   24
Holdaway, Ernest   24–31, 36–7

Holy Ghost Mission   10
homosexuality   113, 123
Hongi Hika   247
Honoré, Abraham   4, 8–11, 15–17, 161, 179
Hoskin, W. T.   29
Houston, Frank   79, 95, 97
Howick   144
Hsi Shengmo   74
Huria, Hohepa   24–5, 31
hybridity   133

I

Iharaira, Kirihaehae   191
India, Salvation Army in   26, 37–8
indigenisation   xi, 24, 75, 195–6, 200
Ingerson, Harold   33
Inglis, John   6–7, 18, 161
Instructions pour les Travaux de la Mission   142–3
Irish, in New Zealand   145–6
Islam   113
Israelites, Māori self-identification as   224, 231, 235, 240, 247
Iti, Tame   210–12, 219

J

Jakes, T. D.   118, 132
Jeffreys, Stephen   77
Jews, *see* Israelites
Johnson, Neville   96–7

K

Kahukura, Meri   191–2
Kāi Tahu   14, 16
Kāi te Pahi   16–17
Kapua, Eramiha   267

karakia signs   68
Kauangaroa   153
Kawerau, Presbyterian Church in   187, 198
Kemp, Major   11
Kemp, Walter   26
Kendrew, Ross   36
Kereama, Calvin   273
Key, John   258
King, Bernice   119
King Country   27, 184–5
kingdom theology   117
Kingi, Karaitiana   155
Kingi, Ranginui   57
Kīngitanga   61, 66, 128–9, 170
Koraki, Hoani Wetepi   17
Korongata   50–1, 70n31
Koroniti   12, 151–2
Kraft, Charles   282

L

Latin America, Pentecostalism in   73, 75–6
Laughton, J. G.
  building school at Ruatāhuna   210
  on Māori leadership   233
  at Maungapōhatu   185
  moderator of THM   196–7
  payment for   186
  on Presbyterian Māori missions   4
  superintendent of missions   193, 196
  and Rua Kēnana   230, 233–4
  and Tūhoe   212, 235
Leeston   24
Levin   265–6
Lewis, Richard   114
liberation theology   129, 235
Life Church   118
Lloyd, Geoff   96–7, 115

Long, Eddie   82, 118–19, 132
The Lotu   174
Lutheran Church   14

M

Macauley, Minnie   204n60
MacDiarmid, Donald   168–9
Macfarlane, James   3–4
Mackie, Robert   27
Magleby, John Ephraim   45
Mana Ariki Marae   129
Manawatū   4, 6–9, 11, 161
Mangakāhia, Hamiora   53–4
Māori
   assimilation of   168, 197
   as dying race   154, 160
   representations of   164, 167, 173
   urbanisation of   31, 75–6, 102, 197–8, **198**
Māori carving tradition   265–7
Māori catechists   17–18, 148–55
Māori children   **166, 173**
Māori costume   41n10
Māori culture, and Salvation Army   38–9
Māori martyrs   169–70
Māori-Pacific Island Council (MPIC)   81–2
Māori Party   114, 128, 258
Māori prophetic tradition   47–8, 59, 129, 152–3, 246–8, 259–60
Māori renaissance   76–7
Māori spirituality   77–8, 126
marae-churches   277, 284n24
Marist Fathers
   conflict with Pompallier   144
   and Māori cathecists   x
   role of in New Zealand   142
   seminary of   146

Marist Māori mission   141, 146–9, 155
Mariu, Takuira Max   155
Marsden, Maori   281–2, 284–5n32
Marsden, Samuel   143, 247
Martin, Debbie   245, 259
Mason, John   10
Masonic Lodge   266
Matahi   **180**, 189
Matakarapa   6
Mataroa   152
Maunga Oriwa   255
Maungapōhatu
   arrest of Rua Kēnana at   208, 211, 239
   Presbyterian mission at   165, 168, 185, 214, 219
   rebuilding of   237–8
   Ringatū Church in   214
   Rua's migration to   231–2
   and Te Kooti's diamond   228
Maungārongo   228
Maxim Institute   112
Maxwell, Earle   35
McCarthy, Joseph (Motu Hinau)   31
McGlashan, John   14
McLean, Donald   7, 17
Medland, Sam   33
Meeanee   145–7, 151
Meihana, Otene   51
Melu, Father   149
Mere (wife of Piripi Tutawha)   25, 27
Mere Eia Mete   51
Methodist Church
   artisan missionaries of   18
   children's material of   174
   and Destiny Church   119, 121
   Māori catechists in   17
Methodist Māori Mission   252
Mihinare tradition   283
Milroy, Miss   **187**, 192

Milson, George 11–12, 179
Miro (Utiku Te Rangi Hikohia) 25, 27
missionaries, artisan 18
missionary literature 160–2, 174
missionary societies 174
Moeraki 16
Mogridge, Ruth 32
Mokai 191
Monfries, Abigail 205–9
Moore, Catherine 31
Moore, George 26, 29, 31–2, 39
Moran, Patrick 145
Morete, Maraea Mohaki 25, 27–8, **28**, 31
Mormon Church
　at D'Urville Island 63–5
　first arrival in New Zealand 44
　Māori conversions to 46, 51–2, 59–60, 66
　and Māori prophecy 56–7, 59, 62–3
　Presbyterian response to 9–10
　role of direct revelation in 47
Mormon missionaries
　and Church of England 51–2
　in Hawke's Bay 50
　intercultural approach of 44–5, 67–9
Morris, Ada 13
Mortimer-Jones, Clive 171
Moses, Harriett 36–7
Moses, Wayne 35–7, 39
Mount Maunganui 36
multiculturalism 39, 80, 84, 93, 99, 106–7
Munro, Himepiri 30, 32

N

Nakada, Juji 252–3
National Church of Christ 130
Native Land Court 43
New Fellowship of Tonga 125
New Life Movement 77, 94
New Zealand, as Christian country 112–13
New Zealand Christian Network 123
New Zealand Company 5, 12–14, 143
New Zealand Missionary Record 159, 162
New Zealand Wars
　church support for Government in 45, 247
　effect on missions 146–7
　Māori grievances from 185
　and North Island missions 13
Ngā Tamariki Puawai 120
Ngā Tau e Waru Marae 58
Ngāi Tuwhiwhia 31
Ngāpuhi 100, 104, 248
Ngata, Apirana 238, 257, 267
Ngata churches 279
Ngāti Kahungunu 56–8, 98, 253
Ngāti Konohi 52
Ngāti Oneone 52
Ngāti Pareraukawa 266, 268–9
Ngāti Parewahawaha 266, 273
Ngāti Raukawa 265–7, 270–1, 282
Ngāti Tauaiti 31
Ngāti Tūwharetoa 13
Ngāti Wairiki 153
Ngāti Wehiwehi 270
Ngāti Whātua 43, 98
Ngatokowaru II 268–72, 275, 280–1
Nicholls, John 26, 29
Niebuhr, H. Richard 282
Nigeria Native Baptist Church 130
Nopera, Eriata 58

North German Missionary Society 8–9, 14–16, 18, 161
Northland, Pākehā settlements in 171
Nūhaka
  Mormon Church in 51
  Presbyterian Church in 167, 186, 188–9, 199

O

Ohanga 65
Ohope 203, 210–11, 215
Old Testament
  and Destiny Church 122
  and liberation theology 235–6, 247
  and Rua Kēnana 230–2
  and Tawhiao 62
  and Te Kooti 224–6
Onehunga 144
Ōpōtiki 171, 190–1
O'Reilly, Father 143
orphanages 171, 183
Otago
  Catholic Church in 145–6
  Māori population of 14–15
  settlement of 13–14
Otago Heads 14–18
Ōtahuhu 144
Ōtaki
  Anglican Church at 6, 266
  Catholic mission at 145–50
  Te Wānanga ō Raukawa at 267
  the Other 171

P

Pai Mārire
  Ngāti Wairiki and 153
  Presbyterian response to 8–10, 165
  and Riemenschneider 16
  and Te Kooti 224
Pakipaki 147–8
Pakuranga 101
Palmerston North 272–3
Panmure 144
Papakura 36
Papawai 54, 60
Parewahawaha meeting house 266, 269, 273, 280
Parewanui 9–10, 249
Parihaka 15–16, 247, 256
Parikino 27
Patea, Joe 23, 37
Pātea 250
Patete, Haimona 66
Paulger, Irene 237
Pentecostalism
  and activism 103–4
  African offshoots of 131
  black American forms of 118–19, 132–3
  and Charismatic movement 97
  church structures in 84–6, 105
  geographical centre of gravity 73–4
  and indigenous people 74–6, 119
  and Māori culture 78, 80, 126
  Pasifika movements 125
  recent evolution of 116–17
  and right-wing politics 112
Peterehema 153
Petit-Jean, Father 144
Petrie, Lord Henry 143
Phillips, Alex 129
Piripi Pauro Tutawha 25, 27
PMMC (Presbyterian Māori Mission Committee); *see also* Presbyterian Māori Synod

expansion of 188–90, **189**
and Hiruhārama 11
and Honoré 9–10
indigenisation of 195–7
Māori staff of 191–2, **192**
payment for missionaries 186–7, 204n60
separation from Foreign missions 161
urban activities of 197–8
women missionaries for 179–80, 183–6, 188, **192–3**, 199
Pohio, Horomona 17
Pohio, Manu 78, 88, 104
Pōkaikaha 228
Pompallier, Jean-Baptiste 141–5, 150, 154–5
Poraumati, Emare 30, 183–4, 191
Pōtangaroa, Paora, *see* Te Pōtangaroa, Paora
Pōtangaroa, Regan 255
Potatau, Hemi 191, 196
Poutini 11, 153
prejudice, formation of 174
Presbyterian Church
Deaconess College, *see* PWTI
deaconesses in 182
engagement of children in x
Māori leaders in 19
men's involvement in 184–5
missions of 161–2
as settler church ix, 3, 17–19
Synod of Otago and Southland 14, 16, 159, 161
and Tūhoe 211–12, 223, 230
women conducting sacraments 194–5
Presbyterian Home Mission 203n37
Presbyterian Māori missions
Break of Day fundraising for 159–60, 163

lack of support for 19–20, 161–2, 179
in North Island 4–7, 9, 11–12
Te Waipounamu 13, 17
Presbyterian Māori Synod/Te Aka Puaho
constitution of 3, 8, 175, 195
employment of women 193, 198–200
ministers of 209–10, 212
Pākehā involvement in 197
records of 4
Presbyterian Women's Missionary Union 162, 186
Presbyterian Women's Training Institute (PWTI) 183, 187–8, 191–2, 198, 200, 204–5
Price, Kem 98–9
Prince, Derek 115
prophecy
interpretation of 53
in Māori tradition, *see* Māori prophetic tradition
in Pentecostalism 76
prosperity teaching 117, 119
Proton Bookshop 120
Prowse, Bessie 33
Prowse, Robert 33, 39
Pu, Patoromu 16–17, 19
Pukekaraka 146–7, 150
Pulepule, Samani 93
Pūtāruru 42n24
PWTI (Presbyterian Women's Training Institute / Deaconess College) 183, 187–8, 191–2, 198, 200, 205

R

race, imagery of 171–2
Raglan 63, 80

Ra'iatea 270
Rangiātea Church 266, 270
Rangikura, Hakaraia 147
Rangiora Pentecostals 125
Rangitakaiwaho, John 59
Rangitakaiwaho, Te Manihera 60
Rangitikei–Manawatū Māori Pastorate 272, 278
Rangitikei River 12, 248
Rangitoto, *see* D'Urville Island
Rangiwaea Island 31
Rātana, T. W. **244**
  death of 257
  early life of 10
  four quarters of 256–7
  gifts to Savage 245–6, 259–61
  leadership role of 127–8, 130
  personal qualities of 243
  prophecies of 87n13, 251–2, 255–6, 260
  at Te Oreore 254
  vision of 74–5, 249–51
Rātana Church
  and African Christianity 130–2
  alliance with Labour 245, 258
  and Apostolic Church 115
  and Destiny Church 83, 126–9
  founding of 252–3
  and Te Potangaroa's prophecies 58
Rātana family, and Presbyterian Church 10
Rātana Ngahina 249–50
Rātana Pā 251–3, 255
Rātana temple, *see* Te Temepara Tapu ō Ihoa
Raukura, Eria 226, 229
Raumati (prophet) 152–3
Rawiri, Rata 203, 207, 210, 215
The Reaper 172

Redwood, Francis 146–7, 151
Reformed Presbyterian Church of Scotland 6–7, 161
Renata, Manuel, as Māori leader 104
revelation, Christian denominations and 47
Riemenschneider, Johann 15–17
Riini, Mona 209, 219
Rikiriki, Mere 10, 249
Ringatū Church
  hymns of 225
  origins of 71n41
  and Rua Kēnana 228
  and Te Toiroa's propechies 49, 53
  in Tūhoe 211, 214, 219
Riverton 8, 24, 205, 220
Rīwaiti 232
Robertson, Fred 194
Roman Catholic Church
  conflict with Salvation Army 25–6
  dioceses of 145–6
  European stations of 144
  Māori ministry in 18, 153–5
  mission to New Zealand 141–3
  Tāwhiao on 66
  and Tūhoe 223
Rongopai 229
Ropiha, Atareta 249
Ross, C. Stuart 162
Ross, John 12
Rua Kēnana
  claims to authority of 228–30, 236–7
  government attacks on 208, 238–9
  leadership of 231–2
  and Sister Annie 207–8
  tangi of 165
  theology of 232–5, 239–40

Ruapuke Island 8, 14, 179
Ruatāhuna **166**, **182**
   Peka Hinau at 170
   Presbyterian Church in 189, 212, 214, 219
   Ringatū Church in 214
   school at 210
   Sister Annie Henry at 205–6, 208–9, 213
Rubie, Syd and Jean 33
Ruruku, Roma Hoera 63–6, **64**
Ruth, Fred 36

S

Sadanand, Samuel 29
Salvation Army
   apology to Māori 23
   beginnings of Māori mission 24
   Council on Race Relations 34–5, 40
   Eurocentrism in 37–9
   at Hiruhārama 25–6
   Māori Division of 26, 28–9, 37–8
   Māori Fellowship of 36–7, 40
   motivations for missionary work 172
   recent Māori work of 33–5
   sixth anniversary meeting of **27**
   social services of 41
Samoans, in Assembly of God 93, 101
Sampson, Robert 31
Savage, Michael Joseph 245–6, 257–9
School of Māori Arts and Crafts 267, 269, 279
Scott, Agnes 26
Seamer, Arthur 29–30, 252

Selwyn, Bishop 247
Servant, Catherin 141
Seymour, William 93
Sister Alison (Jane Spence) 165, 183–5
Sister Annie Henry (Hihita) **182**, **206**
   death of 210, 215–16
   early life of 205
   fostering Māori children 187, 203n48, 207, 210, 216
   gifts for 208
   house in Ruatāhuna 189
   at Maungapōhatu 185
   memories of 211–15, 217–20
   skills of 206–7
Sister Edith (Edith Walker) 188, 191, 203n48
Sister Hercus 198–9
Sister Isabel (Eileen Davidson) **190**, **206**
Sister Jessie (Jessie Alexander) 167, 188, 190
Sister Kearney 176, 193–6, 203n48
Sister Mary Joseph, *see* Aubert, Suzanne
Sister May (May Gardiner) 188
Sister Ross 192, 203n48
Smith, Jack 155, 194
social justice 103
Soulas, Father 148–9, 151–4
Spanish flu 250
St John's College 271, 278
St Michael's Church, Palmerston North 272–3, **272**, **274–9**, 279–81
Stannard, R. G. 15
Stewart, Lionel 99–100
Stewart, William Thomas 50–3, 58–9, 65

323

Stewart Island 8, 17–18
Stirling, Hera 26, 30
Stratford 36
Stringer, Col 113
Sunday schools
　Presbyterian 162
　Salvation Army 32–3

T

Taharangi, Kareti Karioi 31
Tahoraiti 60
Taieri 14, 16
Taikapurua 6–7
Taiwhati 148, 151
Tamaki, Brian
　family background of 129
　founding of Destiny Church 82, 116
　leadership role of 119, 122, 128, 132–3
　as Māori leader 104
　on other Christian churches 122–3, 125
　political statements of 112–13, 115–16
　prophecies of 115
　on secular knowledge 122
　soteriology of 136n31
　and Pentecostalism 118
Tamatea, Maraea 27, 29–30
Tamatea Aurunui 23, 25–8, 30–1, 41
Tanatana 171, 201, 211
Tankersley, Pamela 3
Taonoke 51
Taonui, Aperahama 247
tapu
　and carving 266–9
　deliverance from 77
　integration with Christianity 281–2
　use in Bible translations 109n26
　Winiata's attitude to 268–9, 280
Tarore 169–70, 302
Tate, Henare 281–2
Taumarunui area
　Destiny Church in 116
　mission of Sister Alison 165
　Presbyterian Church in 190, 196
Taupō
　Anglican activity in 13
　Presbyterian mission to 10, 13, 190
Tāwhiao, King **61**
　Mormon missionaries' audience with 65–6
　prophecies of 60–3, 68, 259, 262n14
Taylor, Josiah 25
Taylor, Richard 10, 249
Te Aitanga-a-Hauiti 53
Te Aitanga-a-Māhaki 52
Te Aka Puaho, *see* Presbyterian Māori Synod
Te Amo, Kui Rora 77
Te Ārai 51, 53
Te Atairangikaahu, Queen 62, 128
Te Awahou 6, 10
Te Hahi ō te Ruri Tuawhitu ō Ihowa 66–7
Te Hahi ō te Wairua Tapu 249
Te Hirūhārama Hou 231, 255
Te Hurinui Apanui 229
Te Iharaira 231, 235–6, 238
Te Kahu, Tare Weteri 17
Te Karaiti Te Pou Herenga Waka 278
Te Katera, Hare 66
Te Kere 248–9, 253

Te Kooti
  diamond of 228–9
  and killing of Pera Kararehe 25, 27–8
  Old Testament inspiration of 224–6, 235
  prophecies of 71n41, 212, 223–4, 227, 232, 248, 259
  renunciation of war 227, 248
  successors to xi–xii
  and Te Toiroa's prophecies 53
Te Maari, Piripi 67
Te Māhia 48–51
Te Maire, Rawiri 17
Te Manihera Keremeneta, Rure 154
Te Menehera 152
Te Muriwai 51–2
Te Ope Fish Supply Company 31–2
Te Ope Whakaora 26
Te Ope Whakaora Regional Corps 33
Te Ore Ore 54–8, 253–5
Te Pōtangaroa, Paora 54
  followers of 59, 67
  prophecies of 54–8, 68, 248, 253–4
Te Pōtangaroa, Samuel 59–60
Te Puea, Princess 30, 66
Te Puke 77
Te Puni, Hana Werohu Rangiwhaia 31
Te Raki 14
Te Rauparaha, Tamihana 170, 270
te reo Māori
  renewed interest in 41, 77
  Salvation Army use of 36
  teaching at PWTI 205
Te Tahua, Te Kare ō Mahuru 26
Te Tai Rāwhiti 48
Te Taure, Rikihana 26

Te Teira Marutu 50
Te Teko 190, 192, 198
Te Temepara Tapu ō Ihoa 115, 253, 255, 257
Te Toiroa, Arama 48–53, 68
Te Toko, Hohepa 148, 151
Te Ua Haumene 8, 127, 293
Te Unga Waka Catholic Marae 277
Te Waitaruna, Maraea Te Kehu 28
Te Wānanga ō Raukawa 267
Te Wānanga ō Te Tai Tokerau 281, 285n33
Te Whakapapa ō Te Whakapono viii
Te Whānau-a-Tauwhao 31
Te Whatanui 270–1
Te Whiti 15–16
Te Whiwhi, Matene 270
Temara, Mac 199
Temara, Te Makarini 211
Tembu tribal church 130
Temuera, Paora 266
THM (Te Hinota Māori), *see* Presbyterian Māori Synod
three-self strategy 105
time, Māori ideas of 104
Tirakatene-Sullivan, Whetu 259
Tirikatene, Eruera 245, 259
Tiroa 184–5
Tohu Kākahi 16
tohunga
  prophecies of 43–4, 48–9, 55–6
  resistance to Christianity 95, 152
  social function of 47
Tohunga Suppression Act 96, 238
Toiroa, Arama 49, 51, 259
Toka, Henare 267
Tokaanu 183–4
Tokata-Te-Araroa 32–3
tokenism 39, 80

325

Tokotoko, Hoani   148, 151
Tolaga Bay   33, 53
tongues, speaking in   116
Traill, Arthur   17
translation, theology of   282–3
Treaty of Waitangi
   Destiny Church on   83–4, 126, 128
   Rātana on   246, 251, 258, 260–1
   Salvation Army on   35
   signing of   102, 247–8
   tabling in Parliament   245
Tū Tangata carving school   273
Tucker, Frederick   26
Tuhawaiki   14
Tūhoe
   and arrest of Rua Kēnana   211–12
   churches in   214
   Elsdon Best on   223
   in First World War   239
   and land confiscations   227, 235
   Sister Annie and   206–9, 212
   Te Kooti among   226–7
Tukumaru, Ihakara   6
Tupuhi, Glen   79
Turakina   12, 183, 191
Turakina Maori Girls' School   10, 191, 201n5
Turuwhenua, Hukarere   211
Tweed, Malcolm and Bernice   95

U

Unification Church (Moonies)   132
United African Methodist Church   130
United States
   black Christianity in   235, 240
   right-wing politics in   111–12
   upward mobility   76, 79

Uren, Bruce   95
Urewera area
   Presbyterian Church in   185, 188, 199
   Te Kooti in   226

V

Valdez, A. C.   94
Vanuatu   7, 161
Venn, Henry   105
Viard, Bishop   142, 144–5, 147, 155
Völkner, Carl   8
Vrankovich, Mark   122–3

W

Waddell, Rutherford   162
Waharoa   169
Waiapu   30, 50
Waikaremoana   159, 188, 193, 195
Waikato, Mormon Church in   66
Waikato Wars   61
Waikouaiti   15–16
Waimana   191, 211
Waimate   24
Waiohau   189, 192, 198
Waiomio   80, 95
Wairarapa, Mormon Church in   60, 67
Wairoa   51, 192, 197
Wakefield, E. G.   13–14
Wakefield, E. J.   5
Waotu   65–6
Ward, Edgerton   20
Watkins, Reg   31
Watson, Noel   95
Wehiwehi   270
Wellington, Catholic Church in   143, 145–6

Wells, Margaret   26
Werahiko   148, 151–2
Whaanga, Hirini Te Rito   49–51
Whaanga, Ihaka   51
Whaitiri   228
whakairo rākau   267, 283
Whakatō   224
Whakatupuranga Rua Mano   267
Whangaehu River   25, 153, 248
Whanganui region
    Catholic Church in   148, 151–4
    Presbyterian activity in   11–12
    Salvation Army in   25, 30, 36–7, 153
Whāngārei   69, 94–7
Wharekauri   224–6
Wharekura, Pekahina   207, 210, 215–16
Wharekura, Sam   210, 216
Wheeler, Rob   77
Whenuakura   152
Wi Pere   225
Wi Tako   5
Wi Tapeka, Makurata and Paitini   208

Wi Wereta   229
Wigglesworth, Smith   74, 94
Will, William   15
Williams, Jim   98–9
Williams, William   51–3, 151
Winiata, Alma   268–9
Winiata, Hapai
    attitudes towards tradition   268, 283
    background of   265–7
    theology of   282–3
    and Mangere project   278
    and Ngatokowaru II   269
    and St Michael's Church   272–3, 280
Winiata, Martin   271
Wohlers, Rev.   8, 14–17, 179
women
    employment of   193–4
    as missionaries   180–3, 185–6, 190, 199–200, 202n24

Z

Zionist churches   131–2